International Medical Care

Edited by
Dr. JOHN FRY & W. A. J. FARNDALE

International
Medical Care

*A comparison and evaluation of
medical care services throughout
the world*

WASHINGTON SQUARE EAST · PUBLISHERS
Wallingford, Pennsylvania.
1972

Published in U.S.A. by Washington Square East
Publishers, 109, Logan Lane, Wallingford, Pennsylvania, 19086
Published in U.K. by MTP, Medical and Technical
Publishing Co. Ltd., Oxford and Lancaster.

SBN 852 000 359

First published 1972

PRINTED IN GREAT BRITAIN

Contents

Preface

This is an historic moment in the development of health and medical care services. The United States of America is on the threshold of a new system for health insurance and for the provision of medical care services. In the United Kingdom there is active thinking, discussion and action over a drastic reorganisation of its National Health Service. In the Developing Nations of Africa, Asia and South America there are emerging the beginnings of national and universal health services which have to replace those of past colonial times. In Western Europe and Scandinavia there is a constant struggle with the problems of medical care, and in the U.S.S.R. with its vast numbers of physicians, the great majority of whom are women, there are the beginnings of a questioning of some of the principles on which medical care services are based.

All nations are faced with similar problems and dilemmas in attempting to provide optimal and equable health and medical care services for their people. They are faced with the perpetually insoluble equation of endeavouring to match "wants" and "needs" with available resources.

The public "wants" expressed as the achievement and maintenance of health as a human and civic right are baulked not only by the constant war with medical and social diseases but also by limited economic and manpower resources.

The challenge to us all faced with such common dilemmas and frustrations is how to make the best use of the available resources. What systems of organising medical care are the best? What methods of care are most economic and how may they be deployed most effectively? How many plans are frustrated, not only by shortages of finance and resources but also by the objections raised by various professional and non-professional pressure groups?

This book does not pretend to provide the answers to the many problems and difficulties, but it does aim to define some of the problems in the provision of medical care and to examine how some nations are trying to find solutions.

There are, of course, many ways in which such a complex and

difficult subject might be tackled. We decided on a simple and a clear-cut procedure. A number of acknowledged experts in the field of medical care were each invited to write a descriptive, analytical and critical review on some of the systems of medical care in the world today. The systems selected were those of the U.S.A. (reviewed by Professor Philip D. Bonnet), Canada (Professor Robert Kohn), U.S.S.R. (Dr. John Fry and Dr. L. Crome), U.K. (Dr. A. T. Elder), Western Europe and Scandinavia (Dr. David Stark Murray), Australia (Professor H. N. Robson) and the Developing Nations (Professor N. R. E. Fendall).

A flexible basic plan was followed for each system but the authors were given full range to present the situations and problems as they thought fit.

We were fortunate in having Dr. R. F. Bridgman as a contributor with his unique experience at the World Health Organisation. He provides a truly global view of the whole situation.

It is quite insufficient for technical experts to present their analyses of the existing situations and recommendations on what they believe should be done. The matter cannot be left there. In real-life such proposals and reviews are only a beginning. The administrators, economists and politicians have then to examine the proposals to see how much of the planners' dreams can be implemented. Insufficient attention has been paid to the political "art of the possible" in medical care.

Therefore we invited some eminent and well-known experts in the political arenas in U.K., and U.S.A., to state how they see the problems from their viewpoints.

Kenneth Robinson was for many years a Member of Parliament, and was the Minister of Health in the last Labour Government in the United Kingdom. Professor Wilbur J. Cohen had many years administrative experience in the U.S. Government and particularly in the Johnson administration. Professor Philip R. Lee (Assistant Secretary for Health and Scientific Affairs 1965–9) and Professor George Silver (Deputy Assistant Secretary 1965–8) were brought into the Department of Health, Education and Welfare in President Johnson's period, to head the medical care sections. They write as individuals giving their views and interpretations of the difficulties and achievements at the highest levels of government.

This book is presented to all who are interested in medical care and health services as a contribution and stimulus to the current debates and thinking that is going on all over the world. There are no snappy answers or instructions on how to achieve the impossible. We offer no single best-buy system of medical care that could be applied universally. We have tried to highlight general principles and the common basic ingredients of good medical care. We believe strongly that we can all learn from each other, the west from the east and the east from the west, the developed nations from the developing nations, as well as the more usually believed way round. A continuing dialogue is necessary and international comparisons and studies need to be carried out. It is not enough to leave it all to the World Health Organisation and other international bodies. There are many opportunities for the ordinary people and workers in medical care and health services all over the world to visit each other, to meet, to discuss common problems and then to return to try and improve their own medical systems in the light of what they have learnt.

JOHN FRY.
W. A. J. FARNDALE.

Section One

The Problems of Medical Care

Introduction

Medicine and the Society of Man

JOHN FRY, M.D., F.R.C.S., F.R.C.G.P.

*Consultant, World Health Organisation and
Family Physician, London, England*

With social advancement human attitudes to life are changing and
disease, disability and discomfort are less tolerable and less acceptable.
Mankind is now more expectant and demanding that, in a world
of scientific and technical miracles, death and disease should be
controlled.

Undoubtedly many diseases are being better controlled all over
the world but new problems are emerging as old diseases are being
mastered. Disease patterns are altering and the close relation between
incidence of disease and social progress and development is becoming
increasingly clear. No longer is it possible to consider disease as the
outcome of a single cause. We now realise that most specific diseases
have multiple causes or are associated with a number of factors. Even
in common infections the occurrence, course and outcome are more
related to social and genetic factors than to any simple direct relationship with the causal organism. The great killers of developed societies,
coronary heart disease, strokes and cancer cannot be related to single
aetiologies, and it is becoming increasingly clear that the ways
of life and habits of the victims are of the greatest importance.

It is no longer possible to separate public health from personal
health. In the control of disease the problems of mass medicine
(public health), social, clinical and environmental medicine and personal and family care are indivisible and inseparable. Success in
disease control and improvements in health will come only if these
aspects are unified in a single system of care.

Measures of Disease

The standard measures of disease are those related to the extent
and causes of death at various ages and to the incidence and prevalence of known and diagnosed diseases.

Thus mortality rates are reported from each member of United

3

Nations and these rates are published. Unfortunately the reported data is crude and unrefined and any comparisons beyond gross mortality rates are open to many errors, because of difficulties of nomenclature and lack of accuracy of confirmation of exact causes. What applies to mortality data applies even more strongly to morbidity data. The degrees of error and variability are great in accuracy of diagnosis and in standardisation of medical nomenclature. These potential errors apply more to some diseases than to others and whilst the accuracy of a diagnosis of "chronic bronchitis" is subject to wide variation that of cancer of the stomach will be less variable.

Patterns of disease are related intimately to social factors and conditions and the extent of social pathology in any area should be measured in order to provide a more complete assessment. Such indices as the numbers of severely handicapped, the blind, deaf and crippled; the numbers of known delinquents in prison or other penal institutions; the numbers of known chronic alcoholics; the numbers receiving regular assistance from welfare funds; the numbers of children living in broken families; the extent of marriage, divorce and illegitimacy; and the numbers of deaths from road traffic accidents and suicide – all this data is necessary to build up a composite picture of the challenges facing us all in the control of medical and social diseases.

Another set of data concerns the extent of unmet medical problems as shown by the extent of undiagnosed and untreated disease in the community. It is here that data from pre-symptomatic screening studies should be correlated and presented as comparable statistics.

It is only when all these sets of information are collected and put together that a profile of health and disease of a community begins to emerge (see Appendix on page 334).

Disease Patterns in Developed and Developing Nations

Patterns of disease are very different in developed and developing nations.

The major diseases causing death and suffering in *developed* nations are cardiovascular conditions such as coronary artery heart disease and high blood pressure; strokes associated with atheroma of the cerebral arteries; cancer; acute and chronic infections of the respiratory tract; rheumatism and various degenerative conditions of the locomotor system; mental disorders; congenital deformities and abnormalities; and accidents.

These diseases are the killers and the disablers in a modern developed society. They are conditions associated with ageing and degeneration, as in the case of cancer, heart disorders, strokes, chronic pulmonary infections and degenerative arthritis, and others,

4

such as mental disorders and accidents are related closely to social conditions that have increased the pace and stresses of every-day life and have resulted in breakdown of vulnerable individuals.

The patterns of disease in *developing* nations are related to deficiencies, deprivation and the poverty of all social, medical and material resources that go hand in hand.

In these developing nations many fewer children and young adults are able to survive to be able to become candidates for the more sophisticated degenerative conditions of middle and old age. Infections and malnutrition cause the deaths of many in infancy and childhood.

Prominent amongst these killers are malaria, tuberculosis, gastro-intestinal infections of various types, including cholera, typhoid, dysentery and other less specific infections, smallpox, bilharzia, yellow fever, measles, scarlet fever and whooping cough.

Malnutrition, apart from causing specific deficiency disorders, also results in a general lowering of resistance and a permanent state of debility and depression.

Deaths and disabilities from accidents in developed nations are replaced by deaths and complications from child-bearing in developing situations.

The only diseases that are common to developed and developing nations are infections but the incidence, nature and severity are very different. Degenerative, congenital and mental disorders all fade into the background in developing nations and only come to the fore as the nations move up the ladder of social evolution and advancement.

Deaths

There are approximately 60 million deaths each year in the world. One-half of these (30 millions) are new born babies, infants and toddlers, chiefly in Africa, Asia and Latin America. One-quarter (15 millions) are caused by infections such as malaria, gastro-intestinal infections such as dysentery, typhoid and cholera, tuberculosis, small-pox and pneumonia. One-sixth (10 millions) are caused by cancer and cardiovascular diseases.

These facts speak for the tremendous challenge still facing the provision of medical care throughout the world.

The Physician in Modern Society

Traditionally, "medicine exists to serve" and in the past the art, science and service aspects of medical care were predominant and little was heard of the conditions under which the physicians worked, were paid and were organised professionally. Although the physician must still function as a healer, comforter, guide, philosopher and friend to his patients, he also has responsibilities as a member of a national

5

medical and public health service. He is an integral part of a Greater Medical Profession that is now larger and more composite than ever. No longer can the physician work "solo" and independently, he is a member of a health team working with medical and paramedical colleagues and in cooperation with the public.

It has been traditional for the physician to command respect, power and authority. In the world of the past the university educated and scientifically-trained physician was caring for patients who were lucky if they had managed to achieve more than a basic primary education and were able to read and write. It was easy therefore for the physician to appear and behave as a god-like figure from a different social world. Now within an increasingly well educated, informed and expectant society the physician is looked upon much more as a skilled technician, who is neverthelesss still highly respected, but with less power and authority than in the past.

The modern physician within a changing society is faced with many conflicts and dilemmas that have to be appreciated and resolved if the best standards of care are to be achieved.

Compromises have to be reached between some degree of professional freedom and independence that still is essential if the physician is to continue to be responsible for the care of his patients as individuals and if he is to place this care as of supreme importance, and, controls and directives that are necessary to create changes which are designed to produce a more effective system of care for the population as a whole. It is a compromise between the physician's responsibilities to his individual patient and to the mass society in which he lives.

State Involvement

State involvement in medical care is inevitable because of the high and ever-increasing costs. State subsidies are essential, but their form and nature will depend on national beliefs and traditions.

There is no single system applicable to all. A whole spectrum of possibilities exists from a complete State system as in U.S.S.R., through various types such as the National Health Service in U.K., and Scandinavia to partial subsidisation of special services as in U.S.A.

State involvement leads to problems in relations with the medical profession, over conditions and pay and standards; with the practising physician over controls and directives; with the individual over rules and regulations; and with the medical industry, such as hospitals, pharmaceutical manufacturers and other supporting facilities, over costs, quality and agreements.

With State involvement come decisions on priorities over the use of available resources. Health measures are linked inseparably with social security measures and a general policy has to be evolved to include needs such as child and family allowances, support for the aged and handicapped, unemployment and sickness benefits, services to deal with social problems and subsidies for food, housing, transport, clothes and holidays and leisure.

Public Wants and Expectations

Social surveys suggest that basically the average individual seeks the following from a system of medical care – availability and accessibility to a physician who is known and respected and who has access to specialist services within a reasonable distance. The qualities of care most appreciated are simply kindliness, concern and interest in the individual's problems, time to listen and quality of service.

Individual Responsibilities

What incentives and leads are necessary to encourage the individual to keep fit and healthy?

If the costs of treating the sick are so high how much effort and monies should be directed to health education and disease prevention and how successful are these exercises? Preventive measures are linked inextricably with medical care and public health measures involving sanitation and hygiene and mass immunisation have produced great benefits, but we are now becoming more concerned with more personal measures concerned with the prevention of disease.

Family Kinship

The family is the basic unit in all societies and it is the family that is first involved in medical care. It is remarkably successful since it manages to care for 3 out of 4 of minor symptoms – complexes that occur in a developed nation. Although the family is still of great importance its links and associations are becoming loosened through social changes. Social mobility, industrialisation and urbanisation are all leading to smaller families, working mothers, nurseries and kindergartens and grandmothers who take on the care of young children. There is more emphasis to the voice of youth, which speaks in a rebellious tone and kinship, tribal elders and family councils are being replaced by newer social institutions.

It is therefore in the context of all these apparent changes in the society of man that medical care services have to take their place, and play their part.

B

Chapter 1

International Trends in Medical Care Organisation and Research

R. F. BRIDGMAN, M.D.

*Inspector-General, Ministry of Health and Social Security,
Paris, France
Formerly Chief Medical Officer, Organisation of Medical Care,
World Health Organisation, Geneva*

Whilst medical care is as old as mankind, the concept of medical care organisation is barely 20 years old. For centuries relationships between physician and patient were based on a dialogue. Admission to hospitals was restricted to low income group patients and administration of health institutions was the responsibility of charitable bodies. In many countries, however, local or central authorities long ago shared a part in organising hospitals and welfare services for the poor, beggars, mentally disturbed and infectious patients, but the aim was more to protect society than to care for destitutes.

At the end of the 19th century the views of Chadwick, Pasteur and Lister prevailed, and bacteriology, immunology and public health grew as new disciplines. Röntgen made possible the early detection of pulmonary tuberculosis. Many of the infectious diseases receded and mortality rates changed drastically as well as causes of morbidity.

It is extraordinary, however, that this immense field in which action could be taken by governmental bodies only, did not encroach on the traditional domain of medical care. During the first quarter of the 20th century many hospitals retained their private character and the doctor-patient relationship remained strictly personal.

However, the side effects of the industrial revolution and of scientific development became more and more overwhelming. The relative importance of the various classes in the social structure was modified as the proportion of industrial workers increased and that of white collar workers, agents of the third socio-economic sector, skyrocketed causing the salaried class to become the largest part of the population. The traditional art of medicine was progressively imbued with technology, and became more scientific and thus more costly. The necessity of equalising the cost of medical care among all salary and wage earners led to the Social Security concept which is definitely one of the greatest

8

achievements of modern times in the field of social organisation.

Several trends were observed, which in themselves depended on economic development and also on traditional administrative and cultural patterns, and here we shall point out the salient facts defining these trends in different groups of countries. Any grouping is debatable but from studies on administrative and legislative systems it seems convenient to study successively: —

(a) Countries of western continental Europe (Scandinavia excluded) and Latin America.
(b) Northern American countries.
(c) Scandinavia and the United Kingdom (also Australia, New Zealand, South Africa and Canada).
(d) Socialist countries.
(e) Economically developing countries where genuine historical and cultural patterns are still in force.
(f) Economically developing countries whose patterns were imposed by western powers.

The above grouping is different from the two usual contemporary classifications which are either divided into three, i.e. capitalist and socialist countries and the Third World, or two: i.e. developed and developing countries. These two classifications are much too ambiguous.

There are many common trends between capitalistic and socialist countries as far as technology and research are concerned. However, the so-called developing countries make up a large group which is very heterogeneous. A common characteristic such as economic under-development and its corollary, a low income per capita, hides extensive social and cultural differences. Let us try to define the common trends in each group of countries.

Countries of Western Continental Europe (Scandinavia excluded) and Latin America

The axis of the whole administration is Roman law. The hospital system is thoroughly rooted in the social conscience and its administrative framework is based on local government. There are private hospitals, which are either the remnants of ancient powerful religious voluntary bodies, or profit-making nursing homes mainly used for surgery and obstetrics.

The medical profession has retained its liberal and independent character but since part of the population is salaried or dependant on salaried workers, social security schemes are well developed. In most of these countries social security schemes are not governmental or centrally organised, and often far from unified. Conflicting interests between the medical profession and social security schemes are common but political pressure from the insured population is such that physicians and administrators of sickness insurance funds are condemned to collaborate, even if they continually disagree.

The Government does not control directly either public hospitals nor social security schemes. Its role is to implement a legislative framework, to subsidise capital expenditure and to control both the investment and administration of institutions through local authorities. The results of this complicated machinery may lead to great flexibility and encouragement to local initiative, but can, on the other hand, cause duplication or gaps, sophisticated controls and a certain lack of efficiency.

Health technocrats advocate planning which implies control of all medical care and health services, public and private, full-time personnel and financial and technical supervision. They come across obstacles which are not only traditional and conservative, but of private vested interest and the desire of local authorities to preserve their relative autonomy and possibilities for initiative. The social security organisations, when strictly government controlled, can serve as intermediaries and enable the public authorities to exert pressure on private bodies without encroaching on the principle of constitutional freedom. However, non-governmental social security bodies, enjoying a large degree of independence and benefiting from substantial advantages, develop an empire of their own, erecting powerful institutions for their subscribers, leaving the uninsured to the care of public hospitals or, in the case of the very wealthy, to that of a few luxurious nursing homes.

This lack of coordination leads to very serious overlapping in the more specialised sectors and to gaps as far as basic medical care is concerned. The present trend, in these countries, is to coordinate more closely health and social policy, with the aim of achieving the cooperation of the public and private sectors and to persuade social security schemes to finance not only curative care, but also personal preventive programmes and rehabilitation. It is obvious that from this point of view health authorities and social security schemes have a common interest because the importance of personal preventive services and rehabilitation correspond to savings in expenditure on medical care and invalidity pensions. Moreover, in economic development dependent on manpower, social security schemes are directly concerned with the health of population and therefore productivity.

This brief description encompasses variegated situations prevailing in developed countries of western continental Europe, such as Belgium, France, Germany, Italy, less developed ones like Greece, Spain and Portugal and low income countries of Latin America. It might look strange, at first sight to classify under the same headings France and Colombia, or, Italy and Peru. Actually the Latin American countries inherited their medical care system from the Spaniards and the Portuguese and one can easily find characteristic traits which prevailed in European countries 60 years ago. Latin America is a continent which cannot be classified as developed because of the low level of economical and cultural development of the masses, but it is not certainly underdeveloped if one considers the organisational patterns of the administration and the large number of Universities which exceeds one hundred.

Northern American Countries

Medical care in the U.S.A. has been defined as a pluralistic system matching its pluralistic society. It would be wrong to oversimplify this description in calling it the "American system".

However, being, in fact, non-systematic, the patterns of medical care are open to revision and change as a result of antagonistic pressures from the different population classes and the many professional bodies involved.

The role of the federal government is far from negligible. Most of the large psychiatric hospitals are federal as well as the Veterans institutions. Large sums of money are spent in subsidising health centres and hospitals through the Hill-Burton machinery. There are many small community public hospitals in the U.S.A., largely due to federal aid. However, the limited capacity of these hospitals justifies criticism. Finally, the federal administration gives grants to a host of research projects, and recently developed the extensive Medicare and Medicaid programmes which are an important step towards recognition of the central government responsibility for the public's health. At state level, there is extensive involvement in Public Health, and medical care to indigents is organised by local authorities. However, the great bulk of medical care activities is carried out by the private sector, which, in most of its aspects, is commercialised.

A large part of the $53 billion a year which the Americans are paying for medical care (7·5 per cent of all personal income) is a flow which goes from the private purse of the consumer of health care, to the bank accounts of private practitioners and voluntary hospitals. Half the private hospital bills are repaid by insurance but, as Blue Shield, Blue Cross and many other voluntary and commercial sickness insurances are private, the total amount is still borne by individuals, either by direct payment to the medical care system or through their subscriptions to insurance schemes.

Most of the best hospitals are voluntary and rely partly on private contributions, but when one considers that the hospital's administrative staff receive comfortable salaries and that physicians and specialists demand fees for services, the word "voluntary" is somewhat of a misnomer. For some years the spiralling of medical care costs has been such that influential groups, mostly economists and federal administrators, are seriously considering building-up an American network of planned medical care services according to the regionalisation concept. This is certainly the only way to avoid costly duplication of equipment, to improve the efficiency of the qualified personnel and to bring some rationale into a situation which is no longer merely complex but frankly chaotic.

In modern societies health is no longer the concern of individuals, it is the inescapable responsibility of political authorities. If it is recognised that 25 per cent of U.S. citizens get excellent medical care, then for 50 per cent this care is just passable whilst for the remaining 25 per cent it is more than insufficient.

The building-up of the "great society" implies replacement of the present uncoordinated pluralistic patterns by an organised and efficient system and the problem is essentially to reconcile private interests with a coordinated organisation, for the welfare of all. However, in such an ambitious endeavour, health cannot be considered in isolation; education, social security, welfare and fair equalisation of income must proceed in parallel.

The direction taken by the government seems to use decentralised extensive voluntary bodies to exert their powers through so-called private intermediaries. The accreditation of hospitals is a classical example of remote government control through the American Medical Association, the American College of Surgeons, the American College of Physicians and the American Hospital Association. A similar system was adopted to implement the law on Medicare through sickness and hospital voluntary insurance schemes.

In theory this complicated machinery seems workable in our computer age. However, the medical care system including hospitals still remains a mismanaged business.

Scandinavia and the United Kingdom (including also Australia, New Zealand, South Africa and Canada)

The medical care systems of these countries have in common the fact that they are planned at central government level, but the administration is decentralised either at regional level for hospitals in the English-speaking countries, or at county level in the Scandinavian countries.

In Scandinavia the private sector is limited to a minority of specialists and a few practitioners. Most physicians are employed full-time in hospitals or health centres and the relatively few private hospitals receive considerable support from public authorities. In the United Kingdom the medical profession is at present organised centrally, with decentralised regional boards and executive committees. The profession is represented by elected representatives and the fee per capita for general practitioners is actually a flexible civil servant salary. The role of social security varies. It plays no role in the financing of medical care proper and is largely concerned with sickness benefits and old age and invalidity pensions. The finance for medical care comes from general taxation through the central government budget. In Scandinavia social security funds partly cover ambulatory and hospital care, but the local counties are mainly responsible.

In all these countries the central government has considerable powers. In the U.K. hospital planning and construction is decided upon at central level. However, hospital administration in England is decentralised to regional hospital boards and each regional hospital board decentralises management decisions to smaller hospital management committees.

In Sweden the National Board of Health supervises general health and pharmaceutical services; it exercises control over treatment of the sick in both private and public hospitals. The Central Board of Hospital Planning supervises plans for the construction of hospitals. The State operates three University Hospitals, the Karolinska and Serafimer in Stockholm and the Akademiska in Uppsala. Moreover, according to the regionalisation plan, the counties are responsible for general medical care departments and the State takes over the responsibility for specialised departments in Regional Hospitals. The local administration of all health services is left to the elected County Health Board, and to county borough councils. Similar schemes apply in the four Scandinavian countries. Standardisation and computerisation of data are already implemented and research on administration and utilisation of hospitals and medical care is routinely carried out. Moreover, from an inter-country computer programme, the data can be analysed and compared between the four countries.

In other English-speaking countries, the situation is more complex. Australia and New Zealand have less centralised systems and the social security systems are not nearly so comprehensive as that of the United Kingdom.

In Canada there are important differences between the provinces. Saskatchewan was the first to set up a comprehensive social security scheme to which the hospital administration was entrusted. British Columbia and Alberta are developing systems very close to the English National Health Service, and whilst Ontario retains voluntary hospitals, provincial authorities have organised a powerful hospital committee. In Quebec the medical care pattern is at present closer to the continental European system, but under review.

Socialist countries

The salient fact is the merging in socialist countries of all activities related to population health within a vast hierarchised system in which general practice, hospital and personal preventive care are combined.

The hospital in the U.S.S.R., for example has disappeared as an administrative entity and there are no such things as management boards or municipal hospitals. However, the premises, equipment and technical facilities of hospitals are the focus of the health programme. Take an average general hospital serving a territorial district of 50,000 to 80,000 population as an example. A polyclinic which plays the role of comprehensive out-patient service for preventive and curative work is attached to the hospital and two or three additional polyclinics are established in the district, without beds, physically independent, but linked to the health administration that is located within the general hospital. In each of these polyclinics there is a team of physicians and specialists dividing their activities between out-patient cases and home or domiciliary care. The district is divided up into small territorial neighbourhood areas called "uchastok" with a 4,000 – 10,000 population. Two to five physicians plus two to three paediatricians serve each of these areas whilst screening, follow-up and personal preventive care is given at the polyclinic.

Such schemes are typical of the basic health services in urban areas. In rural areas hospitals are smaller and there are decentralised medical assistants (feldshers) with midwives in villages and serving collective farms.

From this basic foundation a comprehensive hierarchical hospital system is built up. At regional level (oblast) there is a regional hospital with all specialities. At republic level there are specialised institutes for research. Finally, at union level, the Institutes for advanced learning and research are located in the main metropolis.

This schematic description does not give the full picture of the medical care system. Firstly, organisation of paediatric care is quite separate from that of adult care. Children have their own polyclinics, their own hospitals and their own practitioners. Of course, this strict physical distinction is to be seen only in large towns. In smaller towns and rural areas, one finds paediatric departments in polyclinics and general hospitals but it is a principle that all care for children is given by paediatricians. Secondly, campaigns against tuberculosis and venereal diseases are separate from general care. There are no T.B. patients in district hospitals or polyclinics. Mental health is also largely independent.

Finally, a great deal of medical care is organised by large factories, workers' unions and social security (especially for the elderly and convalescents). State responsibility for health care has not suppressed voluntary action. The Red Cross and Red Crescent play a considerable role in health education and follow-up of chronic patients. The whole of the socialist system can be described as an active approach to health protection and promotion, while, in western countries, medical care remains largely passive in the sense that hospitals are rather waiting for the sick than preventing disease.

Whilst the socialist system has a potential in staff, hospital beds, and money to cope efficiently with health protection and promotion, on the other hand, the role of volunteers is considerable in stirring-up demands for health care by the population. Without the army of Red Cross and Red Crescent volunteers and the workers' unions, the health system could not reach the vulnerable groups so comprehensively.

The physical side of the medical care system, as well as the organisational concept is directed towards efficiency and total coverage of the population.

Central institutes determine the number of hospital beds by district, specialised departments, location in the towns, architectural planning and standardisation of all medical equipment. The economic principle of greater return for minimum investment is strictly implemented in order to guarantee total coverage of needs. Therefore, there are no lavish hospitals to be found in the U.S.S.R. and sophisticated equipment is located where it can most efficiently be used. However, the psychological needs of the patient are considered and great attention is paid to his physical and mental rehabilitation.

The trend is to rationalise and specialise the whole system in order to keep pace with scientific progress and to give equal changes to all citizens so that they receive adequate care.

Foreign visitors to socialist countries must understand that behind a somewhat gloomy and standardised outlook, as far as hospital buildings are concerned, medical care organisation is a powerful machine which endeavours to meet the needs of the total population.

Economically developing countries where genuine historical and cultural patterns are still in force

There are a large number of countries in the world in which outstanding civilisations developed and reached a level which was comparable and sometimes superior to that of Europe centuries ago. However, they could not benefit from the industrial technological revolution which brought Europe and North America to the fore, as far as economic development is concerned.

Leaving historians and economists to explain how the wealth of these nations was concentrated in the hands of a few and why most of these eventually came under colonial rule, it is obvious that the people have not forgotten the inheritance of their past history and are still aware of and are familiar with traditional culture. The Arab States, India, and Eastern Asia are examples and these countries have had hospitals for more than a thousand years and renowned medical schools which contributed considerably to the development of medicine in the pre-scientific era. They still, especially in Indian and Chinese spheres of influence, have many traditional doctors who practice an empirical medicine and who are certainly not sorcerers or magicians, the Ayurvedic and Chinese arts of healing for example are effective against many symptoms and the drugs are very cheap. They still have a real value in treating the common complaints of a large number of patients. Culture and learning are valued highly in these countries, this is why modern universities, teaching contemporary scientific medicine have developed so rapidly with hosts of enthusiastic students and teachers. There are for example more than 90 medical schools in India, 46 in Japan, 7 in the Philippines and 3 in Thailand.

Moreover it is noteworthy that the languages of these countries are sufficiently subtle to enable modern technological and medical textbooks to be translated. This considerably facilitates their assimilation by students. Even if English and French books and periodicals are still necessary, there is a growing number of basic books in Japanese, Turkish, Arab, Hindu, Chinese and Thai.

Similarly even if the brain-drain mechanism causes many undergraduates and graduates to be attracted by the Western countries and wish to stay there, a great potential of trained people is on the way. The populations are aware of this trend; they send their children to schools and universities and they respond to health campaigns. More important is the fact that local authorities are receptive because a hospital or an organised medical care health centre is something familiar to the political leaders, and services are deeply rooted in the traditional culture of these populations.

The problem is therefore not that of a lack of receptivity of the population but the uneven distribution of doctors, the low income of the great majority of people, the stringency of health budgets, the difficulties in obtaining drugs and equipment, the dissatisfaction of doctors and the hard living conditions in rural areas where the majority of the population lives.

The development of health services is essentially hampered by lack of money. From one point of view one wonders whether the concept of the Welfare State, born in western countries and developed in the Anglosaxon world, is not the main reason for the slow development of medical care services. It is one thing to declare proudly that free education and free health are the responsibility of the State but it is another thing to put into practice this ambitious declaration.

In countries where the medical system is mainly financed from the state budget one can observe a serious stagnation which is a confession of failure. In countries where Social Security schemes are operating on a reasonable scale, the semi-private sectors flourish as in Japan, Taiwan, Turkey, Iran and the Philippines. It may lead to overlapping and competition but it is a dynamic phenomenon which delivers a greater amount of medical care to certain parts of the population.

Another factor to be considered, is the reluctance of these nations to revise the administrative machinery they inherited from their previous rulers and to adapt it to present day possibilities. This is only partially true for the Arab States which had a strong Turkish administrative pattern easily adapted to a socialist structure. It is a matter of fact that in ancient *Islamic* law the so-called public institutes like the hospitals benefitted from "mortgage funds" but the ownership was delegated to Allah. It was no serious problem to transfer ownership from Allah to the State. However, in Asia the administration patterns imposed by the ruling powers of the 19th century were preserved, even if they were completely foreign to the legislative tradition of the country.

This trait is shared by the last group of countries we shall now examine.

Economically developing countries whose patterns were imposed by Western forces

Most of these countries lie south of the Sahara desert but some of them are scattered in Asia and Oceania.

These countries have in common the fact that they had no written culture before their confrontation with European powers. Their languages are many and are not adaptable to modern scientific concepts. Therefore, students and teachers have to master and to work with foreign languages. Their traditional culture is considered of no value and is despised even if it still flourishes underground.

The western rulers built hospitals of three main types, public infirmaries mainly for the armed forces, mission hospitals and health posts, and hospitals for industrial and agricultural estates. None of these institutions were adapted to the actual needs of the whole population. The public hospitals were located in cities and could not keep pace with the rapid increase in urban populations. They were crowded with local patients, most of them suffering from very severe conditions.

Rural populations, making up 80 – 90 per cent of the country's population were left to missionaries who by natural inclination paid more attention to severely mutilated lepers than to curable adolescents and adults. Moreover, the atmosphere prevailing in these institutions was unfamiliar to the people. It was unavoidable that on occasions the selection of patients occurred only on their superficially abandoning their traditional customs and beliefs. Therefore, private medical care could alienate people from their basic culture. The same could be said for education. After all, the hospitals created and run by industrial or agricultural estates (tin mines, rubber or tea plantations, etc.) were probably the most efficient and often the best planned. However, they were designed for workers only and were available to patients as long as they were registered as workers. Unemployment, long term sickness and strikes amply justified withdrawal of the right to be treated by a given factory or estate's medical care organisation. Workers were often well looked after because they were considered as components of manpower rather than human beings.

Since independence, the situation has changed very slowly. Even if governments want to improve their medical care system they are hampered by lack of skilled personnel, finance, administrative competence and specialised equipment. Despite numerous fellowships and facilities given to students from these countries, the number of doctors is very often less than it was before independence, and practically all rural areas are staffed by foreign doctors who are often of different nationalities from the previous authorities. These have serious language difficulties as well as administrative and family problems.

The few indigenous doctors remain in Europe or in America, or practice in main cities because living conditions in the country are still unsatisfactory. One must also mention the drain to "oil countries" whose companies offer high salaries. The hospitals founded by the previous authorities are decaying because of difficulties of maintenance, deterioration of the central supply system and weakness of administration. Very little effort is devoted to adapting out-moded administrative machinery to modern conditions.

However, a certain number of hospitals have recently been built in Africa. Unfortunately they are seldom properly adapted to local conditions and to the financial resources. The previous ruling countries preserved many commercial ties with their ancient colonies which are not easily severed. Private planning and building firms in developed countries are specialising in hospital equipment and extend their activities to developing countries. Unfortunately the modern type of construction and equipment they offer is too sophisticated. The degree of sophistication is such that tenders allow for considerable imprecision and large profits are possible. Therefore the construction of a hospital is much more profitable than that of a bridge or prison; it is also a much more spectacular achievement guaranteed to please political leaders. In several developing countries there are scores of modern hospitals with paraphernalia often absent from similar institutions in developed countries. The cost of transporting and assembling technical equipment and building material may increase the initial cost by some 200 per cent, finally, the cost of a hospital in Africa may exceed by four or five times, that of a comparable hospital in the developed world. Moreover, the maintenance of electronic machinery and recurrent costs raise insurpassable problems and it is not rare to find a brand new hospital is unable to function and has remained empty since its inauguration.

It also happens that leaders of developing countries, more or less influenced by specialists, wish to have the sophisticated services which are the privilege of developed countries and invest the little money available on prestige departments such as those for heart and brain surgery or cobalt therapy, leaving the medical care services in a serious state of neglect. Therefore in many developing countries the total coverage of the population against health hazards remains a dream more remote from reality than twenty years ago.

Economic losses due to disease and accidents is enormous and obviously jeopardises economic development. A vicious circle is therefore created which could be broken only if the developing countries adopted a more realistic attitude concerning basic medical care. The preliminary stage to the take-off would be the training of auxiliary medical personnel, development of basic health services, adoption of simple type hospital building, centralisation and standardisation of technical equipment, adaptation of administration to staffing conditions and a higher proportion of money allotted to a rationalised health service.

THE COMPLEXITY OF INTERNATIONAL MEDICAL CARE AND FIELDS OF DEVELOPMENT

After this bird's eye view on a very complex situation it seems that there cannot be only one solution to the problem of medical care orgainsation in the whole world. We see that the main organisational patterns depend on many factors of which the social and political structure and the lack of economic development are the main.

The welfare state concept requires either a socialist society as in communist countries, or a high level of economic development from which the Government Health Authorities can obtain the 5 per cent of the gross national product which is the minimum necessary to finance a comprehensive health system. In countries where a large part of the medical care sector is in the hands of the liberal professions and commercial enterprises, the necessity to give each salaried person or wage earner – and his dependents – medical care benefits leads to a comprehensive compulsory social security scheme, which acts as an equalisation system. In a capitalist society where hospitals and medical care services are not nationalised, it is logical that the social security retains a semi-private character. However, if the total budget of social and welfare services amounts to 18 to 20 per cent of the gross national product, partial subsidisation by the state is a means of avoiding the overloading of the productivity sector. This requires an extensive amount of control from the Government which has also to play the role of arbitrator between the liberal and independent medical profession and the social security scheme. In developing countries such a system can be contemplated only when a sizeable proportion of the population is regularly salaried. Peasant farmers always raise a difficult problem because of their low income in cash. Community development and agricultural co-operatives might be an answer to the problem, however, as long as only part of the population is covered by sickness insurance, the insurance funds should not be allowed to build a system of their own, restricted to eligible sub-scribers. A co-ordinating mechanism must be established in order to avoid, by all means, the creation of a dual system, one run by the government, the other by insurance schemes. A private commercial sector can be added for the wealthy.

For the developing countries where governmental resources are low, trained personnel scarce, and where the economy is still at an archaic stage, the nationalisation of the medical care system is practically unavoidable. The result of over-concentration would be preferable to absence of any co-ordination, provided well established planning is carried out. This planning requires considering administrative, financial, architectural and engineering aspects. The amount of competence needed would require the help of inter-country, regional or international planning centres especially where several small countries are involved, because the size of their individual programmes does not warrant full activity of national planning institutes.

In all cases research is indispensable as a basis to planning. We know very little about the relationships between biological needs, "felt" needs, and demands. The perception of disease varies greatly according to the basic culture of population groups. Demands and needs are changing according to education, morbidity, environment, income and availability of services.

If the influence of these factors can be estimated and if it is possible to correlate the demands for medical care with socio-economic and demographic characteristics, the laws governing demand in relation to the level of development can be discovered. Then starting from a certain type of demand corresponding to a given level of development, it would be possible to forecast future demand when the population at risk reaches a further step of development. Planning can be based on scientific observations and facts can be dovetailed to establish a law, that is to say a cause to effect relationship.

We are not yet at this stage but one point is already clear. Traditional statistical studies at national level are of no use because the country average disguises regional differences which are the source for discovering influencing factors. At present many research projects on medical care are conducted by a great variety of methods. Some use utilisation studies through recording patient contacts with the different components of a comprehensive medical care service. Individuals are classified by age group, sex, distance from health facilities, living standards, occupation, marital status, financial coverage, etc. The types of medical care required are classified acccording to disease, group of diseases or medical disciplines. Observations are grouped in order to ascertain how well-defined population groups are actually utilising medical care services. Other studies are focused more on motivation of population demand, behaviour of patients, perception of disease, judgement on medical care services, etc., through household interviews. Combination of these two groups of methods is possible because they actually lead to the same target: assessing population demands and felt needs in relation to influencing factors.

Such studies should be conducted under different conditions and in areas with various socio-economic and cultural patterns. The results will most probably enable the planners to determine with accuracy the priority sectors and the types of investment to be decided by the authorities in order to improve the health status of the productive population and hence facilitate economic development. Based on scientific research, health planning will become a service leading to an exact determination of the strategy of development of medical care services.

Targets being determined, ways of approach can be many. In socialistic societies, planning techniques will lead to reinforcement of the conceptual work at central level and to decentralisation of decision and management. This is already the case in the U.S.S.R.. In capitalistic societies co-ordination between the public and private sectors will be reinforced but this does not mean that voluntary enterprises will become useless or nationalised in the near future. In countries still financially under-developed, but where the brain potential enables, accelerated economic development and a rapid increase in the proportion of salary and wage earners, the trend will probably be towards organised social security schemes participating in capital investment and recurrent expenditure of medical care schemes including personal prevention and rehabilitation. In slowly developing countries central power should be reinstated and technological advice should be sought from inter-country, regional or international research and planning institutes.

This multifaceted approach is a prerequisite for the realisation of the present dream of total coverage of mankind against health hazards, – this aim will be the task of future generations – but if we can lay down the foundations of this ambitious conception before the end of the twentieth century, we can feel we have done our best.

Suggestions for further reading

Journals

Abel-Smith, B., "The major pattern of financing and organisation of medical services that have emerged in other countries." *Med. Care.* (1965), **3**, 33.

Anderson, O. W., "Toward a framework for analysing health services systems with examples from selected countries." *Soc. Econ. Admin.* (1967), **1**, 16.

Bergner, L., and Yerby, A. S., "Low income and barriers to use of health services." *New Engl. J. Med.* (1968), **278**, 541.

Chester, T. E., "How healthy is the National Health Service?" *District Bank Rev. No. 167*, (1968), 3.

Densen, P. M., et al., "Concerning high and low utilizers of service in a medical care plan, and the persistence of utilisation levels over a three year period." *Milbk. Mem. Fnd. Quart.* (1959), **37**, 217

Donabedian, A., and Axelrod, S. J., "Organising medical care programs to meet health needs." *Annals Amer. Acad. Polit. Soc. Sci.* (1961) **337**, 46.

Dwivedi, J. K., "Medical care in India." *World Hosp.* (1967), **3**, 40.

Feldstein, P. J., "Research on the demand for health services." *Milbk. Mem. Fnd. Quart.* (1966), **44**, 128.

Halevi, H. S., "Health services in Israél: their organisation, utilisation and financing." *Med. Care.* (1964), **2**, 231.

Hastings, J. E. F., "Recent developments and current issues in health care in Canada." *Canad. J. Pub. Hlth.* (1967), **58**, 93.

Lafitte, V., "L'élasticité des besoins médicaux et la baisse du seuil de tolérance à la maladie, phénomène de civilisation." *Cah. Soc. Demogr. Med.* (1966), **6**, 66.

Logan, R. F. L., "International studies of illness and health services." *Milbk. Mem. Fnd. Quart.* (1968), **46**, 126

Mainland, D., ed. "Health services research." *Milbk. Mem. Fnd. Quart.* (1966), **44**, *No. 3, Part 2*, 7 and **44**, *No. 4, Part 2*, 9.

Mauro, V., and Cotronei, G., "Evoluzione storica, politica e sociale della assistenza sanitaria nella repubblica cecoslovacca." *Dif. Soc.* (1966), **45**, 75.

Pesonen, N., "Organisation of medical care and public health services in Finland." *World Hosp.* (1966), **2**, 92.

Peyret, "La politique et l'avenir de la santé publique en France." *Rev. Hosp. France* (1968), **32**, 171.

Reinke, W. A., and Baker, T. D., "Measuring effects of demographic variables on health services utilisation." *Hlth. Serv. Res.* (1967), **2**, 61.

Roemer, M. I., "Changing patterns of health services: their dependence on a changing world." *Ann. Amer. Polit. Soc. Sci.* (1963), **346**, 44.

White, K. L., et al. "International comparisons of medical care utilisation. "*New Engl. J. Med.* (1967), **277**, 516.

Zamarippa, C. "Organizacion y funcinamento de los servicios medicos en la seguridad social." *Bol. Med. Inst. Mex. Seg. Soc.* (1966), **8**, 195.

Books

Bridgman, R. F., *L'Hôpital et la Cité*, Techniques Hospitalières, Paris, 1963.

Cuba. Ministerio de Salud Publica, *Red preventivo-asistencial; epidemiologia. Network of preventive and curative medical care; epidemiology; Réseau préventif-curatif; épidémiologie. Ponencias oficiales presentadas al XI congreso medico y VII estomatologico nacional, Habana, Cuba, Febrero 1966*, Ministerio de Salud Publica, Habana, 1966.

National Commission on Community Health Services, *Health is a community affair. Report of the National Commission on Community Health Services*, Harvard University Press, Cambridge, Mass., 1966.

Navarro, V., *Regionalization and planning of personal health services. An annotated bibliography*, Johns Hopkins University, Baltimore, 1967

Roemer, M. I., *Medical care in Latin America*, Pan American Union, Washington, 1963.

U.S.S.R. Ministry of Health, *The system of public health services in the U.S.S.R.*, Ministry of Health, Moscow, 1967.

U.S.A. Department of Health Education, and Welfare. Public Health Service. National Center for Health Statistics, *Medical care, health status, and family income, United States*, Public Health Service, Washington, 1964.

World Health Organisation. Pan American Health Organisation, *Administration of medical care services; new elements for the formulation of a continental policy.* Pan American Health Organisation, Washington, 1966.

World Health Organisation. Pan American Health Organisation. Study Group on Coordination of Medical Care in Latin America, *Relationship between social security medical programs and those of ministries of health and other official health agencies*, Pan American Health Organisation, Washington, 1965.

C

Section Two

Methods of Medical Care

Chapter 2

Medical Care in Europe

D. STARK MURRAY, B.SC., M.B., CH.B.
Consultant, World Health Organisation, and
Consultant Emeritus, National Health Service, England

SCANDINAVIA AND WESTERN EUROPE

Medical Science has a long history and over the centuries a variety of explanations of disease and therefore of treatment, have held the field. The views of the early Greek physicians had a very long life and coupled with some concepts from Arabian medicine merged with those of mediaevel practitioners whose relationship with the Christian church lead to the first development of hospitals. As other scientific disciplines, chemistry, physics and the electrical and optical sciences developed the human body in health and disease came under closer scrutiny and a new way of looking at disease began to develop. Great anatomical discoveries were made, the circulation of the blood was recognised, the dependence of the animal body on oxygen was established and the idea of diseases caused by agents attacking from outside the body slowly proved.

These developments were taking place in many European countries and from an early time, certainly the fifteenth century, there was an international exchange of ideas and a surprising amount of contact between places of learning in all these countries. Out of this there has slowly grown an accepted body of knowledge and opinion as to the normal functioning of the body, of the ways in which it becomes diseased and of the ways in which physicians should study, diagnose and treat ill-health. In this century there has been added the concept of disease prevention and today the European medical professions begin to concern themselves with the preservation and improvement of health.

So when we speak of modern medical science or health care it is to this highly developed system which had its basis in Europe's great teaching hospitals that we refer. In all the countries to be dealt with in this section it is that common body of knowledge, based as far as

possible on scientific methods, which provides the present day system
of health care. The way in which that care reaches the sick has also
been through a long process of development and in most countries
is still under continuous discussion and review. The first attempts at
some kind of organised care was in the hospitals attached to or
part of religious institutions. The Church, therefore, played an important part in the early growth of medical care but it also undertook
a certain amount of what we would now regard as social welfare:
and when the poor became too numerous for any system of alms giving
to operate most countries began some kind of "poor-law system"
which involved housing the needy in "poor houses", or more often
"work houses" as the poor were expected to do some kind of physical
work in return for their shelter. These institutions soon found they
had so many sick people among the poor that they had to provide
medical care and so grew a variety of systems of poor-law medicine.
It is a modern concept that while the poor must be provided with both
food, shelter and medical care it is necessary also to ensure social
welfare benefits and medical services to every citizen as a right.
But history lasts a long time and throughout Europe there are still
remnants, in some cases very large ones, of the church hospitals, of
the poor-law systems and of a variety of attempts to provide care for
those who could not provide it for themselves.

Fundamentally most European countries, indeed all except Eire and
Holland, accept that modern medical care involves both governmental
planning and State subsidies and in both the countries named
practice far outstrips stated policy and much public money goes in to
medical care facilities. The variations are considerable, in organisation,
in amounts spent publicly and privately, in the type of practitioners
involved and in the ultimate quantity and quality of service received
by the sick, but all embody in some form the concept of the sick
making a monetary contribution, but only a contribution to the
cost of their own care at the time of use of the service.

Taking Scandinavia and Western Europe together we are dealing
with a geographical area of great variety and some geographical
features, as in Norway and Sweden, that influence the spread of
services, an area with a wide temperature range, with considerable
variation in altitude and, it follows, with a great variation in conditions
that affect health and the incidence of certain diseases and hazards.
The total area is 1·5 million square miles and the individual countries
vary from Luxembourg with an area of only 998 square miles to
France with over 212,000 square miles. The population is 346 million
with fifteen distinct languages and variations in cultural and educational levels which are quite marked. There is, however, a very great
degree of similarity in the way of life of the urban populations of the

28

larger cities and a great deal of inter-change between them. Most of the countries have today a large tourist industry and millions move around the whole European area so that no longer does any group exist in isolation. Nevertheless differences do exist and are reflected in the health and service security systems in each country.

In Europe the provision of health care has been generally accepted as a community responsibility without carrying that idea in any of the countries except the United Kingdom, to its logical conclusion as to universality and comprehensiveness. The result is that some 80 per cent of the population of Western Europe receive some or all of their health care from a statutory health programme. Historically many of the countries to be discussed started with a variety of voluntary insurance, prepaid and contract types of system for paying for medical care, in the nineteenth century. These developed along-side many schemes, especially hospitals provided by religious bodies, for the very poor; and some of these schemes also became codified in poor-law systems. When the voluntary type of insurance was later changed to a compulsory system, at least for those industrially employed, the poor were omitted as being already provided for and the wealthy were left to make their own arrangements. In time, however, free hospital services became available or were subsidized by the state; and many services connected with wider public health problems, such as infectious diseases and serious mental illness fell outside the insurance system.

But insurance took many forms, developing into a single state system or coming under parastatal organisations or remaining in the hand of numerous small units, as sick funds rather than true insurance carriers. Within these variations the amount of cover given also varied, some items given in full, others being subject to a re-claim system in which the insurance agency would refund part of what had been paid by the patient, the range varying from 60 to 100 per cent but usually around 80 per cent. In some cases the doctors worked to an agreed fee schedule charging no more than the percentages they knew would be refunded, in other instances the refund was based on the schedule no matter how much the doctor actually charged.

The development of health services has been influenced by geography, by the concentration of industry, and by lines of communication. Norway has a population of three and a half millions but in the North they are scattered widely in areas where communication is never very easy and in winter very difficult. The type of services that can be supplied are very different from that in a city and the doctor in some communities is very much more a generalist than one would find in a universtiy city. His income has to be computed differently from that of a specialised physician with a wealthy private practice. A study of the smaller countries reveals how much more personal the health service can be and how much more closely standards can be watched than in a very large country. It also shows that the state has to assume responsibility for a comprehensive service if the natural tendency under a free market medicine system, for doctors to practice in cities where there is wealth, is to be counterbalanced. So long as the attempt is made to maintain a "liberal" medical profession, that is to say not directly employed by the central government, it is difficult to achieve an even distribution of medical care.

The health programme of many European countries is also part of a broader scheme of social security. Social welfare is an accepted responsibility of the state and now covers a very wide range of benefits. The spending of all the countries varies enormously both in its total and in its distribution over different headings of benefits; and the proportions that come from national or local taxation and from insurance also vary.

The total cost of health services has risen steadily over the past forty years, partly as a result of inflation but very largely because so many advances in medicine are increasingly costly, because medical men make bigger demands on supporting services than in pre-scientific days and because all health personnel, but especially the doctors, now demand a bigger share of the nation's wealth. Since at least two thirds of expenditure in most health services is spent on salaries and wages the numbers of health personnel clearly influences the amount of money that needs to be spent. For physicians the range is from three per 10,000 population to fourteen. However, as Table 2.1 shows the variation in other types of personnel is considerable and in the case of dentists and nurses very large. The number of pharmacists is more difficult to assess, local customs and the way in which pharmacy is organised probably account for much of the variation. Of course the number of hospital beds influences the number of nurses needed or who can be trained, and the figures suggest that 10 beds for all purposes per 1,000 of the population which has long been accepted in medical literature might be enough in an efficient service.

Scandinavia

The political climate in Scandinavia has led to a steady development in social welfare and health services. In health there is close co-operation between Norway, Denmark, Iceland, Sweden and Finland. The heads of their health services meet regularly to discuss mutual problems. So far as is possible these five nations co-ordinate their health laws, their standards of education for health personnel and their

TABLE 2.1

	Doctors per 10,000	Hospital Beds per 10,000	Dentists	Nurses and Midwives	Pharma-cists
Belgium	12·5	82·0	—	—	—
Denmark	12·3	91·0	5·2	39·6	3·2
Eire	10·5	205·0	—	—	—
France	11·0	133·9	3·3	20·4	4·5
Germany (West)	14·2	106·0	—	—	—
Greece	14·0	57·0	5·8	26·6	4·5
Holland	11·2	75·7	2·3	12·0	0·8
Iceland	11·6	106·8	2·7	24·1	1·3
Italy	13·3	96·0	—	—	—
Luxemburg	10·0	175·0	—	—	—
Norway	12·0	106·2	7·2	32·0	3·4
Portugal	8·0	58·2	—	—	—
Spain	12·0	44·0	—	—	—
Sweden	9·9	159·1	7·0	107·8	0·1
Turkey	3·1	17·0	—	—	—
U.K.	*11·0*	*105·0*	*2·7*	*31·3*	*5·9*
U.S.A.	*12·9*	*90·0*	*5·1*	*41·5*	*6·3*

social welfare in general. There are still many differences but concepts are similar.

NORWAY

Norway is one of the larger European countries, having 125,183 square miles, but has one of the smaller populations, of around 3·75 million. It is also one of the European countries retaining a hereditary monarchy combined with an elected parliament (Storting). Norway is mountainous, stretches northwards to the arctic circle and as a result is said to have nearly three-quarters of its land which is unproductive. It has a large timber industry, exports iron ore and has a large merchant navy. Its capital, Oslo, is a large prosperous modern city.

The health system of Norway has been developing steadily since 1911. Both World Wars interrupted its growth but there have been repeated revision and enlargement of what was at first only a form of insurance for the lowest income groups. At the same time Norway introduced the idea of people outside the specified groups joining in voluntary health insurance; and in 1956 health insurance was made compulsory for all. Norway's policies are based on a national attitude towards the whole subject of the welfare of the people. The "welfare state" does not hope to do away with sickness, but to prevent much more of it than is possible now. Beyond merely providing medical care, its intent is to help as many as possible from sickness back to a useful position in society.

Politically speaking, this conception of the goal of the "welfare state" in the field of health has been so well understood and accepted by the general public that no existing political party rejects it. Further changes and expansions in Norway may be expected for although it may well be that Norway ranks high among the nations of the world measured by the usual yardsticks of average life-span, infant mortality and occurrence of communicable diseases, no one is ready to rest on their laurels. In discussing and legislating for further advances Norway has the support of the great majority of the medical profession which has up to the moment not opposed the steady development of public services, probably because of the retention of an insurance system coupled with a fee-for-service of which the patient is reimbursed a portion.

Insurance premiums in Norway include a part which provides monetary benefits during sickness in addition to health services benefits and are graduated according to income. There is a National Insurance Institution which governs these services as a whole but the detailed work is in the hands of largely autonomous local insurance funds. There were nearly 740 of these, one to each commune but in recent years efforts have been made to reduce the number. Each local insurance fund is controlled by a small board appointed by the governing body of the commune and can deal with most local problems. But it is the National Insurance Institution which decides upon premiums, ensures the solvency of the local funds, settles disputes and deals with complaints. There is a central equalisation fund which is used to assist small local funds who could not, at fixed premiums, collect money for all their local purposes. In any case the premium paid by "members" supply only half of the total annual cost the remainder is met by employers, the state, and the municipality. For example, the revenue budget for 1966 was as follows:

Members Premium	734	million	Kroner
Employers Contributions	402	,,	,,
Municipalities	183	,,	,,
Central Government	147	,,	,,
Others	7	,,	,,
Total:	1473	,,	,, (approximately $210m.)

It may be of interest to note that the total budget for all the insurance schemes was 4,532 million kroner of which the members paid directly only 1,654 million kroner.

However, the individual still makes a further contribution to the cost of his or her medical care. Treatment and care at public hospitals, sanatoria or obstetric clinics is free. Other kinds of medical care, in particular that given by the general practitioner, is usually on a refund basis, the refund varying from as low as 60 per cent and rising to the full 100 per cent. A doctor may, however, make a contract with the local insurance fund in which case he receives the standard fee from the fund and may or may not expect the patient to pay something more. Injuries and illness come under an Occupational Injuries Insurance Act; confinement (including medical and midwife assistance) and some other special items are free to the patient. The insurance funds pay more for visits or consultations after the first two, with the idea of making it economically worth while for a patient to continue care from the same doctor.

In Norway some drugs, and all drugs for some specified diseases, are free, but others have to be purchased. On the other hand, a measure of the scattered and difficult nature of some rural areas, transport to and from hospital is provided. It is claimed that every kind of transport from reindeer to helicopter can be freely used if a doctor considers it necessary. There is no limit to the time a patient may spend in hospital without charge and every kind of help arising from hospital care is also covered, including convalescent care and rehabilitation.

Insurance premiums vary, as we have noted, according to income and other factors so one can only give average figures for what all this costs. It is about 2·5 per cent of the average premium payer's weekly income, around $55 a year. A wife and family may be covered as "dependents" but a woman in employment or a child over 18 must pay their own premiums. Self-employed persons have to pay a premium and do not necessarily receive the monetary benefits paid to ordinary employees.

Mention has been made of the general practitioner's position in Norway. Essentially the service is based on him and the citizen has complete freedom of choice except that a modification has to be made in the remoter areas. It is of immense interest that whereas in many countries there is still an argument as to whether a citizen has either a legal or a moral right to medical care, in Norway he has a legal and a moral right to *seek* immediate medical aid for any ailment. He must make a positive effort; and when he does the state must see that the care he receives will be of a high standard. But normally he will only receive specialist care when the general practitioner considers it necessary. This and most other aspects of health care in Norway has been agreed with the medical profession which has never opposed the system. From the very first, doctors in Norway have regarded the national program both as insurance of the people's health and an insurance of their own incomes. The doctor is free to practise where he wishes and knows the people are free to make a choice between him and any other doctor. In practice the geography of the country imposes well recognised restrictions.

Because of them, and because all aspects of public health, epidemiology, venereal diseases, food protection, mental health, care of mother and child, are covered by the Norwegian system, there has to exist a chain of public health doctors. The appointment of men to remote areas with a guaranteed income is said to date back some hundreds of years. Those in remote areas could never be working only in the public health fields. They have also to be clinicians ready to undertake a very wide range of medical work. But the individual doctor has also to be an administrator and is the Chairman of the local Board of Health (one to each district) which is an elected body, so reflecting the wishes of the people. He thus represents the national medical administration in his district, but is the servant of the people of that area. He has an income made up by salary from central government and fees for medical services through the health insurance funds.

Norway's hospitals provide 16·2 beds per 1000 of the people, and are mainly owned by local, provincial or national government. There are some private hospitals owned by voluntary organisations or religious bodies. Citizens who use these latter hospitals can still make a claim on the insurance funds but whatever the cost only the standard fees will be paid and the patient must pay any excess. Specialists in most hospitals are full-time members of the staff and responsible for the total care of the patients they admit. However, senior specialists have permission to do limited private practice, normally six hours per week. Specialists outside the public institutions may charge unlimited fees in private hospitals but the insurance fund will pay only the fees set down in the agreed list.

The doctor-patient relationship is not weakened or undermined in Norway by a properly organised pre-paid medical care programme. Indeed, the relationship is often strengthened. The most important reason for this is that the doctor's fee and the cost of hospitalisation no longer cause doctor-patient enmity. Thus the doctor can devote himself fully to his vital professional task and duty of helping his patient in the best possible way without anxieties, doubts or resentments about the patient's ability to pay.

Dental care is largely covered by the insurance funds or, for children and some special groups, by public dental programs. There is a special laboratory service headed by the National Institute for Public Health in Oslo and laboratories for pharmaceutical testing. Retail pharmacies operate in a system which combines public appointment and private practice. Mental health is treated by a variety of hospitals and institutions, the cost being covered mainly by Government in provinces or cities although the insurance funds are contributing increasing amounts to the care of the mentally disturbed.

The quality of medical care depends on many factors, how doctors are educated, what the hospitals are like in design and equipment, how far teamwork is developed and especially whether there is enough money available to give every patient what he needs. On this latter point a basic condition for maintaining high quality medical care is a solid, strong and always available financial source. In Norway the national health insurance programme represents such a source. Certainly the visitor to Norway's hospitals finds ample confirmation that a sound financial source can provide beautiful modern hospitals. Norway's three and a half million people have provided themselves with many first class institutions and compel one to accept the conclusion that medical care has reached a high level amongst prepaid medical systems.

DENMARK

Denmark, "the oldest kingdom of Europe" with a population approaching five million, and an area of 16,000 square miles, mainly in separate and scattered islands, has a long history of developing health services. Today the structure of the health services follows the general line of those already described for Norway, clearly has the same general aim, yields much the same quantity and quality of medical care yet differs administratively.

Denmark has a constitutional monarch and is governed by a single chamber parliament (Folksling) which is elected by proportional representation. The standard of living is high, based on a highly efficient farming system combined with cooperative marketing. There are in addition important shipyards and Denmark has a good merchant navy. Copenhagen is an excellent capital: and the cultural life reflects a high educational standard. Health services are controlled by the Ministry of Social Affairs and are claimed to be based on principles first enunicated in 1892, "mutuality, voluntary membership in State-supervised sickness funds, autonomy with State supervision and state grants to the less well-to-do.' Health services are part of a unified system of social welfare.

Two features are important. The original idea of mutuality remains but "voluntary" has become universal, for 96·7 per cent of the population are today actively insured against sickness. State supervision has become state control for it is clearly easier and better to have the same rules for all citizens especially as those who are not active members of the insurance system must, by law, be associate members; and payments, fees to doctors, can best be settled by central negotiation. The Danish medical profession, like the Norwegian, have never opposed the development of the present services. They are the result of a slow but steadfast evolution, marked by constant undertakings for improvement and extension of the services, which explains the somewhat complicated and erratic pattern of the administrative and organisational set-up, which from the outside view may seem to encounter insuperable problems of coordination. In that co-ordination the Danish Medical Association plays many parts, as negotiator of fee scales, as the recogniser of professional standing without which employment is impossible. The medical profession also provides the body of paid administrators variously called the National Health Service and the Board of Health which must be consulted on all health matters, supervises most of them and through its chief officer, the Director General, advises various ministries on health questions.

The health service now available is fairly comprehensive. It is obtained by the citizen, from whom 75 per cent of the cost of all facilities except hospitals is derived, through membership of a sickness fund of which there is one to every local district or municipality. (There is a scheme to reduce the 700 funds to a more efficient 400.) There are two kinds of members, A and B, the division being purely on income levels. In Copenhagen, in 1968, the dividing line for the head of a family was 43,000 kroner per annum, (approximately $5,700) the figure being fixed once a year according to the cost of living index, and some 88 per cent of the total membership belong to section A. Those in section B pay a higher premium and do not receive the full range of benefits given to members of section A. The insurance funds are organised locally, regionally and nationally and are subject to overall supervision by the Directorate of Health Insurance which acts as the appeal body in any dispute between local offices and members.

The essential difference between A and B members is one of finance, A members receiving most forms of medical care, B members not only paying bigger premiums but being liable to pay a proportion of the cost of some items. It is recognised that a citizen may not always be on the same side of the income level and so benefits must be essentially the same, so that the effect of transfer from one division to the other may be felt as little as possible. Some slight differences may develop between localities as well as between members as local funds have certain options but these are minor in nature.

Danish citizens depend primarily upon their general practitioner. A patient who goes direct to a specialist receives no financial aid. General practitioners are paid by two different methods. In Copenhagen general practitioners are appointed by the sickness fund which divides the city into districts permitting about 1,500 members per doctor. Members are free to choose their family doctor within a certain radius and to do so for a year at a time. The doctor is paid a capitation fee with some extra payments for special services. Outside Copenhagen members also choose their doctor for a year but do so freely from those who have declared themselves willing to do work for insurance funds. In practice very few doctors in all Denmark do not do so. They are paid an annual capitation basic fee plus fees-for-services according to an accepted list of fees. When a B member consults a doctor he pays him directly and reclaims the amount which the fund would normally pay the doctor for attending an A member and giving that service.

Hospitalisation is free to all citizens, is unlimited as to time, and covers acute hospitals and many special services. The hospitals are financed by local and central government and only a part of the actual cost is paid by the sickness fund. This is normally on a flat rate which is a token only, approximately $1 a day although actual costs (1967) were running between $20 and $35. Hospital maternity services are free to both A and B members; so too is midwifery in the home, but in private nursing homes only a part of the cost is paid. Drugs are supplied by sickness funds but only if they are on an official list of some 850 and then only as to 3/4ths of the cost. However, the Ministry of Social Affairs can specify diseases for which the total cost of vital medicines is met.

Experience in Denmark makes it clear that when health services are financed by sickness funds, especially when these are subsidised by central funds, readiness to pay for new developments and treatment is essential. The Danish system is unnecessarily complicated and moves are being made to abolish the artificial barrier of an income level, but both this move and the comprehensive system raised the question of abuse. To meet this Copenhagen has a small committee, of three doctors and three sick fund representatives who can investigate any case in which an insurance fund thinks a doctor has incurred unnecessary expense and can order a guilty doctor to compensate the fund. Outside Copenhagen a number of similar local bodies deal with these cases. The doctor also has the right to refer to such a committee a complaint against a patient or his society.

Repeated mention of Copenhagen indicates the problem that arises even in a developed country in which the capital city is an ultramodern concentration of population while the rest of the country is rural and widely scattered. Basically the same service may be available but it needs to be organised differently. The provision of modern laboratory investigations is an example. In Copenhagen the need for these and the opportunity to provide them arose nearly forty years ago when such provision was in its infancy in most European countries. The doctors of Copenhagen, with remarkable foresight, set up their own laboratory and this has developed to a size than can undertake most of the work needed by local general practitioners or specialists. The health insurance societies pay the cost of such examinations.

In other cities and districts the hospital laboratories undertake this work and payment is made to the hospital by the patients' local sickness fund. Similar arrangements exist for radiology and for physiotherapy. It is to be noted that Denmark and other European countries, have no hospital outpatient departments. Polyclinics are found only in connection with University clinics and the staff are whole-time officers of the hospital. When a doctor refers a case to them the sickness fund pays a small fee for each attendance. At most municipal hospitals patients are seen in a clinic only as a preliminary to admission. Specialists may be permitted to do limited private practice but a great many do not. They have become accustomed to the system which dates back to 1900 and most specialists express themselves as fully satisfied by a system of medical care in which there is no question of money between patient and doctor. Indeed there is some feeling that doctors working as specialists outside the hospital, seeing patients privately but being paid largely by the insurance funds are of lower professional and ethical standing than those doctors who are entirely within the municipal hospital. It is also accepted that a director or manager of the hospital should be a lay officer of the municipality and not, as in Norway, a medical man. Consultation between general practitioner and the hospital specialist might seem a little impersonal as all requests for appointments have to be sent to and are apportioned by a central bureau: but there appears to be a very close relationship between the hospital staff and the family doctors since all are working in a relatively circumscribed area.

Denmark has a comprehensive system for disease prevention, including care of the pre-school child and for regular health examinations in school. B.C.G. vaccination and other immunisation techniques are available free. The family doctor in some areas is employed in this work. Public health nurses, school health nurses, midwives and medical social workers are employed by the local authorites. As in Norway transportation to and from any health facility is paid by the local authority and doctors in the more rural areas receive a conveyance allowance.

Serious complaints about the Danish system are few but doctors still practise very much as individuals and cover at night and during public holidays is not regarded as satisfactory. In Copenhagen and some other large towns "a medical watch" system has been organised for urgent cases at night and during holidays. This service is staffed by young and newly qualified doctors. Group practice is scarcely known, but as Denmark wishes to keep her service based on family doctors, development on the lines of health centres is now actively discussed. Extension of prevention of disease along the lines of regular routine examinations is also actively under discussion and it would appear that the Danish people will continue the steady development of their health service along the lines of comprehensiveness and prepayment by insurance or taxation. That development will be a part of their whole social welfare structure of which it has been said the intention is that the negative aim that no one should be without the resources needed for subsistence must be replaced by the constructive aim: a decent life for all members of the community. Undoubtedly one of the elements of that life is health and Denmark recognises it.

SWEDEN, ICELAND AND FINLAND

Together with Norway and Denmark, these three countries constitute the Nordic Council. In the field of health the Nordic Council has sought to bring their services as closely together as possible and as a result doctors, dentists and pharmacists licensed in any of the five countries may work in any of them. A special school for hospital administrators has been set up at Goteborg in Sweden for students from all five countries. Since 1962 a Nordic Pharmacopoeia has been prepared and the countries are considering uniform regulations concerning the control and marketing of drugs and foodstuffs in the whole Scandinavian area. Subject to certain detailed restrictions citizens of these countries can claim medical care on the same basis as the patients in the country they are visiting. Since all operate refund systems the amount refunded will be that allowed in the country in which they are ill, not necessarily the amount they would receive at home.

Iceland has a system which is very similar to that of Denmark. Iceland became a republic only in 1944 although it had been largely independent of Denmark since 1918 and it has an area of 40,500 square miles and a population of 186,000. Large parts are mountainous and volcanic and are not inhabited, the population depending very largely on fishing. The educational standards are high. Close links are still maintained with Denmark and with the other Scandinavian countries. For health purposes Iceland is divided into 57 medical districts in each of which there is a general physician who has public health and administrative duties but who is also a general practitioner.

D

He is paid partly by salary and partly by the insurance funds. Hospital care is free. For a population of less than 200,000 Iceland has a good supply of hospital beds and an average of 1 doctor to 810.

Sweden divides the great Scandinavian peninsula with Norway. It has an area of 173,436 square miles and is a wealthy country. It has great timber lands in the north and good agricultural land in the south. It has richer mineral deposits than Norway and some highly developed industries. The standard of living is high and much money is spent on education, social services and on health services.

Sweden has probably been the subject of more study in systems of health care than any other country, but this has chiefly been because of its advanced planning and building of hospitals. From quite an early time hospitals in Sweden were provided by local authorities and treatment in public accomodation was free. So it has continued. But from the end of the nineteenth century there had also been a National Board of Health which appointed provincial physicians, to act as a combination of physician and public health officer. There are now 600 such district doctors and they still look after the poor; but they also care for the bulk of the population who are now insured. Fees are those laid down by regulation and 70 per cent of the amount paid is refunded to the patient. Doctors who are outside the district officer system may charge more but the patient can reclaim only 70 per cent of the standard amount.

The pattern, therefore, is similar to that described in Norway and Denmark, a universally available system based on insurance, but comprehensive in what it supplies. There is, however, a much greater tendency to go direct to specialists: and hospital out-patient departments also provide a great deal of primary medical care because there is no system of general family practice. There still exist private wards, but the general level of hospital planning minimises the importance of this. The hospital staff is the same for all patients, and is employed on a whole-time basis. The insurance funds pay an agreed amount per day for every insured member but as in the other Scandinavian countries a high proportion of the total cost is met by the state or the municipality.

It follows that since the Nordic countries have all systems financed in the same kind of way, no serious problems arise across the national boundaries. Movement is free and it follows that services need to be free also. There is little tendency to look on the hospitals of one country as being better than another and indeed the new hospitals of all meet the highest standard of modern planning. In Sweden group practice of specialists is backed as a future development by the Swedish Medical Association while nationally the hospitals are being organised on a regional basis so as to guarantee even higher skills in all parts of the country.

The north eastern part of Scandinavia is occupied by the 130,165 square miles of Finland, a republic with a population of 4·6 million. It is largely a land of forest and timber products form its main industry and export. It is however able to supply most of the domestic goods it requires and the standard of living is high.

Finland stands very much between the Western world and the Soviet Union. Her health services, however, follow the local health insurance office pattern rather than that of a nationally financed service. The State bears about 85 per cent of the cost of hospitals and covers any deficit in the insurance funds which are built up from contributions by employers and employees. Patients pay their general practitioner and get only 60 per cent of the standard fee refunded. The scheme however is relatively new and is still developing.

PORTUGAL AND SPAIN

Spain and Portugal share the Iberian peninsula with areas of 196,700 and 34,500 square miles respectively. In spite of this geographical situation they have been quite separate politically for centuries. Portugal is, for example, a republic: whilst Spain has retained the concept of a monarchy. Both are still very poor countries with low standards of living and low average incomes. They have one thing in common, that they are visited each year by large numbers of tourists, many of whom pass from one to the other. They have, too, similar health hazards arising from their climate. In terms of per capita income they are similar and more closely related in this and other ways than they are with the more northern countries of Europe. In both, hospital services were at one time largely the concern of the Church, but this position has now changed and further changes are taking place. Ineed both countries are contemplating further advances in health cover, especially in rural areas and as their national incomes rise these changes may accelerate. It is a mistake to think that the best services in these countries are lower than elsewhere: but the number of available hospital beds falls very far below for example those of the Scandinavian countries and the concentration of doctors in the cities with medical schools is part of a gross maldistribution of medical care. It is recognised that efforts have to be made to distribute medical care over the whole of these two countries, but there are many rural areas where services are absent or poor. In terms of the proportion of national income spent on health and in terms of the spending per head of the population, Spain and Portugal lag far behind the other more affluent countries.

PORTUGAL

Portugal has a population of 9 million and still large overseas territories. Her industry is poor, the standard of living is low and health records are poor. The present health schemes date from 1945 but there are hospitals that were founded centuries ago, and some are in buildings as old as three hundred years, which have always given services to the poor. Today the indigent are still cared for; but the majority of the population are covered by a system of social insurance which includes health care. In broad terms it is the same kind of insurance as operates in Denmark, financing only a part from the premium paid by employees, about five per cent of their salaries, and deriving the remainder from employers, from the State and from municipalities. Hospital in-patient care in public accommodation is free to most of the population; general practice care may be obtained free at centres set up by the various insurance funds and employing doctors paid by salary or from doctors who will make a small nominal charge at each visit but receive their income from the insurance funds by varying methods, including a basic capitation fee plus payment per item of service. These Social Insurance Institutes are a curious mixture of privately initiated and legally compulsory bodies, most of them on an industry basis but some being district agencies covering a relatively circumscribed area. The most rapid development was inevitably in industry and commerce as joint agreements were made between employers and employees. Today every trade and profession has its insurance institute and in theory each is independent. Those of the liberal professions are financed only by the members themselves since they have no employers to make a contribution. Today it is compulsory for all employed people earning above a certain figure to be members of one of these agencies. Those with a lower income obtain general medical care from public health authorities through salaried communal medical officers. Either way most Portuguese can now obtain medical care. Most primary medical care is given at health centres or as hospital out-patients. The doctors working in both places are salaried employees.

There are in addition special services for particular diseases. A major campaign against tuberculosis has been conducted by a special Tuberculosis Institute through Sanatoria, mass miniature X-ray, prophylaxis and all modern methods of treatment. Treatment may be given at special clinics, preventoria and dispensaries: and when necessary through the local hospitals, the "Misericordias." (These hospitals were first established at the end of the fifteenth century when by the Queen's order local hospitals for the poor were provided.) They are primarily the responsibility of the local authorities and now serve the majority of the people. But all hospitals, local, regional, university and private come under the overall control of the Directorate of Hospitals. The Central Government owns and controls directly the larger hospitals in the university towns, some ten in all. The intention in Portugal is to develop a system of regional hospitals, the country being divided into three zones, to which the more difficult cases and those requiring special treatment can be referred by the smaller local hospitals. The Directorate General of Hospitals has been in existence only since 1962 and at present there is in Portugal a serious lack of hospital beds, less than one-third of the number per 1,000 people that Sweden has, and in particular there is a marked lack of provision for mental health.

In spite of the fact that medical care is available for approximately four-fifths of the population much primary medical care is still obtained at hospital out-patients. In Lisbon hospitals very large numbers of patients are treated every day in the "Urgencia" which accepts not only casualties of all kinds but all patients who simply walk in seeking treatment. Some 40 per cent of those seen are referred to senior specialists for admission. Hospital care is free for about eighty per cent of the people, although nominally those who can afford it should make a contribution of 30 per cent of the cost. A contribution for all members of social insurance institution is, however, paid by these funds. The funds, especially those covering an area, build other health facilities but do not provide hospitals. The cost of in-patient care has, however, been increasing, in common with all other countries, at a steady rate. Private practice takes place within some hospitals, especially in the university centres and the physicians and surgeons are not bound by any fee schedule. However, the hospital collects the accounts and deducts a percentage which goes towards the cost of nursing services.

Lisbon hospitals show to a very marked degree all the combinations of ancient and modern which is still a feature of many other countries. There are departments with a high international reputation. Modern computers are being installed to deal with both the accounts, salaries and wages, patients' bills and general finance and with the intention of centralising records of patients and providing the possibility of good statistical research and medical audit procedures. Old buildings are being altered and modernised, and new hospitals planned and constructed. The medical profession complains that the proportion of the gross national product allocated to health is too low and advances have still to be made in most vital statistics. The newest health facilities are local clinics built by the insurance funds. There is a growing belief that some form of salaried group practice from such centres will be the pattern for the future.

The insurance funds are growing every year as more people join them. Health is considered a right of the citizen but economic development prevents this being completely implemented. Workman's compensation and treatment for certain industrial diseasese are dealt with by a separate system. Most insurance funds, which cover sickness monetary benefit as well as medical service, have arisen by agreement between the trade unions and employers: but once formed they come under the laws governing such bodies. In time all employers will be covered; and now it is proposed to include all agricultural workers although the shortage of doctors in rural areas will probably mean slow progress. The central directorate is a small body of eight, four representing the Government, two the trade union and two the employers. It is strongly argued that a doctor should be actively engaged in these controlling bodies, especially as they have to deal with complaints and a medical opinion is usually necessary.

Portugal has a long border with Spain and it would seem inevitable, indeed is accepted as being so, that any development of health services in one may affect what is done in the other. So far there is not sufficient difference in quantity or quality of medical care in the two countries to lead citizens of either to seek medical care in the other.

SPAIN

Spain has a population of 31·8 million most of whom have a relatively low standard of living although the country has good mineral resources and some industries are well developed. Its main exports are agricultural, citrus fruits and sherry: and today a large part of its annual income comes from the tourist industry which affects the coast and a few centres with a cultural heritage.

The health services of Spain present a very complicated picture and a very uneven distribution of services. However, health plans are part of a general system of social security which has been slowly developing over the past forty years. Social security now covers at least 60 per cent of the population, schemes being compulsory for all below a certain annual income level unless indigent. The basis for their organisation is the trade union, of which membership is compulsory in Spain. The whole scheme is operated by the National Institute of Social Security (Prevision) under the Ministry of Labour. The funds come from employees who pay two per cent and employers who add five per cent of salaries, with the state making a contribution for some purposes. It not only covers medical care in the home, clinic and hospital, but industrial accidents and rehabilitation (for which, the employers now bear the whole cost). Indeed it clearly regards itself as primarily concerned with the workers and is putting considerable emphasis on rehabilitation.

Yet a great amount of medical care still lies outside the social security system, the diagnosis, treatment and prevention of tuberculosis, for example, is quite separate. Mental health care, which is almost entirely institutional, is in the hands of local authorities, some of which have taken considerable interest in mental health but most of whom have done only a minimum.

Local authorities also provide hospitals as do the state, the Church and voluntary bodies. The new hospitals recently built by the National Institute compare with the best in other countries. The variation, however, is from these high standards to very poor institutions which are largely concerned with those who are not eligible for membership of an insurance fund and for the numerous poor. A new hospital law was promulgated in 1961 which set up a central commission for hospital co-ordination and this body has been conducting an extensive survey of the hospitals of Spain. It has also made comparisons with other countries, both poorer and richer, and is evolving a plan to combine all the differently owned hospitals into a regionally planned system.

Meantime those who are insured obtain health care from hospitals and polyclinics. Since 1948 the social insurance has built sixty hospitals, has others under construction, has nearly 400 clinics in operation and many more planned. Patients receive ambulatory care from general practitioners and specialists at these polyclinics and hospitals. As a routine most general practitioners are required to put in a certain time at the clinic and then do their house visits, which are numerous. They are paid according to the number of families on their list, but both to augment the rather poor income that this work provides and because it is the only way in which such duties can be covered, general practitioners are paid extra for public health and preventive work. They are also allowed to do private practice and in the cities this can be lucrative. Many of the smaller health centres are not manned by a doctor but by a nurse who gives a wide range of service.

Hospital care is not necessarily entirely free. Those who are already receiving monetary assistance do not pay. Those who can afford to pay may contribute up to 10 per cent of the total cost of their hospitalisation. Private practice inside hospitals, especially the state owned university hospitals, is permitted but confined to a small number of beds, usually eight for each professor. There is some private health insurance among the well-to-do to cover such events as require consultant care. Social security owns only some 12,000 hospital beds out of a total of approximately 140,000 so they have to pay for use of beds from other hospital owners. These are mainly provincial and other public bodies, although churches own 12 per cent of all hospital beds. Some of the municipal hospitals, such as "Gran Hospital de la Beneficiencia" in Madrid with 1,100 beds, cater largely for those who cannot pay, but social security has a contract to use and pay for 400 of the beds. In the new social insurance hospitals the staffing ratios per bed and the cost per day are very much higher, and it is in the newest of these hospitals that the highest skills, especially in surgery and the greatest care, especially in rehabilitation, are displayed. Spain has still to make progress in maternity services and the care of infants, but the newer social insurance hospitals are well equipped to deal with all aspects.

There appears, as yet, to be no joint arrangements between the social insurance systems of Portugal and Spain. Nor any arrangement about medical education. Spain has a very large number of medical students, but nearly 30 per cent of them come from South American countries. There is much criticism of present medical education as being too theoretical and much talk of the teaching hospitals being over-crowded so that as new hospitals are built changes are likely to be made in the teaching system. Like its neighbour, Spain seems ready for advances which are delayed by the relatively low per capita income of the country.

ITALY

The Italian peninsula together with Sicily and Sardinia has an area of 131,000 square miles and a population just over 50 million. It is a country of great variation in geography, in climate, in standards of living and in distribution of services. In general the south is much poorer than the north which is now highly industrialised and has a flourishing motor car industry, much shipping, textile and other manu-facturing industries. At the same time Italy's famous cities attract large numbers of tourists as do its sea resorts and beaches. The country has been a republic since 1946 but its parliamentary system has remained somewhat unstable.

Italy has a long history in terms of medical science but its present Ministry of Health was only established in 1958. Previously the Minis-try of the Interior had been responsible for health. Many aspects of the Italian system and its future trends are worthy of detailed study. Like the United Kingdom it has a population of 50 million for which nearly half a million hospital beds are available. Medical care had advanced along the lines of insurance groups but these are now re-duced to a few large sick funds which are state supervised and of which membership is compulsory for employed persons and other special groups. Contributions are graduated according to wage and salary but the employed person pays a very small amount in comparison with the employer, only 0·15 per cent of the salary by the employee compared with between 4 and 7 per cent by the employer.

The position is complicated since industrial injuries are covered by a separate scheme which draws its finance from these contributions and because pensions and unemployment benefit also come from the same funds. For independent members of sick funds, small tradesmen and farmers the State covers half of the contribution. The state has also to cover deficits in any of the sick funds and with the rising cost of medical care these are often in deficit. As the government has had to create new legislation to enable it to cover large deficits, there is support for a move to transfer the whole of the finance to general taxation. This would mean big changes in the present arrangements, many of which were made when fewer people were insured. Now nearly 90 per cent of the population have cover.

The hospitals would probably be the first part to be reorganised, and these are operated by many different agencies. Some belong to one or other of the large insurance funds, but others are autonomous institutions with which the insurance funds enter into contracts for beds. Municipalities are the principal owners of hospitals but about one-fifth of the beds are in the private sector. The principal insurance fund which today covers 28 million people (workers and dependents) is known in Italy as I.N.A.M., the National Institute for Sickness Insurance. Other special funds cater for those employed by central government, for those employed by the local authorities and for independent workers, including those on the land. Professional people, including the clergy, also have schemes which do not give the same monetary benefits but cover sickness.

I.N.A.M. gives cover, both financial and medical, for a limit of 180 days and those who are sick beyond that time and those who have not paid contributions must then turn to Public Assistance which can pay for further treatment in a local authority hospital. These are, of course, still in a sense like the poor-law hospitals of the past.

So far as ordinary health care is concerned I.N.A.M. provides this only through its own institutions. It has over nine hundred "ambulatori" which are organised in three main regions and vary in size according to the population they have to serve. In a city a large polyclinic may serve up to 80,000 beneficiaries and have in attendance not only general practitioners but every permitted type of specialist. In communes and rural areas the size is scaled down but all large towns will have full cover, medium size towns only the principal specialities and in small towns none, or what can be made available from nearby larger centres. Payment of doctors is complicated. General practitioners in towns are on fee-for-service according to an agreed scale (a house visit is paid twice as much as a consultation at the clinic,) and general practitioners in the country receive a capitation fee. Specialists working at a polyclinic are paid an hourly rate up to 24 hours in a week.

The specialist working in hospital gets his salary by a division of money for all the specialists received from I.N.A.M. and divided by the hospital according to a formula that allows for many factors including e.g. in surgery, for severity of operations and for status on the staff. A daily sum is paid for every admission and provides the bulk of the money. A per diem rate based on what it costs in a municipal hospital for the poor is also paid by I.N.A.M. to the hospital to cover its costs. As a result I.N.A.M. has not been sufficiently concerned with the quality of medical care, which since it covers more than half the population it should control, but almost solely with the length of stay.

All doctors are free to do private practice and, as in Spain, often do more than one job to achieve a high income. This may be within the hospital where he normally works and the word "clinic" is really applied to a private practice part of a hospital and not, as used here and in many other countries, for a health centre or group practice building.

Mental health care is the responsibility of the provinces and the quality of provision is exceedingly variable. The number of mental health beds is low compared with other European countries. A charge is made on all patients who can afford to pay. Tuberculosis is dealt with by a separate system as is the care of the aged and certain other forms of chronic invalidity. The medical officer employed in this type of service is usually whole-time in the employment of the responsible authority.

Italy, as has been said, is actively considering further changes in its services. As other countries have found, it is economically unsound to have hospitals under many agencies and a five year plan to reorganise the services is being prepared. Hospitals are to be classified according to services available and area covered, in the hope of establishing district hospitals. Two pilot schemes are in operation to try to establish a local health unit which will be responsible for all the services in its area. There is a tendency to favour a nationally financed service with a system of small deterrent payments to be paid on the spot by the patient. But that raises difficulties, for families are still large in Italy and average incomes are not high.

The other schemes mentioned follow similar lines to those we have described for I.N.A.M. But one is quite different, the National Institute for Insurance against Industrial Accidents. This form of care for industrial hazards was started fifty years ago but has grown and been developed in the past ten years until it now covers all workers by hand, including those working in agriculture. It has its own health centres and its own hospitals; but under the new law mentioned above these will be included in the new unified hospital system. The details have still to be worked out.

A weekly contribution for every worker is paid by the employer and all money so collected is managed as one fund. That fund aims to have first-class hospitals fully equipped to deal with emergencies, both accidental and medical, in places to which cases can be easily referred from a wide area. Ten hospitals already exist but dispensaries are spread throughout the country and some departments are established inside municipal hospitals. These deal with cases by first-aid and dispose both of them and of cases returned from the main hospitals. Each hospital has an out-patient department which deals both with cases from the dispensaries and cases from industry in the immediate neighbourhood. The doctors at these hospitals are paid by salary calculated from fees derived as described above but this is generally considered so low that most do other jobs or private practice. Re-education and rehabilitation are the principal purpose of these hospitals, hand surgery takes up a lot of surgical time and all the modern electrical methods of treatment are in use. It is because of this that many people who are not covered by industrial accident insurance seek the services of its surgeons for treatment of injuries, e.g. from motor accidents (in which an expert opinion is also wanted because of the frequency of legal action.)

The Ministry of Public Health is concerned only indirectly with these insurance funds – it is represented on their Boards but they are controlled by the Ministry of Labour. Its main functions, apart from initiating legislation, e.g. on hospital reorganisation, are in prevention and environmental medicine. Vaccination is available against the preventible infections. An anti-smog campaign and an anti-cigarette smoking programme are part of the Ministry's work.

Italy has more doctors per unit of population than any of the other members of the European Common Market, but the figure given – 16 per 10,000 population or 1 per 625 – is inflated by the inclusion of medically qualified dentists. The country suffers, however, from geographical maldistribution of medical man-power and it has no single medical organisation which represents the whole profession. Nevertheless, a federated body of smaller medical societies plays an important part in negotiations with government and insurance funds: and has disciplinary powers in matters of complaint, short of civil legal action, against physicians. With the approach of the fuller implementation of the Treaty of Rome on medical services the medical profession in Italy is faced with many problems of internal organisation which need to be solved to make joint action with the whole of the Common Market simpler and more efficient.

GREECE AND TURKEY

These two countries are linked together solely because in spite of their apparent disunity with European and their distance from the Atlantic Ocean they are nevertheless members of the North Atlantic Treaty Organisation. They have many common characteristics for both are still struggling with a per capita income far below that of all other European countries except Portugal: and both have considerable health problems. Greece has many more doctors per unit of population than Turkey, indeed as many as some other European countries and has more hospital beds. It has not so much of the diseases associated with poverty but still has formidable problems in its rural areas. Turkey is Asiatic rather than European, especially in its more Eastern rural areas and with too little money, too few health personnel and inadequate facilities nearly everywhere which means that medical care, often inappropriate to need, reaches only the few. However, the modern facilities in Ankara are excellent. This only emphasises how much will be needed to raise the standards for the whole of Turkey's 32 million people. It has to work out policies that can serve an over-crowded but perhaps affluent city like Istanbul, and serve also a sparse rural population with a very low per capita annual income. Greece has the same kind of problem with nearly a quarter of its whole population in Athens, and a rural people living very frugally but still tending to adhere to the pervasive patterns of use and belief associated with folk healing.

Both countries have the problem common to all communities where wealth is mainly in a few major cities, that their doctors become concentrated in those cities. This is particularly well seen in Athens where the concentration of over 2 million people attracts 6,000 doctors, more than half the number that serve the country's nearly 9 millions. Both countries have adopted health centres as the way to solve their medical problems and both offer better incomes to rural doctors than to doctors working in the cities but that does not equal urban private practice which in both countries attracts very high fees.

GREECE

Greece has a total area of 50,944 square miles but nearly one fifth of these are in the numerous small islands of the seas surrounding the mainland. The land as a whole is very poor and only about one sixth is said to be arable. Greece is to some extent a maritime rather than an industrial nation and has a very large merchant fleet. Her political instability has made social advance difficult and her general poverty has meant that too little money has been available for health and social services.

The present provision of medical care in Greece is complicated, especially in terms of finance. The Department of Health, under the Ministry of Social Affairs, is responsible for health services but the insurance system, which covers both monetary benefits and health care, comes under the Ministry of Labour. Some 85 per cent of the population is covered by insurance and civil servants also have their own special provisions. The country is divided into health districts each of which has a health committee to carry out plans and programmes prepared and approved by the Ministry. These plans include the provision of health centres and dispensaries, of which some 1,200 give treatment to people all over the country. Some of these in rural areas are really health centres with beds, (usually 10,) for maternity and first aid purposes. Both at hospitals and dispensaries the poor are treated entirely free if their name appears on the social welfare list. The wealthy if they use government owned facilities must pay the full cost; but there are many private clinics.

The service is based upon the general practitioner of which there are 2,800 out of Greece's 11,000 doctors. To attract them to rural mountainous regions and the islands special payments are made to the doctors working in these areas, nearly double the city rate. The plan is to provide 1,200 dispensaries and 100 sanitary or communal stations with beds. The nominal staff of the rural dispensary is one doctor, one nurse and one midwife but many are not fully staffed. Some 4 million people now obtain their medical care in this way. Sanitary problems still need much attention in Greece and the Schools of Hygiene in Athens run courses not only for doctors who can obtain a Diploma in Public Health after one year of full-time study, but for chemists, engineers and nurses.

Hospitals in Greece are either state owned or run as private clinics (which have to be licensed and observe certain standards.) The principal hospitals are in Athens where nearly half of the total number of beds, approximately 50,000, are situated. The staff of these hospitals is paid by salary which is based on a contract for so many hours service to the hospital. This is usually for the whole morning. Afternoons are spent in private practice with later visits to the hospital to see urgent and post-operative cases. A very wide range of cases are seen, as can be imagined, many referred from distant small hospitals. The hospitals suffer more from a shortage of technical staff than of doctors. There is considerable centralisation of laboratory service reflecting the shortage of experts in some fields rather than a planned service.

It is perhaps unnecessary to say that in the present unsettled position in Greece no clear new plan can be expected but everyone considers that developments will be towards a more comprehensive service with the idea of district hospitals backing up the chain of dispensaries and large clinical centres. Staffing remains the greatest problem.

TURKEY

Modern Turkey is the largest country to be considered in this section with a total area of 301,000 square miles and a great variation in almost every feature. The Western part around Istanbul and the Bosphorus is densely populated with many industrial activities which are being rapidly developed; the remainder almost entirely agricultural with a wide variety of products, sultanas, raisins, figs, nuts, pulses, tobacco and wool in addition to the usual cereals. She has also considerable mineral wealth. Differences in altitude are marked and in the higher areas spring comes late relative to countries further north. In some of the eastern areas conditions remain primitive with all the diseases associated with poor village conditions: and even near the cities sanitation and water supplies are far from a modern standard.

Modern Turkey has a relatively short history during which great efforts have had to be made in industry, education and health. With a present day population of over 31 million and great poverty among large sections of that population health hazards have been and some remain very high. Although there were centres of medical knowledge in Istanbul throughout its long and varied history the idea of supplying health care in the rural districts is entirely modern, indeed only began after World War II. It is not surprising therefore that Turkey is still contending with a very low number of hospital beds, (only 1·7 beds per 1,000 people). There is a corresponding shortage of doctors and of course nursing has only recently become a recognised profession which young women can freely enter. Great efforts have been made to create new medical schools; but the capital investment for a school and an associated 1,000 bed hospitals is very high. Ankara now has two medical schools and is building some magnificent hospitals but the number of graduates is still far too low.

When Turkey realised how essential a health service is to a modern nation, a comprehensive scheme was prepared and introduced in 1961. In effect this decision was intended to provide the machinery for delivering medical advice and to provide it free where it could not be covered by expanding the existing health insurance. The country was to be divided into districts and the state was to provide buildings and appoint doctors to cover the district. A start was to be made in the rural areas which at that moment had no medical care. For every 5 – 10,000 people it was intended, and one third of the country was been covered in the first five years, to provide a health centre with a staff of one doctor, one nurse, one sanitarian, one midwife for every 2,500, a car and a driver. The aim was to provide a comprehensive service, prevention, diagnosis and treatment and to do so without charge. There are now over 300 health centres, 250 dispensaries and over 3,000 other kinds of medical aid posts, including mobile units.

Since the teaching hospitals are in Ankara and Istanbul it was felt that students must get practice in such a "socialised service area" and two have been established outside Ankara so that students and young doctors can get experience. One is purely a teaching unit with university staff; both give a full service to the area but the second one is a purely working unit which every medical student attends for one month. At the teaching units young doctors work for a year, return to the department of hygiene to take a diploma and then spend up to six years in a rural socialised service unit.

The working unit mentioned serves a population of 52,000 scattered through 84 villages, a typical Turkish setup. There is a health centre for every 7,000 people. At each health centre of that size the doctor, the nurse and three midwives would live in the buildings; but in some areas "midwife houses" are provided where the midwife lives among her people. The control of the whole district is at a large administration centre, a well designed health centre with clerical staff and in the same grounds a hospital of 50 beds, which serves the whole group. It is staffed by four specialists, an internist, a paediatrician, a gynaecologist and a surgeon who work together as a closely knit team and give each other full assistance. There are still some unresolved questions about payment at the centres and patients may prefer to go direct to the hospital where there are no charges.

The Teaching Health Centre illustrates some of the problems Turkey has to face and the effort she is making to give service to the poor and illiterate. The Centre is in a slum area which has a population of 11,000 but no sanitation. Night soil is still collected and dysentery is very common. The birth rate is high and the infant mortality is very high (but in some socialised service areas it has already been reduced to half the national average.) Both doctors and midwives do a full domiciliary service. But the amount of money available is less than $3 per head per annum and less than that is spent in the rural areas. Turkey expends 9 per cent of its total budget on health but this is clearly not enough to give a full service at modern standards.

The socialised service units are, as we have said, to provide care for those who pay no health insurance as do industrial workers.

There are in addition to the health insurance scheme for workers in industry, special services for railway and municipal workers and there is a moderate amount of private insurance. Citizens not covered by insurance and not living in a socialised area have still to pay. There is a great deal of private practice in the cities. Most hospital specialists have what is spoken of as a whole-time contract but this means from 8 a.m. to 4 p.m. with permission to do private practice ouside these hours. There are some private hospitals but most hospitals have private sections with different charges for single and shared rooms. The insurance fund may own hospitals or it may make a contract with any hospital to take insurance patients. It is not quite clear who pays and when. In theory everybody going into a hospital, state or municipally owned, has to pay a daily charge or prove they cannot. The staff who have to make the assessment know that faced with the prevailing poverty they seldom get the truth about incomes and fees are collected from only a minority of patients. Maternity services are covered by insurance and some excellent hospitals exist where modern midwifery is practised and taught.

One problem faced by the hospitals in the cities, especially the university hospitals, is that any patient can come to them and many come from all over Turkey. There are no uniform salary scales and a very wide range exists between the young doctor and the senior surgeon who has an extensive private practice. There are schemes being tried out to bring private practice into the hospitals on a system which involves sharing the fees between the consultants and the hospital. The large hospitals run their out-patient departments on the clinic system whereby a chief consultant and his own junior staff handle all the cases attending: each team taking a part of a month at a stretch. The cases are seen by the juniors, treated or passed on to their chiefs who order all necessary tests or admit the cases to their wards. These clinics and their staffs are operating at full university standards and much research of a clinical nature is going on.

Research and investigation into health problems, particularly those of an epidemic nature, are carried on at the Public Health Institute in Ankara. There are some smaller laboratories but they can deal only with some types of investigations and must refer the others to Ankara. Food and drugs are analysed and a wide range of vaccines and sera are prepared. Turkey still has a problem with rabies, of which there is a reservoir in wild life; and a special Leprosy Institute has some five thousand cases on its registers and finds some 200 new cases a year. The picture presented by Turkey is that of a country with many health problems but a definite plan to tackle them.

The Ministry of Health and Social Welfare operates through a Directorate with its headquarters in Ankara. It is concerned with all the problems already mentioned, public health and epidemiology, and the directorate controls or sets standards for many other services, for tuberculosis, child welfare and school services. There is a special occupational health service which has its own large hospital. In the factories disease and accident prvention are the chief aim and every factory with over 50 employees must have a doctor whole or part-time according to the size.

Municipal hospitals get their finance from local rates but also from insurance and from patients. Hospitals built for one of the special groups are primarily confined to their own members but usually take all kinds of emergencies. In the directorate itself the deputy directors not only control a section of the work but often have practical work to do as well. Health education of the public is undertaken by all the staff employed at headquarters or by a municipality. Family planning advice, of growing importance in Turkey if poverty is to be conquered, is provided at dispensaries and special clinics.

It has been mentioned that the doctor and midwife in a socialised health service area may visit cases in their home but this is something which the doctor does not normally do. There is no Turkish equivalent of the general practitioner although the men working at rural health centres are, of course, generalists. They are not, as a rule, settling down in an area to look after the same group for years as a family doctor does. The rural health centre teams, it is claimed, are having a big impact on the people in these areas and the scheme will be spread to the rest of Turkey as rapidly as finance and numbers of personnel permit. The cities will for a long time be divided between those using private practice and those using hospital out-patients as their primary source of medical care. Technically it is of a high standard hampered by numbers and in places by lack of equipment. The basis is there, however, for an advance that can fulfil the state's declared desire to give health to all the people.

FRANCE AND BELGIUM

When we turn to these two countries we are dealing with nearly 60 million people who have been close neighbours and allies for a very long time and have provided between them many learned seats of medical knowledge and today stand high in the list of countries when measured by their provision of doctors for the population. Both are members of the European Common Market and free exchange of,

55

E

and between, their medical professions are clearly possible. Their systems of health care have followed parallel lines but with many variations. The medical professions of both countries have been repeatedly at loggerheads with their governments, chiefly about the amount of money the state makes available to the doctors. Their health care arrangements are part of a general system of social security which in some categories of beneficiaries makes quite generous payments. As members of the European Common Market they have accepted those parts of the Rome Treaty which are applicable to workers moving from one country to another, ensure equal treatment for all persons covered by the scheme and allow insured persons and their families to retain the rights already acquired or about to be acquired at the time of moving from one country to another. Both countries have initiated experiments in some aspects of medical care and their social security measures are still growing and seem likely to undergo many developmental changes.

FRANCE

The republic of France has a population of 49 million and an area of 212,700 square miles which make up a rich land with great variations, from the vineyards of the south to the industrial and mining north. In the agricultural areas there is a great variety of farming and there are large areas of forest. In recent years the number of Frenchmen employed in industry has greatly increased and the standard of living has been rising. The country is governed centrally by a Senate and elected National Assembly and administration is highly centralised. France is divided into administrative *Départments* each with a body of administrators responsible directly to Paris, with the result that local government bodies have very few powers. Public education is highly developed and also highly centralised with a high proportion of students going on to universtiy education. Medical services are also largely controlled from the centre.

The basis of the protection in France of the population by social schemes is that medical expenses are very heavy: often they could not be met by the individual alone. The progress recorded in the country's standard of health is in great measure due to the organisation of schemes that tend to distribute the financial burden over the whole community.

The principal scheme is the national system of social insurance, started in 1930 for low income wage earners but extended in 1946 to all wage earners and some special categories. Then in 1961 agricultural workers were brought in; and other groups are covered by non-compulsory mutual benefit insurance which can be held in addition to Social Security; and for those without financial support, for war victims and the disabled, a system of social aid. In brief, everybody is or can be covered for health care as well as social security payments. The schemes are operated by regional offices, controlled by a central organisation, and this permits some flexibility to meet local conditions. Central government covers any deficit in those funds from general taxation. Nearly nine-tenths of the population is covered by one or other of the schemes, over 75 per cent by the principal national scheme but 99 per cent of the lower income groups. The premiums paid in France, by employee and employer are graduated according to salary. Service benefits cover all illness except those for which special schemes operate, for example, tuberculosis. Medical aid covers the admission of the mentally sick to institutions, either public or private.

One very big field which is covered separately is occupational health for which France has a highly developed system which includes both a great variety of regulations on industrial hazards, factory doctors and compensation. All factories must have medical cover, jointly if they are small, full-time if they have over 3,500 workers. Something between 9 and 10 million workers are protected in this way and a new law now brings agriculture workers into the scheme. At the end of 1966 over 2 thousand doctors (about 10 per cent women) were engaged full-time in industrial medicine and over 2,500 were employed part-time. Salaries vary in different areas but are satisfactory enough compared with other kinds of medical specialities to keep recruitment high. The building industry is included in the service for occupational health and mobile medical units are used on building sites.

The benefits for occupational accidents are higher than for ordinary sickness and the scheme is autonomous inside the general organisation of social security so that better grants can be made to someone injured in the performance of a task which contributes towards the national production effort. Among the benefits are payments to a surviving wife and children and they may also go on having medical care without making themselves eligible by working. Normally there is a condition attached to health care through sickness insurance that the insured person must have worked for at least 60 hours during the three months preceding the illness. But once the right has been established treatment can go on as long as the illness lasts, without limit.

Payment for treatment is, however, rarely 100 per cent. All ordinarily recognised medical needs are covered and the patient is free to choose his doctor but he must in the first instance pay the fee demanded. The fee should be the fee laid down in a tariff agreement made with the medical profession of the area (but following lines laid down nationally) and which is the basis for re-payments, usually 80 per cent but more or less for drugs according to how essential they are considered. This is where there has been so much trouble between government and doctors. If a tariff scale cannot be agreed after negotiation, it can be laid down and enforced by the government and doctors may decide to accept it or not. There are areas where only 50 per cent of the practising doctors have accepted the tariff, thus restricting the patient's free choice. There is also the problem of distinguishing between general practice and specialist practice which is paid more. A doctor is not allowed to charge more than the scale for any unjustified reason such as his own reputation or the fact that the patient is wealthy or thought to be. There is a hidden punitive effect in the fact that when a compulsory tariff has to be introduced it is lower than the tariff paid to doctors voluntarily agreeing to the standard rates.

The general practitioner in France still practises as an individual and it is only recently that group practice has begun to appear. The present insurance arrangements would not affect the development of group practice. The general practitioner in France appears to do both office and home consultations as in many other countries but he has no list of patients and has not that authority which in some countries permits specialist care only through referral by the general practitioner.

Throughout France, however, there is a chain of over 700 dispensaries, which may be administered locally or regionally, for maternity and child welfare, and the school medical service; and the social insurance offices can use their funds to add to these, especially in fields such as the treatment and prevention of tuberculosis, advice on cancer and on one of France's chief problems, alcoholism. The same dispensaries also carry on health education and propaganda. Clinics and other facilities for mental disorders are also provided from the social security funds.

The funds are also used to some extent to provide capital, between 30 and 40 per cent of the annual spending on construction and modernisation of hospitals. France has 500,000 hospital beds, 100,000 for mental disorders and a similar number in private hospitals which may be profit-making but are mainly of the voluntary non-profit-making type, often religious. The public hospitals may be autonomous, like university hospitals, or owned by local authorities but all are co-ordinated by a central department. The Ministry of Social Affairs, since 1966, has been responsible for the whole social security pro-gramme. Recent laws have the particular object of subjecting the establishment of any new institutions and any extension of an old one to previous approval by the Ministry in order to avoid duplication and thus give greater effectiveness to the health equipment plan. France operates by systems of five-year economic planning.

The hospital system as it developed was, naturally, unplanned but it is now hoped to bring it into a pattern, to rationalise and grade the hospitals within a regional framework. The regional hospital centre will be the place capable of and equipped for a complete hospital service and will be linked with the many smaller hospitals around. One of the important fields is that of road and work accidents, burns, and poisoning and the Ministry of Social Affairs has a whole section dealing with these problems. Special arrangements, reflected in some first-class modern units, for emergencies and trauma are laid down by the Ministry and autonomous hospitals have to provide, for example, mobile accident units where they are thought to be necessary. Central funds are, however, available for the purchase of equipment. Ambulances may be public or private but cost is covered, as with all other essential services, by social security, although the patient may still have to pay 20 per cent. France has built many first-class hospitals and in these the medical staff are engaged on a whole-time basis. Usually about 8 per cent of beds are available to chiefs and assistants for private cases. There has been a great increase in the number of specialists who do no private practice, which is necessary if the hospitals are to utilise fully the complex and costly technical equipment and installations purchased by the administration. It offers the doctors the advantages arising out of a single plan of work and has made it possible to take a step forward in "humanising" the hospitals. In the teaching hospitals similar arrangements are being made and at twenty-four centres there is a single medical staff, exercising in consequence a dual hospital and university function. In the smaller hospitals the staff arrangements may be salaried or they may be on some local basis in units which are, essentially, general practitioner medical and maternity centres with midwives attached.

The budget of hospitals is completely independent of local authorities. Almost the total cost is derived from payments by patients for the services rendered, that is, the cost of staying in hospital and the fees for out-patients consultations. But for nearly all patients, indeed for all except those being treated as private patients, the payments are not made personally but by a third party, the social insurance funds or social aid for the non-insured. The method by which the hospital collects the money is that every individual is given an account, based on the cost per day which is then passed on for payment. This account covers every hospital expense but the medical fees are the subject of a separate account.

France aims at a truly comprehensive service in which present gaps arise from the problems of personnel and finance. The medical profession has perhaps not been so constructive or co-operative as the general political democratic spirit of France might have led one to expect. There has been a continuous attempt to maintain the liberal and independent concept of the medical profession. Since a high proportion of the cost of medical care is now paid by third parties of which the government is the largest many doctors are now taking full-time salaried positions and the opportunities for independent actions are becoming less.

The future plan is not only to provide better cover in hospital out-patient clinics but to build and staff town clinics, a form of polyclinic, at which any medical pratitioner will be able to obtain every kind of technical examination and test. This scheme is to be coupled with a form of specialist care in the home so that patients need not always be admitted to hospital.

All these advances will need a great amount of money and health is only now being given its proper place in the country's spending. The state and its social security organisation co-operate to work out the needs and where the advance can be most rapidly made. The up-grading of the medical educational system has already cost a vast sum but the future need for beds is still considered to be very high. For the moment France is putting much more money into hospitals than any other section of medical care and it is not clear whether it is accepted that hospitals are tending more and more to become the mainstay of the health organisation as a whole or whether the general practitioner working from group practice premises will be seen to have a vital primary care function.

BELGIUM

The densely populated 11,780 square miles of Belgium have a population of 9·5 million but produce a country which in spite of its devastating experiences of war is highly industrialised, textiles, engineering, iron and steel and ship building all being important. At the same time it has extensive farming activities. It has some affinities with its Dutch neighbours to the north and its French neighbours to the south but suffers from having two official languages: and since feeling about language is intense those who, like doctors, have to deal with both French and Flemish speakers, have to use both. Belgium is a constitutional monarchy with a two chamber system of government.

Medical care in Belgium follows a familiar European pattern with a combination of government control, governmental provision and social insurance which pays both public and private purveyors of health care part of the cost, leaving the remainder to the patient. Special services exist for groups such as railwaymen or for diseases such as tuberculosis and cancer. Public health services are provided and backed up by state laboratories. Hospitals, which are not considered to provide nearly enough beds, are the subject of a new plan for better and more organised provision.

Belgium has, however, suffered very much from the independent attitude of the medical profession and from the continued retention of hospital facilities by private societies and private persons. Only 40 per cent of the hospital beds are in public institutions and of hospitals just over one-third are owned by public authorities plus a few owned by insurance organisations. Sickness insurance was put on a national footing in 1945. The Act which established this cover for industrial workers, and dependents, below a certain income level, agreed to pay for hospitalisation and gave the patient free choice in public or approved private hospitals.

Although the Ministry had not been given powers to re-organise hospitals, by hinting at rejection of approval, standard requirements for all hospital departments were established and subsidies were offered, both to public and private institutions, to enable hospitals to bring themselves up-to-date. In time it led to a new law, which became active in 1964, and which replaced the previous indirect influence on hospitals through sickness insurance with a state guardianship. The important new authority given to the Ministry of Public Health was that aid for hospital building, for modernisation, for new equipment would be given only within the framework of a nation-wide programme. The state, it will be seen, has not taken over the hospitals but left them in the hands of the previous owners. It is up to municipalities or voluntary agencies to promote new buildings or reconstruction. The state contents itself with setting the standards, ensuring the plan and subsidising the scheme by 50 or 60 per cent of the cost according to the status of the project. A rational hospital system, obtaining most or all of its daily costs from patients or third parties is thus expected to grow and develop in a few years.

There are still many hospitals controlled by religious bodies but increasingly the staff of nurses are no longer recruited to the religious order but are trained nurses and nurses in training. Mental hospitals come under control of the Ministry but are still needing much improvements. Only 4 mental hospitals are actually state owned, 46 others being owned partly by lay and partly by religious organisations.

The aim of the hospital services financially is to balance the budget. The patients are billed by the usual technique of a fixed charge per day which is laid down by a department of the Ministry after considering all the facts and figures. In those communal hospitals managed by the sickness fund all treatments, including medicines, are free. In private hospitals the whole cost is not reimbursed, the usual amount being 85 per cent of the total. As in other systems based upon an overall social security insurance system, those of low income or not insured are paid for by the social aid scheme, so that in effect all but a few people of high income are covered. The patient can choose his own hospital, but usually takes the advice of his general practitioner.

The general practitioner constitute nearly half of the doctors in Belgium, and although solo practice has been the rule, group practices are now being formed. Any practitioner may accept patients and is paid by a set scale of fees, fixed by a negotiation between the Ministry and the profession. The patient recovers between 75 and 85 per cent, particular groups (e.g. widows and the tuberculous) getting the higher figure. Doctors may only prescribe medicines included in an approved list but this is extensive. The patient pays the pharmacist and reclaims if the cost is over a certain amount.

Belgium has had great trouble over schedules of fees. Anyone discussing the point will meet a great deal of cynicism about the attitude of the profession. The profession's reaction to the scale of fees last proposed is regarded as quite unjustified since few doctors adhere to the scale of charges and patients often pay much higher than in theory they should. As a result charges can be quite a drain especially to those whose only income derives from the other side of social insurance, the monetary benefit for sickness. Those who are sick for more than eight days receive 60 per cent of their normal wage and if their doctor exceeds the scale of fees, this can absorb a large proportion of their reduced income.

Just as many hospitals are privately owned so too are many of the diagnostic services. These send their bills to the social insurance fund, again according to a fixed scale, and as a result build up quite impressive units. As a rule they combine work for a private hospital with work for both general practitioners and specialists.

Belgium is a member of the European Common Market and may have to make considerable adjustments to fit into future schemes. This may prove as difficult as has the solution of her own internal language problem which necessitates every medical document being in two languages. It is not clear that she has categorically accepted that the State is responsible for the health of every citizen but she approaches that position in a variety of ways with 90 per cent of the population covered by sickness insurance and almost everybody able to obtain a comprehensive service by prepayment combined with paying a proportion at the time of use.

THE NETHERLANDS

Holland with an area of 13,500 square miles has a population of 12 million and has shown a standard of living that has been rising steadily since the country was returned to a constitutional monarchy after five years of German occupation. Medicine has always had a high place in Holland's social structure and in its universities.

The Netherlands have a long history of both state intervention in matters of health and attempts by the people to organise prepayment for health hazards on a voluntary basis through sickness funds which before World War II covered about 50 per cent of the people. Although today no country can provide medical care without the state intervening Holland still boasts of the efforts of Public Authorities and Private Initiative in the organisation of Public Health. Today sickness insurance is part of a very full system of social welfare which is compulsory for all below a fixed income level, but others are free to join the scheme. 70 per cent of the population join the compulsory scheme but another 10–15 per cent will join one of the sickness funds while 15–20 per cent of people carry private insurance either as their whole protection or in addition to social insurance. It is said that only 2 per cent have no insurance with a central Sick-Fund Council. This Council controls the finance of the sick funds through an equalisation fund into which all premiums (of which the employer pays a greater part than the employee) are paid and to which the Government adds an amount which may be up to 20 per cent of the total. This covers various groups of insured who do not pay the normal premium, for example the aged poor who pay only a half or a quarter of the usual amount according to their income. A sick fund cannot refuse them membership on the gounds that the old have a greater chance of sickness than other age groups.

The Dutch sick funds are more than a way of guaranteeing free medical care; they are intended also to guarantee the quality of the care their members get. There are a variety of ways in which this is done but partly it is through the long asssociation of the medical profession with the funds. Some of them were set up in the last century by the doctors' own organisation, The Royal Netherlands Society for Promotion of Medicine. Others had an industrial origin, a means whereby employers could assist those of their workers whose earnings were low.

So far as medical care is concerned a member of a sick fund can consult any doctor within his areas who has an agreement to treat sick-fund patients, but patients register with the doctor of their choice when the method of payment is on a capitation basis. The aim is 3,000 sick-fund members per doctor in any given area but the capitation fee is higher for the first two thousand patients than it is for the remainder. The quality of service is supervised by controlling doctors employed by the sick funds. These controlling doctors have a number of duties aimed at avoiding abuse and waste. The doctor's first entry into practice has to be agreed by the Provincial Inspector for Public Health, but discipline on ethical matters is enforced by the Medical Association. Drugs are prescribed free if they are on the official list but others can be prescribed with the agreement of the controlling doctor. It is interesting that patients also register with a pharmacist who receives a payment for every one who does so, as well as the payment for the drugs prescribed.

Holland today is the most densely populated country in the world. There has a very low death rate and a high birth rate. The three largest towns are densely populated but the bulk of the people live in small towns and villages, which necessarily affects the organisation of medical care. The medical profession plays many official and semi-official parts. Thus the distinction between specialist and non-specialist is very sharp and is defined both in general and for every individual doctor by the Registration Committee. Sick funds and hospitals will accept a doctor as a specialist only if he has been accepted by this Committee.

But the country depends upon the general practitioner and usually accepts him as a family doctor and so much the first line of medical care that, except for some emergencies, the sick funds pay the fee for a specialist only if the patient has been referred by his general practitioner. There are no binding regulations about a family all having the same doctor but this is something the Dutch people adhere to; and the Dutch name "house doctor" indicates that home visiting is the rule. The general practitioner, although he normally gets most of his income from the sick funds is, of course, free to take private fees or do other work.

General practitioners in the Netherlands are nearly all in solo practice but in one of the most newly reclaimed polders, (land that was formerly under the sea) group practice has been initiated. In most places free co-operative mutual aid rather than definite group practice seems to be the rule. A great need is felt for continual re-education and there is a strong College of General Practitioners, the work of which is sufficiently important to be financially supported by the state. The general practitioner has increasing responsibility and skill. He has to take a leading part in integrated and co-ordinated health care, the essence of which is to be close co-operation between the various workers in the front line of health care; the general practitioner, the district nurse, the midwife, the pharmacist, and the dentist, and in the future probably also the social worker. These workers must have the opportunity to enter into a good consultative and referring relation with the workers in the second line of health care, the medical specialists, the hospitals and the various organisations in the field of mental and social health care. This cannot happen while the general practitioner is in solo practice and the establishment of group practices will probably play an important role in these developments.

General practitioners often employ a medical aid who has special training in their consultative work. For the nursing of patients in their own homes Holland has district nurses who are employed by what are known, from their symbol, as the Cross organisations. There are three, in addition to the Red Cross, one Roman Catholic, one Protestant and a general one. These Cross organisations employ over 1,500 district nurses and have other kinds of workers who assist practitioners, and deal with special cases. General practitioners also have in many towns laboratory services organised by the sick funds, or by the hospital. In some but not all places open access for general practitioners is given, the sick funds paying the laboratories per item of service.

Midwifery in Holland has always been regarded as a normal procedure and nearly 70 per cent of births still take place in the home. It is a little strange that the general practitioner who is expected to be the family doctor is not involved in obstetrics. In a very large number of cases a midwife is solely in charge, is paid by the sick fund for each case she does, and need only call in the doctor in case of difficulty. There is competition between doctor and midwife for cases. One feature of home midwifery which is of great assistance to midwife, doctor and patient is that the Cross organisations train and employ girls as maternity aids who act as nursing home-helps. A member of these organisations who has paid the appropriate fees can have the service of such an aid during and after the birth of a baby.

The general practitioner can refer his patients to recognised specialists who will be paid their fees by the sick fund. The specialist may admit his cases to hospital knowing that the patient will get free treatment for one year. There are 276 hospitals officially recognised and over 160 are denominational, Protestant or, more numerously, Roman Catholic. The University hospitals are owned by the state which has to subsidise them heavily as the charges made to the sick funds, fixed by a special board, are much less than the true daily cost. Non-teaching hospitals, public or private, have to meet all their costs from the sick funds but the payments are calculated on an average bed occupancy of 90 per cent, not always easy to achieve. The specialists in most hospitals have private practice facilities inside the hospital or in their own consulting room. But with the building of great new hospitals which are also teaching hospitals there is a move to have a closed hospital system of salaried officers.

Holland also has a system of health care in industry which is almost entirely set up and financed by employers. One such service has been in operation for forty years; but now there is a move to cover the whole of industry. The social welfare system covers all kinds of disability with special schemes for seamen and agricultural workers, and a very large number of medical men and women are engaged in public health preventive work and in administration. In preventive work the sick funds also play a part by making money available for this purpose.

The Netherlands achieve a comprehensive health cover by a very complex combination of public and private bodies. There is no complacency although in terms of vital statistics Holland can show some excellent results.

WEST GERMANY

The Federal Republic of Germany, usually referred to as West Germany, is very similar in size and population to the United Kingdom, 95,744 square miles and 59 million people. Its remarkable recovery from the devastation of World War II is based largely on its coal, iron and steel and on industrial products in engineering, motor vehicles and chemicals. It has at the same time quite large agricultural and fruit areas. It has a two chamber system of government but the ten states (*Länder*) which make up the country have their own governments and a considerable autonomy in education and in health matters. The standard of living is now high but in some respects its social services are not so developed as in some neighbouring countries.

Sick Fund insurance systems were established in Germany between 1880 and 1890 and were consolidated by a Social Insurance Act in 1911. Today compulsory schemes cover all wage earners and salaried workers below a certain level, but others may join. There are for higher income groups and at higher premiums, private sick insurance funds. All of the schemes combined probably cover about 90 per cent of the population. The Ministry of Health of the Federal Republic of Germany supervises the sick funds but they are administered by the provincial (*Länder*) governments. The funds are never entirely solvent, although the aim is that they should be and the federal authorities give certain subsidies. The provincial governments vary very much in how much they spend on health and how full a public health service they give. Each district has a public health office which is directed by a medical officer of health. He is responsible for sanitary and hygiene services, welfare of school children, expectant mothers and infants and persons suffering from tuberculosis and other conditions. These medical officers have educational duties and in some places act as forensic physicians. Although these medical officers are closely linked with the federal public health system they are largely independent and responsible to their local council.

General practice is almost entirely based on the sick fund arrangements, which now cover 90 per cent of the population. Employed and employers pay contributions to the funds, graduated according to salary and covering benefits both in service and in money: dependants are also covered. Those citizens not members of a sick fund because they are unemployed or poor are given a medical card, which entitles them to medical care, by the office for service welfare. General practitioners may establish their practice wherever they like and solo practice has been the rule. Every member of a sick fund can choose his own doctor, general practitioner or specialist from those who have a contractual agreement with the local sick fund. The doctors themselves organise the payment of the individual doctor, claim fees for all of them on a set amount for each consultation plus extra payments for special types of treatment, of which a very common one is giving injections. The local association of doctors on the panel receive a total amount which they disburse among the members.

Although it has been said the doctor is free to practise where he likes he has to make a contract with a sick fund, which need not necessarily accept him. Each sick fund constitutes a panel of doctors who will be paid by the fund for the patients they see. Doctors can be accepted only after they have been medically qualified for three years and have undergone further training, including a special preparatory course for panel doctors. All panel doctors are members of an official association which among other duties deals with all payments to doctors, as mentioned above. It is a source of complaint among the general practitioners that they do not earn enough from the sick funds alone and must do private practice or other work; but some studies suggest that the average income is about DM 22,000 a year which is said to be adequate in relation to the cost of living in Western Germany. It is in fact said to be higher than the income which is earned by the full-time hospital officer who has no private practice. At the same time the panel doctor is subject to close scrutiny, and the doctor who exceeds the average fee claims for any particular field, or who appears to be over-presenting may be challenged by the board of his panel association.

The general practitioner has few restrictions on his practice except for the care he is expected to observe in prescribing costly medicines. His relationship with the sick fund is a purely financial one and he has received very little help through the funds to raise his standard of care by the use of x-rays, laboratories and advanced techniques of treatment. The sick fund will pay for these things but the general practitioner has to make his own arrangements with a university hospital department, with a private laboratory or by providing his own facilities. This is now becoming a recognised method and general practitioners are grouping together, to build, staff and use diagnostic and treatment centres. The attitude of the fifteen to twenty doctors in Cologne who have combined is that in modern times the G.P. must have enough apparatus and knowledge to be able to give to the specialist to whom he refers a case, a full "work-out" of all the necessary tests. This is not group practice although the doctors work very closely together and can consult with colleagues known to have special skills, but is a convenient way of building up a laboratory, with clerical and other staff to enable them to obtain what in other countries is provided on an open access principle. The hospitals in Germany have not organised their laboratories in that way and it is held that the chief stumbling block is the much criticised German Chief-of-Staff system which keeps lucrative private practice in the hands of the head of the department. The general practitioners who are running such diagnostic centres all maintain their own private consulting rooms, even their own smaller laboratories, but pay the centre their due proportion of the cost based on what has been claimed from the local sick fund. The tests available are not only biochemical but include electrocardiograms.

It is also interesting that once such a centre is established it is possible to add all the range of treatments that require technical assistance and special equipment, electro-therapy, all kinds of physiotherapy and various forms of inhalation for respiratory tract complaints.

Germany has a fairly high ratio of hospital beds to population, the majority being in public institutions or in non-profit making hospitals largely supported by the sick fund payments. Here again the relationship is a purely financial one, the sick funds exercising very little control over the voluntary hospitals and none over the public hospitals; but there are some owned by the sickness insurance bodies themselves. All members of sick funds and their dependents get completely free hospital care with a limit of eighteen months. Although the sick funds do not control the hospitals they use, all hospitals are supervised by the Board of Health. The sick funds also employ their own doctors who can visit any hospital to check on cases of chronic illness who are, naturally, a drain on the sick funds.

A very high proportion of doctors working in hospitals are employed on a full-time basis. There are nearly 80 university hospitals which gives an indication of how many centres of the highest medical standards there are in the country as a whole. Since World War II there has been of necessity a very large amount of hospital building, the capital being found by the federal or provincial governments. We have said that a patient may consult any doctor who has a contract with their own sick fund and that includes specialists as well as general practitioners, but it appears to be a fairly general rule that it is the general practitioner who is first seen and he refers his cases to the hospital specialist.

Although a highly industrialised state, Germany has not developed an occupational health service as has France. The insurance system covers compensation but has no separate funds and organisation. Safety officers are appointed in all factories and factory medical officers carry out routine inspections aimed at seeing that the provisions for the protection of labour are carried out.

Germany has a high ratio of doctors to population and has a very large output of qualified medical men. Medical education has not escaped its share of student unrest and even revolt as to the way in which they are taught. The sick fund system has become static and the newly qualified men seem to feel it has no quality control mechanism and no social content such as is necessary today. The Chief-of-Staff tradition in hospitals is much criticised both for its finanacial and psychological effects and because it tends to produce pockets of medical care of a supposedly high standard but plays no part in the overall planning of health services. The provincial autonomy in health organisation appears to be so firmly adhered to that there is difficulty in developing a national strategy on health matters.

EIRE

The Republic of Ireland with an area of 27,135 square miles and a population of 2·9 million has many health problems some of which arise from and are related to the low standard of living and general underdeveloped state of the country. Eire has only slowly become industrialised and still has some 30 per cent of her working population engaged in agriculture, forestry and fishing. Emigration from Eire over the past century, chiefly to the U.S.A. but also to England and Scotland, has given a different population distribution from many other European countries. Indeed it is estimated that Eire has the lowest percentage of population in the economically active age group, 57·8, of all the European countries, contrasting for example with 65·4 in England and Wales and 67·1 in Western Germany. Population is now increasing and the median age at death has risen rapidly in the past twenty years. Disease prevention, especially in the case of infectious diseases, produced very rapid falls in deaths and as the general environment, sanitation, water supplies and so on improve Eire should rapidly improve its overall health position. Industrialisation is advancing rapidly, financed to a considerable extent by foreign companies setting up factories where labour is fairly readily available.

All these factors are affecting thinking and planning of health services in Eire. Up to the present its health services have developed on lines very different from the United Kingdom, of which it was once a part, and from most European countries. Its Poor-law system and services for disease prevention, maternity and child welfare had been very similar to those in England but hospitals had been few and there was no health insurance system. Since Eire became a republic many new hospitals have been built, chiefly with money derived from the world famous Irish Sweepstakes, lotteries based on horse-racing in England.

The Government of Eire not only does not attempt to provide a universally available service and does not accept the proposition that the State has a duty to provide unconditionally all medical, dental and other health services free of cost to everyone, without regard to individual need and circumstances. However the preventive services being designed to protect the community as well as to succour the individual, are to be available to all without regard to means.

The services are organised, financed and administered by local health authorities but changes to a form of special regional health bodies are to be introduced. The above statement of attitude has in practice divided the population into three groups of which only the 30 per cent in the lowest income group obtain all services free and 10 per cent are eligible only for infectious disease services, and rehabilitation. The great majority in the middle income group do not get the General Medical Service, provided at dispensaries and in the home by salaried medical officers but are eligible for hospital and other institutional care, for mental health care, maternity and infant welfare and some other items. The distinction between the lower and the middle income groups is purely financial but the limit is set at such an income that over 90 per cent of the population falls into these two groups and therefore obtains a large part of its health care from the State schemes. It has been the continuing policy of the Government and the health authorities to improve facilities by building new hospitals, clinics and dispensaries, by providing better equipment, by making specialist services more readily available throughout the entire country, by increasing the numbers employed in the health services. It is also policy to ensure that no one is prevented from having any service they require for those outside the groups statutorily entitled to the services can use them if they can show hardship.

The finance of the health service in Eire and the way in which general medical services are provided for those eligible are both unusual. Poor law medicine was originally locally financed: but since 1947 the central government has taken over more and more of the burden and by 1965–66 was paying half out of the total of £30 million which was the expenditure on local health services. Having reached this position the Government announced that it considered that the local rates were not a form of taxation suitable for collecting additional money on the scale now needed. Capital expenditure however has been quite a different matter for between April 1948 and April 1965 a total of £35 million had been spent, only £6 million by local authorities and £7 million by the State, the remainder £22 million being provided from the Sweepstakes. There has always been a danger that capital expenditure from this type of fund might out-run the growth of expenditure on daily maintainance and the ability of local health authorities to meet all the continuing demands of new hospitals and the Government, while still welcoming the money from the Sweepstakes, is taking a stronger hold on the total to be spent on new hospitals when the service is taken over by the new regional health boards.

The general medical services, as indicated above, are supplied by district medical officers, usually one to a dispensary district. He has the duty to attend and see patients at the dispensary at fixed times and to visit a patient at home when required. The district medical officer is part-time and also engages in private practice, attending to the 60 per cent of the people who form the middle income group: but Eire is determined to move away from the poor law atmosphere maintained by the old dispensaries and to insist that there will be no distinction in future between those whose general medical care is paid for by the health authorities and those who pay for it directly. It is hoped that this will give all patients some choice of practitioner although it is admitted that Eire has areas so sparsely populated that choice must be limited.

The position on hospital services is not quite so clear as the division between lower and middle income groups would suggest. Although the middle income group are expected to pay for hospital services the amount asked is a purely token sum but the health authority has an option whether to make this charge at all. As a result in 1965 for example no charge was made for 60 per cent of middle income group patients and only half of the remaining 40 per cent were charged more than five shillings a day. Charges were also made for certain out-patient services but they brought in a very small sum and as it is considered desirable to encourage out-patient attendances

71

rather than treatment as in-patients the Government propose to abolish charges for out-patient specialist services.

SWITZERLAND

Switzerland is a country different in many ways from other European countries and its health services are also different although following the general pattern of insurance coupled with the patient paying his own fees and claiming back up to 80 per cent. Switzerland has a population of just over 6 millions, an area of 15,941 square miles. It is the most mountainous country in Europe, the Swiss Alps covering more than half the country and producing the problems that arise in any country where communications are difficult. The country is divided into 22 cantons or more correctly these 22 units are federated as the Republic of Switzerland, each having its own government for most matters with a consequent variation in services, finance and so on. Although having only a few industrial centers Switzerland is prosperous and is the international centre for many organisations, including the World Health Organisation which has its headquarters at Geneva.

The health services are based on insurance against illness, a federal law passed in 1911 which entitles every citizen to insure through one of the numerous mutual aid socieites or through sick funds set up by a canton or even by the smaller communes. Much of the scheme is left to the cantons but there is pressure from the centre as a subsidy is paid by an annual grant per member to those cantons which come up to certain minimum standards. Each canton has to decide to which groups of citizens the compulsory type of scheme is to be applied and in some the figure is low: for the country as a whole it is about 80 per cent. The amount they pay into the sick funds also varies, as do the benefits obtained.

All Swiss physicians, there are about 5,000, are paid fees by the sick funds for each consultation they make. Sick funds may also pay part, usually 75 per cent, of the cost of prescribed drugs and must make a contribution towards the cost of medical care in hospital. The sick funds show considerable variation in the hospital benefits they provide.

LUXEMBURG

The smallest European country has an area of 998 square miles and a population of 335,000. In spite of its size it is an important steel-producing country and is the headquarters of the European Coal and Steel Community and is a member of the European Economic Community. Its population is served by only 20 hospitals with some 3,500 beds and has had a health insurance scheme from the beginning of the century. This is a compulsory system which draws its funds from contributions based on salaries, employees paying approximately four per cent and employers two per cent. The money is paid to sick funds each of which has considerable autonomy. As a result the benefits vary and so do the amounts the patient has to pay. Hospital treatment is usually free but the patient may have to pay up to 25 per cent, but never more, of the cost of medical treatment and medicines. As with so many other countries the patient has to reclaim fees he has already paid and the exact amount refunded varies up to that 25 per cent. The same rules apply to care of the eyes and to dental treatment.

AUSTRIA

Austria has been an independent republic since 1918, being only a little larger than Eire, 32,376 square miles, but with a population nearly three times as large, 7·2 million. Although largely agricultural, including forests, it is today highly industrialised with a large steel output and many engineering activities. Its standard of living has risen rapidly in the past ten years. Its political administration has changed many times but under some of these she made many advances in the social services, including housing and health. Indeed at one time Vienna was one of the foremost cities in Europe for medical education and high quality medical skill. Medical literature is full of the names of Vienna's most famous surgeons, physicians and psychiatrists: but the organisation of many preventive services and the attempts of education for mothers and children in matters of health was also noteworthy.

Health services are provided now for all workers and employed persons through a compulsory system of health insurance. As in West Germany the states into which Austria is sub-divided have certain local powers and in some areas the insurance system may also cover the self-employed and farmers. The organisation is however not on an area basis but on a group concept by which groups of the population come under one scheme: and so people in analogous employment but not covered by the compulsory scheme may join on a voluntary basis. Taking the country as a whole over 90 per cent are insured in this way. The sick funds and compensations are controlled by central Government regulations but still operate independently of each other. Thus although both employer and employee pay about 2 per cent of the employee's salary there are variations: in some cases, especially lower paid workers, cash benefits are also included in the benefits.

Austria still has a high proportion of general practitioners, all of whom may accept patients under the existing scheme but the method of payment is very complicated and differs with different groups. In most the general practitioner is paid a form of capitation fee but receives a further payment for services given and that fee may be paid by the corporation or directly by the patient who then claims it back. Almost 85 per cent of prescriptions are paid for but there is a list of drugs not approved by the sick funds and for them the patient has to pay. A second list also includes expensive drugs and for treatment with them the doctor has to have the prior consent of the sick fund.

Hospital care is also paid for by the sick fund insurance but the amount paid varies among the funds. There are some state hospital and some private hospitals but most are municipal. Both hospital and general practitioner care can be provided free for those who are below a certain income level or an indigent and for this purpose the Government subsidises the sick funds. The preventive services are usually municipal and very fully developed.

Suggestions for further reading

Auster, Richard, et al., "The production of health, an exploratory study." *Journal of Human Resources* (1969), **4**, pp. 411–436.
Bice, T. W., and White, K. L., "Factors related to the use of health services: An international comparative study." *Medical Care* (1969), **7**, 2, pp. 124–133.
Broyelle, J., et al., "Recherches sur les besoins de santé d'une population." *Bulletin de l'INSERM* (1969), **24**, 3, pp. 613–732.
Hyman, J., "Empirical research on the demand for health care." *Inquiry* (1971), **8**, pp. 61–71.
Roemer, Milton I., "The organization of medical care under social security." *Geneva, ILO* (1969), 241p.
Somers, Anne R., "The rationalization of health services: A universal priority." *Inquiry* (1971), **8**, pp. 48–60.

Chapter 3

Medical Care in the United Kingdom

A. T. ELDER, PH.D., M.D., F.R.C.P., F.R.S.H., D.P.H.
Ministry of Health and Social Services, Belfast, Northern Ireland
Formerly Ministry of Health, Whitehall, London, England

Introduction

The United Kingdom has a population of over 55 million 2·5 million of whom live in Wales, 1·5 million in Northern Ireland and some 5 million in Scotland. Historically the laws governing health in Great Britain and Ireland between 1801 and 1948 can be classified as, in effect, the relief of destitution, but it was no accident that the National Health Service Acts in the various parts of the United Kingdom came into force simultaneously on the 5th July, 1948, this being 100 years from the passage of the first great Public Health Act of 1848.

Control of the environment was consolidated in an important Act of 1875, but it was not till the early part of the 20th century that state-aid for medical research and medical benefits by way of national insurance schemes came into being.

This was the legislation of 1911 promoted by Mr Lloyd George, being, in substance, the beginning of a state-aided general practitioner service outside the ambit of the then existing Poor Law Legislation.

The year 1907 had already seen the introduction of a school medical service, this being in England and Wales, and also in Scotland, an integral part of the educational system. The value of free meals and milk to necessitous children was being appreciated, though the real value of milk as a protein food was not fully realised until 1928 when Dr. Boyd Orr (Later Lord Boyd Orr of Brechin) was carrying out research in this field on school-children in Belfast, Northern Ireland. In the Second World War, under the guidance of Lord Woolton, the nation came to a full realisation of the importance of adequate nutrition in the maintenance of sound health, and food values were very accurately assessed.

The year 1918 saw the introduction of a Maternity and Child Welfare Act which gave authority to local councils to establish preventive clinics which would care for the health of expectant mothers and young children, and the Act, or similar legislation, operated at that time throughout the whole of the British Isles and included what we now recognise as the Republic of Ireland.

Just as important as nutrition and infant and maternal care, was the housing of the population, and for some years this aspect of environmental health absorbed the attention of medical officers of health, and council officers generally, till housing legislation was consolidated in an important Act, the Housing Act of 1925 (England and Wales).

In England and Wales the Public Health Act of 1936 consolidated the major public health and environmental health legislation, while the Local Government Act of 1933 established without equivocation the position of the medical officers of health, and health inspectors, and from then on they were to take a very firm control of infectious diseases, including tuberculosis.

Thus long before the introduction of a national health service, a health service seeking to maintain a healthy environment and clean food was well established.

The idea of a welfare state had been gaining ground throughout the Second World War and reached maturity with the publication of the Beveridge Report on Social Security. From this came the publication of a White Paper on the need for a national health service which was presented to Parliament in 1944.

Thus in Britain the year 1948 saw the beginning of an era of great adventure, and indeed the establishment of the National Health Service was itself a unique adventure for it set out to provide comprehensive care for all sections of the population and for all purposes, without payment at the time of use. Whatever form of treatment was to be carried out, the cost would be borne by the State, including the cost of medicaments and appliances, with a few exceptions. For example, there would be some charges for the renewal or repair of spectacles, dentures and other appliances where repair or renewal was made necessary through negligence. If the patient's medical condition was such that his general practitioner recommended that it was necessary for a specialist to attend to him in his own home a specialist would visit his home for this purpose at the State's expense.

Total community care of course includes certain services outside the concept of the National Health Service, such as some services provided by the Home Office and Home Departments (Offenders and Training Establishments), Department of Education and Science (Health of the School Population) and, say, Industrial Health

Services and Inspection but even here for the supply of doctors and paramedical personnel these services are to a certain extent integrated with the National Health Service Provision.

Also some small amount of private health insurance exists in the United Kingdom for hospital and family doctor services.

What follows in a description, first of all, of existing services in England and Wales, with a brief mention of any differences in Scotland, Wales and Northern Ireland, and then a glimpse into the future proposals for the British Health Services in the years 1973–75 and beyond.

International relationships through World Health Organisation and the Council of Europe are not dealt with in this chapter.

THE NATIONAL HEALTH SERVICE OF ENGLAND AND WALES

General

Under the National Health Service Act 1946, it is the duty of the Minister of Health to "promote the establishment in England and Wales of a comprehensive health service designed to secure improvement in the physical and mental health of the people of England and Wales", and the service "shall be available to all citizens". Though changes have occurred in the administrative arrangements of Government departments over a few years now, the operative provisions of the main legislation remain in force.

Thus the Ministry of Health is now the Department of Health and Social Security under a Minister of State for Health and Social Security, having taken over responsibility for social insurance and pensions, covering a wide field. Outside direct Government control but under various financial controls of greater or lesser degree by the central government departments the service is divided into three parts

   (a) hospital and specialist services;
   (b) local authority health services;
   (c) executive council services;

All hospitals, municipal and voluntary, had been transferred under the National Health Service Act 1946, to the Minister of Health, and the Minister and Parliament is the nation's trustee for the hospital service, the cost of which is met by taxation.

Taxes are collected from, and applied by, two main sources in Britain. Income from central Inland Revenue taxation is applied to the upkeep of hospital and family doctor services, either by direct or indirect payments to the authorities responsible, but public health (i.e. preventive health) services are financed by local taxation (rateable taxes) supplemented by direct and indirect government grants under various statutes and regulations.

The hospitals are grouped in regions under Regional Hospital Boards, the members of which are appointed by the Minister, and there are 15 such Regional Hospital Boards in England and Wales. Hospitals designated as teaching hospitals are administered by Boards of Governors directly responsible to the Minister. Within the areas supervised by each Regional Hospital Board there are Hospital Management Committees. Every year a Hospital Management Committee must prepare estimates which are the basis of the annual budget submitted by the Regional Hospital Boards to the Minister. While the teaching schools keep gifts and legacies and other endowments which helped them so much in the past before the setting up of the National Health Service the endowments of other hospitals were pooled by the State in a special hospital fund from which Regional Boards and Hospital Management Committees receive a share of the money. The endowments of Teaching Hospitals were pooled to a limited extent.

The Minister of State has direct responsibility for –

(a) the provision on a national basis of all hospital specialist services;

(b) the mental health functions previously in the hands of a Board of Control – except for the quasi judicial functions designed to safeguard the liberty of the patient;

(c) the conduct of research work into matters relating to the prevention, diagnosis and treatment of illness or mental defect;

(d) a public health laboratory service; and

(e) a blood transfusion service.

He has indirect responsibility for family practitioner services in that the family doctors though in contract with the Executive Councils are remunerated, according to the size of their patient panel lists, from central funds. Local authority services are financed partly by local taxation.

He is advised in the discharge of his responsibilities by a Central Health Services Council which reviews the general development of the service and makes a special study of any subject to which, in its opinion, the Minister's attention should be called, and by a number of standing advisory committees which he has established on the recommendation of the Central Council.

The Hospital Service

It has been said that "whatever may be the prevailing tint of its current politics, at any time, the British race champions in its daily life of a deep-rooted conservatism and love of tradition". (H. W. C. Vines)

When the Health Service undertook responsibility for hospital planning and building it inherited an astonishing admixture of older voluntary hospitals, some very famous ones such as St Bartholomew's, St. Thomas' and Guy's of London, dating back to the 18th century, voluntary infirmaries, poor law hospitals (from the 19th century) and many small cottage-type hospitals and private maternity and nursing homes.

The local Government Act of 1929 had abolished boards of guardians (former Poor Law Service) and as local authorities had already in their charge some 36,000 beds in isolation hospitals, 21,000 beds in sanatoria for tuberculous persons, and 2,600 maternity beds in lying-in institutions, together with the 120,000 beds inherited from the poor law service, they had now responsibility for 180,000 beds excluding beds in mental hospitals and mental deficiency institutions.

Thus, under the Act the first attempt was made to provide one unified hospital service in place of this former multitude of unrelated and independent voluntary hospitals and hospitals provided by the local authorities. Certain private nursing homes or hospitals run by religious orders, private companies, or others were disclaimed under the provisions of the Act, but a total of some 3,000 hospitals became available with a total potential of approximately 500,000 beds (including mental health and mental deficiency).

Teaching hospitals were to be administered by boards of governors, and in addition some of the former voluntary infirmaries were joined into groups such as the United Leeds Hospitals, or United Cambridge Hospitals. There were altogether 36 teaching hospitals – 26 of them in London (under-graduate and post-graduate). Non-teaching hospitals are grouped in local districts, each group under the aegis, as already said, of a hospital management committee (H.M.C.) and each group is theoretically able to offer within it a balanced range of normal specialities.

The exception is that hospitals dealing with mental illness or mental subnormality still tend to be independent groups, although this practice is now in decline. There are 336 *H.M.Cs.*, this number being reduced annually as administrative amalgamations take place. Much discussion of recent years has taken place on the need for a thorough review of accommodation for the mentally ill and for the care of the mentally subnormal, and for a review of this work the reader is referred to several papers which have issued of recent years on the requirements of a comprehensive mental health service. (See Bibliography)

In addition to the teaching and general district hospitals of each region, there are numbers of specialised hospitals dealing with such matters as cardiology, diseases of eye, ear, nose and throat, dermatology, cancer, to mention but a few. The district hospitals provide a full range of out-patient facilities together with pathology services, rehabilitation services, and training schools for nurses and the professions ancillary to medicine. The latter are not necessarily located in every region but most regions have some facilities for training in one or other of these supplementary professions.

The Council for professions supplementary to medicine supervises the various Boards which individually register and control the separate professions.

At present these include –

Chiropodists	Physiotherapists
Dietitians	Radiographers
Medical Laboratory Technicians	Remedial Gymnasts
Occupational Therapists	Orthopists

At the start of the Health Service it was clear that not only did many anomalies exist in area provision of hospital beds by categories but also in the standards of hospital buildings. This led to a great deal of re-assessment.

Gradually the conception of a multipurpose District General Hospital emerged, (Hospital Building Programme 1962) culminating in the publication in 1969 of a Report by a Select Committee of the Department of Health and Social Security, set up by the Central Health Services Council on the "Functions of the District General Hospital".

The idea of the district general hospital, incorporating provision for all the ordinary acute general specialities, can be traced to the Hospital Surveys undertaken during the Second World War.

District general hospitals would, of course, contain a fully developed accident and emergency department.

The reader is referred to this report for detail, but the plan envisaged that separate hospitals would continue to be maintained or provided in the following roles : —

(i) Long-stay geriatric annexes.
(ii) Some of the existing mental illness hospitals (mainly for long-stay cases).
(iii) Mental Subnormality hospitals.
(iv) Small hospitals in peripheral towns (for normal maternity cases, long-stay geriatric cases, some medical cases, and out-patient clinics).

The Local Health Authority Services

Administrative counties are in the main the geographical counties and their councils are appeal and supervisory authorities so far as the municipal boroughs, urban districts and rural districts within their counties are concerned. They are local health authorities under the National Health Services Act 1946 and are responsible for all the Part III services and for certain mental health functions under Part V of the Act. County Councils also have a variety of duties under the Public Health Act of 1936 and other Acts. Large boroughs, known as "County Boroughs" have similar comprehensive responsibilities to the Counties.

Local Authority health services provide for control of the environment under the Public Health Acts and various special Acts covering water, drainage and the like, but apart from this miscellany of health and welfare functions provided under the various Acts, the National Health Service Act itself covers broadly maternity and child welfare arrangements, home nursing, health education, local ambulance services, home help services and all matters dealing with the prevention of illness and aftercare. The additional duties of the Health Committees are covered in the following list:

(a) Prevention of illness and after-care (*N.H.S.* Act, 1946).
(b) Prevention of the spread of infectious diseases (Public Health Acts, 1936 and 1961).
(c) Vaccination of smallpox contacts.
(d) Health Education (*P.H.* Act, 1936, and *N.H.S.* Act, 1946).
(e) Registration and inspection of private nursing homes (*P.H.* Act, 1936, and Nursing Home Act, 1963).
(f) Registration of charities for disabled persons (National Assistance Act, 1948).
(g) Registration of homes for disabled, elderly, and mentally ill (National Assistance Act, 1948).
(h) Port Health (Shipping and Airports) (Public Health Regulations, 1966).
(i) Imported Food (Food and Drugs Act, 1955).
(j) Hygiene, unfit food, meat inspection, and slaughterhouse inspection (Food and Drugs Act, 1955).

Health Committees are advised by a Medical Officer of Health with a full range of nursing, dental and public health staff, and the duties and powers of the medical officers of health are set out in a Local Government Act (1933) by which each medical officer of health must possess a *registered* Diploma in Public Health.

The Family Doctor Service

Family doctor services are provided under the general direction of executive councils advised by medical committees whose area of jurisdiction is coterminous with the boundaries of existing county and county borough councils. The doctors are independent contractors. The trend of recent years has been for doctors to become grouped for general practice in group practices, a growing number of these now being located in health centres.

Some of these health centres simply possess consulting rooms for the family doctors and ancillary services for record keeping and clinical testing, while other have modified diagnostic facilities such as radiology and laboratories; others again are linked with local authority services such as antenatal and child welfare clinics and/ or the school medical service, and finally some are located in the grounds of, or adjacent to, hospitals and work very much in collaboration with out-patient departments. These group practices are tending more and more to become linked to the local authority health service, particularly with health visitor services to provide, together with the medical officer of health and his staffs, a comprehensive system of community care.

The general practitioner services may now be seen as an important and integral part of the growing concept of Community Care or Community Medicine. One of the most important changes has been the integration of public health into the total socio-medical complex, that is to say, the attachment of health visitors, district nurses and social workers to family doctor groups, and an improved relationship between medical officers of health and family doctors.

The total concept of community care is, of course, incomplete without reference to the care of the mentally ill and the mentally subnormal in the population and the relationship of medicine to the great variety now of social and medico-social workers and ancillary professions.

Health Centres

The recent growth in the number of health centres throughout the United Kingdom is worthy of special note. At first slow in development there has been a rapid move forward recently in the number of centres building or in the planning stages.

A scheme for providing health centres was first proposed in the Interim Report of the Consultative Council on Medical and Allied Services (Lord Dawson of Penn's Report, 1920).

Experience was gained during the inter-war years by a number of local authorities who built centres for housing the services provided by them prior to the passing of the National Health Service Act 1948. The White Paper (Cmd. 6761 of 1946) which explained the National Health Service Bill stressed the importance of the Health Centre, and the suggestions then made for the unification of all medical and allied services, curative and preventive, provided for people in their own homes are embodied in the National Health Service Act (Section 21). Provision is made for general medical and dental services together with pharmaceutical services for the local health authorities own services and for specialist services to be be made available at health centres. One estimate places the number of health centres in service by 1972 at around 300.

In most planning regard is had to existing local authority clinics and general practitioner group practices and existing local hospital out-patient departments, so that a present lack or obvious need can be met in any further planning of buildings. By 1972 it is estimated that about 6 per cent of all principals in general practice will be practising from health centres.

The Mental Health Services

The National Health Services Act 1946, brought mental and physical health together for the first time in one comprehensive service. The Central Government is now responsible for –

(a) hospital and institutional accommodation and all services, including nursing, for the mentally ill or for mentally subnormal persons free of charge (subject to payment only for those received as private patients);

(b) services of specialists (free of charge) for the mentaly ill or for the mentally subnormal.

The local health authorities are responsible for the community care of the mentally subnormal and their initial care and conveyance to hospital, together with aftercare.

The majority of the mentally subnormal are brought to the notice of the local health authority through the schools, but others are referred from courts, probation officers, infant welfare clinics, hospitals, family doctors, parents or friends. Since January 1958 it has been possible, within existing legislation, to admit patients to mental deficiency hospitals on an informal basis and training and occupation for subnormal living in the community at occupation centres, home teaching schemes, supervision in protective employment, care and aftercare. By the end of 1957 there were in England and Wales 157,291 hospital beds for mental illness, 57,036 for the mentally subnormal compared with 268,446 beds for all other types of illness. 98·3 per cent of all patients suffering from mental ill-health were cared for under the National Health Service, and 82·6 per cent of patients were admitted directly to mental hospitals on a voluntary basis. At the end of the year 37 per cent of all in-patients were voluntary patients.

Of course, where necessary in the interests of society or of the patients themselves, mentally disordered patients can be compulsorily detained in hospital, compulsion in England and Wales being regulated by the Mental Health Act 1959.

Special rehabilitation facilities exist to help patients return to life in the community, and most hospitals have a department staffed by medical social workers (psychiatric social workers and almoners) specially trained to apply the principles of social case-work to the problems of the hospital patient.

The total number of beds required for the mentally ill has fallen to around 120,000 but for the appreciation of the arguments for and against housing patients in hospitals for the mentally ill or in psychiatric wings of general hospitals or in the community in hostels or day hospitals, the reader is referred to special books and articles such as those of Tooth and Brooke (1961); Jones (1963); Thompson (1963); Farndale (1963); Elder (1964).

There is a wide variety of units available throughout the United Kingdom, ranging from highly specialised or long or short stay hospital diagnostic units to psychogeriatric rehabilitation, day hospitals and clinics, centres for the subnormal and university teaching and research centres. An adequate total assessment of need is only possible if each facet of the psychiatric service is examined in isolation, and in detail (Elder, Mulligan, Heaton-Ward).

The Care of the Aged

Hospitals, in general, have wings for geriatric patients, local authorities provide houses and hostels, welfare authorites have extensive social care services, and many voluntary bodies make this a prime interest of their existence.

One point for special consideration is how far facilities for temporary sickness should exist in welfare and health authority homes for the able-bodied elderly, as these are all served by family doctors of the national health services. Removal to and transfers to and from hospital must be as flexible as possible and the British Health Services make a point of enabling this pattern to emerge.

The School Medical Services

These are in no way intended as a substitute for the National Health Service but are in addition, cosely co-ordinated but continuing as a separate entity organised by local education authorities in Great Britain. Services include medical inspection, dental inspection, maintenance of health record cards, minor ailments, dental service, child guidance. There are 300 clinics in England and Wales for child guidance though not all are full-time.

Education of Handicapped Children

Education authorities have a duty under the 1944 Education Act in England and Wales to provide special educational treatment for these children. Special schools exist for the following 10 categories of handicapped pupils: –

Blind	Epileptics
Partially sighted	Maladjusted
Deaf	Physically Handicapped
Partially Deaf	Pupils suffering from speech defects
Educationally subnormal	Delicate

Day and Boarding schools exist for each category.

An important function of the School Health Service is to ascertain which children of school age require special educational treatment, or are unsuitable for education or training in a special school.

Occupational Health Services

These services are essentially preventive in character, and include first-aid treatment for cases of accident or sickness. Employers have a general responsibility not to endanger the life and health of their employees, and many have excellent arrangements for the employment of doctors and nurses to achieve the wider aims of enlightened management policy (see Central Office of Information pamphlet – "Labour Relations and Conditions of Work in Britain" *R.F.P.* 5120).

In general the Factories Acts appoint Inspectors and provide extensive regulations for health and safety, ranging from the screening of entrants into industry to highly specialised consultant services for industrial diseases. Certain prescribed industrial diseases are notifiable by law to the Chief Inspector of Factories.

It should be noted that industrial services are as yet maintained privately by industry itself, and are not financed by the Treasury.

Special extra-governmental services exist but are controlled by legislation, such as the National Coal Board industrial medical service, the Atomic Energy Authority service, London Transport Authority services and others. The Central Government supervises the Mines and Quarries Inspectorate which operates the powers of the Mines and Quarries Act 1954.

Comprehensive industrial hygiene services are also provided on a fee basis by the North of England Industrial Health Advisory Service, the Occupational Hygiene Unit at the University of Manchester, and the Scottish Occupational Health Laboratory.

It may be mentioned that a factory inspectorate appointed and paid by the Central Government was first created by the Factories Act of 1833. During the first ten years there were 18 inspectors, and this figure has now risen to over 500.

About 220,000 industrial premises, and about 30,000 building and civil engineering sites come under the Factories Act, while about 70,000 premises are subjected to the Offices, Shops and Railway Premises Act.

The safety, health and welfare of agricultural workers is safeguarded by the Agricultural (Poisonous Substances) Act 1952, and the Agriculture (Safety, Health and Welfare Provisions) Act 1956. Regulations are enforced by inspectors of the agricultural departments.

Professional personnel throughout the United Kingdom consist of: –

(a) Medical Inspectors of Factories – Central Government;
(b) Appointed Factory Doctors – to carry out statutory medical examinations, investigate cases of notifiable industrial disease and certain accidents;
(c) Industrial Medical Officers appointed by employers;
(d) Industrial Nurses.

A committee on Industrial Health Services estimated that in 1951 there were 230 doctors engaged whole-time on factory work. If one includes part-time doctors there were 1,287 in addition to 1,789 Appointed Factory Doctors. There were about 2,600 state registered nurses and 1,400 other nursing staff employed in factories. There is evidence that the numbers have increased in recent years.

THE NATIONAL HEALTH SERVICE IN OTHER PARTS OF THE UNITED KINGDOM

For the most part the service operates as in England and only minor variations exist in Wales, Scotland and Northern Ireland but a few of the interesting ones are mentioned here.

Wales

In 1969 the administrative structure was slightly altered in that there is now, under the Secretary of State for Wales, a Health Department of the Welsh Office in Cardiff with a Chief Medical Officer and staff. There is one Welsh Regional Hospital Board and a separate Board of Governors for the Welsh National Medical School. This latter is being rebuilt on a new site on the outskirts of Cardiff and will constitute the Welsh National School of Medicine together with the University Hospital of Wales and will provide comprehensive facilities for medical education and research.

The Report of a Survey of the Hospital Services of South Wales in 1945 demonstrated that the time had come for establishing a Medical Teaching Centre in Cardiff on a completely new site, to include a new Dental School and Hospital.

Eventually a new hospital of 800 beds was agreed with medical and dental schools and an entry of more than 100 medical and 50 dental students.

At the beginning of the National Health Service there were 5 institutions recognised as health centres, but thereafter progress was slow, only 4 more being opened between 1965 and 1967, but during 1968 4 were opened and 5 more in the first half of 1969, with 18 more either being built or in planning. A rapid expansion is expected after 1970.

Scotland

The National Health Service (Scotland) Act of 1947 transferred ownership of almost all the hospitals to the Secretary of State for Scotland.

The Scottish service is organised in the three main divisions outlined as for England. The country is divided into 25 areas in each of which there is an executive council which arranges with doctors, dentists, chemists and opticians to provide services for patients.

To provide hospital planning units of reasonable size Scotland is divided into five regions, each under the control of a Regional Board. Four of the regions are centred on the Scottish university cities of Edinburgh, Glasgow, Dundee and Aberdeen where there are teaching hospitals for the training of medical students. The fifth region is based on Inverness and serves the Highlands. There are about 400 hospitals in Scotland with accommodation for some 64,000 patients. Approximately 27,000 of these beds cover mental illness and mental deficiency.

Ambulance services and the blood transfusion service come within the scope of the Regional Boards, but in both of these activities the Boards co-operate with the St. Andrew's and Red Cross Scottish Ambulance Services, and the Scottish National Blood Transfusion Service. The smaller islands and remote parts of the mainland are served by an air ambulance service.

There are 55 health authorities providing care as in England and Wales.

Scotland is served by its own Health Services Council which advises the Secretary of State. There is a difference from the Regional Hospital Board arrangements in England in that the Regional Boards have responsibility for the Teaching Hospitals, but, through the medium of separate Advisory Committees for Medical and Dental Education.

The Secretary of State, through his Home and Health Department, is advised by a Scottish Hospitals Endowment Research Trust.

In Scotland the primary responsibility for building health centres rests with the appropriate Government Department but powers are

87

sometimes delegated to local authorities. By the end of 1968, 11 health centres had been opened in Scotland with accommodation for 58 general practitioners, representing 2·3 per cent of all principals. Four centres provided general dental services and one had a National Health Service pharmacy. By 1969, of the 11 Health Centres, 7 had been provided by the Secretary of State and 4 by local health authorities under delegated powers.(17)

The most striking contrast with the rest of Great Britain is that hospital outpatient services are provided in all but two of the Scottish Health Centres and 3 of them are actually attached to hospitals. During 1968 plans were approved for 9 centres and a further 25 reached planning stage. Thirty-eight other proposals were under consideration at the end of the year.

At this point it should be mentioned that on 17th November, 1969, there came into operation in Scotland, the Social Work (Scotland) Act 1968. At the centre, functions, formerly and primarily the responsiblity of the Scottish Home and Health, and Education Departments, have been merged into a single administrative division, the Social Work Services Group an independent entity directly responsible to Ministers (though formally attached to the Scottish Education Department for financial accounting) and headed by a Chief Adviser.

A Statutory Advisory Council on Social Work will replace former advising councils on child care and aftercare and the Scottish Probation and Training Council.

At local level the large burghs and County Councils have elected social work committees to replace the former welfare, children's and probation committees, have appointed directors of social work, and have prepared for the integration in the new social work departments of staff previously employed by these separate committees and those employed in social work by local health and education authorities.

Some health legislation exists on a wholly United Kingdom basis with option for the component parts to delay involvement or to opt out. Thus, by way of example, the Clean Air Act 1956 applies also in Scotland through a separate inspectorate under the Alkali Act of 1906. The School Health Service operates in Scotland under a separate Act – the Education (Scotland) Act 1962.

Northern Ireland

The health services of Northern Ireland are provided under separate legislation – the Health Services Acts (Northern Ireland) 1948–67. Under the social services agreement between the United Kingdom and Northern Ireland Governments the scale and standard of the services are kept in general conformity with those in England and Scotland.

It is the duty of the Ministry of Health and Social Services to promote a comprehensive health service which is administered in three parts – hospitals, general health services, and personal health services, the latter by eight local authority health committees which also provide school health and environmental health services. Ambulance services and all services for the mentally subnormal are administered by a Hospitals Authority in Northern Ireland, and financed from the General Exchequer.

Welfare services, home help and child care services are provided under separate legislation by eight local authority welfare committees.

The Health Education Council for England and Wales, and Northern Ireland has operated from the beginning of 1968. (A separate Council and Health Education Unit have been established in Scotland.)

Capital development in the hospitals service in Northern Ireland is still running at a higher rate than in Great Britain. A hospital plan was published in 1966, defining a 10-year building programme and a review has since carried the plan forward to 1978. The basis of the future pattern of services is the development of comprehensive area hospitals (corresponding to district general hospitals in England and Wales).

Capital programmes are also in train in the community health and welfare services. Health centres are being developed from which family doctors and local authority nurses and other staff provide comprehensive community care. At the end of 1968, 10 such centres were in operation and when the full programme is completed it is estimated that two-thirds of the family doctors in Northern Ireland will be practising from health centres.

In Northern Ireland School Health Services are mainly a matter for the local health authorities.

In England and Wales the term "mental subnormality" is in use, in Scotland the term "mental deficiency" is used, while in Northern Ireland a person suffering from arrested or incomplete development of mind (whether arising from inherent causes, or induced by disease or injury), which renders him socially inefficient to such an extent that he requires supervision, training or control in his own interests or in the interests of other persons, is known as a "person requiring special care". This category covers both "subnormality" and "Severe subnormality". Some of these "special care" cases require insitutional care; many can be looked after in the community. Of the latter, a certain proportion are looked after in special care day training centres. These should not be confused with special schools for the educationally subnormal under Education Authorities, because this situation is the same in Northern Ireland as in Britain. But, so far as Northern

Ireland is concerned, whether special care cases are in institutions, a village community, or at home in the community they are, at present, the responsibility of the Northern Ireland Hospitals Authority. To this extent therefore there is, at the time of writing, a slight variation from the British pattern.

THE ECONOMICS OF THE HEALTH SERVICE

When estimating originally in his famous report, the then Sir William Beveridge considered that a comprehensive health service might cost £177 million annually. Contributions would be exacted from employees and employers, the state would bear part of the cost, and there would be a "hotel" charge for residence in hospital. The latter proposal was never accepted by the Government but certain charges were made for spectacles, false teeth and various appliances. This list and costs of prescriptions have varied with Government and the pound sterling has progressively suffered from inflation. The total allocation for England and Wales from the social security contributions towards the annual cost of the Health Services amounted to £32 million in 1948, while the estimated total given by the Government Actury in 1946 was £152 million.

Even so, now at nearly £2,000 million, equivalent to £40 per head of population the cost has soared in the last 20 years, accounted for by augmented personnel, higher salaries and wages, vastly improved specialised services and expensive hospital equipment, together with ever increasing costs of drugs.

The greater part of the cost falls on the Exchequer, and the services now account for more than one-tenth of total public expenditure and about $4\frac{1}{2}$ per cent of the gross national product.

The following are the items for which there are charges: (certain exemptions or refunds are made and anyone who finds hardship in paying the charges may apply to the Department of Social Security for a grant); dentures (except for children under 16 or still in full-time attendance at school, and expectant and nursing mothers); spectacles; (except children's spectacles in standard frames); treatment in the dental services (but not for examination only, nor for arrest of bleeding, domiciliary visits and denture repairs, nor for treatment given to people under 21 or to nursing or expectant mothers).

There are also small charges for milk powder, orange juice and other welfare foods and for some local authority health and welfare services. Prescription charges at a nominal rate (currently 20p) were re-introduced in June 1968. Exemptions are made for children, people aged 65 and over, expectant and nursing mothers, patients in specified medical categories needing medication for long periods, war

pensioners and people with low incomes who are receiving supplementary benefits.

The National Health Service Act 1946 allowed for charges for a
limited number of hospital beds for patients desiring privacy or private
treatment and the National Assistance Act 1948 allowed charges for
welfare services to the handicapped. Some hostels and residential
homes require payment at varying rates.

Expenditure on the National Health Service rises annually with an
increasing population, among whom are large numbers of children
and elderly people who make the heaviest demands on it. Purely
administrative costs are low, being about 4 per cent of the total cost.
Members of the hospital boards and committees executive councils and
committees of local authorities serve in a voluntary capacity and are
paid only their out-of-pocket expenses.

Value for Money – The Health Statistics

The reader should consult the first of a new series of Digests of
Health Statistics for England and Wales 1969, published by the
Department of Health and Social Security, and future publications
of the kind, for factual details, and also "Local Government Medical
Staff" by Warren and Cooper (1967).

As an example of comparative analysis, it is suggested that the
increase in family doctor partnerships (77 per cent of principals compared with 69 per cent ten years earlier) and in collaboration with
local health authority staffs, has helped to meet the additional load
of the increased average panel list of patients of 2,477 per doctor
compared with 2,326 in 1963.

There has been a clear and substantial increase in the number of
cases attended by home helps, and local authorities have substantially
increased residential accommodation for all groups in need over the
past decade.

There clearly cannot be any economic saving or return in costs of
caring for the elderly and the severely handicapped. This is a manifestly
humanitarian service, but there can be returns in terms of cost in
preventing sickness so as to keep people fit and at work, in speedier
rehabilitation and return to work, and in speedier and more accurate
diagnosis of disease.

It is postulated that savings will accrue if patients can be treated
at home or in health centres but this presupposes a strengthening of
community services to take over much of the less intensive care now
given in hospital.

It means the extension of certain hospital diagnostic services and
physiotherapy to extra-hospital premises and greater availability of
diagnostic resources to the family doctor.

Closer association of family doctors and local authority staffs leads to a greater degree of integration of community care services.

A faster turnover of patients per hospital bed increases the usefulness of the hospital and incidentally reduces the cost of treatment per head of the patient population. That this is already happening is shown by the fact that at the start of the health service in England and Wales there were 500,000 beds or approximately 11·3 beds per 1,000 of population against a present complement of 9·6 beds per 1,000 of population. Hospital admissions, on the other hand, have increased by 60 per cent since 1965. There is also some evidence of a change in the disease situation in the community.

"The health services will begin to go out positively to seek ill health (especially in the elderly) so that disorders can be treated in cases where at present they would never be brought to the doctor. Research is likely to reveal ways in which the early diagnosis and presymptomatic treatment of many chronic progressive illnesses can improve their prognosis; this will lead to a general demand for regular screening, using new methods of automated biochemistry. Results from the screening rests, as well as patients' records from both hospital and general practice, will be stored centrally in computers. Many of the social problems of today – alcoholism, child delinquency, matrimonial disharmony, sexual difficulties and motiveless crime and violence – will be regarded increasingly as medical problems to be treated instead of being ignored or punished.

These two problems compound each other; as we lose more national earnings through sickness absence we are forced to regard more strictly the health services we can afford to provide. This basic economic dilemma is one facing all nations of the world" (The Royal Society of Health).

A partial solution rests in better evaluation of organisation of the health services, and a re-appraisal of hospital costs. According to the Hospital Plan for England and Wales (Cmd. 1604 – HMSO) of 1962, the hospital building programme would require some £700 million. A more recent estimate by the Central Office of Health Economics placed the figure at £1,000 million. At present hospital beds are occupied by many who do not need hospital care. A quarter of all patients in British hospitals have been classed as "self-help" patients needing, at most, minimal nursing care. In addition, many patients are kept for long periods after surgery while other hospitals discharge similar patients within a few days. Few medical or surgical procedures have been subjected to the sort of clinical evaluation which is routine for new medicines; hence the value of these procedures is unproven, and in some cases is seriously doubted.

One urgent priority is to reassess the capital investment programmes in the health services. It is true that many of the health problems of today – and particularly those of tomorrow – could more appropriately be tackled in the community than in large expensive hospitals. Diagnostic facilities, and even beds for day care, might be provided in local health centres. The hospitals being built may have to last for fifty or a hundred years (*R.S.H.* Journal Vol. 89 No. 5 1969).

But, looking broadly at the subject of value for money, let us remember with gratitude the virtual disappearance of infectious diseases over the twenty years, particularly crippling ones like poliomyelitis, the rapid decline in illness and deaths from tuberculosis, the improved overall health, the reduction in infant deaths (34 per 1,000 live births in 1948, 18·3 in 1967), and the reduction in maternal mortality (1·04 per 1,000 live births in 1948, 0·20 per 1,000 total births in 1967).

Though some chronic non-communicable diseases such as cancer and cardiovascular diseases show increasing morbidity and mortality, the average span of life nevertheless continues to increase.

It is interesting to record that the crude death rate for 1967 for England and Wales at 11·2 per 1,000 was the lowest since 1948, when, in fact, it was 11 per 1,000. The overall crude death rate has not differed all that much because improved controls in some directions are offset by increasing mortality in others, as mentioned above.

There is no question but what the nation is reaping rewards by way of improved preventive and curative facilities but control of nugatory or less fruitful expenditure must always remain of paramount concern to those controlling a national health service.

Health Education as an aspect of all philosophies within the total Health concept has contributed its share, but will assume an even greater prominence with the passage of time.

PROPOSALS FOR THE FUTURE

The Special Reports

Education and Research – The Todd Report

Since 1920, while clinical research is sponsored and financed out of the exchequer in Great Britain and Northern Ireland largely by the Medical Research Council as advised by its Clinical Research Board, there are many other Foundations such as the Nuffield Trust and the British Empire Cancer Campaign for Research which award grants to suitable applicants (See B.M.A. Handbook on Research Grants).

Recently the central Government departments under the banner of Research and Development have increased the scope and amount of direct grants for research other than through the medium of the Medical Research Council.

Medical Education has since the first Medical Act of 1856, been an increasing concern of the General Medical Council. The Council controls the registration of doctors after qualification and lays down the broad pattern of medical education which is given effect by the various medical schools.

New Government proposals to change the law as it effects the registration of the doctor follows in fact the reform of medical education in the light of the tremendous advances in medicine itself. It is true that a comprehensive review of medical education was undertaken by the Goodenough Committee in 1942–44, but for a variety of reasons its recommendations had less effect than might have been expected.

It was, therefore, not surprising that in 1965 the Government appointed a Royal Commission under the Chairmanship of Lord Todd, and it is their report, published in 1968, which has now triggered off these further legislative proposals.

The Royal Commission's first conclusion was that in terms of present-day advances in medical knowledge and the growth of specialisation, there is no longer any substance in the assumption that at the end of undergraduate training the emergent doctor is sufficiently experienced in medicine, surgery and midwifery to engage in independent practice. The Royal Commission recommended a pattern of postgraduate training designed to ensure that doctors, whether they choose to take their careers in general practice, the hospital service, in industry or preventive medicine, shall be fully trained for the work they undertake, and be regarded as "specialists" in their own field. It was for this reason that the Royal Commission has proposed a system of vocational training and registration, on top of registration as it exists today.

Other professions whose future education and administration are under close study are –
  (a) Nursing (Salmon Committee)
  (b) Hospital Scientific Services (The Zuckerman Report)
  (c) Professions Ancillary to Medicine (Registration Boards)
  (d) Public Health Inspectors – New University degrees in Environmental Health Sciences.

Administration

The Royal Commission on Local Government Administration – Maud Committee

The Royal Commission on Local Government Administration (Redcliffe-Maud Committee) was not concerned in replanning the

National Health Service, but since its Report has been accepted in principal by the Government, it must be assumed that the National Health Service will take cognisance of it and will not develop in isolation.

Briefly the Commission's main provisions (which relate only to England and Wales and exclude London) are for 61 new Local Government areas each covering town and country; in 58 of them a single authority for all services, the three largest in Birmingham, Liverpool and Manchester being differently regarded.

At lower level there will be local councils with a duty to represent local opinion and a right to be consulted on certain questions.

The whole country, including Greater London, will be divided into eight provinces with a provincial council. Broadly speaking planning for housing, transport and major environmental services will co-exist alongside the new health service programme about to be described.

The Green Papers

Changes in the administrative structure of health and personal social services are underway in the United Kingdom.

It would not be appropriate therefore to close this chapter without making due reference to these sweeping changes foreshadowed for the British Health and Welfare Services. The Secretary of State for Scotland reviewed the proposals in his Green Paper of December 1968 in the light of comments received and the consideration being given to the report of the Royal Commission on Local Government in Scotland.

The new Green Paper (E & W) (1970) set out three firm decisions by the Government on matters of principle, as follows:

(i) The National Health Service to be administered, not by local government, but by Area Health authorities directly responsible to the Secretary of State and closely associated with the local authorities.

(ii) The division of services between local authorities and the National Health Service to be organised on the required skills to effect integration of hospital, specialist and general practitioner services, and services at present controlled by the local health authorities.

(iii) In general the number and areas of the area health authorities would match those of the unitary areas and metropolitan districts outside London proposed by the White Paper on the Reform of Local Government (Eventually 5 such conurbations were conceded). All told there would be about 90 such area health authorities coterminous with new local government

95

boundaries and catering for populations varying from 200,000 to 1,300,000.

The area health authorities were to administer the following services:

the existing hospital and specialist services;

the existing family practitioner services;

the following services at present provided by local health authorities:

ambulances;

epidemiological work (general surveillance of the health of the community);

family planning;

health centres;

health visiting;

home nursing and midwifery;

maternity and child health care;

prevention of illness, care and after-care, through medical, nursing, and allied services (including chiropody, health education – other than its place in the school curriculum – and screening), residential accommodation for those needing continuing medical supervision and not ready to live in the community;

vaccination and immunisation;

the school health service.

The Government would consider further where responsibility for the child guidance service should lie. There would be a statutory committee for family practitioner services. Each area health authority would have about 20–25 members. One-third of these would be appointed by the medical profession, one-third and the chairman by the Secretary of State, and the other third would be local authority nominees or members.

A Green Paper was also issued in Northern Ireland. Following these provisional papers which were the subject of widespread consultation and discussion, there came finally, in 1971, as preludes to legislative proposals, Consultative Documents for England and Wales and for Northern Ireland, and a White Paper (Cmd. 4734) for Scotland.

A summary of these proposals gives a picture of the administrative changes envisaged throughout the United Kingdom to take place between 1973 and 1975. It is interesting to note that the year 1975 in exactly one hundred years from the major consolidating Public Health Act in Britain of 1875.

The Consultative Document and Scottish White Paper

On 5th November 1970 the Secretary of State for Social Services stated in reply to a Question in the House of Commons by Dr. Gerard Vaughan –

"The Government intend to unify the administration of the National Health Service. Legislation will bring the change into effect at the same time as alterations are made in the structure of local government.

The National Health Service will be administered by health authorities outside local government working closely with the local authorities responsible for the personal social services and the public health services. The Government are not satisfied however that the detailed administrative proposals in the Green Paper of February 1970 would create an efficient structure of a unified service. They are studying the comments made on the proposals, and before reaching final decisions of their own, will consult with the organisations concerned."

The Government has announced its decisions on the future structure of local government in England in Cmnd. 4584. This states that the local authority personal health services will be transferred to the new area health boards, and that the aim is to bring the reorganisation of local government and of the National Health Services into operation on 1st April 1974.

Work is now starting on the preparation of the legislation needed to unify the administration of the National Health Service. The unified structure will incorporate the personal health functions which, since the 1946 Act set up the Service, have been exercised by local authorities, including the provision of health centres, the health care of mothers and young children, midwifery, health visiting, home nursing, ambulance services and the prevention of illness. It will not however incorporate the functions which (although they derive from the original National Health Service Act) are now discharged through the new local authority social service committees, set up following the Local Authority Social Services Act 1970, namely home help, certain other social care services and certain residential services. These personal social services will continue to be the responsibility of the local authorities. Future arrangements for the school health service will require special consideration.

The decision to have certain social services discharged under the Local Authority Social Services Act 1970 by the local authorities rather than the Area Health Boards arose out of the report of the Seebohm Committee set up following the 1965 White Paper (The Child, The Family and the Young Offender).

The not dissimilar recommendations contained in a White Paper published by the Secretary of State for Scotland in 1966 had already been translated into legislation by the Social Work (Scotland) Act of

1968, providing for the establishment of comprehensive social work departments by local authorities in Scotland.

"The administrative arrangements *will fully preserve the clinical freedom of those who provide services to patients*; they will help to ensure that the services are provided quickly and effectively; and they will secure a close co-ordination of aims and of day-to-day action both within the unified National Health Service and with related services, especially those run by local authorities. Collaboration with voluntary organisations, too, will continue to be developed."

Area Health Authorities (Boards)

The area health authorities will be the operational National Health Service authorities, with responsibility for planning, organising and administering comprehensive health services to meet the needs of their areas. Each area authority will also be responsible for the management of the integrated health services in the various parts of its area ("districts") served by separate district general hospitals and the community health services associated with them.

The boundaries of the area health authorities will be the same as those of the counties (other than the metropolitan counties) and the metropolitan districts proposed for local government in Cmnd. 4584. On this footing there will be about 70 of them in England, outside London. As the Green Paper of February 1970 recognised, there must be firm links and arrangements for close collaboration with the matching local authorities. But the Green Paper did not make comprehensive proposals for achieving this. An effective mechanism is essential for the mutually agreed planning of, and investment in, the health and related local authority services. There will be provision for working together in day-to-day operations and for sharing supply and other ancillary services. The arrangements should cover, too, the provision of advice and services to the health authority by the local authority through its social services department and its staff, and to the local authority by the Health authority's community physicians and other medical staff, dentists and nurses including those transferred from local authority to health authority employment. In particular, it will be necessary to ensure that local authorities continue to have the medical advice they need for the effective discharge of their functions in education, the personal social services, and the environmental health services.

Regional Health Authorities

The regional health authorities will be responsible for the general planning of the National Health Service (including the specialities and, in consultation with the Universities, the service facilities to be provided in support of medical teaching and research) in each region; for allocating resources to the area health authorities; and for co-ordinating their activities and monitoring their performance (including the effectiveness of their links with the matching local authorities) to ensure that national and regional objectives are achieved and that the desired standard of service is provided. This will place on the regional authorities a real management responsibility within the chain of command and will give them a very different function from that of the regional health councils proposed in the 1970 Green Paper. In addition the regional authorities will themselves provide some services and will be the building authorities for all major projects.

The areas of the regional health authorities will be based on the 14 planning regions hitherto adopted for the hospital service, except that, subject to consultations with those concerned locally, it is proposed to divide the present Sheffield hospital region into two health regions based on the medical teaching centres at Nottingham and Sheffield respectively.

Central Department

In discharge of the Secretary of State's responsibility to Parliament for the National Health Service as a whole, the Central Department will determine national objectives, priorities and standards and allocate resources to the regional authorities. These responsibilities will – as at a lower level with the regional health authorities in respect of the area health authorities – not involve detailed control but will inevitably carry with them an ultimate responsibility for the quality and effectiveness of management and for the monitoring of performance. The existing Hospital Advisory Service has demonstrated the value of expert visiting advisory teams in psychiatric and geriatric hospitals, which contain over half the hospital beds in the National Health Service. Ways of gathering information, and disseminating advice, on successful arrangements for linking together the planning and operation of health authority and related local authority services will also be studied.

Membership of Authorities

The chairman and all the members of the regional authority will be appointed by the Secretary of State after consultations with the interested organisations including the universities, the main local authorities and the main health professions.

The chairman of the area authority will be appointed by the Secretary of State, and the members (who might number 14 in addition to the chairman, except that areas which include a teaching district will need a few additional members) will be appointed as follows –

(a) Some by the corresponding local authority;
(b) One by the university providing medical and dental teaching facilities;
(c) The rest by the regional authority;

Community Health Councils

The area health authority will be required to set up a community health council for each of its constituent districts. This will ensure that in making plans and operating services, area authorities take full account of the views of the public they serve. The council will be appointed after consultation with a wide range of interested local organisations. It will be consulted on the development and operation of the health services in the district, and its members will have the right to visit hospitals and other institutions. It will produce an annual report.

Family Practitioner Services

The family practitioner services occupy a central position, and the area health authority will be closely concerned with plans for their development – for example, at health centres and by attachment schemes, in which nurses and health visitors work together with practitioners – in close collaboration with other parts of the unified National Health Service and with the personal social services.

Endowments

The public will be encouraged to continue to support endowment funds; and provision will be made in the legislation to protect their local character and control.

London

The arrangements in Greater London will be based on the general regional and area structure set out above but will need to be specially shaped to meet conditions there, including the already established pattern of local government services, the distribution of hospitals (including teaching hospitals), the presence of separate postgraduate teaching hospitals and the wide coverage of the existing executive councils. There will be separate consultations on these problems with the organisations concerned.

Special arrangements for teaching districts

These districts will be administered as part of the areas in which they are situated. To secure that the inclusion of the teaching hospitals will benefit all the health services in the districts in which they are

situated, to retain hospitals' individual identities and historic traditions, and to maintain the special services they provide, there will be
the following arrangements: –

    (a) the regional health authority will appoint a special regional
        committee to deal with planning matters relating to teaching
        and research;

    (b) expenditure for the services in a teaching district will be separ-
        ately identified in the regional health authority's approval
        of expenditure for the area;

    (c) the area health authority will be required to appoint a district
        committee to manage the services in each teaching district
        (which will normally carry the teaching hospital's name). This
        committee will consist partly of members of the area authority
        itself and partly of others; in the early years of the reorganised
        service, the Secretary of State will appoint the chairman and
        some members; it will doubtless usually hold its meetings at the
        teaching hospital;

    (d) when a consultant is being chosen to serve in a teaching district,
        the advisory appointments committee will always include in
        its membership one or more members nominated by the district
        committee; and

    (e) arrangements will be made for one or two members of existing
        boards of governors and university hospital management
        committees to be appointed to each of the area authorities
        concerned and to each teaching district committee.

The Medical Officer of Health

The Consultative Document is subject to further discussion before
legislation is promoted but the previous Green Paper proposed that
there will be one corps of administrative medical staff serving both
the area health authority and the local authority. Most of the present
work of the Medical Officer of Health will be included in the wider
functions of the chief administrative medical officer in his capacity
as chief "community physician".

He will have four main tasks –

    (1) To develop the quantity and quality of information about
        health needs and the working of area health services;

    (2) To act as adviser on the health of the community to the area
        health authority;

    (3) To advise the local authority on the heatlh aspects of all its
        services and particularly to give a lead in health education;

    (4) To perform the public health duties of the present Medical
        Officer of Health.

However, though the area health authorities could provide services for people who suffer injury or ill-health however caused, and would be responsible for preventive health measures of many kinds, they would not have a specific responsibility for occupational health.

The Local Authorities

Local authorities will retain their responsibilitites for public health matters and the following public health services will continue to be administered by them: –

the prevention of the spread of communicable diseases other than by specific prophylaxis or treatment;

food safetly and hygiene;

port health;

the public health aspects of environmental services;

diseases of animals in so far as they affect human health;

enforcement responsibilities relating to environmental conditions at work places;

health education (a power concurrent with that of the health authorities).

All these responsibilities both of Area Health Authorities and of local authorities are to be read alongside those which the Government has decided should be exercised by the local authority social services.

In addition to the social services at present provided for the elderly, the handicapped, and the homeless, and the children's services, local authorities will be responsible for the following services which are at present provided under health powers: –

family case work and social work with the sick and the mentally disordered;

day centres, clubs, adult training centres and workshops for the above;

the day care of children under five, day nurseries, and child minding;

the care of unsupported mothers, including residential care;

residential accommodation for those who cannot live at home but do not need continuing medical superivision;

home helps;

[See Local Authority Social Services Act (1970)]

The local authority will carry out its functions in these and other matters relating through the medium of a social services committee, and will appoint an officer to be known as the director of social services, for the purposes of their social services functions.

Reorganisation of the Scottish Health Services

Proposals are contained in Cmnd. 4734 published in July 1971. This White Paper takes account of the previous Green Paper and proposals offered following its publication, and also the report of a Joint Working Party on the Integration of Medical Work – "Doctors in an integrated Health Service" published by *H.M.* Stationery Office on 27th July 1971.

Scotland accepts also the conception of Area Health Boards – there will be 14 such Boards for Scotland.

Six of the health board areas are identical with proposed local government regions, while a further six are formed by the sub-division of the two largest local government regions along district boundaries. Orkney and Shetland are to be recognised to be special cases for geographical reasons.

Local health councils will be established for the separate districts and there will be a Scottish Health Service Planning Council with statutory status as an advisory body to the Secretary of State.

Wales

The reorganisation of the Health Service in Wales was forecast by the publication of a Green Paper by the Welsh Office in 1970.

The proposals are consistent with those proposed for England but framed to take account of the special circumstances of Wales: –

(a) The Secretary of State for Wales is solely responsible for the administration of the health service within Wales and is jointly responsible for aspects of health policy common to Great Britain.

(b) Wales must be treated as one unit for the planning and control of the health service. It is too small to be split into two or more regions.

(c) The pattern of local government in Wales will differ in some ways from that in England.

The principle of Area Health Boards is accepted and the Green Paper speaks of seven such boards, four for new proposed counties plus three unitary areas into which it is proposed some existing counties should be divided.

These areas vary in population from 116,000 to 432,000 with the special exception of Cardiff (the capital City of Wales) and East Glamorgan – population 919,000.

Over-all planning will be a function of the Welsh Office with direct responsibility to the Area Boards but a satisfactory system of local participation will be maintained in the running of the service.

The special interests of the Medical and Dental Teaching School in Cardiff will be preserved.

Northern Ireland

The Ulster Consultative Document of March 1971 accepts the

H

general United Kingdom pattern and proposes four Area Health Boards, three with a population of around 250,000 people, together with the Belfast Area which because of its size will stand on its own (750,000).

A single set of Area Boards will however administer both personal health and personal social services through two statutory committees.

There will be 26 district local authorities, grouped in such a way as to render it possible for each Area Health Board to be coterminous geographically with a specified number of districts which will be caring for the environment.

Education Areas will be coterminous with Health Board Areas except that Belfast and surroundings will be divided probably into two Education Board Areas.

Undergraduate medical and dental education and links with the University Medical School will be maintained by the Belfast and South-Eastern Area Board.

One Housing Executive (of a N.I. Housing Council) will service the whole Province, and for economic reasons some services for the Provincial population of $1\frac{1}{2}$ million will be discharged centrally.

Summary

This chapter has dealt with the historical background of the introduction of a National Health Service in the United Kingdom. It has outlined the existing services in being up till the end of the year 1971, and has thereafter given in broad outline the Governments proposals for the restructuring of the administrative pattern of the personal health and personal social services for future years.

Much is still under discussion but it is envisaged that between the years 1973 and 1975 legislation will bring the new conception into being in the various parts of the United Kingdom so as to be effective everywhere by probably the year 1974–75.

The possible links between control of the environment through continuing local authorities and the new Area Health Boards has been outlined, and some discussion has been offered on the economics of the National Health Service in the United Kingdom.

Conclusion and the Case for Unification

Perhaps we could do no better than quote from the notes of the Chief Medical Officer for England in Health Trends (No. 1 Vol. 2 Feb. 1970) as follows: –

"In our field we can discern objectives though it must be allowed that to some cynics, looking at us from afar, we might appear in the Health Service to be operating a very expensive personnel maintenance organisation, concerning ourselves largely with people nearing the end of their lives, the prolongation of which merely involves the community increasingly, in numbers and time, with the need for further care.

This might be represented to be true in the more civilised or advanced communitites but even here there are many opportunities of prolonging life and activity for the young and active worker both by prophylaxis and treatment. In truth, it is neither possible nor profitable to pursue the comparison between our field and the field of commercial life; we must just allow that in a general way it is our role to bring the best and most effective remedies to bear on a situation, whether it be personal or in the community at large, with as little delay as possible."

Bibliography

B.M.A. News No. 20, "Future Role of the G.M.C." (1969, Oct.).

Central Office of Information—"Health Services in Britain", (1968), H.M.S.O. London.

Central Office of Information—"Health Services in Britain", (1958), H.M.S.O. London.

Churchill, Randolph S. "Winston S. Churchill", (1967), Vol. 2, p. 304–305. Heinemann, London.

Department of Health and Social Security and Welsh Office (Central Health Services Council)—"The Functions of the District General Hospital", (1969), H.M.S.O.

Department of Health and Social Security "The National Health Service Reorganisation", (1971), Consultative Document (May).

Department of Health for Scotland—"The National Health Service in Scotland", (1959), H.M.S.O.

Elder, A. T. "A Comprehensive Mental Health Service", (1964), Papers of Health Congress, Royal Society of Health (Torquay).

Elder, A. T. "Mental Health Services in Northern Ireland", (1968), Trends in Mental Health, Farndale, W. A. J., Pergamon, London.

Farndale, W. A. J. "Day Hospitals", (1963), 13th International Hospital Conference, Paris.

Godber, Sir George "On the State of the Public Health", (1969), Departmental Report of the Department of Health and Social Security, H.M.S.O.

Government of Northern Ireland, "The Administrative Structure of the Health and Personal Social Services in Northern Ireland", (1969), H.M.S.O. Belfast.

Heaton-Wood, W. A. "Psychopathic Disorders", (1963), Lancet 7273, 121.

Hill, C. and Woodcock, J. "The National Health Service", (1949), Christopher Johnson, London.

Jones, Kathleen, "The Community and Mental Health", (1963), World Federation for Mental Health, 16th Annual Meeting, Amsterdam.

Lycett, C. D. L. "The Seebohm Report", (1969, Oct.), B.M.A. News No. 19.

Mackintosh, J. M. "Trends of Opinion about the Public Health 1901–51", (1953), Geoffrey Cumberlege, Oxford University Press.

Maybin, R. P., Health Centres in United Kingdom. Personal Communication. (1969, Nov.).

Ministry of Health and Social Services "Restructuring of the Personal Health and Personal Social Services in Northern Ireland", (1971, March).

Ministry of Home Affairs (Northern Ireland). Departmental Annual Report, (1921–39).

Mulligan, J. A. S. "County Armagh Mental Health Services", (1963), Personal Communication.

Owen, D., Spain, B., Weaver, N. "A Unified Health Service", (1968), Pergamon Press, Oxford.

Report of Royal Commission on Medical Education and Research, (1965).

Roberts, L., Shaw, K. M. "Synopsis of Hygiene", (1952) (Jameson & Parkinson), Churchill, London.

Scottish Home and Health Department, "Health and Welfare Services in Scotland, (1969), Report for 1968, H.M.S.O.

Scottish Home and Health Department, "Reorganisation of the Scottish Health Services", (1971, July), H.M.S.O. Cmd. 4734.

Secretary of State for Scotland, "Social Work and the Community", (1966), Cmd. 3056, H.M.S.O. Edinburgh.

Thompson, D. "Mental Health—The Shape of Things to Come", (1963), Public Health LXXVIII, 2, 94.

Tooth, E. C., Brooke, Eileen "Trends in Mental Hospital Population and Their Effect on Future Planning", (1961), Lancet 1, 710.

Vines, H. W. C. "Background to Hospital Planning", (1952), Faber and Faber Ltd., London.

Warren, M. D., Cooper, J. "Local Government Medical Staff", (1967), The Medical Officer, 118, 185.

Welsh National School of Medicine, "New Medical Teaching Centre", (1966), Cardiff.

The Welsh Office, "The Reorganisation of the Health Service in Wales", (1970), H.M.S.O.

Suggestions for further reading

Calouste Gulbenkian Foundation Report, "Community Work and Social Change", (1968), Longmans, Green & Co. Ltd., London.

Central Office of Information, "Health Services in Britain", (1968), H.M.S.O. London.

Curwen, Michael, "Health Centres: Some Facts and Figures", (1969), Paper read to a Conference on "A New Framework for Community Care", at the Hospital Centre, 9 January 1969.

Medical Care in the United Kingdom

Department of Health and Social Security, "Digest of Health Statistics for England and Wales", (1969), H.M.S.O. London.

Government of Northern Ireland, "Prescribing and Sickness Benefit Costs in Northern Ireland", (1969), Pemberton Report, H.M.S.O. Belfast.

Government of Northern Ireland, "The Re-shaping of Local Government", (1969), (Further Proposals), H.M.S.O. Belfast.

Laidlaw, A. J. "Outlines of General Practice", (1963), The College of General Practitioners (Midland Faculty). E. & S. Livingstone, Edinburgh and London.

Ministry of Health, "A Hospital Plan for England and Wales", (1962), H.M.S.O. London.

Minister of Health and Secretary of State for Scotland, "Report of the Committee of Enquiry into the Cost of the National Health Service", (1965), (Guillebaud), H.M.S.O. London..

Radiographers Board Publishers—Radiographers Board under Section 2 (4). Professions Supplementary to Medicine Act 1960, (1963).

Rosenheim, Sir Max, "The Unity of Medical Services", (1969), Public Health, Vol. 83, No. 6, September 1969, Academic Press, London and New York.

Smith, Duncan N. "A Forgotten Sector", (1969), Pergamon Press Ltd., Oxford (The Training of Ancillary Staff in Hospitals.)

The Political Quarterly "Future of the Social Services", (1969), Vol. 40, No. 1, Jan.–March.

The Medical Officer, "Health Services and Local Democracy". (1969).

The Medical Officer, "The Middle-Aged and Health Education". (1969).

Thompson, W. "Eight Scottish Health Centres", (1969), The Medical Officer, p. 128.

Thompson, W. "Health Centre Care in Scotland", (1969), The Hospital, 65, 1, 11.

Thompson, W. "Health Centres and the Hospital", (1969), Health Bulletin, Scottish Home and Health Department, Vol. XXVII, No. 4, p. 18.

Yellowlees, H. "The Boundaries of Community Medicine with the Hospital Services", (1969), Public Health, Vol. 84, 1, p. 18.

107

Chapter 4

Medical Care in the United States

PHILIP D. BONNET, M.D.

The Johns Hopkins University, Baltimore, Maryland, U.S.A.

The area of the United States is 3·6 million square miles and in 1969 the population exceeded 200 million. Particular characteristics of the population are shown in fig. 4.1

U.S. POPULATION PYRAMID
PERCENTAGE DISTRIBUTION BY AGE AND SEX
UNITED STATES

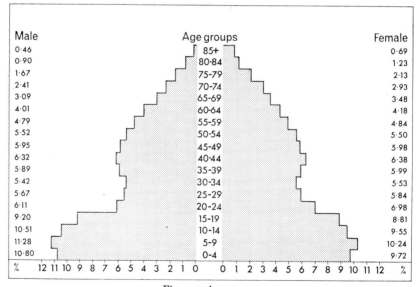

Male	Age groups	Female
0·46	85+	0·69
0·90	80-84	1·23
1·67	75-79	2·13
2·41	70-74	2·93
3·09	65-69	3·48
4·01	60-64	4·18
4·79	55-59	4·84
5·52	50-54	5·50
5·95	45-49	5·98
6·32	40-44	6·38
5·89	35-39	5·99
5·42	30-34	5·53
5·67	25-29	5·84
6·11	20-24	6·98
9·20	15-19	8·81
10·51	10-14	9·55
11·28	5-9	10·24
10·80	0-4	9·72

% 12 11 10 9 8 7 6 5 4 3 2 1 0   0 1 2 3 4 5 6 7 8 9 10 11 12 %

Fig. 4.1. Age groups.

(Source: Population Estimates, Series P–25, No. 352, (Nov. 18, 1966), U.S. Dept. of Commerce, Bureau of the Census. Table 3, p. 16: "Estimates of the Civilian Resident Population of the United States, By Age, Color and Sex, July 1, 1966, with comparable Figures for April 1, 1960.)

THE PRINCIPLES AND PHILOSOPHIES UNDERLYING THE HEALTH SERVICES IN THE U.S.A.

There is no coherent set of principles or philosophies which have guided the development of health services in the United States. If one tried to find a single attitude which most nearly covers the present situation, it would be a pragmatic, materialistic improvisation. Although philanthropy and religious good works have been and remain a strong influence, science and technology have become steadily more influential. The power and influence of government have been slowly but steadily increasing as communications and transportation have increased in speed. Responsibility for health and health services is diffused and dispersed throughout society with no crystallisation or focus for the whole.

There is a rising dissatisfaction over the disarray and the lack of coherent system in the health services of the United States but there is no consensus as to the appropriate solutions. Compulsory national health insurance is being advocated with increasing frequency but it is recognised that increasing the availability of money to pay for services without greater rationalisation of the organisation and the distribution of health services will only increase the costs without equivalent benefits. Among the problems which stand in the way of change, not the least are the categorisations and rigidities among the many programs of the Federal Government each of which is supported by a special constituency with political power. Then too the size, diversity and individualistic traditions of the United States make rationalisation difficult.

Physicians for the most part are engaged in private practice but under a wide variety of organisational arrangements. The office attached to the physician's home is a phenomenon that is rapidly decreasing. It is more usual for physicians to cluster in small or large medical office buildings, some of which are being located in close proximity or even attached to general hospitals. The majority of physicians are in independent private practice. It is the physicians collectively and a smaller number of other health practitioners who are implicitly responsible for assuring the availability of health services. All other agencies, private or governmental, function in a secondary role. Therefore, there is no central health authority which can be formally identified.

In recent Federal legislation, there has been a declaration that health services have now become a right of all citizens. In other legislation, such as Regional Medical Programs, there has been a declaration that the law does not provide authority to interfere or make changes in the manner of practising medicine. Reconciliation of these two viewpoints is difficult indeed and therein lies much of the problem of greater rationalisation of health services.

From an historical viewpoint there was, over the years, a slow development of Federal health activities which culminated in the U.S. Public Health Service, so named in 1912, but remaining as a portion of the Treasury Department, until transferred to the Federal Security Agency in 1934 and then to the Department of Health, Education and Welfare when created in 1954.

It was only in the depression years of the 1930's that the Federal Government began in earnest to become involved in social legislation including health affairs.

In the meantime, the states individually adopted legislation regulating various aspects of health services, such as licensing of professionals, licensing of institutions, authorization of health insurance, establishing health departments and setting standards. The emphasis however, remained on individual responsibility, local government supervision and minimum of government interference.

For nearly 50 years, there have been recurrent debates about national health policy, national health insurance and a more rationally organized medical care and health services. There has been each time some new legislation but it has been pragmatic in nature and an attempt to deal with a specific problem rather than the development of a national program.

The history of Medicare and Medicaid is illuminating. They are the most recent Federal enactments dealing with the payment for health services for certain population groups. Payment is chosen as the means to assure availability of services. It does not in itself provide the services. Medicare is a compulsory national hospital insurance program, with an associated voluntary option to elect medical insurance also, for all citizens who are 65 years of age or over. Medicare is financed by a compulsory payroll tax for the hospital part and a premium payment matched by Federal general revenue funds for the "voluntary" medical part. To cover older people who had not qualified for annuity payments, the Federal Government bought eligibility for them by using general tax funds. The benefits are quite comprehensive but are strictly limited to benefits based on medical need and do not pay for either preventive or health maintenance services. Medicaid, on theother hand, is not social insurance. There are no payroll taxes or premiums paid. It is a welfare program financed jointly by the Federal Government and the individual states. Federal standards were established both for eligibility and for benefits. They were generous and proved to be more expensive than states could afford and even the Federal share proved to be greater than anticipated and therefore burdensome. Thus, in one piece of legislation three different philosophies were embodied: traditional welfare or "poor law" provision and compulsory social insurance, and voluntary insurance.

New Proposals

Because Medicare has proved more costly than anticipated, because Medicaid has proved to be unsatisfactory, expensive and in some respects unworkable, because of the continued rise in health services costs, and because of efforts to eliminate or reduce poverty with which health problems are intimately associated, there is a large amount of political interest in the Federal Government in finding better arrangements and better controlled expenses. Many proposals have been and are being made. Most prominent among the proposals are those advocating National Health Insurance. There are at least four proposals similar in objectives but differing in detail. In addition, there are proposals to expand Medicare to include the disabled and to add out-patient prescription drugs as a benefit, to offer incentives for the establishment and use of "health maintenance organisations" (essentially group practice and hospital service on a capitation basis), to introduce "Preventicare", a program of screening and periodic examinations. There is interest among the states to have the Federal government take over a larger share of health services costs, especially under Medicaid. This is because financially they are hard-pressed and are seeking any possible form of relief.

There is little doubt that there will be new legislation in the direction of a more uniform national program. Many believe that the first step should be to create a Council of Health Advisors, to propose a coherent national health policy, before trying to add patches to the present jumble.

Health Insurance – Present Status

The chief reliance for solving or ameliorating the financial burdens of illness and injury has been placed on prepayment and health insurance. Both are really sickness insurance in principle and have done little to include true health supporting services. Prepayment is voluntary and chiefly offered by the 80 Blue Cross plans. Prepayment provides service benefits rather than money benefits as insurance does. The distinction between prepayment and insurance has diminished over time, each becoming more like the other and nearly meeting at a mid-point. Prepayment is always "voluntary" or non profit. Insurance is usually a profit organisation, though many are mutualised and dividends are paid to the policy holders. All health insurance and prepayment are regulated by the states. There is no Federal policy or legislation dealing directly with either, though proposals have been made to permit reinsurance of excess risks for special population groups.

Coverage of the population by some form of health insurance is extensive. In the northern part of the country 90 per cent or more of the people are covered. In the South and West, the population covered varies between 75 and 80 per cent. In 1968, over 169 million people (85 per cent) had some form of private or voluntary health insurance. The highest number have hospital coverage, with surgical benefits the next highest. Half of those over 65 years of age continue to have supplementary private insurance benefits, since Medicare through limitation of benefits, co-insurance and deductibles covers only about 50 per cent of all medical care expenses on average. Total Health Insurance benefits were $12 billions in 1968, representing about one-third of all private health services expenditures and 14 per cent of total health expenditures. Although the amount and extent of coverage is impressive it is regarded as insufficient and further growth is expected to be slow. The chief shortcomings of present health insurance are considered to be: too limited coverage of long term disabling illness, too limited coverage of ambulatory care, too great emphasis on expensive in-patient services, inability to reach and provide continuous coverage for low-income people and marginal workers.

Present private insurance is financed wholly by premiums. Some are fully paid by employers, some are paid partially by employers and some are wholly paid by the employee or individual policy holders. Group policies cover about 90 per cent of all insured and the total coverage is nearly equally divided between Blue Cross – Blue Shield prepayment and commercial health insurance.

It is estimated that about 8 million people are covered by organised group practice plans or consumer co-operative plans. This represents 4 per cent of the population and growth has been slow in part due to scarcity of venture capital. In the last two years, there has been increased interest in expanding the organised group practice movement and some new plans have been initiated but the acceleration in growth so far has been modest.

Other new forms of health insurance which have recently become available in some areas have been: Dental care coverage and Out-patient Drug coverage.

Among the new patterns of provision of services has been the financing of Children and Youth Programs by the Childrens Bureau, and the organisation of Neighbourhood Health Centers by the Office of Economic Opportunity (the Anti-Poverty Program). Both of these are aimed at poor disadvantaged groups in large cities and in rural areas. Both endeavour to provide comprehensive health services to a defined population in a defined geographic area. Both are directed at prevention of severe illness and reduction of hospital use. There has been wide variation in the activities and the success of these new programs. In many cases they go beyond the usual concerns of health to include legal aid with housing problems, provision of jobs for people in the area served, improvement of educational opportunities. One new ingredient in these programs has been the inclusion of mandatory "consumer" participation. In some instances, this has led to the program being converted to a political power base in which health services become secondary or incidental. On the whole, these programs seem to be beneficial and productive in many ways but measureable effects in health status have yet to be documented.

In summary, the philosophy and principle affecting health services remain traditional American self-reliance and independence. These have been tempered by many facilitating and standard-setting activities of both a voluntary and a governmental nature. Many programs exist to assist those who for one reason or another do not succeed in being self-reliant and self-supporting. The philanthropic impulse remains alive and active but the magnitude of the problems now requires that they be largely met by public philanthropy and social insurance. The efforts to date have been fractional, categorical, and uncoordinated by a systematic philosophy. New efforts toward a more rational comprehensive and integrated health services system are now being made. The pattern of the future is not yet visible.

STRUCTURE AND ADMINISTRATION OF HEALTH SERVICES

In the United States, responsibility for health remains primarily with the individual. During the last hundred years, there has been a slow steady shift toward the assumption of more and more responsibility by society through government but this has occurred mostly in categorical programs to deal with special problems or specific groups of people but without any clear national health policy. As a result, there is an array of activities which are only loosely interrelated and integrated, and which are frequently characterised as a "non-system".

It may be important to clarify the phrase health services at this juncture, since there is much confusion between services dealing with sickness and injury and services directed toward health through prevention and control of the environment. To be sure, these cannot be wholly separated but it is helpful to recognise the differences in the objectives and the appropriate methods between those two major aspects of health services. Traditionally, the sickness services have received the largest amount of attention and concern. Health improvement services have generally received less attention and less financial support.

Responsibility for health services varies in accordance with the specific type and may be considered in two ways:

1. Individual versus group or collective responsibility
   a. Treatment and care of the sick and injured.
   b. Maintance and promotion of health
      1. Personal health
      2. Environmental control
2. Private versus governmental responsibility
   a. Treatment and care of the sick and injured.
   b. Maintenance and promotion of health.
      1. Personal health
      2. Environmental control

In general, individual responsibility and private sector responsibility apply to the treatment and care of the sick and injured, with limited exceptions for special groups – the poor, the American Indians and the Military. In addition, there has been recent (1966) acceptance of collective and government responsibility for assuring to other groups the financial means to obtain care – especially the aged. Individual and private responsibility applies also to maintenance and promotion of personal health, with the exceptions of special disadvantaged groups and of the general but feeble efforts in health education of the public school system.

Group responsibility is undertaken in the private sector by employers, especially in large industries with respect to occupational health, such as control of hazards, and with respect to financial participation in the cost of health (really sickness) insurance. In addition, voluntary agencies conduct health education as a part of their fund raising campaigns.

Collective responsibility in the public sector has been primarily directed to monitoring the performance of health related activities in both private and public sectors: enforcement of sanitary codes and control of industrial hazards. The only legal requirements applicable to individuals are: vaccination against smallpox for school entrance, for reentry after foreign travel, and pre-marital blood tests for syphilis. In addition, there are licensing requirements for both individuals and for institutions.

Today in the United States, there is a pluralistic potpourri of organisations, programs, agencies, activities and individuals, some private, some public which in the aggregate provide all of the health services. There is no single descriptive classification which fits the many varieties of services. Philosophically, the primary responsibility remains with the individual and with the private sector. All collective and public responsibility is secondary, adjunctive, advisory, supplemental and constraining. As noted previously, there is a steady trend toward increasing the extent of public intervention and assumption of responsibility but the scales are still predominantly weighted on the side of the individual and the private sector. In the beginning of public responsibility, it was local governments which were involved. As time has gone on, there has been a shift from local government, to state government, to the federal government. This has not involved a transfer of responsibility as much as an increasing superimposition of standards, constraints and financial supplementation by higher levels of government.

Licensure

Among the more pervasive influences of government in health service are licensure of both health service workers and health service institutions. There are now some thirty health services occupations which are legally recognised through licensure, registration or certification. In addition there are other occupations with health implications such as barbers, beauticians and plumbers which are licensed. In each case, the majority of members of most licensing bodies are members of the occupational group being licensed. This has raised questions of conflict of interest, self-protective guild attitudes, and whether they do function in the public interest. Since each group endeavors to identify an exclusive function for its members, health service activities become fragmented and rigidified. On balance licensure probably has been beneficial. Whether it will remain so in the future is another matter.

Licensure of health service institutions is relatively recent and originated in concerns for building safety and fire protection. As time has gone on, licensure concerns have expanded to including staffing patterns, staff qualifications, quality control activities and other operating standards. Because of the problems of increasing specialisation among health service workers, there are proposals to abandon much of the licensure of individuals and hold the institution which employs the workers responsible for their performance.

All licensure is the responsibility of the individual states. There are reciprocity arrangements among states for licensing of personnel but on the whole, the states jealously maintain this modest evidence of residual sovereignty. Under the Medicare law, a higher standard than licensure was required of institutions which wished to participate and Federal certification of "providers" was introduced. This undoubtedly foreshadows the time when there will be uniform Federal standards for both institutions and personnel.

HEALTH RESOURCES

Personnel

There are nearly 300,000 active physicians in the United States. The active physicians are classified in table 4.1.

TABLE 4.1

In Practice		274,190
Civilian (Non-Federal)		249,273
Solo or Group Practice	190,079	
Full-time Hospital Practice	16,604	
Interns & Residents & Fellows	42,590	
Federal		24,917
Full-time Hospital Practice	20,651	
Interns, Residents & Fellows	4,266	
Not in Practice		
Civilian (Non-Federal)		17,247
Medical Faculty	11,166	
Research	3,352	
Administration	2,729	
Federal		2,635
Research	1,243	
Administration	1,392	
The population per active physician is:	1/700	

The ratio of physicians to population varies widely among the 50 states. The difference from high to low is of the magnitude of 3:1. The states vary markedly in size and in density of population. Neither of these factors correlates well with the physician population ratio as shown in the following table:

TABLE 4.2

	Physician-Population Ration per 100,000 population	Population (000's)	Density
United States	150		
Massachusetts	208	5,437	691
California	184	19,221	123
New York	222	18,113	378
South Dakota	86	657	9
Mississippi	76	2,342	50
Alaska	74	277	0.5

A high population-physician ratio seems to be related to high per capita income and the amount of medical education available within a state. There is no correlation between physicians and the mortality or morbidity statistics of a state.

Even within a single state, there may be wide variation in the availability of physicians, especially of family or general practitioners. Older style practitioners have been dying out in rural areas and in central poverty areas of large cities are not being replaced. Like the population generally, which is becoming increasingly concentrated in metropolitan areas, physicians too are becoming concentrated.

There is widespread belief that there is a substantial shortage in the number of physicians and there are many proposals to increase the number and size of medical schools. Since large numbers of foreign-trained physicians come to the United States for additional training and then a substantial proportion remain in the United States, there is need to consider an increased production of physicians if only to reduce the dependence on other nations. Some observers of the United States health scene believe strongly that there is no absolute shortage of physicians and that all of the problems relate to mal-distribution, imbalance among specialties, and inefficient organisation of medical care services.

The numbers of specialists in active practice are approximately as follows:

TABLE 4.3

General Practice	65,000
Internal Medicine	26,000
Pediatrics	11,000
Cardiology	1,500
Other Medical Specialties	5,000
General Surgery	20,000
Thoracic Surgery	1,000
Other Surgical Specialties	25,000
Obstetrics – Gynecology	14,000
Psychiatry	13,000

It has often been viewed with concern that the proportion of physicians in general practice has decreased from 76 per cent in 1940 to 36 per cent in 1965. Some internists and pediatricians have taken up significant proportions of family type practice formerly carried by the general practitioner. Renewed efforts are being made in some medical schools to offer specific education for general or family practice. In addition, a specialty certifying American Board of Family Practice has been created within the past two years to make available special recognition of family practice as a specialty. It is too early to know what influence these activities will have on the career choices of medical graduates. Some present day medical students are showing a new concern for social problems and renewed interest in people in addition to science and technology. Whether the character of the medical profession will be markedly altered by these attitudes is not yet known.

Group practice in its many forms is regarded by some as the pattern of the future. Its growth, however, has been slow, especially among those groups which offer reasonably comprehensive services for an annual capitation fee.

The number of active dentists in the United States is nearly 100,000. The population per active dentist is 46 per 100,000 population. There is the same variation in the distribution of dentists, ranging from a high of 66 to a low of 23 per 100,000 population. Although relatively there appears to be a greater shortage of dentists, there is little public concern about the availability of dental care.

The number of active nurses is nearly 700,000 of whom about 65 per cent were employed on a full time basis. This represents a population-nurse ratio of 313 per 100,000. The distribution of types of registered nurses and their employment are as follows:

TABLE 4.4

Employment of Registered Nurses 1966

Hospitals and other Institutions	67·0 per cent
Private Duty Nursing	10·0 per cent
Physicians' Offices	8·0 per cent
Public Health Departments	4·5 per cent
School Nursing	3·5 per cent
Industrial Nursing	3·1 per cent
Nursing Education	3·6 per cent
Other	0·3 per cent
TOTAL	100·0 per cent

A greater variation (4:1) among the states in the population-nurse ratio occurs than in physicians and dentists, varying from 536 per 100,000 population in Connecticut to 133 per 100,000 population in Arkansas.

Nursing is undergoing a transition, the directions and outcome of which are by no means clear. The drive seems to be on the one hand to identify an autonomous and independent role for nurses and on the other hand to establish nursing more clearly as a scientific and technical discipline. In spite of the many expressed dissatisfactions and criticisms by and of nurses, the numbers continue to grow. A substantial improvement in the economic rewards of nursing since 1967 has facilitated the increase in the numbers of nurses.

Facilities

1. *Ambulatory facilities*

Two-thirds of all physicians in practice maintain their own individual offices. Although in years gone by, it was common for the office to be several ground floor rooms in the physician's residence, this practice has never been universal and now it is quite uncommon. The minimum office consists of two rooms: a waiting room and a consulting room. More often it has a separate examining room in addition. Some physicians have large suites with several examining rooms, a laboratory and special treatment rooms. Many physicians have their offices in a Medical Office Building, which facilitates the availability of diagnostic procedures and specialist consultations. Except in a few rural areas, physicians do not dispense drugs.

Hospital Clinics

Many hospitals conduct out-patient departments, originally for poor patients as a charity but in recent years, as a community service and for specialist consultation. These clinics tend to be the source of primary care for large numbers of the city's poor. They are most frequently associated with large urban hospitals and much less frequently with hospitals in small cities or towns.

Health Department Clinics

Traditionally, these clinics have been primarily for the prevention and control of communicable diseases. They include well-baby clinics, immunisation clinics, tuberculosis control clinics. In recent years, clinics devoted to the control of chronic disease have appeared, though are not yet widespread. They include: cancer clinics, heart disease clinics and arthritis clinics. A special group of clinics sponsored by the Federal Government is: The Crippled Childrens Program for assuring the availability of orthopedic and related services to all children in the nation.

Industrial Clinics

All large industries and responsible employers make provision for emergency care of employees, for pre-employment examinations and in some cases for periodic health examinations. Small businesses are unlikely to make direct provision for health services, although all do make some arrangement with a nearby practitioner or a hospital for the care of industrial accidents. Only in very large industries with special hazards are physicians employed full-time to staff the industrial clinics. Mostly they are staffed by industrial nurses, with a physician on-call. The same physicians who are responsible for the medical care services are also usually responsible for plant sanitation, although in situations of special risk, there are often special technical personnel to monitor the level of exposure and to make regular inspection.

School Clinics

The regular day schools have a small clinic room and if large enough a school nurse. A physician is on call. The only functions of the school clinic are disease detection and "First-Aid". They are empowered to provide no treatment. Parental permission is required even for immunisations. Periodic screening exams quite superficial in nature are undertaken to identify gross defects in vision or hearing and significant impairments. If such are discovered, recommendations are made to the parents. The record of parental response and compliance with the recommendations is surprisingly low especially among the poor where the incidence is greatest. Apathy rather than inadequate funds seems to be the chief problem.

The school health services were established when acute epidemic disease and parasitic infestations were common. Now that those problems have nearly disappeared, there is reason to question the justicfication for the traditional type of school health program. The nurses have a very low productivity, do almost no nursing and would be better employed elsewhere in the health services. Health education in schools would seem to be more urgent than health services other than "First-Aid".

Residential schools have usually a small infirmary with a nurse on duty and a nearby physician on call. Scheduled sick-call is held in the infirmary.

Independent Clinics

There have been a few free-standing independent dispensarys or out-patient clinics. The first organised medical institution in the United States was the independent Boston Dispensary but now merged into the New England Medical Center. In recent years, there have developed two new types of independent clinics – The Neighborhood Health Center (in poverty areas) and the Community Mental Health Center. Both are too recent to permit any judgement about their long-term durability or performance. For the present, they are offering reasonable responses to some urgent problems, many of which are more social in nature than medical or health-related.

Emergency Services

One of the traditional obligations of the general hospital has been to provide emergency services. In cities, this included the operation of ambulances. Since World War II, hospitals have ceased to operate ambulances for emergency services because of economic considerations. Now the emergency ambulance services are most often operated by police departments or fire departments. Hospitals have continued to operate emergency units. It is now being questioned whether every hospital should try to operate an emergency unit. They are expensive, difficult to staff adequately, and often not well equipped. Considera-tion is now being given to the development of a single coordinated regional emergency service, though there seems to be little monentum being generated. In the meantime, the public is turning more and more to the emergency ward of the local hospital as the simplest, most direct and convenient way of being sure to be able to locate a physician whether or not the problem is urgent. The visits to emer-gency units in hospitals are rising 1 per cent each year even though less than half of the visits can be considered urgent and only about one-tenth are life-threatening or pain emergencies. In the considera-tion of new patterns of organisation, the emergency unit and the demands being made on it require a high priority.

In-Patient or Hospital Services

The supply of in-patient beds of all types in 1968 was as follows:

TABLE 4.5

	Total Beds	Beds per 1,000 pop.	Occupancy Percentage
All Hospitals	1,663,000	8·4	82·9
General Short Term	806,000	4·1	78·2
General Long Term	67,000	0·3	82·6
Metal	594,000	3·0	89·6
Tuberculosis	22,000	0·1	65·1
Federal (all types)	175,000	0·9	83·7
Nursing Homes	846,500	4·3	89·2

As for the case of personnel, the distribution of in-patient facilities is uneven among the states, even though the variations do not correlate with morbidity or mortality statistics.

In-patient facilities have three kinds of possible sponsors and the proportions among sponsors varies by type of facility. The sponsors are: (1) Non-profit community or church related organisation – pre-

dominant among short term general hospitals; (2) Government –
may be local, state or federal – predominant among mental and other
long term hospitals; (3) business profit organisations – predominant
among nursing homes.

The time trends in the availability of in-patient facilities are
interesting. There has been a steady increase in short term hospital
and nursing home beds, a rapid decrease in tuberculosis beds, and a
slow decline in mental hospital beds. The trend is for hospitals to
become larger and more comprehensive. Specialty hospitals have
tended to disappear by merger or by becoming general hospitals.
Strenuous efforts are being made to reduce the use of the short-term
general hospital. Suffice it to say here, that since the 1930's public
opinion and financial arrangements have favoured hospitalisation as
more convenient and more effective. The rising cost of the acute
hospital is now viewed with apprehension and therefore attention is
being given to finding new incentives, to developing effective alternatives, and reducing or controlling the increased use of hospitals.
Success to date has been meagre. Organised prepaid group practice
associated with a hospital seems to be the favored and most hopeful
pattern, though objective evidence on the performance of prepaid
group practice is mixed and by no means conclusive with respect to
productivity, effectiveness, efficiency and economy.

The rapid growth of the nursing home industry, predominantly on
a profit-making basis, is a recent development. The growth has been
10 per cent per year since 1960. Living accommodations and family
arrangements in the United States have evolved in a way which makes
care of a disabled parent at home more and more difficult. With
major disability, the response has been to provide nursing home care,
at government welfare expense when necessary. Originally, the nursing
home was a converted dwelling, operated by a nurse or occasionally
by a physician. In the former case, it provided a modest living for
the owner-operator and in the latter case, a break-even operation
but some opportunity for professional fees. After World War II, there
was a rapid rise in the numbers of disabled old people and the
proprietary nursing was the only available rapid response. Neither
governments nor non-profit organisations accept risks and therefore
respond slowly to new needs. Perhaps a contributing factor was
ambivalence about whether the needs were primarily social or pre-
marily medical. This ambivalence persists and the nursing home remains a hybrid. Under Medicare legislation, the concept of extended
care facility was advanced as an alternative to "expensive" general
hospital care. In practice, it has had the effect of trying to establish
many nursing homes as medical facilities rather than social facilities.
The picture is confusing but it appears that the nursing home is

becoming identified more and more as a social institution, needing some medical support services, and less and less as a health or medical care facility.

So varied are the health and medical needs of a large population that the varieties of needed facilities have by no means been exhausted. Rehabilitation facilities perhaps are the most important ones to recognise. The concept of rehabilitation should function in all health service facilities. The need for specialised rehabilitation facilities is based on the numbers of severely disabled individuals for whom medical care offers no immediate cure and who require special opportunities and facilities to assist them to regain the maximum possible function.

Home Services

Traditionally, physicians have made home visits, though their frequency has steadily declined. Many specialists now make no home visits but family physicians do. Over 27 million home visits were made by physicians in 1966/67. These represented 3·3 per cent of all physician visits.

Visiting nurses have been available for many years in certain sections of the nation but not all. Originally established by voluntary auspices in large cities to care for the poor in their homes, the benefits to all classes became evident and were made available. In some locations, the health department has undertaken to make home nursing available.

Home health services were included in the Medicare program under certain conditions and as a result there has been a substantial increase in their availability. In July 1969, there were 2,200 home health agencies certified under the Medicare program and about 45,000 claims per month were being made. It is interesting to note that certification requires that at least one service in addition to nursing be available through the home health agency. Such additional services are usually nutrition or physical therapy.

In a few cities, there are organised home care programs, usually associated with a large hospital. Many of these accept only patients discharged from the hospital sponsoring the program as a means of avoiding repeated hospitalisation. Others accept referrals from other institutions on practicing physicians. There programs accept complete responsibility for all services which can be provided in the patient's home including physician's service, nursing service, physical therapy, drugs, social service, equipment and appliances. In some cases, the program includes everything but the physician's services. This however is not the true form of a comprehensive organised home care service.

First Contact Services

A majority of Americans claim that they have a family physician but the strength of the relationship varies widely. Since people move quite frequently, the association with the same physician over long periods is unusual.

Increasingly, hospital emergency units are functioning as first contact services especially for those without an identified family physician but also as a matter of convenience for many who do claim to have a family physician. Because of the steadily rising demand on hospital emergency units for first contact services, hospitals are employing fulltime physicians to staff those units and in addition are establishing general practice units separate from the emergency unit.

Other possible first contact services include: industrial clinics, school health services, out-patient clinic, pharmacists.

There is relatively little known about the frequency of first contact services and the kind of health worker with whom first contacts are made. Of all visits to physicians, 72 per cent are made to his office, 11 per cent by telephone, 9 per cent at hospital clinic or emergency room, 3 per cent at home and 1 per cent at place of employment. One survey revealed that 69 per cent of people had seen a physician within an 11 month period, 5 per cent had not seen a physician for 5 years or longer or had never seen a physician ($\frac{1}{2}$ per cent). Of those who had seen a physician during the year previously (69 per cent), the distribution of the number of visits was:

TABLE 4.6

1 visit	20·5 per cent of total respondents
2–4 visits	26·9 per cent
5–12 visits	15·4 per cent
13–24 visits	2·8 per cent
over 24 visits	1·5 per cent
unknown	1·0 per cent

In organised group practices and in many individual practices, advance arrangements are made for a physician to be available on call at all times.

There is little known about the types of physicians who are approached for first contact services or those who respond when called.

Perhaps equally important to the question of first contact services is the question of primary physicians. This involves the question whether the majority of individuals have a single physician who is requested and accepts responsibility for arranging for any indicated type of health services and maintaining a complete record of all services. Except in the case of organised group practice, it is rare for a single physician to be able to function as a primary physician. Most families who have physicians are apt to have several primary physicians at anytime. A different one perhaps for each member of the family. The physicians will change from time to time with changes in residence, in age or in the specific medical problems. People in the U.S. are very mobile, travel much and move their residence often. Continuity of primary care is exceedingly difficult. There is little evidence that Americans place a high value on it. In fact, the evidence is more in the opposite direction. People are free and exercise their freedom to consult any physician of their own choosing regardless of prior relationships. There is no implied criticism of physicians in these choices. They are manifestations of independence. Even in prepaid group practice, in spite of required additional financial payments, members obtain about 12 per cent of all covered services outside of the group practice services. Under these circumstances, continuity of medical record, record linkage and fully developed primary care is impossible because it is neither demanded nor appreciated.

General Practice and Family Care

The general practitioner is a declining proportion of all physicians in practice. At one time, he represented 90 per cent or more of all practitioners. In those days, he delivered the babies, did the surgery and treated the pneumonias. Now he represents 25 per cent or less of all active physicians. He does little or no surgery, may or may not deliver babies. His claim to being a generalist rests on his willingness to care for patients of all age groups and to try to advise with respect to any kind of problem but not claim to be an expert specialist in the treatment of any group of diseases or any specific organ system. Recent studies of medical students indicate that only 10 per cent plan careers in general or family practice.

Specialist Services

There is no requirement that patients be referred to specialist. They may be consulted directly or may be referred. There are courtesies and amenities to be observed among physicians but since patients are free, there is no method to restrain self-referral to specialists. When a patient is referred to a specialist, professional ethics requires that the patient be sent back to the original physician.

Specialists tend to concentrate large proportions of their work in and around hospitals. Dermatologists and psychiatrists are notable exceptions. Specialists usually are paid directly by patients on a fee basis or indirectly through a prepayment plan such as Blue Shield. Remuneration on other bases is an exception.

Hospital and Extended Care Facilities

Hospitals and other in-patient institutions all have appointed members of their medical staff who are authorised to utilise the facilities of the institution for the treatment of patients. Practitioners who do not hold hospital appointments must refer patients to a physician who does have such an appointment. Hospitals have a concentration of the apparatus of medical science and therefore exert a powerful attraction to both physicians and patients, as the place where the best diagnosis and treatment is likely to be obtained. For this reason, hospitals have steadily increased in popularity and in utilisation.

Extended Care

Extended Care Facilities are a special type of nursing and medical care facility derived from the progressive patient care principle. They are intended to substitute for the convalescent hospital days or the days of low level of medical care between major episodes of treatment. To some extent, they also provide terminal care. Initially they were regarded as an extension of the hospital at a lower level of cost because of less intensive requirements. In practice, they were a new intensive type of nursing home. In order that continuity be promoted, one of the Medicare requirements was a transfer agreement between the extended care facility and the hospital to facilitate the movement of patients.

In July 1969, there were 4,849 extended care facilities with 342,000 nursing beds certified for Medicare patients, which represent about one-third of all nursing home beds. Medicare claims are running at the rate of about 50,000 per month. It is not yet clear whether or not extended care saves either hospital days or expense. The chief difficulties have arisen in defining appropriate levels of need for care and differentiating between medical need for treatment and social need for care.

Nursing homes are available to serve the severely disabled and disabled elderly. Their function is primarily nursing care and a sheltered place to live. The quality varies widely. Except for the special extended care type of service, there is no insurance to pay for nursing home care. Welfare eligibles may receive nursing home care at government expense. With the exception of a few who receive private or church charity, all others pay for nursing home service for members of their family from their personal means.

Community Home Care

About 500 hospitals offer organised home care services, primarily for their own discharged patients. The objective is to minimise re-peated hospitalisation and to maximise patient comfort and self-sufficiency. Such programs may include physician services, nursing services, physical therapy, nutrition, drugs, social service, loan of equipment.

It is more common for home care to be provided by community-based organisations, either the visiting nurse association or the health department. Originally, only nursing visits to the home were available. In recent years, other services such as physical therapy and nutrition services have been added. Meals-on-wheels provides food to the shut-in and elderly home bound patient in a certain number of cities and towns. All requests for service must be approved by a physician to be honored by the agency.

Medicare gave an impetus to the expanison of home care services by providing payment. This like extended care was intended to save hospital days and reduce expense. It is not known whether or not it has accomplished those objectives. Its social objectives of improving patient morale and self-sufficiency have been at least partially attained.

There are 2,209 home health agencies certified by the Medicare program but they are unevenly distributed. New England has 16 per cent of the agencies but only 6 per cent of Medicare beneficiaries. The Pacific States have 7 per cent of the agencies and 12 per cent of beneficiaries. Claims are running at a rate of about 90,000 per month.

Home care is considered to be desirable but not absolutely essential. It is constrained by the home conditions and the availability of relatives or neighbors to provide continuing support or assistance between visits.

Provision of Drugs and Appliances etc.

The most wide spread means of obtaining drugs and appliances, glasses and equipment is on a direct purchase basis. This simple pattern is modified and tempered. Hospitalisation insurance covers most if not all drugs used during the hospital stay. It does not cover "take-home" drugs. Welfare programs for the poor will pay for most of the necessary accessories of medical care. In recent months, new plans for prepaying the cost of prescription drugs outside of hospitals have been established. There are voluntary philanthropic organisations which provide equipment on a loan or modest rental basis for use at home.

It is significant that the Medicare law specifically excluded the payment for glasses and hearing aids, in addition to examinations for glasses or hearing aids and other "preventive" or "protective" services for the aged. This exclusion did not apply to Medicaid, the program for the poor, though the individual states were free to define the level of benefits within certain limits. Only a few states tried to provide comprehensive benefits and they soon encountered severe financial difficulties which led to retrenchment.

Public (Environmental) Health

The problems of the environment traditionally have been the responsibility of the "local" health department, at either a county or municipal level. Because many counties are small, there have developed some regional health departments but generally county pride has prevented or delayed such advances.

Until recently, environment has included: water and therefore sewage, food, pests, parasites, rodents and therefore waste disposal, housing and premise sanitation, and acute infectious diseases. All of these could be handled on the basis of local jurisdiction. But now the new environment problems of air pollution, radio-activity, drug abuse, excess population density are not as easily amenable to local solutions. Thus the responsibility for environmental health is moving to the state level from the local authority level.

State responsibility until recently has been limited to setting standards, financial assistance and laboratory services.

Because of wide variation in the size of states and their financial resources, there is considerable variation in the amount and quality of public health services. The Federal Government provides financial assistance to the state on a basis which more nearly equalises the available resources in relation to population.

Among the unsolved problems are highway accidents. Although the health services monitor the frequency and severity of highway accidents as well as caring for the victims, the responsibility for highway conditions, quality of motor cars and code enforcement lie entirely outside of the health services. This is occurring more and more as technology advances. The control of conditions – industrial waste, radioactivity and the like are outside of the health services, the functions of which become more and more those of monitoring and reporting incidence, prevalence and severity, and caring for the victims.

Community and Regional Planning

The first effort at any formal health service planning was embodied in the Hill-Burton legislation of 1946, which offered Federal financial assistance in the construction of hospitals in return for each state establishing a regional plan for hospital bed requirements. The three-tiered hospital region was the Hill-Burton concept – recognising base hospital, regional hospital and local hospitals. This concept was never formalised but has influenced practice continuously, though it is difficult to apply in large multi-hospital metropolitan areas.

The most effective planning device has been the money market and the availability of financial support. Borrowing to build hospitals is a very recent development. But fund-raising campaigns have been common in both private and public circles. The decisions have been ratified by public support either as donations or votes in favor of a bond issue.

From state Hill-Burton plans, there developed area-wide hospital planning agencies and more recently comprehensive health planning agencies in each state. The information available is steadily improving in quantity and quality but as yet the problems of political and financial leverages necessary to implement plans have not been solved. Complicating matters was the creation of a National Regional Medical Program which was categorical in nature – heart disease, cancer, and stroke – and which created strange new regions with little rationality or political validity. Therefore, the Regional Medical Programs are a wholly Federal enterprise with only money as leverage and without any ability to alter the organisational status quo.

There is much talk of planning and considerable planning efforts, but the fruits are difficult to find. There is substantial ability to block an unwise project or even a good project, but little ability to fill gaps or bring about constructive change.

No formal arrangements exist for allocating patients. State boundaries tend to be limiting with respect to state-provided services, such as mental hospital care. In prepaid group practice with formal contractual arrangements, there are defined limitations. Generally speaking, freedom-of-choice prevails and no attempt is made to impose arbitrary constraints.

Rural Health Services

It is difficult to identify a special aggregate as rural health service. Areas of low population density, areas of rural poverty, special groups such as the Amerindians, certain regions like Appalachia, all influence the pattern of health needs, demands and services but none have any unique characteristic which could be called rural. There are special problems and difficulties in each of the circumstances but a rural health service pattern does not exist.

As farming has become industrialised, there is no special problem of rural health services. Where farming has not become industrialised, there are pockets of difficulty. Among these are the problems of migrant farm workers, those who harvest a soft perishable crop and move on with the seasons. In time, machine pickers will replace them but in the meantime they persist as an exploited mobile peasant class, carrying their diseases, their parasites and unborn babies from place to place.

There are very few counties in the United States which are more than one hour from a large town or small city. The rural problem is identical with the core city problem – lack of availability of emergency and primary care services. The solutions may be different but the problems are the same.

The United States in this regard is different than Canada. The United States has some wide open spaces left but they are mostly desert or mountain crag. Because of the mobility of people in the United States by means of the internal combustion engine, there is no part of the United States far away from an urban area, except Northern Alaska. In other words, an industrial technocratic society has a very difficult time recognising any special problem of rural living. There are problems of poverty, of ignorance and others but they are not problems of the rural life.

Specialised Health Services

a. *Diseases*

It is inevitable that to some extent health services will be organised around categories of people or categories of diseases or categories of medical specialisation. Usually, categorical services are considered to be those organised around specific diseases, such as Cancer, Tuberculosis, Poliomyelitis. Such diseases often do require special facilities, special equipment, special treatment modalities which leads to specialised services and institutions.

Perhaps the earliest and most persistent categorical services were for mental patients, Similarly, however, there were categorical services for infectious diseases – isolation hospitals and tuberculosis sanitoria. In these instances, the motivation for categorical service was public fear and the need for segregation of patients to protect the public. As medical specialisation developed, other categories based on technological requirements emerged – the Ophthalmic or Eye Institute, The Lying In Hospital. The childrens' hospital was an expression of social concern for the differences between children and adults. As time has gone on, the impetus for new categories has waned. Because people are regarded as indivisible and may in fact have more than one kind of condition, the recent trend has been toward greater coordination, more comprehensively organised services. The tension between generalisation and specialisation remains. Categories are necessary but they do change as concepts and priorities change. Most medical research is highly categorical in nature and will likely remain so. The provision of medical care services will likely become better coordinated and less categorical.

b. *Population groups*

In the absence of a national program, different population groups have obtained health services in different ways.

The most notable special population group are the American Indians for whom the Federal Government adopted a paternalistic role and has provided an Indian Health Service for those living on reservations. This was fully financed by the Federal Government. The record is a mixed one. Present day health statistics for the American Indian are nothing to be proud of. The problems are social, cultural and economic as well as medical.

Special attention has been given to handicapped children, veterans, pregnant women and the new-born, poverty groups, migrant farm workers and most significantly under Medicare, all citizens 65 years of age or over. In most of these instances, the provision was through payment by government for services rendered rather than the direct provision of service.

The industrial worker has been protected against the hazard of loss of income and medical expense arising from accidents and injury at work. Employers have insured against this risk with private companies.

c. *Rehabilitation*

The concept of rehabilitation has been most closely allied with the specialty of physical medicine. It received a great impetus during World War II from intensive study of the injured and new efforts to restore active function as soon as possible. Early ambulation after surgery was an associated concept.

Every good physician practices rehabilitation and is concerned with helping patients to regain normal activity or maximum functions. For some serverely disabled individual special programs, services and facilities are needed. And further for some with significant residual disabilities, sheltered workshops are needed.

Rehabilitation centers have developed in recent years in several different patterns. There is the day center, the residential center and the comprehensive rehabilitation center. The latter incluces physical rehabilitation, speech therapy, and vocational retraining. In 1968, out of 680,000 patients provided services, 208,000 were restored to gainful employment through the services financed by the Federal Vocational Rehabilitation program. A few over 1,000 hospitals (15 per cent) have Rehabilitation In-Patient Units.

d. *Preventive Services*

Preventive services provided to individuals are primarily the responsibility of the family physician but school physicians, and employer health services all have a share.

There are three legal requirements:

1. Vaccination against smallpox for school entrance;
2. Vaccination against smallpox for readmission to the country after travel abroad;
3. Premarital Serology Test.

There are special requirements for school teachers and food handlers.

Immunisations are generally administered by the family physician or pediatrician. From time to time, special immunisation campaigns are undertaken by health departments and special clinics are organised in convenient locations such as schools, industry, shopping areas. Most health departments will provide immunisation at anytime by appointment.

Screening is not widely practiced and is declining in popularity. Mass screening for tuberculosis has steadily declined as the number of new cases discovered has declined and the radiation risk has been given more weight. Most screening now is done by individual physicians in the regular course of their work. Cervical cancer screening is widely practiced by hospitals and physicians. But organised campaigns on a large scale are rare.

Multiphasic screening of well populations is currently in a research and development stage. This is no doubt that present day technology permits rapid automated multiphasic screening at a reasonable cost. It is not, however, clear as yet what the cost-benefit relation may be. It provides systematic information to the physician but the interpretation of the data remains a matter of judgement. and the decisions about treatment are also a matter of judgement. The number of new conditions identified by automated screening are not impressive. The frequency with which a new condition (mostly chronic in nature) can be treated is low. More evidence is needed to permit evaluation of automated screening. Better answers are needed to such questions as: Does an elevated blood glucose always mean diabetes? When is an elevated blood pressure indicative of essential hypertension? There are enthusiasts for multiphasic screening but experience reinforces the view that the practice of medicine still requires the art in addition to the science.

The Role of Voluntary Organisations

In the absence of a national health policy and a coordinated government health service, the majority of health services are provided by voluntary (non-governmental) organisations and activities. The relative importance of physicians in private practice and of voluntary non-profit hospitals has already been indicated. In addition to those manifestations of voluntary effort, there are the voluntary fund-raising organisations, the oldest of which is the Tuberculosis Association and its Christmas Seal campaign. Such organisations raise money by donations and use their funds to expand services, to improve services, to inform the public about their special interest and concern.

There are differences of opinion about the benefits and costs of relying on the voluntary principle. The advocates argue for the advantage of flexibility, adaptability and innovation. The critics argue on grounds of duplication of effort, extravagant overhead expense, lack of uniformity in performance, imbalance between the funds raised and magnitude of the problems to be served.

The public by its continued response and giving to voluntary causes of all kinds seems to favor the continuation of the voluntary principle. Their multiplicity, however, does raise questions about possible coordination of efforts. Some areas have adopted the United Fund approach to reduce the number of appeals. Such an approach is necessary if payroll deduction is to be involved. It does not however seem to be very effective in door-to-door individual appeals.

Financing of Health Services

a. *Payment by Consumer*

Having evolved from a private practice and fee-for-service system, the main emphasis remains on payment by the consumer of a fee, which is due at the time the service is rendered. This arrangement reinforces and sustains the special, individual, private and privileged relation between doctor and patient. The trend is distinctly toward increased insurance benefits and toward increased public expenditures. The changes since 1959/60 in the proportions of expenditures have been impressive:

TABLE 4.7

Per cent Private and Public Health Expenditures

	1959/60 Per cent	1968/69 Per cent
Private	78	64
Direct Payments	53	38
Insurance Benefits and Expenses	22	24
Philanthropy	2	1·5
Public	22	36

A major shift to public expenditures occurred in 1966/67 with the initiation of the Medicare program for those over 65 years of age.

By 1968, over 169 million citizens, 85 percent of the civilian resident population had some form of private health insurance. The majority of the remaining citizens are eligible for some type of government medical assistance. The proportion of medical expense covered by all programs whether private or public varies substantially. The most comprehensive plans – prepaid group practice and Medicare – cover approximately 50 per cent of total medical expenditures of their beneficiaries. In general private prepayment and insurance covers about one-third of medical expenses, hospital expense and surgical expense being covered to the greatest extent.

Payment for insurance coverage is by an annual premium paid to the insuror. For employed groups there is a group rate which may be related to the experience of the group itself or to the experience of the whole plan. It is customary for employers to pay part or all of the premium for employees and their families. The amount paid by the employer is determined by the negotiated contract where a labor-management agreement exists. The employees' shares are handled by the employer through payroll deduction. Individual insurance coverage can be obtained by those who are not members of a group. As a rule, premiums are somewhat higher because of adverse selection factors and higher administrative costs. Aggregate premiums for private health insurance represent 2·5 per cent of disposable personal income.

In addition, every working person employed and self-employed contributes to the Social Security Trust Funds through compulsory earnings tax. The employer pays an equal amount to that paid by the employee. Specific portions go to the Annuity Trust Fund for cash pensions, to the Disability Trust Fund for cash pension to the prematurely retired due to disability and to the Medicare Trust fund for health services benefits to those aged 65 or more.

Thus total financing of health services is a mosaic of sources and channels which include fees, premiums, payroll taxes, general taxes, and philanthropic donations.

Income Maintenance during Disability

There are two provisions of a private voluntary nature for income maintenance: (1) formal or informal provision for payment of all or part of regular remuneration during work absences due to sickness or injury; (2) provision of insurance to provide for income during short term or long term disability. It is estimated that 56 million people (70 per cent of the labor force) were covered for short term disability in 1968. About 8 million (10 per cent of the labor force) were covered by insurance for long term disability.

There are four governmental programs relating to income maintenance during disability: (1) Workmen's Compensation for work related injuries; (2) Compulsory Disability Insurance for all employed individuals in two or three states only; (3) Social Security Disability Payments, originally a waiver-of-premium to prevent loss of accrued benefits at a future time, subsequently converted to cash annuity payments; (4) Welfare Assistance to the Totally and Permanently Disabled. Altogether these programs seem to reasonably cover the short term disability problems quite adequately and some long term disabilities. But benefits are not unlimited in time or amount. When benefits are exhausted and work is impossible, welfare is the only remaining resource.

Cost Estimates

Total expenditures for health service of all types in 1970 are over $63 billions or approximately $310 per person per year. This represents about 6·8 per cent of the gross national product, a high proportion. Comparisons with other countries are difficult because of variations in the way the expenditures are aggregated. The United States figures include such things as all drugs including those sold "over-the-counter", military medical expenditures, industrial expenditures for health services, which are not always included in other national aggregates. These and other variations do not explain the whole difference between the United States figure and that of other Western Nations but they do account for a part of it.

Total expenditures have increased 5 times in 20 years. The increase can be accounted for as follows:

Population growth	19 per cent
Price increases	50 per cent
All other such as	
increased use, new services	31 per cent

The largest factor in the increased expenditures has been the rise in institutional care costs which now account for 50 per cent of the personal health care dollar.

The Training of Medical Personnel

a *Physicians*

Following award of the M.D. degree, at least one year of hospital experience as a house officer is customary and is required for licensure in a few states. Formerly, the first hospital year was called the internship and subsequent years were called residencies or fellowships. The latter usually related to acquiring of specialty qualifications. In the last year or two, it has been possible to enter directly into a specialised

135

K

residency program immediately after obtaining the degree. This is another trial effort to reduce the total time required before entry into practice but it is too early to render a verdict on the merits of such a plan.

Each recognised specialty prescribes the qualifications, duration of special training and experience, and the requirements of an "approved" residency, for candidates to take the certifying Board examinations in that specialty. These examinations are given in two parts – a written part and an oral/demonstration part. A passing grade in both parts is required for certification. The newest certifying board is that for "Family Practice". This board is unique in two ways. When established, there was no "grandfather" provision to certify certain individuals with long experience without examination. There is also a unique requirement of periodic recertification by examination to retain qualified specialty status.

Many opportunities for continuation education of practicing physicians are available through medical schools, medical societies, and specialty societies. A substantial proportion of practicing physicians take advantage of these opportunities. Perhaps a third of practising physicians, however, do not avail themselves of these offerings. It is not known whether those who do not participate are able to keep themselves up-to-date in other ways.

Opinions on the existence of a shortage of physicians are mixed. In any event, federal funds have stimulated the expansion of existing schools, and the creation of new medical schools. These efforts are expected to increase the graduates of United States Medical Schools from 8,400 to 1970 to 10,400 in 1975. To these are added an average of 1,600 foreign medical graduates who obtain medical licenses in the United States each year.

b. *Dentists*

There has been a modest decline in the ratio of dentists to population and efforts have been to increase the number of dental graduates. One factor is different than the physician situation. No foreign dental graduates are accepted except from Canada which may account for 10 graduates per year. Applications for dental school are not as great in proportion to those accepted as in medicine. Some schools report unfilled vacancies.

Projected expansion of dental schools is estimated to increase graduates from 3,600 in 1970 to 4,200 in 1975.

A dental degree requires a minimum of 2 years of college and 4 years of dental school but a college degree is not uncommon. There is no required equivalent of the internship, though it is not uncommon for a recent graduate to work in the office of an older dentist for a time. Specialties of dentistry are developing and these require post-graduate training and certification by specialty boards.

The introduction of improved dental equipment and the greater use of dental hygienists and dental assistants has increased the productivity of dentists to a noticeable extent. With increasing fluoridation of water supplies, better nutrition, and better oral hygiene, it is anticipated that the demand and need for dental services will grow at only a slightly greater rate than the population itself.

c. *Nurses*

Professional nurses are recruited from secondary school graduates and at the present time, there are three patterns of nursing education: (1) the traditional hospital diploma school, requiring three years; (2) the collegiate program of four or five years, leading to a baccalaureate degree; (3) the newest is an associate degree in a junior community college, requiring two years. To qualify as Registered Nurse, it is necessary to pass the examination prescribed by each state, which is the same for all three patterns of education. Although the nursing enrollments are increasing at a modest rate they are nearly balanced by nurses withdrawing temporarily or permanently from the field.

Since 1967, there has been a substantial improvement in the economic status of nurses which appears to have attracted some nurses back to the field. The degree of increase has not yet been documented.

The licensed Practical Nurse or Vocational Nurse receives a training in a vocational school or a hospital for 18 months or two years and then may take the licensing examination. Licensure, however, is mandatory in only 9 states.

d. *Other Health Service Personnel*

Special education, training and registration or licensing exist for many other health service personnel, such as: physical therapists, laboratory technicians, radiology technicians, optometrists, podiatrists, nurse anaesthetists, inhalation therapists. Each month a new group emerges which seeks recognition of formal training requirements and legal registration.

There is much debate about the development of new types of health personnel. Among those most rigorously discussed are proposals for "physician assistants" or "physicians substitutes". The discharged military medical corpsman is mostly frequently mentioned for the former and the nurse-practitioner and nurse-midwife for the latter. There are trial demonstration programs being carried out but there are as yet no clear patterns emerging.

New types of auxiliary personnel include the community health aide or indigenous health worker. These have emerged primarily in the OEO Neighborhood Health Centers in poverty areas. They serve as cultural liaison officers, home visitors, health educators and general expeditors. They have been successful when wisely chosen and most importantly, these opportunities have made new jobs for people who were themselves disadvantaged but had a native wisdom to be put to effective use.

Research

a. *Medical Research*

Although medical schools and hospitals have engaged in research for many years, and although drug companies have undertaken to develop new drugs, it was only after World War II that significant expenditures for medical research were identified. The earliest research activities were supported by private foundations and individual philanthropists.

Although the U.S. Public Health Service had undertaken special research projects in its Hygiene Laboratory since 1880, it was not until 1930, that it was renamed the National Institutes of Health. The first institute, The National Cancer Institute was created in 1937. The Second World War because of its impressive scientific and techno-logic developments including the mass production of penicillin gave a tremendous impetus to medical research and the rapid growth of the "NIH" began in 1950 and reached its peak in 1967/68 with total appropriations exceeding $1 billion. Many of these funds were distributed to medical schools and universities in the form of extra mural research grants. Some believe these funds shifted the objectives of medical schools too far toward research and away from educating practitioners. In addition to the National Institutes of Health, the Department of Defense, the Atomic Energy Commission, the National Aeronautic and Space Administration and the National Science Foundation have all supported health related research.

Total expenditures for medical research amounted in 1968/69 to $1,735,000,000. of which only 11 per cent was derived from private sources.

Included in research support have been grants for research training and grants for construction of research facilities.

Although many impressive advances have been made in the science and technology of medicine, the majority have been refinement and more detailed exploration of known fields. The identification of molec-ular diseases is one of the more important accomplishments. There have not been any major breakthrough with respect to the major diseases afflicting mankind. Progress against cancer has been made but the hoped-for "cure" is not yet at hand. Anti-hypertensive drugs and anti-cholesterol drugs are at hand but heart disease, especially coronary artery disease remains a serious and unsolved problem. Often the effect of medical research advances has been to make medical care somewhat more effective but considerably more expensive.

Reconsideration of priorities is under way and a slow reduction of the priority heretofore given to medical research is in process. It is not likely that there will be a major reduction in expenditures but it is clear that there will not continue to be a steady rise in research support for the foreseeable future.

b. *Health Services Research*

Among the areas for research recognised by the Public Health Service was that of Health Services Organisation. Authorisation for research and demonstration was included in the Hill-Burton hospital construction program but the appropriations were always modest. National Institutes of Health supported research conducted in recognised academic disciplines but did not readily support anything considered to be applied research or a demonstration. Although the figures vary somewhat, the total expenditures for Health Services Research have never exceeded $200,000,000, which represents only 1/2 of 1 per cent of total medical care expenditures.

Prior to 1968, support of health services organisation research was divided among several divisions of the Department of HEW. In that year, the National Center for Health Services Research and Development was created and currently has appropriations amounting to $45 millions. It is expected to grow rapidly as the emphasis is shifted from emphasis on formal research to emphasis on development and introduction of innovative changes in the "delivery" of medical care. This is a shift of emphasis only and not a substitution. To date, the problems have been sufficiently complex and the solutions sufficiently controversial so that no clear pattern for the future has yet emerged. The search appears to be for a mechanistic and fiscal solution to problems which may prove to be more in the realm of concept and social values.

It is interesting to note that few private organisations, whether foundations, prepayment or insurance agencies, have invested substantial funds in health services research.

c. *Information System*

There is no national standard mandatory system of records or information, either financial or clinical. As a result, most studies involve the gathering of new data, the making of special surveys, and are ad hoc in nature.

The National Center for Health Statistics a part of HEW makes continuing sample household surveys, analyses of hospital discharges, analyses of mortality statistics, and a limited periodic health examination surveys among others. These give valuable national estimates but are not applicable for small area studies.

The organisations of providers gather and publish certain statistics. Prepayment agencies report their experience annually on an aggregate basis.

There is general agreement that better and more complete information is needed but there is little agreement on the nature of the needed information. The computer is regarded as a new opportunity which will in time facilitate more complete data with record linkage possibilities but the issues of privacy and a unique identification number are far from solved.

Planning, Evaluation and Quality Control

There is widespread concern and interest in planning many aspects of modern society: educational systems, mass transportation systems, urban planning. Health services are not immune. Since the passage of the Hill-Burton Act in 1946, there have been formal efforts to develop plans for the distribution of hospital facilities in relation to need. This led to the creation of area-wide hospital planning agencies for a more refined effort to relate services and facilities to the needs of people. The results on the whole have been good but meager. Shared services have developed. Underutilised obstetrical units have been discontinued. More national decisions based on better and more complete information have been possible. Planning efforts generally have been more effective in opposing unwise moves than in stimulating action to fill gaps.

In 1966, a Federal law was enacted creating under the title "Partnership for Health", a program of Comprehensive Health Planning. This was intended to stimulate each state to create a single agency for planning the development of all health and health related activities on a coordinated and comprehensive basis. Each state has designated such an agency and plans are being developed slowly. Other programs, categorical in nature or well-established traditional ones, have received greater financial support but progress is being made. The problems are complex, social patterns are slow to change and planning takes time. The concept of planning is well-established and accepted. Its form and methods are in the development stage. In the absence, of a central authority to carry out plans and to mandate change, progress will continue to be slow. Planning will continue to be a combination of voluntary and government action.

Evaluation is much discussed but very loosely used. It can mean anything from a popular opinion poll to a sophisticated research design. Generally, it means the establishment of specific objectives, specific criteria in relation to those objectives and measurement of the extent to which the objectives have been attained. Because of the well known difficulties in defining and measuring the outcomes of health services, especially medical care services, most evaluation efforts are applied to the process rather than to the outcomes. Many efforts are being made to develop new methods of evaluation involving health indices, health status in relation to services provided. None is wholly satisfactory but progress continues slowly toward a distant goal.

Quality of care is estimated in a variety of ways. Methods for so doing are farthest advanced in organised institutional settings such as hospitals, nursing homes and prepaid group practice. The care given in practitioners' offices being largely invisible to observation and only lightly documented if at all, can only be judged indirectly by patient satisfaction, and by other physicians to whom patients may be referred. All of the methods involve the application of peer medical judgement in one form or another. Traditionally, among the members of a hospital staff, there has been a certain amount of informal "looking over each others' shoulders". Peer review is a method for formalising such overseeing of what other physicians do, though most often it is done retrospectively on the basis of the medical record, rather than while the care is in progress.

The oldest methods employed to assure quality of care were licensure of practitioners and licensure of institutions. These were indirect means aimed at eliminating the "unqualified" and "irresponsible" and at encouraging a safe environment and institutional conditions which would not impede quality of care and hopefully would facilitate it. Although licensing of professionals has occurred for nearly 100 years, widespread licensing of institutions is only 25 years old. Public confidence has been placed almost entirely on the practitioners to assure quality. They established the standards for qualification of licensed physicians. They examined the candidates. Professional societies provided grievance procedures, reviews of physician's conduct and disciplinary procedings. Loss of license was a legal action by the State but only for some criminal conviction or mental incompetence legally certified.

Before licensure of institutions became widespread, voluntary accreditation of hospitals was established by the American College of Surgeons to improve standards and facilitate high quality surgical care. One of the requirements was an adequate medical record on each patient. Accreditation of hospitals and other institutions remains voluntary and has had a powerful effect on quality of care in hospitals. It is not a solution to every problem but is aimed in the right direction. Hospital visits are made by teams, one of which is a physician. The evidence of medical staff organisation and responsible concern for quality of care is reviewed and a sample of medical records is examined. For many years, review of tissues removed at surgery has been a requirement. Recently a full utilisation review procedure has become a requirement. Medicare legislation recognised utilisation review and made it mandatory for hospital certification. Utilisation review includes such questions as: Was hospitalisation necessary? Was the diagnosis promptly made and substantiated in the record? Were services employed appropriate? Was the length of stay appropriate? Several methods have developed for conducting utilisation reviews. Among them are: a medical staff committee; an external committee; an employed consultant; a regional committee etablished by the medical society. One of the principal questions involves the selection of cases for individual review. Random sampling may be used. Development of length of stay profiles by diagnosis permit selection of those cases which fall outside some agreed variation from the mean. Use of criteria established by committees of recognised specialists for specific diagnoses permits individual review of those patients whose care differs from those criteria. The specific effects of utilisation review are difficult to measure. The effort to examine questions of quality and the evidences of concern for quality have been beneficial. Since standardisation of people and their care is not possible, variations will occur and applied judgement will remain essential.

Significant Corresponding Features of Other Systems

Comparisons of health service arrangements among advanced Western Countries in spite of their obvious differences in organisational or financial arrangements, and in the quantities of men and facilities, reveal the same set of problems confronting them all. The relative magnitude and importance of each problem varies from country to country. None has a complete answer to the complete set of problems, for the choice seems to rest between equality with inflexibility at the price of mediocrity or quality with flexibility at the price of unequal distribution.

Suggestions for further reading

Freidson, Eliot; "Profession of Medicine." (1970), New York, Dodd, Mead & Co.
Glaser, William A.; "Social Settings and Medical Organization: a Cross-National Study of the Hospital," (1970), New York, Atherton Press.
Roemer, Milton; "Doctors in Hospitals." (1971), Baltimore, Johns Hopkins Press.
Somers, Anne Ramsay; "Health Care in transition: directions for the future." (1971), Chicago, Hospital Research Educational Trust.

Chapter 5

Medical Care in Canada

ROBERT KOHN, M.A., DR.JUR.

The Johns Hopkins University, Baltimore, Maryland, U.S.A.

Canada with its area of 3·9 million square miles is somewhat larger than Europe or the United States but has only about one-thirtieth of the population of Europe and about one-tenth of that of the United States. Particular characteristics of its population are demonstrated by an age and sex breakdown (see. Fig. 5.1).

POPULATION PYRAMID

PERCENTAGE DISTRIBUTION BY AGE AND SEX

Total population 20 millions

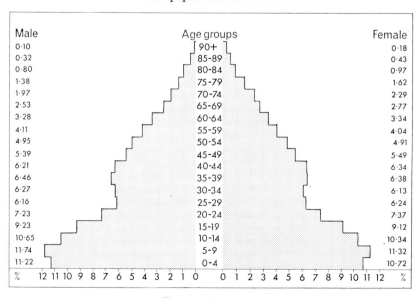

Fig. 5.1. Age groups.
(Source: Census of Canada, 1966.)

PRINCIPLES AND PHILOSOPHIES UNDERLYING MEDICAL CARE

Until about a decade ago Canada and the United States remained the only two countries in the world where the provision or at least the financing of health services for large groups of the population, if not the entire population, were not considered a responsibility of the state. Both countries are young in terms of the beginning of settlement by Europeans and also in terms of the age composition of the population brought about in part by a substantial influx of immigrants in the younger or middle age groups.

Expectations of a better world to come after World War I resulted in some political suggestions in favor of the state assuming greater responsibility for the welfare of its citizens, but it was not until the depression years that the demand for a measure of social security became stronger and at the same time more acceptable to the policy makers. Some basic social security legislation originated in the 1930's in both countries initiating a development towards gradual extension varying considerably, however, between Canada and the United States in scope, direction, and speed. World War II and the immediate post-war period accelerated the movement, more strongly on the Canadian side of the border parallel to and stimulated by the Beveridge Report in Britain and the objective set by the announcement of the "four freedoms."

The principle of assistance to the needy had always been accepted in the tradition of the poor law philosophy. Unemployment insurance was the first measure to be introduced under which benefits were provided, based on contributions, and regardless of demonstrated need. It was also the first social security measure which, under a constitutional amendment, the federal government was empowered to enact and administer. Old age pensions and allowances for children followed. The idea of universal and compulsory health insurance under government auspices has a long and varied history in Canada. A federal government committee submitted a draft health insurance bill in 1943, which was never acted upon. Two of the western provinces introduced hospital insurance schemes for their respective territories in the early post war period.

In addition, there had been for some decades arrangements to deal with local situations. Examples are the municipal doctor scheme which originated in the Province of Saskatchewan attracting doctors to small rural communities by offering them a fixed annual income, and the cottage hospital scheme in Newfoundland providing health services to isolated outlying settlements along the coast.

Existing Voluntary insurance can be traced back to the Blue Cross plans developed in the United States in the depression period, to insurance plans for industrial employee groups as fringe benefits to compensate for wartime wage freezes, and as far as physicians services are concerned, to voluntary prepayment plans sponsored by organised medicine on a much more comprehensive basis than their United States counterparts. With the advent of hospital and medical care insurance legislation, these plans either disappeared gradually or moved to insurance for services not covered by government plans. In all cases, however, their experience assisted the planning of the new governmental schemes; their organisational and administrative know-how is being used by either government agencies taking over the existing organisation or channelling their insurance through these agencies.

The federal government first entered the health field, apart from its exclusive responsibility for certain selected population groups, through the device of categorical grants to the provinces. The first step in the direction of a national policy towards universal insurance coverage was taken by the passing, in 1957, of the Hospital Insurance and Diagnostic Services Act. This Act authorises contributions by the federal government "in respect of programs administered by the provinces for hospital insurance and laboratory and other services in aid of diagnosis." By 1961 all provinces had implemented the Act.

In 1964, a Royal Commission of Health Services recommended the institution of a universal and comprehensive health insurance scheme for Canada, and also made recommendations regarding fiscal and organisational aspects of the health services complex.

The next major step came with the passing by the Canadian Parliament in 1966 of the Medical Care Act which provides for federal contributions to provincial plans for medical care, i.e. physician care, insurance. As in the case of the earlier hospital insurance plan, the provinces have joined this federal plan one by one, as financial arrangements were made and the political situation warranted.

Both these plans are basically provincial in nature. While the provincial plans adhere to some broad standards required by the federal legislation, they differ in many other respects which are left to provincial jurisdiction. These differences and the fact that even the hospital insurance and medical care insurance taken together still fall substantially short of covering all health care needs, render a brief description of the Canadian health care system very difficult. Furthermore, both federal plans are closely related to the state of federal-provincial relations generally. These relations are in a state of transition at this time and it is difficult to say in which direction they may develop. All this is closely tied in with Canada's constitutional problems which are most evident in the controversy between the predominantly French Province of Quebec and the federal government and the predominantly English speaking provinces, but which also have important economic and political undertones in regard to all provinces. Like in other federal states, the balance between federal and provincial rights is a delicate one with critics of the present situation on both sides. In Canada the situation is very much in a state of flux: on the one hand, there is agreement that the constitution – now in the form of a statute of the British Parliament – should be "repatriated"; on the other hand, there is wide disagreement as to how a new constitution should deal with the cultural and social differences, and how the economic needs of all parts of the country could best be served. It is obvious then that the financing and organisation of health services are bound to be affected by whatever solutions will be adopted for the broader issues underlying federal-provincial relations.

The Current status of the Health Services

The provision of actual services by government (i.e. by personnel employed and facilities owned by government) is limited to comparatively small groups for whose health services the federal government has assumed responsibility. The federal government thus provides services for registered Indians and Eskimos (a responsibility gradually shifting to the provinces), for certain categories of seamen and immigrants, and for members of the armed services and veterans.

Health departments at the local and provincial level assisted by the federal health department have traditionally been concerned with environmental health and certain preventive measures such as immunisation, maternal and child care, and certain categorical programs such as the operation of mental and tuberculosis institutions.

With these exceptions, health professionals are private agents represented by their respective professional organisations, and hospitals are mostly operated as voluntary, mostly non-profit agencies. The existing programs under federal or provincial auspices are aimed at the financing of health services, leaving their provision and organisation basically to the private sector but with certain controls exercised by the public plans. While these plans cover basic hospital and physicians services, they are not comprehensive in the sense of covering all necessary health services: drugs and dental care are notable exceptions for which only very limited private voluntary prepayment plans are available in most provinces.

Hospital Insurance

The federal Hospital Insurance and Diagnostic Services Act of 1957, which all provinces had joined by 1961, provides for the federal

government to share with the provinces the cost of providing specified hospital services to insured patients. The Act now covers over
99 per cent of the population of Canada. It provides insurance for
in-patient services which must include accommodation, meals, necessary nursing service, diagnostic procedures, pharmaceuticals, use of
operating rooms, case rooms, anaesthetic facilities, and use of radio-
therapy and physiotherapy if available. Out-patient services may be
included in the plans and all provincial plans do include at least
some out-patient services.

It should be noted here that in Canada, as in the United States,
the physician responsible for the care of hospital in-patients is usually
not employed by the hospital and his bill, therefore, is not covered
by hospital insurance.

Care in tuberculosis hospitals and institutions for the mentally ill
is not covered by the Act. The cost of patient care in tuberculosis
hospitals is met from tax funds in every province, except one where
the patient may be required to pay a nominal fee. In regard to mental
institutions too the major part of the cost of in-patient care is
borne by the provinces. Some of the provinces pay the entire cost;
others have these patients covered by the provincial hospital insurance
plan but without the cost being shared by the federal government.
In all, about four per cent of the operating income of mental hospitals
was received from or on behalf of paying patients. The cost of in-patient
care for tuberculosis or mental patients in general hospitals comes
under the provisions of the Hospital Insurance and Diagnostic
Services Act.

Medical Care Insurance

The Medical Care Act, passed by the federal Parliament in 1966,
came into force on July 1, 1968. It provides for provincial insurance
plans for physicians services in and out of hospital on a cost sharing
basis between provincial and federal governments; additional health
services may be added eventually to these federal-provincial agreements.

The federal legislation stipulates the following criteria for a provincial plan to qualify for federal contribution:

a) the plan must be operated on a non-profit basis by a public
authority in the province,
b) it must make insured services available on uniform terms and
conditions to all insurable residents of the province,
c) it must cover at least 90 per cent of the eligible residents of the
province during the first two years, and at least 95 per cent
thereafter,

148

d) it must provide for the portability of benefits in all participating provinces for Canadian residents.

These standards have been applied with some degree of elasticity in the existing federal-provincial agreements. The services provided under the Act are defined as all medically necessary services rendered by medical practitioners, but some provinces offer additional services not shared by the federal government.

Two provinces (British Columbia and Saskatchewan) entered the plan on its inception in 1968. The others followed gradually and by now all provinces are participating in the plan The two basic health insurance plans, the Hospital Insurance and Diagnostic Services Act and the Medical Care Act, are supplemented by a number of other government as well as private voluntary plans applying to certain categories of beneficiaries or health problems. Foremost among such plans are the provisions under the Canada Assistance Plan of 1966 and the provincial Workmen's Compensation plans. The former provides for federal-provincial cost sharing for health services provided to public assistance recipients who amount to about 5 per cent of the population. Workmen's Compensation legislation, dating back to as early as 1914, provides industry financed insurance for workers suffering from work connected injury or occupational disease. In addition, there are numerous public and private voluntary plans covering geographic areas and benefits not now included under the hospital and medical care insurance plans. These plans are continually being adjusted to fit into the two expanding basic plans.

As will be seen from this description, health insurance in Canada is in a state of transition, and this not only because of the ongoing developments in the health field itself but also because of the unsettled constitutional issues concerning the division of federal and provincial jurisdiction and financial responsibility generally in all areas.

It will also be seen that the present multiplicity of agencies and auspices under which services are provided and financed renders an adequate summarization for the country as a whole very difficult. Furthermore, it must be remembered that about three-quarters of Canada's territory lie outside the area of organized community services, where not only distances and communications but also the harsh northern climate create great problems in the delivery of health services.

Income Maintenance During Illness

The schemes described so far deal only with the cost of health services. Canada has as yet no universal scheme to compensate for income loss due to illness or disability.

There are programs providing for federal-provincial cost sharing of allowances to the blind and the permanently and totally disabled but these allowances are limited to the needy below certain income limits. Provincial Workmens' Compensation plans provide for income maintenance during disability due to work-related injury or disability. There are provisions for limited paid sick leave and for early retirement in the case of permanent disability in the public service and in some industries but on the whole the provision for income mainance during illness is left to private insurance either on an individual basis or by employment connected group insurance.

At one time consideration had been given to some kind of disability benefit scheme within the framework of the unemployment insurance system. A recent government background paper prepared for a federal provincial conference proposed constitutional powers for the federal government to operate national public income insurance schemes such as sickness insurance but this is still in the hopper of the constitutional, fiscal, and cultural power play between the provinces and the federal government.

Financing

Both the previously described federal-provincial hospital and medical care insurance plans are in fact provincial plans whose cost is shared by the federal government which by and large pays about half of the specified costs with some adjustment in the cost sharing formula for circumstances in each province: the federal contribution is higher for provinces with a lower per-capita cost of services, and lower for provinces with higher costs.

The federal share is financed out of tax revenues. Provincial plans display a wide variety, however, in the methods of financing the provincial share for the two programs, and some provinces have changed their systems of financing over the years, especially in the direction from premiums to general tax revenue and, as will be seen below, several provinces combine various methods of raising the necessary funds.

Alberta finances hospital insurance from an addition to the property tax as well as direct charges to patients (other than new born infants). The medical care plan is financed through premiums and direct charges to patients.

British Columbia finances hospital insurance out of the general revenue fund to which part of a provincial sales tax accrues. It also levels direct per diem charges to patients. Medical care services are financed through premiums on a voluntary basis.

Manitoba finances hospital insurance through a combination of

premiums, in addition to the personal and corporation income tax. Medical care services are entirely financed by premium.

New Brunswick finances both hospital insurance and medical care services out of general revenue.

Newfoundland also finances hospital insurance out of general revenue and employs the same method for medical insurance.

Nova Scotia finances hospital insurance through a sales tax, but medical care insurance from general revenue.

Ontario finances hospital insurance through premiums with compulsory payroll deductions from employees in establishments with fifteen or more employees. The medical care plan is also financed through premiums.

Prince Edward Island finances both hospital insurance and medical care services out of general revenue.

Quebec finances hospital insurance from general revenue. It collects a payroll tax from employers and employees, and a tax on earnings from the self employed.

Saskatchewan finances hospital insurance through an annual hospitalization tax which is augmented from general revenue funds. Medical care insurance is financed through premiums, a special tax augmented from general revenue, and direct utilization charges to patients. The latter are likely to be discontinued after a recent election victory by the former opposition party which, by the way was the party in power when hospital and medical care insurance were first introduced in the province.

Trends: Future Plans and Policy

Reference has been made to the state of transition in Canada not only of the organisation of health services and their financing but of the division of responsibility among different levels of government generally. There is, on the one hand, the see-saw between federal and provincial prerogatives but, on the other hand, a continuing trend of responsibility – particularly financial responsibility – being shifted from the local level to higher levels of government where greater resources are available for the ever expanding public services of any kind. In addition, there is a continuing reassessment of the respective roles of the public and private sector, of individual and collective responsibility for the well-being of the people. Here, the general trend seems to be away from the old concepts of the poor laws and public assistance to social security, i.e. the guarantee of certain minimum standards to all members of the community. This refers particularly to the various forms of income maintenance but the same trend can be decerned also in regard to the provision of health services.

Canada has a blue print for its health services system in the report of the Royal Commission on Health Services of 1964. Since that time the situation has changed in some respects and nowhere is there an explicit commitment to its implementation by the policy makers. Nevertheless the recent developments have been along the lines recommended by the Commission and it can be assumed that while there may be differences in specific proposals, the basic philosophy of the report is generally shared and accepted, i.e. that the objective is a universal and comprehensive health insurance scheme aimed not only at paying for what services exist but also at their more rational organisation and use. "Universal," to use the definition of the Commission, means that adequate health services shall be available to all Canadians wherever they reside and whatever their financial resources may be, within the limitations imposed by geographic factors. The term "comprehensive" includes all health services, preventive, diagnostic, curative and rehabilitative, that modern medical and other sciences can provide.

University has been a characteristic of all national and provincial plans, unlike the programs existing in the United States which are aimed at and available only to the aged, the poor, or certain other selected groups.

Comprehensiveness, it would seem, will be achieved step by step. All Canadians are now covered for in-patient hospital services (exclusive of physician services). Now that all provinces have joined in the federal medical plan, they are also covered for services provided by physicians both in and out of the hospital. The act provides for the future extension to other services and some provinces already provide under their plans coverage for certain services other than those of the physician. It may be assumed, therefore, that gradually the comprehensiveness proposed by the Royal Commission will be achieved.

There is, at present, no serious plan to change the basic condition under which health professionals and institutions operate. Even under new systems of financing, they will continue generally speaking as free agents but will be subject to greater control and coordinated planning.

STRUCTURE AND ADMINISTRATION OF THE CANADIAN HEALTH SERVICES

Because of the multiplicity of auspices and jurisdictions under which the various parts of the Canadian health services system function, the aforementioned Royal Commission on Health Services referred to it as the "health services complex" rather than a "system." Nor is there any one axis around which the various agencies and jurisdiction may be grouped.

Broadly speaking, it will be helpful for the understanding of health services in Canada to observe their development and relationship along three axes:

1. personal vs. environmental health services
2. individual vs. collective responsibility
3. private vs. government responsibility.

By separating environmental from personal health services, we can readily describe the former by their very nature as being the responsibility of the public authority, i.e. government. The traditional concern of health departments in such areas as sanitation, water supply, food inspection, housing and industrial standards, has been extended into the emerging problems of air and water pollution, radiation, and similar potential hazards resulting from the changing social and technological scene. On the other hand, the actual operations of services such as sanitation and water supply have become public utilities with health departments retaining supervision of the health aspects. The health department's involvement in these matters results from two aspects: first, the necessary measures are beyond the individual's capacity, and second, they require regulatory power which only government can provide.

The second set of criteria, i.e. the distinction between individual and collective responsibility, will help to explain the increasing substitution of collective for individual effort in the field of health services, without the latter necessarily being provided by government. Examples of such collective but largely private and voluntary effort are the various health insurance or prepayment plans which, at the time of the introduction of the federal medical care plan, extended to some 60 per cent of the population providing some protection against the costs of physicians' services. Similar private and voluntary plans for hospital insurance existed before the introduction of universal hospital insurance and still continue to cover benefits not provided by the government plans. One notes here the gradual assumption by government of previously private but collective activities concerned with health services.

Finally, the distinction between private (individual or collective) and government responsibility helps one understand the changing role of government in the field of health services, particularly of personal health services (environmental health services traditionally having been the responsibility of government). Governments, meaning in this context health departments, operate at three levels within the existing federal constitution: local (municipal), provincial, and federal. Traditionally, the role of government in Canada – as in the United States – has been residual to individual and private responsibility.

Government has stepped in, or been allowed to step in, only where a problem became too big to be dealt with by the individual, either alone or collectively. Thus, the early boards of health and later health departments were concerned with the control of epidemics and the environment. Certain personal health services also resulted from that: for instance, the immunisation measures and other preventive activities such as maternal and child care. Before effective treatment for mental disease and tuberculosis was known, government built and operated institutions for these patients, originally mainly to protect the community from the patients and later also because individuals could not be expected to pay for their long stay in these hospitals. Hence, provincial governments had shouldered the main responsibility for patients in mental and tuberculosis institutions. This has been stated as the reason for excluding mental and tuberculosis hospitals from coverage under the Hospital Insurance and Diagnostic Services Act. In time, the factor of protecting the community from certain categories of patients gave way to assisting patients in meeting the high cost of complex and often prolonged services; thus, some provinces assumed the financial responsibility for cancer diagnostic and sometimes treatment services (voluntary agencies provided similar assistance for certain categories of diseases). All along, governments have accepted the responsibility of assisting the indigent in obtaining health care, with medical indigency assuming greater and greater proportions as the cost of health care increased. This has resulted in the present overriding role of government in the area of health care financing. The Royal Commission on Health Services, basically sympathetic to the idea of government intervention only on behalf of the indigent, found that the number of people requiring subsidies to meet the high cost of health services would be so large that no government could impose a means test on so many citizens or would be justified in establishing a system requiring so much unnecessary administration. Rising costs in health services as in most other community services are also the reason for a gradual shift of responsibility from lower (local) to higher (provincial, federal) levels of government which under the existing tax system obtain larger revenues.

Personnel

Since health is a matter under provincial jurisdiction, licensing of health personnel is subject to provincial measures. In regard to physicians, provincial medical acts have transferred this function to licensing boards whose composition varies among the provinces: some consist of elected members of the medical profession; some are made up of some elected members of the profession, some appointed by the provincial government and university faculties of medicine. In most provinces a candidate must submit a certificate of registration with the Medical Council of Canada, ensuring a uniform standard of educational attainment. Before receiving a license, the candidate must have obtained a medical degree and completed a year of internship in an approved hospital. Foreign trained physicians are also required to pass the Council examination and satisfy certain provincial requirements which vary from province to province. Similar provisions provide for the licensing of dentists.

Members of the other health professions generally qualify for practice by registering or membership with a recognized professional organization based on the attainment of a certain required standard of education or training.

Licensing of Institutions

Licensing, generally speaking a function of provincial authorities, is a prerequisite for the operation of hospitals. It is aimed at ensuring the maintenance of minimum standards of safety and patient care, and it is coupled with periodic inspections of the institutions.

Licensing, however, is but one form standard setting. Another is the approval of a hospital for participation in the provincial hospital insurance program. There also is the voluntary program of hospital accreditation. The Canadian Council of Hospital Accreditation, formed by the national hospital and medical associations, surveys hospitals requesting accreditation and examines the physical facilities, medical records, operating room facilities and procedures, safety standards, sanitary controls, disaster plans, organization of the medical staff, and administrative procedures and records. The surveys are repeated every three years to ensure that accreditation standards are maintained and recommendations carried out.

HEALTH RESOURCES

Personnel

Canada had 22,816 active civilian physicians in its ten provinces in 1967, which means a population of 894 per physician. Not covered by these figures are the two northern territories, Yukon and Northwest Territories, which have a total of about 30 physicians, both private practitioners and government employed, amounting to a population of about 1,500 per physician in this area with small populations scattered over a huge and intractable area.

The distribution of physicians varies considerably from province to province. The respective ratios of population per physician were as follows in 1967:[1]

TABLE 5.1

Province	Population per Physician
Alberta	927
British Columbia	824
Manitoba	877
New Brunswick	1,303
Newfoundland	1,506
Nova Scotia	937
Ontario	840
Prince Edward Island	1,346
Quebec	893
Saskatchewan	986
Total all provinces	894

While these ratios provide a rough basis for comparison, they do not indicate the adequacy of the supply of physicians. One reason is that most of Canada's provinces are large in size – some cover about twice the area of France – so that even a province presents a very heterogeneous picture regarding health services. Thus, urban areas have a disproportionate supply of physicians compared to rural areas, a situation which is aggravated by the fact that rural physicians are generally older and have less logistic support than their urban colleagues in terms of auxiliary personnel and facilities.

In 1965, there were 6,396 dentists in Canada. This means 3.3 dentists per 10,000 population, or a population of 3,070 per dentist.[2] Schools of dentistry are separate from the medical schools in Canada.

In the same year there were an estimated 58,000 nurses (using WHO criteria), or 30 nurses per 10,000 population, or a population of 340 per nurse.[3] There were about 9,000 pharmacists, or 4.6 per 10,000 population, or a population of 2,180 per pharmacist.[4]

Facilities

The term comprises a wide variety of physical structures designed to accommodate health services of one kind or another such as physicians' offices, dentists' offices, clinics of various kinds, laboratories, as well as hospitals. The latter, however, are the only ones that are well documented in Canada but they are also the most important in terms of cost – both capital and operating costs – and in terms of their role in the health services system.

As in the case of health personnel, ratios of hospital beds to population, or vice versa, are not very good indicators of the adequacy of supply but, as in the case of personnel, they permit broad comparison among countries.

The following table shows the supply of hospital beds in Canada in 1966:[5]

TABLE 5.2

Rated Bed Capacity and Percentage Occupancy in Operating
Hospitals, by Type of Hospital
Canada 1966

Type of Hospital	Total	Bed capacity per 1,000 population	Percentage Occupancy
General and allied special			
General	114,591	5·7	80·1
Chronic, convalescent,			
rehabilitation	19,543	1·0	90·9
Other	2,742	0·1	61·9
Total	136,876	6·8	81·3
Mental	65,265	3·2	100·0
Tuberculosis	5,168	0·3	68·2
All hospitals	207,309	10·3	81·5

The number of beds in mental hospitals has remained fairly stable between 1961 and 1966, showing a slight decrease in the absolute number in the last report year. The number of beds in tuberculosis hospitals, on the other hand, was less than half in 1966 of what it was five years earlier. It should be remembered here that mental and tuberculosis hospitals are mostly owned and operated by the provincial governments, which also bear most of the cost of treatment in these hospitals. They are excluded from the federal hospital insurance scheme which, however, does cover mental and tuberculosis patients in general hospitals. With the decline of the incidence of tuberculosis and the shift towards active treatment and with the shift of psychiatric treatment from the old large mental hospital to psychiatric units in general hospitals, the emphasis in hospital construction and care has been more and more on the public general hospital which is the mainstay of the hospital insurance program.

The following table shows the rated bed capacity of public general hospitals, its trend, and differences among the provinces:[6]

Prince Edward Island, the smallest of the provinces, is the only one where bed capacity has decreased in relation to population.

TABLE 5.3

Province	Rated bed capacity per 1,000 population	
	1961	1966
Canada	5·51	6·11
Alberta	6·59	8·05
British Columbia	5·60	5·60
Manitoba	5·96	6·18
New Brunswick	5·20	5·91
Newfoundland	3·78	6·27
Nova Scotia	4·94	5·78
Ontario	5·53	6·16
Prince Edward Island	6·83	6·61
Quebec	5·02	5·52
Saskatchewan	7·41	7·56

MEDICAL CARE – Personal Health Services

The conventional first contact, still is with the physician. This, in Canada, is not necessarily one considered as a primary physician. Even the notion of what a primary physician is, varies: it may be the general practititioner, but could also be an internist or pediatrician. Canadians are generally free to consult directly any physician, generalist or specialist. Some specialists, however, do insist on seeing only referred patients.

There are no data available on the respective role of general practitioners and specialist as first contact physician in Canada. Although physicians are about evenly divided into general practitioners and specialists, and although patients generally do have ready access to specialists, those who have a personal or family physician are likely to consult him first. Internists, pediatricians, gynecologists and obstetricians – a group of specialists who in many ways act as generalists for their clientele – account for about one-quarter of all specialists.

There is a good deal of soul searching going on, in Canada as everywhere else, about the future role of the general practitioner, personal physician, or family physician, a search which eventually will have to dove-tail with the development of a physician's assistant among whose functions may be some of the screening and other procedures now performed by the general practitioner.

The General Practitioner

It may be noted that some general practitioners specialise in the sense that their interest focuses on certain categories of conditions or patients but formal recognition and certification of specialty status are conferred by the Royal College of Physicians and Surgeons of Canada, with some special arrangements in certain provinces.

Little is known of the pattern and content of general practice in Canada. One study, however, gives some indications of the general practitioners' work, mostly in solo practices.[7] Since that study was undertaken there probably have been certain trends such as towards wider participation in group practice, or towards still fewer home calls but these trends would not offset the general pattern found earlier.

According to that study, the average working week of general practitioners was 52 hours, with a patient visit load of 159 per week. Of these visits, about 14 per cent were home calls, about 60 per cent office calls, the remainder hospital visits. The average size of practice was about 1,700 persons. The time spent per office call was about 15 minutes.

General practitioners employed few auxiliary personnel. Those in solo private practice had, on the average, one person working for them. This would be a nurse in about half the cases, the remainder being divided between technical and clerical personnel.

Looking at the picture from the patient's point of view, we cannot distinguish between general and specialist practice. In all, Canadians had 5.4 physician's visits on the average per year, of which 2.9 were office calls, 1.8 hospital visits, and 0.6 home calls; the rest were telephone calls, etc.

The Specialist and his Patients

Specialists may be serving as primary physicians in the sense of being directly approached by patients as well as providing continuing general care to certain groups of patients, e.g. the pediatricians or internists. Also, specialists treat their own patients in hospitals so that in this respect there is no clear dividing line between ambulatory and in-hospital care.

According to the above quoted study, the average work week for specialists was about 43 hours, with a patient load of about 100. Home calls accounted for 5.2 per cent of the weekly visit load for specialists and 0.7 per cent for consultants. About half their visits were made at the hospital.

The Changing Role of the Physician[8]

Some of the changes in medical practice in Canada correspond to similar changes elsewhere: they are part of the general social and scientific evolution. The health problems that patients bring to the physician have changed from largely acute and infectious diseases to chronic conditions, including the wide range of psychiatric disorders. The more medical practice is specialised, the greater the need for synthesis and hence the soul searching about the future of general practice in some new form such as the "specialty" of family medicine. The methods employed by the physician change with technical advances, shifting more and more from the art to the science of medicine. There is a concomitant division of labor not only among physicians but also among physicians and other health personnel. It is interesting to note, for instance, that the Canadian Medical Association and the Canadian Nurses Association have met jointly to review this division of labor between them. Physicians tend to outrun the general population trend towards the larger urban areas thus adding to the problem of bringing health services to the scattered rural population left behind. The physician's relationship with his patient is changing from that of a friend and mentor to that of a scientific consultant, with the patient no longer looking up to physician as superior in education and upbringing but often at least matching his educational status. The organisation of modern medical practice is affected by the increasing need for equipment and auxiliary personnel, one of the factors in the slow but steady growth of partnership and group practices.

The new forms of health insurance, described earlier, are changing the physician's relationship to the hospital.[9] One of the changes has been the increasing use of emergency departments as sources of primary care for reasons of convenience, difficulty of contacting a physician, and last but not least insurance coverage of care in the hospital but not outside. The old indigent outpatient clinic is being replaced by teaching-hospital-based family clinics, providing teaching hospital privileges for some general practitioners whereas previously such appointments were largely reserved for specialists. The independent role of the Canadian physician from the hospital is reflected in the separate financial arrangements. Even pathologists and radiologists in hospitals, although paid members of the hospital staff, are in most cases still remunerated on a fee-for-service basis. There are various forms of medical staff organisations in hospitals arranging for group billing systems in regard to "non-private" patients. And there is also a tendency to get physicians more concerned with the financial position and operation of hospitals.

Community Care

Many agencies and types of personnel provide services for patients outside the hospital, both ambulatory and homebound. Besides the physicians and a very small number of private duty nurses acting as independent entrepreneurs, there are numerous clinics dispensing mostly categorical care in accordance with the objectives of the particular public or private agency; examples are mental health; the traditional public health department functions like venereal disease, immunisation, maternal and child care, tuberculosis, and others; cancer; rheumatism and arthritis, cystic fibrosis, and various others. Other agencies, mostly private and non-profit, are organized to provide a certain type of service such as visiting nursing.

An interesting development is the institution of what is referred to as organised home care plans. Variously defined, these are basically organisations which coordinate and make available to the patient and his physician the services of at least two agencies serving the sick in the community outside the hospital.[10] Foremost among the services provided are nursing, homemaking, various forms of therapies, X-ray and laboratory services, social services, and such other services as may be available in the community. The plans are organised either by a hospital to facilitate earlier discharge and appropriate after-care, or they may be organised on a community wide basis. The aged constitute the majority of patients of these plans representing, as may be expected, largely the chronic diseases. The scale of operation of the formalised home care plans is still very limited. It was estimated that in 1965 only about twenty such plans existed in the country serving not more than a few thousand patients compared to the several million who pass through the hospitals annually. In other cases, however, the visiting nurse may make arrangements for certain services needed without the existence of a formal plan and other informal referral arrangements serve a similar purpose.[11] In a system where so many different agencies under a great variety of auspices exist, the organised home care plans serve an essential purpose because without them it is extremely difficult for the patient or the physician to avail themselves even of the services that exist. Thus, while these plans have been slow in developing – largely due to lacking enthusiasm on the part of the physicians and inadequate insurance coverage, they do constitute a model by which the now badly proliferated and fragmented services could be effectively organised.

Dental Care

Generally dental care is not covered by the existing public insurance plans.

There are, however, provisions for public assistance recipients to receive dental care. Comprehensive government financed programs exist in the four western provinces, in some cases the patient having to contribute to the cost of dentures. In the remaining provinces some dental care, mostly emergency, is provided under the various welfare programs.

In the absence of universal and comprehensive programs, various schemes exist to provide some dental care to children. Provincial health departments have dental health divisions. Some provinces employ travelling clinics to serve particularly children in outlying areas and provide at least some emergency services to adults. Some health departments provide dental services for school children, and two regions in the Province of Saskatchewan have prepaid programs for children up to age 12.

The provision of drugs, and appliances etc.

The existing national medical care insurance plan is presently limited to the payment for physicians services. Several provincial plans provide for such additional services as optometry (but not glasses), chiropractic, or certain nursing services. There is provision for the extension of these plans to other services such as those listed in the title but for the time being there are only limited private and voluntary plans which provide such coverage.

Public (Environmental) Health

Matters of environmental health are the responsibility of health departments. This responsibility may be discharged in various forms. It is mostly regulatory (by legislation, licensing, standard setting) leaving the implementation to the agencies or individuals concerned subject to inspection or testing by the public health authority. The engineering aspects of the public water supply and sewerage systems, for instance, have been taken over by other municipal departments. The new dimensions of the pollution problem, however, have involved other areas of the public domain in the concern for these matters and in some cases boards or commissions with broader representation have taken on the responsibility for all aspects of water supply and sewage disposal.

Air pollution and control have been added to the functions of most provincial health departments. Radiation control and protection is carried out by the federal health department with the assistance of provincial inspection officers.

Most provincial health departments have occupational health divisions whose function it is to assist in the prevention of occupational diseases and the elimination of other work-related hazards. Food and milk sanitation at the various stages of processing, sale, and consumption in public places is another responsibility of provincial and municipal health departments.

It should be noted in the discussion of provincial health department activities that they do not vary from province to province as much as one might expect because of the provincial jurisdiction in health matters. There are two factors which account for a very considerable degree of uniformity in provincial health legislation and activities in such public health fields as those discussed here. One of these unifying factors is the role of the federal Department of National Health and Welfare which provides consultation, technical assistance, and in some cases grants. The other element is the institution of the Dominion Council of Health, composed mainly of the federal and provincial deputy ministers of health, i.e. the top ranking civil servants, who meet regularly to discuss technical and policy matters of common concern without, however, making binding decisions. The ministers of health also meet periodically to discuss matters of policy.

Community and Regional Planning

Because of the multiplicity of auspices under which health institutions, agencies, and professionals operate, no rigid formal system of regionalisation or health services planning exists. Hospitals (with the exception of those owned by governments), physicians, dentists, and other facilities and independent professionals are established and operated basically at their own initiative. The fact, however, that most hospital construction is supported by government grants and that hospital operation takes place within the framework of the national hospital insurance scheme implies some effective controls. Thus, the provincial laws implementing the hospital insurance plan within a province must provide for arrangements for the planning and development of hospital resources and services. This gives the provincial agency certain veto powers and there are also beginnings of regional hospital planning on a voluntary basis. In regard to other services, however, there is little or no planning, except again where – like in outlying areas – all services are provided by government.

Rural Health Services

The small cottage hospitals which several decades ago filled the needs of rural areas cannot provide the services expected of a modern hospital and these hospitals are disappearing. The daily press not infrequently carries stories about small towns being without a physician or dentist, and various attempts by the community to entice someone to settle there are reported. The basic difficulty remains attracting personnel to work and live in rural areas. Among suggested solutions are strategically located group clinics, and various transportation and ambulance services, travelling clinics, and various combinations thereof, but so far the problem remains largely unsolved.

The difficulties increase as one moves northward into the very sparsely northern parts of the provinces and the northern territories which are administered by the federal government. There one finds about one per cent of Canada's population scattered over more than three-quarters of its vast territory, exposed to a hostile climate and forbidding topography.

Provincial health departments have instituted special services for the outlying areas within their boundaries: air ambulances, floating clinics in the coastal areas, outpost hospitals and nursing stations, two way radio communications.

In the Northwest Territories, where the population density is about one inhabitant to 50 square miles, and the Yukon, where there are about 18 square miles per inhabitant, the federal health department maintains nursing stations trained lay dispensers in localities where professional personnel could not be maintained, and it has developed family medical packs for families and small bands of people who have no regular contact with any of the established services. Parts of the Arctic are visited annually by a ship carrying medical personnel and supplies. There are plans to cover the entire northern territories by flying circuits which would also provide for regular visits by professional personnel to the various settlements.[12] Religious and lay voluntary organisation also have brought health services to these areas.

Categorical Health Services

Categorical health services owe their existence only partly to the fact that certain health problems require specific facilities, equipment, or skills which would not be applicable to general health care. Very largely, and this is particularly true of North America, they have been due to the absence of a universal concern with health or ill health as such. They have developed as particular problems arose, became recognised, and stirred public interest. As comprehensive plans develop they gradually absorb some of the categorical services.

a *Disease and Rehabilitation*

The care, and in particular the institutional care of the tuberculous and mentally ill has traditionally been a function of the provincial health departments which have been operating mental and tuberculosis hospitals. This historical development was the reason for excluding these two types of institutions from the federally supported national hospital insurance scheme.

The mental health services provided through public programs include mental hospitals, community mental health facilities, and special services for the mentally retarded and other specific groups. Each provincial health department now contains a mental health division or branch.[13]

Tuberculosis control programs have been conducted by provincial health departments for many years, greatly assisted by the voluntary tuberculosis associations. Diagnosis and treatment are largely the function of the health department, while the voluntary agencies concentrate on case finding programs, health education and rehabilitation.[14]

Communicable disease control, the original raison d'être for public health activities and administration, still remains one of the main-stays of local and provincial health departments. This includes immunisation programs, surveillance, case reporting and epidemiology generally, as well as general prevention and health education. Venereal diseases receive special attention. The larger provinces maintain separate venereal disease divisions in their health departments.

Cancer has become a matter of public concern because of its great impact in terms of mortality. Both health departments and voluntary agencies, as well as semi-public commissions share in the financing of research and services, including diagnosis, treatment, and health education.

Similar arrangements exist for the registration, treatment, and habilitation of handicapped children. Rehabilitation services for adults also have been receiving attention. One of the specific matters of concern in this field is the need for coordinating the wide range of community services required, often involving not only the health department but also social services, education, vocational training, and job placement. To accomplish this, all provinces have established committees or commissions with representation from the public and private agencies concerned.

A number of specific health problems have become the object of voluntary effort, linked to varying degrees with health departmental activities, the former being particularly concerned with fund raising for research, health education, and also the provision on financing of certain services. Examples of such problem areas are alcoholism, drug addiction, arthritis and rheumatism, cerebral palsy, cystic fibrosis, diabetes, epilepsy, hemophilia, and certain impairments such as hearing, speech, and vision defects.

b *Population Groups*

There are certain groups of people who have been recognized as particularly vulnerable to disease, injury, or the financial burden of illness. In the absence of a universal and comprehensive health care program, these groups have been singled out from time to time for public attention by government or voluntary agencies. Not infrequently the latter pioneered programs, identifying needs and demonstrating the feasibility, and government eventually accepting responsibility for such projects. As in the case of disease categorical program, here also as comprehensive programs develop, they gradually absorb categorical services although some of these display a remarkable stamina for survival even after they have outlived their usefulness and original purpose. In some cases this leads to shifting contents of categorical programs such as tuberculosis agencies concerning themselves with all chest diseases, or poliomyelitis programs being broadened to cover all handicapped children and even adults.

The federal government has statutory commitments for the care of members of the armed forces and veterans, mariners, to some extent immigrants, and it has traditionally assumed responsibility for the health of Indians and Eskimos who, however, are likely to be gradually integrated into the provincial health care programs.

Mother and child health services have received early attention from voluntary groups and health departments, the latter providing for prenatal and postnatal supervision, well infant and child care, and health education. A high and probably increasing proportion of these services is carried out by private physicians and clinics.

School children receive varying degrees of health supervision, examinations, and various tests, as well as limited first aid care at school, the care being under the auspices of the local health department or education authority. The value of these programs has been disputed and is under review in some areas.

There are special programs for the protection of industrial workers in their work environment. The health departments of the larger provinces have occupational health divisions whose main function is to require or at least recommend measures which would prevent hazardous situations. In addition, every province has Workmen's Compensation legislation in effect which provides compulsory, industry supported, prepaid insurance for workers suffering from work-related disease or injury. The Workmen's Compensation boards are remarkable not only as early prototypes of health insurance agencies, but also because of the good working relationship they have developed with the medical profession, and last but not least because of their pioneering in the rehabilitation field. Besides these public plans, individual industrial establishments frequently provide health services for their employees ranging from first-aid stations to fairly comprehensive services provided by some larger industries especially in outlying areas such as mining towns.

a. *Rehabilitation Services*

Rehabilitation is a philosophy or objective rather than a new type of service although greater emphasis on this objective and increased scientific knowledge in the various related fields have led to the development of new disciplines and services specifically oriented towards rehabilitation. The purpose of rehabilitation is to go beyond the halting or controlling of the disease process by restoring the sick and injured to a maximum of his social functions. Thus rehabilitation involves not only the wide range of medical services needed for the patient's medical rehabilitation but also the services necessary for social rehabilitation whereby the dividing line between these two stages is a very thin and fluid one.

Under the Vocational Rehabilitation of Disabled Persons Act of 1961, the federal government shares with the provinces (except the Province of Quebec) the cost of rehabilitation services coordinated by an inter-agency coordinator. Assessment of disability, counselling and placement services are provided free of charge; other services have to be paid for by those who are able to pay and to the extent that they are not covered by an insurance program.

b. *Preventive Services*

As already described, preventive services such as immunisation, well mother and child care, dental examinations for children, etc., have traditionally been the domaine of the local and provincial health department. To the extent that they are personal health services, their provision is shifting gradually to the private sector, especially due to the expansion of more comprehensive insurance plans.

Role of Voluntary Organisations

Elements of voluntary organisation, limited here to the non-profit agencies, have been described earlier in various contexts: e.g. the voluntary hospital, voluntary prepayment plans, and generally in the discussion of the respective role of government and voluntary effort. Many of the existing voluntary organisations have categorical objectives, aiming at the control of certain health problems or the assistance of the sick or disabled in certain population groups. In 1962, there were 20 national organisations, most of whom concerned with specific disease categories (e.g. cancer, tuberculosis, arthritis, multiple sclerosis) but others such as the Red Cross, visiting nurses associations, and others aimed at general health problems. In addition to the national organisations, usually with provincial or local branches, there are many organisations of purely local or provincial scope. There are basically two types of voluntary health organisations:[15] (a) those organised by citizens to help other people (e.g. the Canadian Tuberculosis Association or the Canadian Cancer Society); and (b) those organised by patients, their relatives or friends, to help themselves with their common problems (e.g. the Multiple Sclerosis Society or the Cystic Fibrosis Foundation).

Voluntary organisation has played a very important role in Canada's

167

health services by identifying problems in need of public action, by pioneering new types of services and demonstrating their feasibility so that government agencies could take over, and by supplementing the efforts of government agencies. These functions will certainly continue even with the growth of coverage under various insurance schemes.

Because of the multiplicity of voluntary agencies there is a strong demand for their closer coordination in order to rationalise their funding as well as their operation.

Financing

The already referred to state of flux in the Canadian health services scene makes it difficult to describe specific methods of financing or to indicate prevailing patterns, but some general statements will help to clarify the underlying nature of payment mechanisms.

a. *Payment by Consumer*

The methods of payment for in-hospital care have been described in the context of the national hospital insurance scheme. The same applies to consumer payments for physicians services under the public medical care insurance plans in the provinces.

Even before the advent of the federal medical care insurance scheme, some 80 per cent of the population had some insurance coverage against the cost of health care. The extent of this coverage varied widely among the large number and variety of these private insurance plans. There have been basically two types of plans: the non-profit type, mostly sponsored by provincial medical associations offering "service" contracts whereby participating physicians accept payments by the plan as payment in full; and the "indemnity" contract underwritten mainly by commercial insurance companies and undertaking to reimburse the patient at stipulated rates regardless of the actual cost. Most of these plans cover only the services of physicians.[16]

Another type of insurance which had become quite common in recent years – it covered some 6 million people in 1966 – has been the so-called "major medical expense" insurance which covers a wide range of services including drugs, appliances, etc., but requiring a certain deductible of the subscriber each year and in addition payment of a certain percentage only (usually about 20 per cent) of the remaining claim.

There are some limited and largely still experimental prepayment plans for dental care and prescribed drugs. An important recent development, though still very limited in terms of people covered, are prepaid group practice plans. They are consumer-sponsored (by labor unions or on a cooperative basis) group clinics which provide a comprehensive range of health services only for their subscribers.

On the whole, dental care, drugs, appliances, and other incidental services are still subject to direct payment by the consumer. The Royal Commission on Health Services, however, had recommended comprehensive coverage by a national health insurance plan, and the present federal Medical Care Act provides for its future extension to services other than those of physicians.

b. *Remuneration of Provider*

With the exception of physicians in government departments and those in group clinics, physicians are paid on a fee-for-service basis. This applies to medical care insurance plans as well as to direct consumer payments. The existing provincial medical care plans negotiate fee schedules with the professional organisations. Physicians on the staff of group clinics, an as yet relatively small group, are remunerated in a variety of ways ranging from salary to various forms of profit sharing.

Hospitals, to the extent that they are not owned and operated by governments, are generally reimbursed in accordance with the provisions of the hospital insurance legislation. Reimbursement is made not on the basis of individual patient claims but on the basis of the annual budget of the hospital which is reviewed by the provincial hospital insurance authority and on the basis of which, once approved, monthly or semi-monthly payments are made to the hospital. This procedure relates only to the operating costs of the hospital. Capital costs are financed through private fund raising, supplemented by government grants.

c. *Income Maintenance During Disability*

Reference has been made earlier to the provision of government pensions for the totally and permanently disabled who meet certain criteria of need.

With the exception of Workmen's Compensation for occupation – related disability, there are no public programs of income maintenance during temporary disability. The only provisions that exist for these contingencies are provisions for paid sick leave for employees in many industrial enterprises, provisions for sick pay as part of collective bargaining agreements, and private insurance.

Medical Personnel – Physicians and Paramedics

Physicians

The Royal Commission on Health Services pointed out that the recruitment of entrants in the medical school has declined in proportion to total university enrollment. The high cost of medical education is described as a significant barrier as is the length of time required to qualify as a physician.

Some provincial governments provide financial assitance to medical students.

The education of the physician includes two years pre-medicine following graduation from secondary school, four years medicine, one year of internship, and several additional years for specialisation. Medical schools are integrated parts of a university headed by deans appointed by the Board of Governors of the university. The responsibilities of the school are divided among clinical departments each with its own chairman or head. Department heads in fields such as medicine, surgery, obstetrics and gynecology, psychiatry, and pediatrics are appointed so that there main responsibility relates to the department with limitations on private practice.[17]

Dentists

The dental student also faces the problems of the high cost of education, the highest of all professional schools. Consequently, a high proportion of students is recruited from higher income families. Another deterrent is the high cost of establishing a dental practice. Less than two per cent of registered dentists are women and it is felt that more women could be attracted into the dental profession.

Dental schools in Canada are separate from the medical school. Entrance requirements are secondary school graduation plus one or two years in a general course in arts and sciences at a university. The dental course itself covers four academic years, about one-third of which is devoted to basic sciences and two-thirds to clinical disciplines. Specialty training requires from one to three additional years depending on the speciality.[18]

Nurses

Attracting students into nursing schools has not presented major problems for the large urban schools. Any active recruitment undertaken by these schools is usually in response to requests by schools or community organisations to counsel girls graduating from secondary schools. The small rural schools find recruitment more difficult and this has led to the institution of recruitment programs in many of these schools. Among the means used are literature, lectures, hospital visits, and improvements in the residential facilities. Selection procedures review in addition to academic performance generally also health and personality of the candidate. Thought has been given to attracting more men into the nursing profession; among the barriers now are not only job content and remuneration but also the perception of the occupation as primarily female.[19]

Nursing education has taken place traditionally either in the university schools of nursing, generally a four year course following graduation from secondary school and offering the B.Sc. degree, or in a three year hospital diploma program resulting in a certificate; both types of graduates qualify for resgistration. New programs have been introduced, however, shortening the period of study by reducing the time spent by student nurses in service functions. This renders it possible to provide nursing education in community college type schools. A special program is available at some schools for the training of psychiatric nurses. Postgraduate programs may lead to master's degrees, public health degrees (usually required for visiting nursing), and some universities offer midwifery training to graduate nurses.

Other Health Services

There is an increasing number of other health professions requiring university education: pharmacists, dietitians, social workers, optometrists are among these but new ones are being added as formal training replaces apprenticeship in various health occupations.

Vocational schools and community colleges also have been taking on the training of a growing variety of technicians and therapists resulting from the use of more and more complex equipment and the development of new techniques.

RESEARCH

(a) Medical

Federal government agencies have steadily increased their funds allocated for both intramural and extramural biomedical research to $44·7 million in 1967–68. Funds designated in the estimates for these purposes in 1968–69 totalled $53·5 million, an increase of over 19·7 per cent. The principal agency engaged in intramural medical research is the Department of National Health and Welfare, which spent $8 million on research and development studies and related scientific activities in the fields of radiation protection, air pollution, occupational health, environmental health, biochemistry, epidemiology, and health services. The Department of Veterans Affairs continued a variety of clinical studies in chronic disease problems including a psychiatric research program, that amounted to $357,000 in 1967–68. The National Research Council also conducts intramural investigations of importance to health in radiation biology and the biosciences.

Federal grants supporting the development of biomedical research and research personnel in universities and hospitals have been channelled mainly through the Medical Research Council, although significant outlays are made by other agencies in special fields such as public health, defense, and dental research. Moreover, the expansion of research plants is one of the key objectives of the Health Resources Program of the Department of National Health and Welfare.

The Medical Research Council spent $20.5 million in 1967–68, of which $7,759,000 was allocated for annual grants-in-aid, $4,991,000 for three-year term research projects, $2,638,000 for equipment grants, $3,760,000 for research scholarships and fellow-ships, and $1,351,000 for other research promotion. Its 1968–69 budget for these programs has been increased to $26,943,000.

Under the Public Health Research Grant, the Department of National Health and Welfare allocated $4,090,000 in 1967–68 to applied and developmental research projects, conducted by universities, hospitals, health departments, and other non-profit health organisations; in addition, it gave $424,000 for physiological research under the Fitness and Amateur Sport Grant, $152,000 for research and demonstration projects on health aspects of mental retardation, and $23,000 for smoking-and-health research. It is estimated that $10 million, or 30 per cent of the Health Resources Fund expenditures in 1967–68, were used to build research facilities as an integral part of this program to expand the training of health personnel at medical and dental schools and affiliated centres.

Other substantial grants-in-aid of research were made to the universities by the Defense Research Board for studies in arctic medicine and climatic physiology, aviation medicine, radiation protection and treatment, toxicology, and other special areas. In 1967–68 this support totalled $473,000. The remaining extramural program, for dental research, which has been administered by the National Research Council's Associate Committee on Dental Research, spent $419,000 in 1967–68.

The principal voluntary agencies supporting medical research in Canada, related to their special interests, are the National Cancer Institute, Canadian Arthritis and Rheumatism Society, Multiple Sclerosis Society, and the Muscular Dystrophy Society. The Inter-departmental Committee on Medical Research provides a forum for the sharing of information and support of medical research to which the voluntary agencies are invited. The Medical Research Council now reports to Parliament through the Minister of National Health and Welfare.[20]

(b) Health Services Organisation

With the growing cost and complexity of health services and the expanding involvement of public agencies and public funds in the delivery of health services, there has been an increasing demand not only for public accountability but also for close attention to the effectiveness and efficiency of these services. When the Royal Commission on Health Services submitted in 1964 its recommendation for a universal and comprehensive health services system, it made also numerous recommendations regarding the rationalisation and organisation of such a system and its component parts. It recommended as an essential part of the system the establishment of a Health Sciences Research Council which would absorb the present Medical Research Council and broaden it so as to be able to study the many problems of a social, administrative and purely technical nature which confront the health services and, in particular, to evaluate the effectiveness, efficiency, and coordination of the various elements of the health services complex.[21]

Such a central research agency still awaits implementation but research activities in the field of health services organisation have increased considerably in recent years with the development of new public programs, especially those for hospital and medical care insurance. The federal health department maintains a research and statistics directorate as well as research branches directly related to its various programs, such as a Hospital Services Study Unit related to the hospital insurance program. The introduction of the medical care program was accompanied by the work of several task forces to study the various aspects of the program. Provincial departments also have research and statistics units which, in some of the larger provinces, have reached a considerable degree of sophistication. Schools of public health and related departments in medical schools across the country complement the picture. Federal grants and the federal health department's consultative and technical services contribute greatly to research activities in centers across the country. The National Public Health Research Grant, for instance, amounting to about $5 million dollars per year, supported a wide variety of research projects relating to the prevention of disease, disability or death; epidemiology; hospital administration; community based health care; operational research; environmental health and sanitation; the training and utilisation of manpower.[22]

(c) Information System

One of the recommendations of the Royal Commission on Health Services concerned the developing and maintaining of a continuing system of health statistics in Canada to be supplemented by ad hoc studies as required. The Commission was critical of the present fragmentation and inadequacies of health information which, however, is largely due to the proliferation of responsibility for services among many agencies and auspices. Canada has a central statistical agency, the Dominion Bureau of Statistics, which in addition to being responsible for the quinquennial census also acts as the statistical arm for the various departments of the federal government. In practice, however, the Bureau is limited generally to the collection of certain large scale continuing series of statistics and the various departments also maintain their own statistics branches. The Bureau has a health and welfare division which collects and publishes the national vital statistics, a very comprehensive set of hospital statistics based on annual reports submitted by individual hospitals and including hospital morbidity statistics based on individual discharge records. It also compiles mental health, tuberculosis and communicable diseases statistics. The collection of data on physicians' services is under consideration. The federal health department has its own statistics branch covering the various programs for which it is responsible. Correspondingly, provincial health departments have their statistical offices to process data related to their programs. The possibilities of a coordinated system of health statistics for a general population are demonstrated in the Province of Saskatchewan where a hospital and medical care insurance system has been in operation for many years and where data from these two systems can be linked. Experiments with record linkage are also carried out elsewhere but still rather limited in scope and purpose.

The introduction of the hospital insurance program has resulted in better and more complete hospital statistics and it may be expected that the medical care insurance program will similarly stimulate improved statistical coverage in this area.

PLANNING, EVALUATION, QUALITY CONTROL

Planning, evaluation, and quality control are functions of authority and responsibility, and they are therefore correspondingly divided and proliferated in the Canadian health scene. Strong fiscal participation by the federal government in health insurance programs and in grant supported projects have given the federal government leverage in standard setting and control. The same is true of the provincial governments in their relationship to the providers of services, i.e. particularly hospitals but also local health departments which are under provincial jurisdiction. By approving hospital budgets, for instance, the provincial hospital insurance agencies have a strong hand in surveilling hospital operations. Licensing of personnel and institutions serves to ensure certain minimum standards although these have little effect on the actual operation of a service. It may be anticipated that rising public involvement in the financing of health services and rising costs will bring about greater attention to planning, evaluation, and quality control since these are essential to maintaining effectiveness and efficiency of the services.

SIGNIFICANT CORRESPONDING FEATURES OF OTHER SYSTEMS IN SAME CATEGORY

Apart from Canada's northern regions which present unique problems demanding unique solutions, it may be said that in its social and economic institutions Canada very closely resembles the United States. This applies also to the basic structure of the health services and the philosophies underlying their organisation and operation. The providers of services, hospitals as well as physicians and other personnel, are independent agents, entering now and then into contractual arrangements with governments but remaining free within the limits of such arrangements. The hospitals are largely voluntary non-profit community agencies; physicians in private practice largely remain individual entrepreneurs.

Both Canada and the United States have in recent decades witnessed developments towards government participation – or intervention – in the form of public systems of health insurance systems. While these are in priciple only new methods for paying bills (third parties instead of the individual patient), they do necessarily bring about some measure of control by the fiscal agent. This control, so far, has been somewhat stronger and more effective in Canada than in the United States. Canada's medical care plans, for instance, operate on the basis of fee schedules agreed on between the profession and the intermediaries; the United States medical care programs are still groping for ways of controlling payments to the providers of services.

Probably the most important difference between the approaches to health care in the two countries is their respective development of a national health insurance system. Up to about two decades ago, after World War II, the movement towards social security ran roughly parallel in both countries; so did abortive attempts to implement health insurance against the opposition of the medical profession. Then Canada instituted its national health grants program, avowedly aimed in part at providing the necessary resources for a national health services program. Ten years later Canada introduced its universal national hospital insurance program, and another decade later the medical care program. Thus, the approach was to provide step by step, one service at a time to the entire population.

References

1. Department of National Health and Welfare (Canada). *Health and Welfare Services in Canada 1969*. Ottawa: the Department, 1969, p. 116.

2. World Health Organization. *World Health Statistics Annual 1965*, Vol. III. Geneva: the Organization, 1969, pp. 9, 33.
3. Ibid.
4. Ibid.
5. Based on: Dominion Bureau of Statistics (Canada). *Hospital Statistics*, Vol. I, 1966. Ottawa: Queen's Printer. 1968. p. 39.
6. Op. cit., p. 53.
7. Judek, Stanislaw. *Medical Manpower in Canada*. Ottawa: Queen's Printer, 1964.
8. Kohn, Robert. *Emerging Patterns in Health Care*. Ottawa: Queen's Printer, 1966.
9. Snell, Bernard. "The Changing Position of the Physician in Canadian Hospitals." *Medical Care.* 7:43–49, 1969. (supplement).
10. Kohn, Robert, op. cit.
11. Ibid.
12. Kohn, Robert, op. cit.
13. Department of National Health and Welfare. *Provincial Health Services by Program*. Health Care Series No. 23. Ottawa: the Department.
14. Ibid.
15. Govan, Elizabeth, S. L. *Voluntary Health Organisations in Canada*. Ottawa: Queen's Printer, 1966.
16. Department of National Health and Welfare. *Provincial Health Services by Program*. Health Care Series No. 23. Ottawa: the Department.
17. Royal Commission on Health Services, op. cit.
18. Paynter, K. J. *Dental Education in Canada*. Ottawa: Queen's Printer, 1965.
19. Robson, R. A. H. *Sociological Factors Affecting Recruitment into the Nursing Profession*. Ottawa: Queen's Printer, 1967; and Kohn, Robert. *Emerging Patterns in Health Care*. Ottawa: Queen's Printer, 1966.
20. Department of National Health and Welfare. *Health and Welfare Services in Canada 1969*. Ottawa: the Department.
21. *Royal Commission on Health Services*, Vol. 1. Ottawa: Queen's Printer, 1964, p. 35.
22. Department of National Health and Welfare. *Health and Welfare Services in Canada 1969*. Ottawa.

Chapter 6

Medical Care in the U.S.S.R.

JOHN FRY, M.D., F.R.C.S., F.R.C.G.P.
Consultant, World Health Organisation and
Family Physician, London, England

and

L. CROME, M.C., M.R.C.P.
Chairman, Society for Cultural Relations with the U.S.S.R. and
Neuropathologist, Queen Mary's Hospital for Children,
Carshalton, Surrey, England

The population of the U.S.S.R. the largest country in the world (8·6 million square miles) is now (1971) more than 242 millions, but occupying such a vast land mass the U.S.S.R. is relatively sparsely populated with a population density of 27 per square mile. Many ethnic groups make up the population and schools have to teach in more than 61 local languages, and whilst the largest ethnic group are the Caucasian Slavs of the west who make up three-quarters of the Soviet population, other sizeable groups are Turks, who comprise Uzbeks, Kuzakhs and Turkumen, Mongolians and Asiatics.

The U.S.S.R. is still a "young" nation. Less than 10 per cent of the population are over the age of 60 and the problems of caring for an ageing population have not yet presented. The post-world war II boom in babies occurred in U.S.S.R. as in all other nations of the world and the age group of 15–40 is the largest section of the population. Retirement from work at present is at 60 for men and 55 for women.

Constitutional Structure

The 240 millions of U.S.S.R. are members of a Federation of 15 Republics, the largest being the Russian Federation in the west, with well over 100 millions, and the Ukraine with over 45 millions.

Each Republic has certain degrees of independence with its own elected Soviet Councils and Ministries with local regional duties.

Since 1917 the constitutional structure and organisation have followed the Socialist pattern. There is a single political party, the

Communist Party. There is State ownership and State responsibility for most productive and cultural activities.

The political system centres around the Communist party which has 14 million members. This represents some 12 per cent of the working adult population. Entry is competitive and is based on merit and achievement and service to the State.

Admission to the Party usually follows participation in the Pioneer movement for children between 10 and 16 years of age and in the Young Communist movement (the Komsomols) for the 15–26 year olds. As entry to the Communist party, so entry into these groups is competitive and progress depends also on achievements and service.

Administrative Structure

The administrative structure is made up of units of decreasing population size from national to local levels. Each administrative unit level has its own similar organisation corresponding to the level above – very much like the Russian wooden doll, of the same pattern and shape but of decreasing size.

1. The topmost level is the *National* administration which plans and directs policies for the whole of the U.S.S.R. and its 240 million people.

   At this level is the *Supreme Soviet* in whom all legislative powers are placed. The Supreme Soviet is made up of two chambers of elected representatives, almost all of whom must be members of the Communist Party.

   One chamber is the *Council of the Union* with representatives (1 to 300,000 people) who are elected from a single party list by the people direct. The other chamber, the *Council of Nationalities,* consists of representatives from the Federated Republics; these representatives are persons who have been elected to serve on the Republic councils. Thus, both of these chambers consist of elected members, one directly and the other indirectly.

   The Supreme Soviet elects its own administrative body, the *Praesidium,* with a chairman and some 35 other members and the praesidium then appoints the executive Soviet Ministers who work together in the *Soviet Council of Ministries.*

   Within this Council, and a member of the Cabinet, is the *Soviet Minister of Health* who is responsible eventually to the Supreme Soviet for the administration and organisation of the national health services.

2. The Union is divided into 15 *Republics* and their general administrative structure mirrors that at the national level. Thus each of the 15 Republics has a Minister of Health who is a member of

the Government of the Republic and who also reports directly to the Minister of the Supreme Soviet.

3. All the larger Republics are composed of a number of *regions, or oblasts,* whose population ranges from 1–5 million.

The general administration of the oblast is made up of an Administrative Council of about 40 members, comprising representatives of the people, Trade Unions and other branches of local activities. The oblast council nominates an oblast executive committee of some 12 members, who then have to be elected by the whole local population.

The Chief Medical Officer of the oblast is a permanent member of the Administrative Council and often is also elected to the Executive Committee.

4. Each oblast is made up of *districts or rayons.* The number of rayons in each oblast varies from 10–50 and the population of each rayon ranges from 40,000 to 150,000 depending on the density of the population.

The Rayon represents the basic level of administration and in the large towns the rayons are part of the City Council administration, which acts as an oblast in cities such as Moscow, Leningrad and Kiev. The Council of each rayon consists of elected representatives. The rayon medical administration is under the charge of a chief medical officer who is responsible to the oblast medical department for all the medical services in the rayon.

5. The most peripheral medical levels are the *uchastoks or local neighbourhood wards.* These represent territorial divisions of a convenient size designed to provide personal care for the people. The size of each uchastok will vary with the speciality and form of care. Thus the uchastok paediatrician will have a population of up to 1,000 children to care for, the uchastok therapist an adult population of 2,000, the tuberculosis specialist one of 8,000 and the psychiatrist one of 20,000.

There is no special formal administrative structure for these neighbourhood units but they do form an essential functional part of medical and social work.

ECONOMIC AND SOCIAL SECURITY SYSTEMS

Since 1917 the Soviet Union has been economically organised on the Socialist pattern with ownership of almost all productive and many cultural activities vested in the State. There are exceptions. Some collective farms are owned by the former occupiers with sharing of profits. Many cultural activities are dependent on local initiatives with a considerable degree of freedom of choice.

Medical Care in the U.S.S.R.

The concentration of central power and decentralisation of executive administration have been designed towards the development of a planned economy with priorities being decided on scientific and pragmatic bases. A special feature is the mixture and working together of the State Administration and the Communist Party in parallel and side by side. Policy decisions as distinct from matters of administration are made by the Party and its Praesidium and are implemented and supervised at each administrative level by a corresponding committee or representative of the Party.

The Soviet system of national accounting differs from that employed by the Western nations in that it is based only on material products in calculating gross national income. Therefore no true comparisons can be made, although it has been suggested that the Soviet gross national product (G.N.P.) was approximately one-half that of U.S.A. in 1968.

Health and social security have been accepted as essential factors in sound Soviet economic development since successful economic progress can be achieved only by a healthy and confident community. The support of health, culture and social security occupies a large slice of the national Soviet budget.

By 1966 it is stated that the social and cultural budget accounted for 40 per cent of the total Union budget.

This budget supported three main and somewhat distinct sectors – education and science; health, sport and physical culture; and social security and welfare.

It is difficult to be precise on the exact amounts and proportions of this budget that is devoted to health, but it was stated to the W.H.O. Travelling Seminar on organisation of Medical Care in 1967 that approximately 7·2 per cent of the total Soviet budget is devoted to health and associated activities.

In the Soviet system it is assumed and planned that there will be no real unemployment because work is allocated and shared by all. There are no special plans therefore to care for the unemployed. Those who are "unemployable" either because of medical or social disabilities are registered as such and receive state grants.

Special grants are available also for war veterans, maternity grounds, for sickness absence from work and for retirement pensions.

Vital Statistics

Birth Rate	18·4	per 1,000
Death Rate	10	per 1,000
Maternal Mortality	32	per 100,000 births
Infant Mortality	28	per 1,000 births
Divorce Rate	2	per 1,000
	18	per 100 marriages

180

PRINCIPLES AND PHILOSOPHIES UNDERLYING MEDICAL CARE IN THE U.S.S.R.

Medical care services and the health programmes are part of the overall national socio-economic plan and take their place with other national policies and developments. All such activities are based on forward planning, regular systematic reviews and assessments of quality and standards related to many indices prepared by the Soviet Ministry of Health. The financing of the health services is largely from central national funds and not through taxation or by any form of personal insurance. In addition certain special facilities are paid for by trade unions, collective farms and industries.

Free Medical Care

Medical care and services are free to all. The whole population is covered. Services include regular medical examination and screening for preventive and therapeutic purposes, hospitalisation, specialist services at polyclinics, treatment of mental disorders, industrial and occupational health services, rehabilitation and recuperative holidays and health education.

Although for all purposes services are "free" there are some that carry with them nominal charges for the individual patient. Thus some fees are paid for drugs, dentures, spectacles and surgical appliances. Excluded from all or part of such fees are war veterans, children and adolescents and persons undergoing "dispenserisation" care and chronic invalids, thus in fact, more than a half of the total population is exempt from all fees.

In large cities there are also a small number of private fee-paying polyclinics, where people can receive private care from a panel of eminent specialists appointed by the State. These fee-paying clinics are part also of the national medical service and exist to provide opportunities for individuals to seek additional medical opinions to those available in local polyclinics.

Universal Availability and Accessibility

Medical care is available freely to all Soviet citizens throughout life and this applies also to foreign visitors.

Services are planned and organised on a territorial basis so that all those living in specific localities, rayons and oblasts are able to receive care from those facilities in that particular sector. There is no free choice of doctor and patient. Allocation is on a geographical basis according to place of residence and the physicians and associated staff appointed to care for that particular area.

The principles of ready availability and accessibility have applied to rural as well as urban regions. In urban communities ready and easy access has been provided to the local polyclinics through good public transport facilities. In rural areas the widely dispersed and small communities have created problems of access which have been overcome through the use of trained medical auxiliaries, "feldshers", who work under the direct supervision and responsibility of physicians from the local polyclinic and who provide care and supervision at local rural medical outposts.

The wide use of modern transport services such as helicopters and small airplanes, has made the provision of care for outlying communities much easier.

Specialisation

All physicians in the U.S.S.R. are considered as "specialists" in their work. "Generalists" disappeared as a group some 30 years ago.

Specialisation is a salient feature of the Soviet system of medical care and there are now 75 specialities recognised after appropriate training and examination.

Specialisation begins with the student on entry into medical school. The young student of 18–19 has to select one of four faculties in a medical school – therapy (general medicine), paediatrics, hygiene and public health, or stomatology (dental surgery). Having selected one, he eventually qualifies either as a therapist, paediatrician, hygienist or stomatologist, and he works as such in the profession.

Further postgraduate specialisation is open to all physicians. A 2-year specialist course exists for "ordinants" or doctors who do not aspire to an academic degree and a 3-year course for "aspirants" or trainees in teaching hospitals seeking further academic qualifications such as the degree of candidate of medical science.

Prevention

Great emphasis is placed on prevention of disease in all fields of medical care in U.S.S.R., preventive work involves all physicians.

Techniques of prevention include compulsory prophylactic immunisation, regular screening and supervision of vulnerable groups (dispenserisation), preventive admission to hospital of certain individuals with conditions such as peptic ulcer, chronic chest conditions and high blood pressure, group therapy and rehabilitation for persons with certain disorders at prophylactoria sited at large industrial units, environmental controls and energetic and widespread health education.

Public Participation

Medical care is ineffective unless there is full public participation and support and in the Soviet Union this principle is being put into practice.

More than 45 million (out of 100 million adults) have taken courses in first aid and hygiene and approximately one-quarter of these, or one to every 10 households, serves voluntarily as a *health volunteer*.

These health volunteers give their services freely in hospitals, polyclinics, emergency units and blood transfusion stations and they also play an important role in maintaining local hygiene and sanitary standards. They are used also in encouraging individuals to attend follow-up clinics at polyclinics for dispenserisation purposes.

The organisation of these services are through Councils of Voluntary Public Service. These councils are attached to most medical, curative and prophylactic units and pharmacies. On each Council there are representatives of trades unions, collective farms and industrial undertakings together with members of the public including housewives, pensioners and others.

The Red Cross and Red Crescent Society has a membership of more than 70 million and trained members man health and first aid posts on farms, factories and offices.

BASIC MEDICAL STRUCTURE AND HEALTH ADMINISTRATION

The Soviet medical services are part of the total social and economic structure and as such follow the general administrative pattern. Within the medical services there is no separation of personal and public services.

The aims are to meet the stated principles and to ensure that services are available to all.

1. At the summit there is the *Council of Ministers of the U.S.S.R.* in which the Minister of Health is a member of the Cabinet.

2. The *Ministry of Health of the U.S.S.R.* is headed by the Minister of Health who has been traditionally a practising physician and who undertakes his ministerial work in a part-time capacity. He is assisted by 4–6 deputy ministers, who are also physicians, each of whom has charge of a department with departmental tasks. The total staff of the Soviet Ministry is around 900 of whom 600 are physicians. The total may seem small for a nation of 240 millions but it must be remembered that the Ministry is a policy-making body and is not involved actively in local administration. The fact that two out of three of the Ministry staff are physicians, and that they occupy most of the senior positions, illustrates that the U.S.S.R. medical administration is carried out by trained physician-administrators and not by lay-administrators.

3. *Ministries of Health of the Soviet Republics*
   Each of the 15 Republics has its own Ministry of Health headed

N

by a Minister of Health appointed by the elected Central Soviet of each Republic.

Each Ministry collaborates closely with the national Ministry. The functions of the Republic Ministry of Health are to implement the national policies in their own territory and to prepare and administer the budget.

Almost all funds come from central sources and there is no local taxation. Each republic is involved in medical education and is responsible for a number of medical schools for physicians and paramedical staff.

4. *The Region (Oblast)*

Republics are divided into administrative regions or "oblasts" with populations of 1–5 millions. A large city of this size, functions as an "oblast".

The head of the Regional medical services is the chief medical officer who is a member of the Executive Council.

The medical appointment is usually full-time but the physician is encouraged to continue in some medical work or research in addition to administrative duties.

He (or more often she) is responsible for all the health services in the oblast – this includes hospitals, polyclinics and public health services. There is no independence of any professional group or sector within the oblast.

Clinical responsibilities rest with the chief physicians at the main Regional hospital. In each speciality there is a chief physician who is responsible for the organisation and quality of services within his speciality in the whole region. Thus the chief Surgeon will be responsible for the provision of regional sergical services. He will be involved in planning, continuing training, quality controls and regular liaison. In this work he will pay regular visits to the hospitals and polyclinics and ensure that appropriate services are available. This includes the organisation of cooperation between hospitals and staff so that patients may be placed in the correct hospital or unit in the region appropriate to the patient's needs.

5. *District (Rayon)*

Each Region is divided into 10–50 districts or "rayons". The population of each district ranges from 40,000–150,000 depending on the population density.

The District is the basic formal administrative unit, and in rural areas it has a seperate administrative structure, but in large cities and urban areas it is part of the city administration.

Within each district there is one or more hospital, a number of polyclinics and at least one public health unit. The chief physician of the district, who is appointed by the District Council and is usually the senior physician at the hospital, is responsible for all the medical services in his district. Thus, he supervises hospitals, polyclinics and public health services as a single service. And whilst he has considerable freedom of action, he is still responsible to the chief medical officer of the Region for general policy organisation.

6. *Neighbourhood (Uchastok)*

The neighbourhood unit, has no formal political or administrative representation but it is a convenient territorial and operational subdivision on which to base general and personal services. The size varies according to the speciality, but for the basic specialities of child care and general medicine (therapy) it is around 4,000 persons.

Each administrative level has two prime functions – the implementation of national agreed policies and the preparation of a budget. This creates some limitation of independence at each level but makes for clearly recognised responsibilities and duties.

Community and Regional Planning

Planning medical care services is a total operation in U.S.S.R. involving all administrative levels from the rayons to the supreme Soviet.

It is based on definition of standards and objectives to be achieved and assessments of local needs and deficiencies that have to be corrected.

The norms and standards of quantity and quality of resources are set by the Soviet Ministry of Health and the local assessments are carried out through regular, 5-yearly, "health inventories" or censuses by public health (sanepid) units in the rayons and oblasts. Discovered deficiencies are recorded and corrected wherever possible.

Budgeting

The preparation of the health budget is an overall annual experience. The work involves all levels from the district upwards. Starting at there the chief physician with the executive officers prepares a statement of his expected needs for the coming year. This is sent to the Regional authorities for approval and correlation, and in turn submitted to the Ministry of Health of the respective Republic thence to the Ministry of Health of the U.S.S.R.

The budgeting is based on running costs and capital expenditure and approval is usual.

The funds allocated are administered by finance officers at the various levels.

Although there is considerable local independence for executive functions there is no financial or economic autonomy for any of the institutions. All are part of a great system and have to fit into it.

THE MEDICAL PROFESSION

In the Soviet Union physicians and other members of the medical profession are recognised and accepted as skilled professional technical experts. They are considered to be on the same level as other skilled professional and technical groups. No special privileges are granted to physicians but they obviously occupy a reasonably high social status since there is keen competition for places in medical schools.

The "rights" of the medical profession and individual physicians are protected by their professional representation body on a trade union basis.

A feature of the Soviet medical profession is that nearly three out of every four (70 per cent) of physicians are women, but the proportion is changing since 40 per cent of medical students now are males. This high proportion of women as physicians is explained partly by the needs for men to undertake more arduous work in the early days

TABLE 6.1

Medical Resources of U.S.S.R.

Population	240 millions	
Total Physicians	*550,000	(including 70,000 dental surgeons)
Physicians per population	1 : 415	(1 : 480 if dental surgeons are excluded)
Physicians per 10,000	24	(21 per 10,000 if dental surgeons are excluded)
Medical Education Medical Schools	85	
Annual Number of medical graduates	30,000	(12 per 100,000 of population)
Nurses	35 per 10,000	
Other Paramedical workers	37 per 10,000	
Hospital Beds	9·6 per 1,000	

*70 per cent of all physicians are women.

of the Soviet Union, partly by the fact that this great increase in numbers of physicians trained in the immediate pre and post-war periods found an insufficient number of suitable male candidates and partly the relatively low salaries of many doctors.

TABLE 6.2

Percentages of Physicians in Specialities

Speciality	Percentage of all Physicians
Uchastok Physicians (unchastok therapists and paediatricians)	25
Medical Specialities (general medicine, infections diseases, paediatrics, radiology and pathology)	30
Surgical Specialities (general surgery, orthopaedics, ear, nose and throat, ophthalmology, thoracic and neuro surgery)	25
Psychiatry (neurology and psychiatry)	5
Others	15

Although 70 per cent of all physicians are females, in the top level medical administrative and clinical and research posts there are more men than women.

There are 75 recognised medical specialities, each with its own course of training and pattern of work.

The rates of physicians per 10,000 population in the different republics of the U.S.S.R. vary considerably:

Middle Grade Medical Workers

There are approximately 2 million "middle grade medical workers" in U.S.S.R., a rate of 80 per 10,000 of the population. These workers (Table 6.4) include nurses, paramedical auxiliaries in the recognised specialist fields of radiology, pathology, public health and dentistry. But there is also the group of "feldsher", or medical assistant, which is a special Soviet category that has existed since the last century.

The roles of these workers are to work in collaboration with and under the direction of physicians.

TABLE 6.3

Physicians per 10,000

U.S.S.R.	23·9
Western Republics	
Georgia	34·6
Latvia	31·4
Estonia	29·8
Armenia	27·2
Russia	24·9
Ukraine	23·1
Asiatic Republics	
Tadznik	14·9
Uzbek	16·9
Kayakh	18·4
Kirgiz	18.8

TABLE 6.4

U.S.S.R.—Middle Grade Medical Workers
per 10,000 of the population

	Rates per 10,000
Nurses (all grades)	33·9
Feldshers & Feldsher midwives	20·5
Midwives	7·4
Radiographers	0·9
Pathological laboratory assistants	2·8
Public Health Workers	4·2
Dental Technicians	0·8
Pharmacists	5·5
Others	3·5

Nurses in U.S.S.R. correspond to nurses in other systems but in addition to traditional nursing care they undertake a good deal of ward cleaning and organisation and much of the routine clerical and office work in the hospitals and polyclinics. They are less involved with technical medical procedures.

Technical assistants in the radiological, pathological, dental and public health services carry out routine technical tasks leaving anything more to the large number of physicians available.

The feldsher is unique in the Soviet system of medical care. The feldsher category is that of an all-purpose middle-grade worker who assists physicians in the medical, social, preventive and health educational fields. He, or more often, she, works in close collaboration with and under the supervision of a physician.

Historically the feldsher originated in the 17th century as a stop-gap for shortages of military physicians. Peter the Great innovated the grade of feldsher, who was a quickly-trained physician-substitute. The grade continued and spread to rural districts and until 1917 the feldsher had to function as a second-best physician, because there were no physicians available.

The grade was not abolished with the Revolution of 1917, but the roles of physician-substitution stopped. The feldsher was to act as an assistant to physicians and to undertake duties for which she would be specially trained.

There are now some half a million feldshers in U.S.S.R., who have been trained specifically to serve as middle-grade medical assistants. Their work is well defined and is supervised by a physician.

In rural areas they staff some 75,000 feldsher posts in outlying collective farms and villages and are linked closely with a local rural (uchastok) polyclinic – hospital. A physician based at this hospital visits the feldsher post regularly and is available for emergencies.

The work of the rural feldsher includes the care of minor medical and surgical conditions, supervision and follow-up of more major conditions under the direction of the physician, routine and regular preventive care, including immunisations and pre-symptomatic screening, health education and supervision of sanitation and public health services.

In the urban districts feldshers undertake more specialised duties in medical and social fields such as in polyclinics and special dispensaries, attached to industrial units, public health departments and in staffing the ambulance services.

Training for Physicians

Undergraduate Period

There are 85 *medical schools* in U.S.S.R., which in 1965 were graduating 28,000 physicians each year with a target of 40,000 by 1975. This means that in 1965 the graduating class in each medical school averaged 330 students. At present two-thirds of medical graduates are women.

All medical schools (medical institutes) are state-owned but have a certain degree of local autonomy and independence. The Soviet Ministry of Health is responsible directly for 10 schools and the others are administered by the Ministry of Health of the various Soviet

Republics. There is no common pattern of association with a university and most medical schools have only tenuous links with local universities.

Medicine is a popular career and there are up to 10 applicants for each place in a medical school. Selection is on merit, personal qualities and certain previous experience.

Merit is assessed on the results of an entrance examination in physics, chemistry and Russian language, literature and philosophy.

Personal qualities are assessed at interviews. Some priority is given to feldshers who are encouraged to switch to a medical training after three years or more work as a feldsher. In fact, between 20–30 per cent of all medical students are ex-feldshers. Consideration is given also to any public service that the potential medical student may have undertaken in the social, welfare and youth leadership fields. Medical education is free and students receive adequate maintenance grants.

Having been selected, the young student has to select one of three medical faculties in which he is to study and there may be different numbers of vacancies in each. Thus he must decide even before commencing on his medical training whether he is to enter the general therapeutic faculty, the paediatric faculty or the faculty of public health and hygiene. Once he has entered a faculty he will be trained as a therapist (general medical and surgical training), paediatrician or hygienist (public health medical officer).

The curriculum is standard and is followed by each medical school, lasting six years.

MEDICAL CARE – FLOW, COMPONENTS AND ROLES

Flow of Medical Care

The various levels of medical care are the family and personal self-care, first-contact care at the polyclinic, specialist care for the ambulatory either at the polyclinic or dispensary and care in hospitals of various degrees of specialisation.

There are differences in rural and urban districts.

In urban areas the situation is that the individual's first contact with medical care services is through the neighbourhood or "uchastok" physician, who is usually different for various members of the family. Thus a paediatrician will care for children, a therapist for adults and a gynaecologist for the feminine ailments of the mother.

The polyclinic services combine those of first-contact and specialist ambulatory care but the specialists who work at the polyclinic do not have hospital appointments. The local district hospital that provides general hospital services is staffed by a different staff from that which provides care in the polyclinics and the hospital is not involved in outpatient care.

In rural districts the first medical contact is usually the feldsher or feldsher-midwife based at a feldsher-midwife post in a village or collective farm.

The feldsher is supervised by and is in contact with, physicians at the local neighbourhood polyclinic-hospital. This structure combines the services of a polyclinic and hospital. The hospital beds generally are limited and rarely number over 100.

First-Contact Care

There is no free choice of first-contact physician in U.S.S.R. There is division into territorial neighbourhood units or uchastoks, each with an average population of 3,000–4,000, and the first contact medical care of this population is allocated to the local physicians. Thus there is a "uchastok" therapist who is responsible for the 2,000 or more adults in this locality and a "uchastok" paediatrician who cares for the 1,000 or so children. There also may be others involved, such as the industrial physician who provides care for those in industry and other occupations and whose patients may overlap to a certain degree with those of the therapist.

Each of these physicians will have a nurse attached, whose function is to assist not only in medical care but also to act as a receptionist and clinical assistant.

Neighbourhood physicians based as they are on a polyclinic will be able to have professional contacts with colleagues but to a considerable extent they work independently. Recently it has been decided to encourage the formation of groups of 4 physicians to work together and so to provide a team of doctors to care for a larger population and for this team of first-contact physicians to be associated with a regular specialist gynaecologist, surgeon, general physician and ear, nose and throat and eye specialists.

The work of the uchastok physicians will be concerned chiefly with the management of the more common and less serious medical and social problems, but in addition a considerable proportion of their time, perhaps more than one-third, will be spent in preventive work, routine screening for early stages of disease, health education and rehabilitation.

Rural Areas

The problems of providing accessible, available and quality medical services in rural areas are those of distance, scattered populations and attracting physicians and other staff to such areas. Conditions vary and there has to be flexibility of organisation.

These problems have been tackled in U.S.S.R. by breaking down the services into units staffed by medical assistants (feldshers) specially trained to undertake a certain degree of responsibility for therapeutic and preventive care and to work under the supervision of a physician.

In this way it has been possible to provide a system of complete accessibility and availability of medical services to all Soviet citizens.

Thus each feldsher or feldsher-midwife post may provide first-contact care by medical assistants for from 500–2,000 persons. Each feldsher is responsible for from 200–1,000 persons, depending on the population dispersal.

Feldshers are trained and able to manage minor medical ailments and the definitive care of less minor conditions such as pulmonary infections, strokes, cardiac failure and other chronic and longterm conditions under the direct supervision and control of the doctors who are based at the local uchastok polyclinic-hospital unit. Other work undertaken by feldshers is maintenance of public hygiene and sanitation, implementation of certain health screening and preventive programmes, including immunisations, antenatal and postnatal supervision and cervical cytology, and health education through cian(s), therapist(s), surgeon(s), obstetrician(s), and technician(s), for the diagnostic facilities. The numbers of medical staff will depend on the population cared for but the minimum will be a paediatrician, therapist and surgeon (and obstetrician) for a population of 4,000 persons.

Facilities for all units include a minimum of an operating theatre able to deal with most general surgical emergencies, diagnostic equipment such as x-ray machines, a small pathological laboratory and electrocardiogram.

Each rural polyclinic – hospital unit is related closely with a base rayon (district) hospital and there are good air, road and sea transport facilities that will either take patients to the larger hospital centre or specialists to the rural units.

The rural polyclinic-hospital combines the facilities of the polyclinic as a medical centre for amulatory patients with hospital beds for those requiring admission.

Depending on the locality and population density so each unit may care for populations between 4,000 and 20,000 persons, with hospital beds at a rate of 7–8 per 1,000 that is from 25–150 beds. The present trend is to close down the small units with fewer than 100 beds, to establish larger units and to develop better transport facilities to enable persons to travel further to better-equipped centres.

Urban areas

In urban areas the implementation of availability, accessibility and care by specialists takes on somewhat different patterns from that in rural areas.

The main features in urban areas are:

1. Those living in a defined geographical neighbourhood division are allocated (without choice) to the 'uchastok' physician responsible for that area.

2. These physicians are all recognised as trained "specialists". Each has been trained since the student undergraduate period as either a paediatrician or therapist, and deals with the medical ailments of adults. They confine their care to the group of population or diseases in which they have been trained.

   There has been no system of "general practice" or "family medicine" since the late 1930's.

3. The work base for first-contact-care is the *urban polyclinic.* These are the community centres for primary medical care and for specialist care for amulatory cases.

   In large cities there are separate polyclinics for the various specialities.

   Thus in cities such as Moscow, Leningrad and Kiev there are separate polyclinics for adults, one for 40,000–50,000 persons and for children one for 10,000–15,000 children.

   There are also other polyclinics or dispensaries that provide care for tuberculosis, obstetrics and gynaecology (women's consultation clinics) and other specialities.

   Since there is no emphasis on "family medicine" there are no all-purpose general family polyclinics in large cities providing care for all the members of one family.

   In small cities there are general polyclinics that combine adult, child and other specialist services, but even in these there is definite distinction between the various services for children, adults, etc.

Specialist Care for Ambulatory Patients

In U.S.S.R. the specialist "outpatient" care that is necessary for ambulant patients is available at polyclincs and special dispensaries. The differences between polyclincs and dispensaries are largely in the degrees of specialisation. Thus, whereas a large number of specialities may function from a polyclinic, a dispensary is restricted to a single speciality. These dispensaries exist only in large cities with populations large enough to warrant their existence. For example, in Moscow there are dispensaries for tuberculosis, mental illnesses, skin and venereal diseases, cancer, rheumatism, heart ailments and "women's consultation clinics" for obstetric and gynaecological conditions.

The polyclinic provides the central core of specialised care in the community outside the hospital.

It combines first-contact and specialist services. The polyclinic doctor is a recognised specialist who has undergone a set period of postgraduate training and examination and he acts as a specialist for ambulatory cases. He restricts his work to his speciality and patients may be referred to him by neighbourhood physicians (doctors-of-first-contact) or by other specialist colleagues, or the patient has direct access to him. Thus, it is quite acceptable for persons to attend directly any of the specialists in a polyclinic or at a special dispensary. There is no rigid system of inter-professional referrals.

As a rule the work of the polyclinic specialist is restricted to out-patient care and he has no duties in or access to hospital beds although some polyclinics have beds for short-term care. If a patient requires admission to hospital then he comes under the care of another set of hospital specialists. Inpatient and outpatient work, services and staff are separate. For educational and training purposes there are regular exchanges of junior and middle-grade staff between polyclinics and local rayon hospitals.

The organisation and planning of polyclinics and allied services is a major task of the oblast health department.

In Moscow with its population of $6\frac{1}{2}$ millions there are 600 polyclinics and 500 dispensaries.

There are special industrial polyclinics either within the community or at large industrial units. At these polyclinics great emphasis is placed on prevention of disease and health maintenance and a special and interesting feature is the prophylactorium. This is a residential unit where those at work who suffer from certain chronic conditions such as chronic bronchitis, heart disease, peptic ulcers, rheumatism or psychiatric illnesses can be brought together for resi-

TABLE 6.5

Speciality	Ratio of Polyclinic Specialist per population
General Medicine	1 : 2,500
General Surgery	1 : 8,000
Dermatology	1 : 17,000
Ophthalmology	1 : 20,000
Psychiatry-Neurology	1 : 17,000
Ear, Nose and Throat	1 : 4,000
Gynaecology	1 : 8,000
Tuberculosis	1 : 8,000
ALL	1 : 550

dential group therapy after work and rehabilitated and re-educated for health. Not only are the patients treated but relatives also are invited to learn how their health may be maintained.

Polyclinics are well utilised. In urban areas it is estimated that the annual attendance rates are 9–10 per person. Of these one-half are for general first-contact care and one-half are for specialist care. In rural areas the proportions are the same but the attendances are lower, at 5–6 per person per year.

There is a high staffing ratio of specialists in polyclinics and the ratios in table 6.5 are representative.

HOSPITALS

Soviet hospitals are primarily inpatient units, and staffed by different physicians and nurses from the polyclinics which are the centres for specialist care for ambulatory patients, the hospital's relations with the community are through the polyclinics. In urban districts one polyclinic is generally sited within the district hospital's grounds and exchanges of staff take place regularly with this and other local polyclinics.

One in five of the population is admitted to hospital each year. This high rate of hospitalisation is explained partly by the large numbers of general hospital beds available (almost 9 per 1,000) but also because of the policies relating to hospital admission. There is a much more liberal attitude and many patients are admitted "prophylactically" in attempts to prevent the conditions deteriorating.

Hospital Administration

Medical administration in U.S.S.R. is carried out by specially trained physicians. Not only are all top hospital administrators physicians but they are also in active practice and combine administration with clinical work. Even the Minister of Health of the U.S.S.R. is by tradition a working physician.

There is competitive selection for these hospital administrative appointments that carry extra remuneration, privileges and status within the profession. Selected trainees undergo a 3–6 month training at special institutes.

Emergency Medical Services

There is a national system organised and designed to deal with all forms of medical emergencies, from everyday accidents and transport of the sick, to major disasters such as earthquakes.

The service, as is all medical care in U.S.S.R., is free and generally available and also concentrates on prevention as well as service.

The services are organised on ambulance stations each of which covers an urban population of 50,000–80,000, and in a rural area is based on the neighbourhood polyclinic – hospital unit. The establishment, at present, consists of one ambulance to 15,000 persons in an urban area and one to 10,000 in a rural area with the greater difficulties of distance and terrain.

Ambulance stations are generously staffed with physicians and trained auxiliaries. For example, the central ambulance station in Kiev has a staff of 300 physicians and 400 feldshers for a population of $1\frac{1}{4}$ millions. For routine transport of "cold" cases one or two feldshers man the ambulance in addition to the driver, but for all emergencies a physician has to travel in the ambulances.

The ambulance stations have functions that extend beyond the transport of persons to and from hospitals and polyclinics. They are a part of a national system of medical care.

All modern forms of land, sea and air transport are used and in a country as large as U.S.S.R., air ambulances are a prominent feature transporting not only patients but also physicians to the sick.

Planned hospital admissions, including maternity cases, and the transport of road traffic accidents are the common types of calls, but with these and in other situations there is considerable specialisation. Thus, special teams are used to transport maternity cases, children, infectious diseases and psychiatric cases.

There are special groups which travel in specially designed ambulances to deal with cardiac, neurological, mental, traumatic and obstetric emergencies. Their purpose is to take modern emergency and resuscitative care and equipment to the patient. These units therefore are staffed by two skilled physicians and two feldshers. The cardiac ambulance, for example, will include an electrocardiogram, defibrillilator, electronic pacemaker and drugs and equipment for intravenous therapy and anaesthesia required to resuscitate cases with sudden cardiac collapse. The special prevent accidents and teach the public in early and first-aid measures of all emergencies, are all a part of the work of these ambulance stations.

These stations also function as central public medical information centres. The public are able to 'phone them direct and get advice on management of emergencies, on nursing persons, who may have been involved in accidents and admitted to hospital, and on other more general medical matters.

Resources and Utilisation

In the U.S.S.R. in 1966 there were 9.6 hospital beds per 1,000. These were not equally distributed throughout the nation. The range was from a low of 8.1 in Soviet Armenia to a high of 11.6 in Soviet Latvia.

This rate of 9.6 beds per 1,000 included 0.93 per 1,000 for mental illnesses (a rate that is four times lower than those of U.S.A. and U.K.). Future plans are already in operation to aim for a national rate of 13.2 per 1,000 hospital beds and of these 11.2 per 1,000 are to be for general care and 2.0 per 1,000 for mental illnesses.

In addition to hospitals there are many "sanatoria" or convalescent homes which are used either as nursing or welfare homes for long-stay chronic diseases or for rehabilitation, convalescent or recuperative holiday purposes.

Future trends in the hospital field include an increase in the overall number of hospital beds to reach 13.2 per 1,000 and 3 per 1,000 in sanatoria (to meet an annual hospitalisation rate of 64 per cent); parallel with the increase in quantity more emphasis is to be paid to quality criteria and controls, and efforts are to be made to improve the turn-over and occupancy rates; larger hospital units of 1,000–1,200 beds are to replace small units; this increase in the size of hospitals will be associated with more 'diversification' – there will be more special units in district (rayon) hospitals and also more 'special' hospitals in large cities to concentrate on specific medical problems; a high priority is to be given to rural areas where there are many old hospitals in need of replacement; and all hospital development is to be carried out in close harmony with other community services.

COMMUNITY AND HOME CARE

In U.S.S.R. considerable emphasis is still placed on home care. For example almost one-half of the daily work of the uchastok doctors is set aside for home-visiting. In addition involvement of the public as volunteer health activists ensures considerable public interest and participation in preventive care, health education and self-management of minor conditions.

Although admission to hospital presents no difficulties as there are so many hospital beds available, the polyclinics and dispensaries serve as important community health centres and the uchastok principle of territorial responsibility enables continuing care, interest and participation by a few doctors who become well known to the community.

As well as providing medical care the polyclinics are involved actively in health educational programmes, in preventive care, including screening of the population and follow-up of vulnerable individuals, and in rehabilitation of the chronic sick and those recovering from acute illnesses.

In all these community and social exercises in public health the "sanepids" play an important role.

PUBLIC AND ENVIRONMENTAL HEALTH – THE SANEPIDS

The "sanepids" (sanitary-epidemiological units) are the basis of public health in U.S.S.R.

There are 5,000 of these sanepids, or one to 50,000 persons. Thus there is approximately one public health unit for each polyclinic area and 1–3 for each district, depending on its size and geography. They are staffed by 40,000 "hygienists" (or 7–8 per cent of all physicians). Hygienists are physicians who have undergone a specialised training and education for their work in the public health field. This training extends from their entry into medical school as undergraduates right through their postgraduate period.

The *roles* of the Public Health Units are three-fold.

1. *Supervisory* to ensure high levels of local hygiene and sanitation and for this they have considerable powers of inspection and direction; powers that are independent of all other local authorities.

2. *Organisational* – They are involved actively in positive steps to improve the living and working conditions of their community. For these purposes they are involved in maintaining a system of notification of infectious diseases and of analysing regular morbidity records and data that are sent to them from polyclinics and hospitals. They also supervise the standard programme of preventive immunisation. They are concerned with environmental standards at schools, creches and nurseries, at home and at all the various working establishments in their territory. They are responsible for ensuring safe food, clean air, provision for leisure and rest. They are involved in the organisation of the health education, coordination of local health services and in the liaison of certain social services such as housing and social welfare.

3. *Economic Forward Planning* They also have the important and responsible function of preparing plans for the future development and growth of local medical and social services. This planning is based on regular reports and data and on the 5-year "health inventory" which is carried out by each public health unit into its own area. This exercise involves visits and inspection of all medical facilities and assessing their quality in relation to certain provided norms and standards.

SPECIALISED SERVICES

Dispenserisation and other Preventive Services

Prevention of disease and health maintenance is one of the basic principles on which Soviet medical care is founded. Amongst the preventive services are the general attention and care paid to public and personal hygiene and sanitation and the more specific programmes of immunisation against accepted conditions such as diphtheria, tetanus and pertassis, smallpox, poliomyelitis, tuberculosis and measles. Others are the preventive screening and follow-up under the "dispenserisation" scheme and the efforts at health education.

Dispenserisation

Originally a feature of the work of the specialised dispensaries the scheme has been extended to cover the whole medical system and is an important part of the work of all polyclinics. Working the scheme accounts for 10–20 per cent of the time spent by the neighbourhood therapists and for 50–60 per cent of the paediatrician's time.

The special features of the scheme are as follows:

1. Early diagnosis of clinical and social disorders through regular screening and examination.
2. Definition of "vulnerable" individuals who may require special care.
3. Correction of underlying medical and social causes and early treatment of detected conditions.
4. Regular and continuing follow-up of specified conditions such as high blood pressure, peptic ulcers, coronary heart disease and other cardiac disorders, obesity, glaucoma, chronic bronchitis, asthma, tuberculosis, cancer, strokes and others.
5. Health building through special rehabilitation and various social and medical supplements.

At present the "dispenserisation" scheme covers some 85 million out of all 240 million Soviet citizens, but it is aimed to extend it to cover all the population, hence the need for more physicians and medical auxiliaries. The present groups selected for annual examination and follow-up include – all children, adolescents and expectant mothers, active sportsmen, those in specified occupations and those suffering from specified diseases.

The various steps in the programme are: selection and call of the individuals from a central register; examination and screening by the polyclinic physicians; assessment and definition of personal problems; correction of underlying medical and social defects, the latter may

o

include housing, marital problems and work conditions; action is taken at the polyclinic or through the sanepid unit, in case of social problems, to remedy defects where possible; and follow-up of specified individuals and groups of diseases either at polyclinics or dispensaries.

Health Education

It is estimated that more than 45 million or one-half of all adult Soviet citizens have taken special health educational courses in first-aid, hygiene and simple medicine. They provide a sound base on which further and continuing health education can be organised.

The volunteer health "activists" are a part of the scheme of public health education. These are as the name suggests, unpaid volunteers who are further trained in elementary hygiene, first-aid and the structure and organisation of the medical care system. There is one such "activist" to every ten dwellings and their role is to assist in maintenance of hygiene and sanitary standards and to help in organising the "dispenserisation" scheme by encouraging attendance for screening and follow-up examinations.

RESEARCH

Formal medical research in U.S.S.R. is carried out at specialised Research Institutes and Academies. Some units at Regional hospitals also undertake clinical research, but this depends, as anywhere, on individual interests and enthusiasm.

All research activities are supported by grants from the Ministry of Health. Research projects have to be approved by a standing committee of the Ministry before a grant is given and regular assessment and reports are required for continuing support.

Operational research is a continuing exercise affecting all levels of the Soviet medical systems. From the very peripheral feldsher-midwife posts and polyclinics right through to the Ministry of Health there is constant collection and analysis of data relating to work-load, its volume and nature, its quality and end results.

From the polyclinics and district hospitals daily records and data are sent to the local records and statistics unit at the rayon sanepid stations. There they are analysed and sent on to the Regional medical department and finally to the Ministry of Health in Moscow.

At the Ministry of Health there is a constant exercise taking place of assessing the present operational state, as shown by on-going records, and working out and developing optimal standards, indices or norms which should be arrived at in the future.

SPECIAL SERVICES

Maternity and Child Care Services

If there is any "privileged" class it is the children, and considerable efforts have been and are being made to develop high standards of care for children right from the antenatal period through to infancy, childhood and adolescence.

Maternity Care

Maternity care is completely free and services are readily available accessible to all women in all areas, and all obstetric deliveries are planned to take place in special maternity hospitals or homes. The importance and pattern of antenatal care is understood and accepted by the public and an important field of health education is during this antenatal period. Mothers are instructed on the need for regular supervision, on health maintenance and on child care after delivery.

Provisions for the social welfare of expectant mothers are written into Soviet law. There are generous maternity grants and leave from work is expected for at least six months, three months before and three months after delivery. In certain cases this leave may be extended with full pay for a period of twelve months.

There has always been a liberal attitude towards voluntary termination of pregnancy and birth control. If a pregnant woman wishes her pregnancy to be terminated she sees the obstetrician at the women's consultation clinic. It is the obstetrician's duty to try and dissuade the woman from such action but if she remains adamant and insists on termination this is carried out on payment of a fee by the woman. Family planning advice is also available also at the Women's Consultation clinics. Until now mechanical "check" methods such as sheaths, caps and intrauterine devices have been standard methods used. Hormonal tablets have not yet been accepted beyond the experimental stage.

With this organisation the quality indices show a good level of maternity care. The overall birth rate in U.S.S.R. is 18 per 1,000, maternal mortality rate 32 per 100,000, and infant mortality 28 per 1,000.

CHILD CARE

Families are smaller, birth rate is falling, more mothers are working and the grandmother has a more responsible role as "housekeeper". All these are social happenings in U.S.S.R. Added to this are continuing, but easing, housing difficulties in large cities, such as Moscow and Kiev, to which many from the countryside have migrated.

There are nevertheless generous family grants for children and a national pattern of child care has been evolved. Before school there are creches for infants in their first year and 10 per cent of all such infants attend these; nurseries care for 25 per cent of all children aged 1–3 years; and kindergartens are attended by more than 3 out of 4 pre-school children aged 3–7. All these establishments are provided by the State and are supervised by the local children's polyclinic and the educational authorities.

The local paediatricians are the children's doctors-of-first-contact. Each such physician is responsible for up to 1,000 children under 15, with between 40 and 50 first-year infants. Working with each paediatrician are one or two nurses who have special roles in this work.

The pattern of child care that has been evolved is as follows.

1. During the antenatal period, mothers, particularly the primiparous, are educated and prepared for child care, and during the month preceding delivery they are visited at home by the locality's paediatrician and nurse who will look after the baby, and general discussion and preparations made.
2. After delivery and during the week's stay in the maternity hospital they are shown how to care for their new born baby.
3. Within two days of returning home the locality's paediatrician and nurse visit the mother at home and arrange for continuing supervision at the local polyclinic.
4. During the first year of life monthly visits to the polyclinic are arranged and regular examinations and immunisations carried out.
5. During the second year of life 3-monthly attendances are encouraged.
6. During the third year, two attendances for assessment of development are expected.
7. From 3–7 years an annual visit is arranged.
8. A pre-school examination (at 7) is carried out by a group of specialists at the polyclinic, i.e., ear, nose and throat, eyes, etc.
9. At school an annual examination is carried out.

Mental Illness

Because of the belief that the environmental influences of a socialist regime reduced the prevalence of mental illness there have been fewer resources available in U.S.S.R. for hospitalisation.

In fact reports suggest that the prevalence of psychoses and neuroses is not very different from that in U.S.A. and U.K. Thus data from

Shepherd et al., (1966)[1] and Field (1967)[2] show that the annual prevalence of psychoses in U.S.S.R. is 4 per 1,000 and of neuroses 59 per 1,000, and the corresponding rates for U.S.A. are 6 and 53, and for U.K., 6 and 89.

The care of the mental sick in U.S.S.R. follows a recognisable pattern of flow, with the common and less serious mental illnesses being managed by the neighbourhood physicians in the polyclinics. If the patient requires more specialised attention then he is referred either to a "neuro pathologist" (psychiatrist) at the polyclinic or to a psychiatric dispensary, if there is one in the area.

The psychiatric dispensary is a special polyclinic that deals only with the mentally sick. It is staffed by psychiatrists, some of whom are also on the staff of the local mental hospital. Patients have direct access to these psychiatric dispensaries and referral through a general polyclinic is unnecessary. These dispensaries are able to carry out long-term care and supervision of patients in the community and their psychiatrists and nurses are able to visit patients at home and to organise various rehabilitation and health educational programmes.

Mental hospitals in U.S.S.R. tend to be large and removed some distance away from the city centres. Standard methods of psychopharmacology are used and in addition there is considerable emphasis on group therapy and application of Pavlovian principles.

In terms of resources there are in U.S.S.R. 9 psychiatrists per 100,000 and 0.93 psychiatric hospital beds.

Comment

It is reasonable to recognise that what the U.S.S.R. has achieved in the last 50 years in its medical services has been brought about by continual analysis, direction of work forces, and specialisation. Nevertheless, the importance and influence of the U.S.S.R. and its systems of medical care range well beyond its own boundaries. Its system of care being an integral part of socialist philosophy has created similar patterns in Eastern Europe and China and could in the future be the basis of medical care services in many developing nations of the world.

References

1. Shepherd, M. et al. *Psychiatric Illness in General Practice*. London: Oxford University Press, 1966.
2. Field, M. G. *New Aspects of Mental Health Services*. London: Pergamon Press, 1967.

Chapter 7

Medical Care in the Developing Nations

N. R. E. Fendall, M.D., B.SC., D.P.H.

Professor of Tropical Community Health,
School of Tropical Medicine, Liverpool, England

Formerly, Director, Medical Services, Kenya; Staff Member, The
Rockefeller Foundation; Regional Director, the Population Council,
New York, U.S.A.

The roots of backwardness lie not in a lack of knowledge, but in an inability to harness such knowledge to the benefit of humanity.

Health is a purchasable commodity; and health plays a major role in economic development. The industrialised nations are now benefiting from years of investment in health services. The underdeveloped territories have hardly begun to participate in the scientific revolution; being still in the pre-agricultural era of hunting, fishing and a shifting agriculture. Others are experiencing the agricultural revolution with settled land tenure and consolidated holdings. Yet others have still large sections of the population nomadic. Still others are entering the era of the industrial revolution, with some prime industries, but most secondary industries. There is not one "underdeveloped" world, but many countries in differing stages of development.

No single index can reflect adequate differences in standards of living between nations. A United Nations Expert Committee listed twelve factors which would need to be improved if levels of living were to be raised. These are: Health, including demographic conditions; food and nutrition; education, including literacy and skills; conditions of work; employment situations; aggregate consumption and savings; transportation; housing, including household facilities; clothing; recreation and entertainment; social security; and human freedoms. Conversely, all these factors are involved in the striving for better health.

The common factors that comprise the state of underdevelopment are limited economic resources, paucity of educational services and trained manpower, excessive fertility levels, malnutrition, a common disease pattern, and an entrenched conservative peasant agricultural society.

It is evident from many studies that 70 per cent of the world population still lives in extreme poverty, with great disparity between the rich and the poor. Two types of economies exist in most of the underdeveloped territories, the monetary economy of big business and mechanised farming, and that dependent upon subsistence farming. It is the latter that supports the bulk of the population: some 60 per cent or more.

The situation is not improving to any material extent, even though incomes per head of the underdeveloped territories increased by between a fifth and quarter during the 1950s. This rate has subsequently slowed down: much of it being absorbed in a rapid population growth rate. During the same period (1950s) average income per head in the developed countries rose by a third and in the 1960s has accelerated. Thus, the gap between the underdeveloped and developed nations grows wider. The rate of growth is not such as to inspire any optimism, but rather to indicate that unless traditional methods of fostering development can be appreciably improved this harsh poverty of 70 per cent of the world's people will continue for many generations (Figure 7.1).

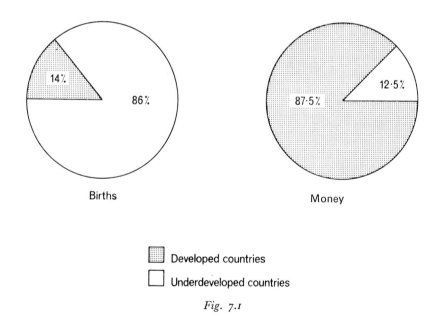

Births

Money

Developed countries

Underdeveloped countries

Fig. 7.1

When it comes to the deployment of economic resources to health; such expenditure is still regarded as "non-economic" and health services suffer as compared to resources made available to agriculture and industrial development. There is also a disparity between the proportion that developed and underdeveloped territories allocate to health – the former exceeding 4 per cent of the Gross National Product; the latter rarely achieving 2 per cent (see Table 7.1). Much of this difference is accounted for by differences in the availability of

TABLE 7.1

Table of Health Expenditures
C 1962

Country	Proportion of GDP/GNP Spent on Health	Proportion of Budget Spent on Health	Per Capita Expenditure on Health
U.S.A.			
Total	5·7 GNP		§162.00
Private	4·3		
Public	1·4	5·0	
		Per cent	
Sweden			
Total	4·4 GNP		80·00
Exp. of Govt.			
Oper. Services	2·7		
Exp. for Comp.			
Health Ins.	1·7		
United Kingdom	3·85GNP		56·00
Jamaica	2·1 GDP	11·0	9·60
Guatemala	1·4 ,,	9·1	2·36
Senegal	2·0 ,,	6·6	3·47
Thailand	0·5 ,,	3·4	0·65
Kenya	2·1 ,,	6·2	1·54*
Uganda	1·7 ,,	7·6	1·33
Tanzania	1·4 ,,	9·2	0·77
Malawi		11·8	1·03
Ghana	1·16 ,,	7·1	4·00
Ethiopia	1·35 ,,	6·8	0·72
N. Nigeria		12·0	0·50

*For 1964/65 reduced to $1·09.

U.S.A.   Merriam, Ida C., "Social Welfare Expenditure," Social Security Bulletin, October 1965. U.S. Department of Health, Education and Welfare.
Progress in Health Services, Health Information Foundation, University of Chicago, Illinois, November/December 1965, Vol. 14, No. 5.

Sweden   Seldowitz, E. and Brewster, A. W, "Sweden's Health and Cash Sickness Insurance Program," Public Health Reports, Vol 79, No. 9, September 1964.

United   "Monthly Digest of Statistics," Central Statistical Office, H.M.S.O.,
Kingdom London, May 1962.

health insurance and welfare schemes. In terms of per capita expenditure on health the disparity is even more stupendous. Highly industrialised countries spend between $50 and $250 per head per year, whereas the underdeveloped countries expenditure is between $0·50 and $10 per head per year.

Health, Manpower and Training

Trained health manpower is desperately short throughout the underdeveloped world, and with the present imbalance between population growth rates and professional health educational institutes, it is likely to remain so. The table 7.2 shows the estimates of physician by continents. At one physician per 770 population, the world needs a further 3·5 million doctors.[1] At $25,000 cost per physician, this would mean a total of $87·5 billion to remedy the deficiency. Maldistribution makes the situation worse; of the one and half million physicians in the world only three hundred thousand are in the underdeveloped world which contains nearly three quarters of the population. Of the world total of nearly 450,000 dentists, only a quarter serve the underdeveloped world.

TABLE 7.2

Physician Manpower and Education Situation

Area	Population (thousands)	No. of Medical Schools	Number of M.D.s	Graduates	Pop. per Med. School (Millions)	Pop. per Physician
Latin America	211,795	100	117,543	6,104	21	1,800
Africa	253,950	17	31,500	1,193[a]	15	8,000
Asia[b]	874,690	128	153,422	7,401[c]	6·9	5,900
Europe[d]	406,577	182	476,557	18,929[d]	2·2	850
U.S.S.R.	214,400	77	364,324	26,452	2·8	580
Oceania	15,684	8	16,014	582	1·9	980
Japan	93,200	46	99,793	3,200	2·0	930
North America	198,585	98	253,994	8,023	2·0	780

Source: World Directory of Medical Schools, W.H.O.,
Geneva, 3rd Edition, 1963.

[a]Excludes Algeria.   [c]Excludes Pakistan.
[b]Excludes Japan and Mainland China.   [d]Excludes Bulgaria, France & Federal Republic of Germany.

Nursing is in no better shape, for three quarters of the world's nurses are in the Americas, Europe and the U.S.S.R., leaving the remaining quarter to serve Asia, Africa and Latin America. Europe has one nurse to 330–1200 inhabitants depending on the country. In the Americas the range is from 230–600 persons per nurse; in Asia there is one nurse to between 430 and 8,200 persons; and in Africa one nurse serves 800 to 12,500 inhabitants.[2] In many of the developing nations there are fewer nurses than doctors. For example, India where there are two physicians for each nurse and Latin America where in 1966 there were 147,959 physicians but only 83,631 graduate nurses.

Such tables, however, do not reveal the whole picture since distribution, population growth rates and migration distort the apparent availability. The distribution of physicians and people as between urban and rural areas are in almost inverse proportion for under-developed territories. This maldistribution is illustrated by the table (7.3) showing the situation in selected countries. That this maldistribution does not apply only to physicians can be seen from the table (7.4) showing the distribution of various health personnel in Thailand – a picture that is representative of other underdeveloped areas.

TABLE 7.3

Maldistribution Tables 1964
Table of Distribution of Physicians by Proportions

Country	Capital		Rest of Country	
	M.D. per cent	Pop. per cent	M.D. per cent	Pop. per cent
Jamaica	70	26	30	74
Guatemala	82	15	18	85
Senegal	63	15	37	85
Thailand	60	8	40	92
Kenya	54	5	46	95

Such patterns of maldistribution of health personnel inevitably reflect the patterns of availability of medical care and health services as between urban and rural areas; and give rise to large pockets of people being very ill-served, meagerly served, or served not at all.

The population growth rate makes attainment of satisfactory ratios of health personnel well nigh impossible to achieve. In Africa, for example, approximately 1,200 doctors graduated in 1960, whereas the births alone that year were in excess of ten million, i.e., one doctor produced for every 8,000 children born. In Latin America during the decade 1957–66, physicians increased from 100,000 to 148,000. During the same period the population increased by 31 per cent leaving a net gain of 0.8 physicians per 10,000 persons over the period. In the underdeveloped world, as a whole, excluding China,

TABLE 7.4

Table of Distribution of Personnel: Thailand
1964

	Bangkok (Pop. 2·3M 8 per cent Total)	Rest of Country (Pop. 26M 92 per cent Total)
Physicians	60 per cent	40 per cent
Dentists	79 per cent	21 per cent
Pharmacists	77 per cent	23 per cent
Nurses	67 per cent	33 per cent
Midwives	57 per cent	43 per cent
Lab. Technologist	90 per cent	10 per cent
Dental Hygienists	86 per cent	10 per cent

in one year 14,698 doctors graduated and 54,000,000 babies were born. That is, one doctor for every 3,600 babies born.* To put it more succinctly, in the underdeveloped world doctors are increasing at a net rate of 2·1 per cent and the population at 2·6 per cent. An estimate of the supply of physicians has already been given to correct deficiencies at an absolute level (3·5 million). It is apparent that training costs alone render the attainment of an adequate physician population ratio well nigh impossible in most of the developing countries.

POPULATION TRENDS AND IMPLICATIONS

Overcrowding relates to the effective deployment of available resources. Population control programs are aimed at achieving a more equable balance between growth rates of people and their resources so that improvement in living standards can be achieved more rapidly. Allusion to some of the implications of imbalance between rates of growth of economies and high level manpower has already been made.

The present massive increase in the population of the world – the major increase coming from the underdeveloped areas of the world – will result in a consequential and proportionate shrinkage of total biological resources. Overcrowding, whether it relates to rural and/or urban areas brings in its train economic insufficiency, social tensions, and violence.

In the industrialised world, though the poor have large families, they remain a minority segment of the population, and it is the

*By contrast in the developed world 1 doctor graduates for every 350 babies born each year.

Fig. 7.2. *Percentage of physicians in relation to percentage of population in capital cities and remaining areas of 25 countries*

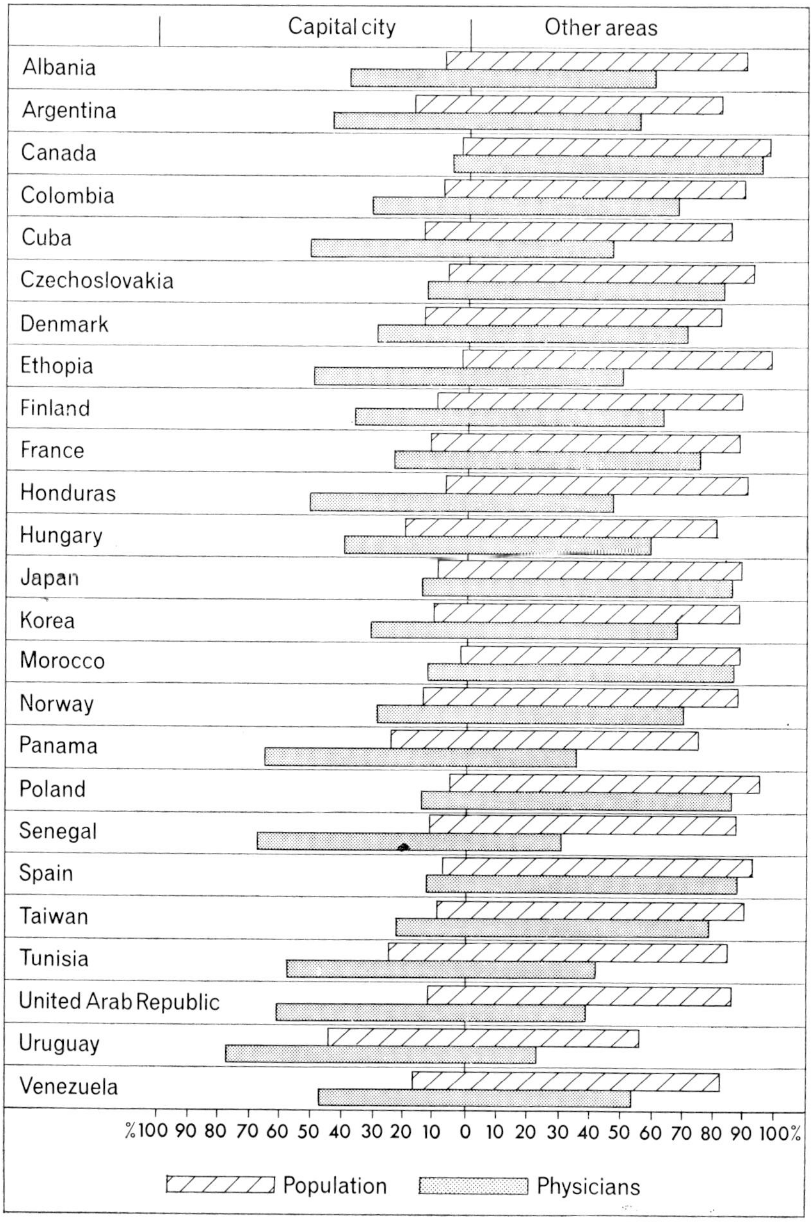

	Capital city	Other areas
Albania		
Argentina		
Canada		
Colombia		
Cuba		
Czechoslovakia		
Denmark		
Ethopia		
Finland		
France		
Honduras		
Hungary		
Japan		
Korea		
Morocco		
Norway		
Panama		
Poland		
Senegal		
Spain		
Taiwan		
Tunisia		
United Arab Republic		
Uruguay		
Venezuela		

%100 90 80 70 60 50 40 30 20 10 0 10 20 30 40 50 60 70 80 90 100%

Population   Physicians

World Health Organisation Chronicle, Vol. 22, No. 3, March 1965.

urbanised middle and professional classes who contribute most to the total increase of people. In the underdeveloped world, it is the rural poor who make the greatest impact on population growth. They constitute a difficult segment of any nation's population to reach with services.

If the world population continues to grow at the present rate of 2 per cent, it will double in 35 years, reaching a total of nearly 7 billion (high projection rate). The previous doubling took nearly twice as long – 61 years – a rate of 1 per cent. Each year some 125 million babies are born and 55 million die, leaving a net gain of 70 million. By 1980 the net gain will be 100 million per year, and by the year 2,000 some 200 million will be added each year.

The underdeveloped areas contribute 71 per cent (2.5 billion) to the present world total, and by the year 2,000 will constitute approximately 85 per cent since the rate of growth of these areas is 2·6 per cent per annum compared with 1·1 per cent for the developed areas. Yet, the underdeveloped areas are the areas which can least afford this increase in terms of improvement of the quality of life rather than the quantity.[3]

In the next 35 years, Latin America's population is expected to triple: it is the fastest growing area in the world. Africa is expected to increase by nearly 180 per cent and Asia by 140 per cent. By contrast, Europe will increase by about one quarter.[4] China will be the largest single nation with a population approaching 1,500 million. India will be the next at nearly 1,000 million and a long way behind will be the U.S.S.R. with 400 million and the U.S.A. with some 355 million.

Density and Urbanisation

Only about one third of the earth's surface is habitable so that overall density figures do not reveal the whole picture. Presently there are 63 persons per square mile of the world's habitable land surface: by the year 2,000 there will be 142. Asia has a density of 177, Latin America 31 and Africa 27. By contrast, Europe supports 233 persons per square mile. By the year 2,000 Asia will support 423, Latin America 96, Africa 75 and Europe 301.

Europe, however, because of its industrialisation can support its population even though there are only three acres of land per person. But the underdeveloped areas with their living linked to subsistence farming cannot. Asia is moving towards only one and a half acres per person. In Africa, despite the low population density, it is estimated that 47 per cent of the area and 45 per cent of the population are experiencing population pressures.[5] One of the great contrasts between the underdeveloped and the industrialised nations

lies in the degree of urbanisation; and in consequence their dependence upon a monetary economy or a non-monetary land subsistence.
Urbanisation is increasing at approximately twice to thrice the rates of
national growth rates; rates that put great strains upon the national
economy in developing housing, sanitation, water supplies, community
amenities and transport.

Defining urbanisation as areas of over 20,000 persons or more,
Latin America has approximately 30 per cent urban population, Asia
under 20 per cent, and Africa less than 15 per cent. By contrast,
North America has nearly 50 per cent of its population urbanised
and Europe over 40 per cent. In terms of individual countries the
contrast is even greater with the United Kingdom having an urban
population of 80 per cent and Kenya 7 per cent (U.S.A. 65 per cent).
Even in the developed countries the strains upon the economy in
promoting better urban living conditions are obvious. Slum clearance,
purer air, adequate and safe water supplies, public transport, social
unrest and violence, noise, infectious diseases, welfare services, high
risk sickness groups, all are obvious areas of economic distress. In the
developing countries the peri-urban "septic fringe" borders on human
chaos and desperation. Urbanisation is probably the most visible
phenomenon of human want and distress.

Age Structure

Differentials in population growth rate resulting from high birth
rates and declining mortality rates undoubtedly place a strain on
economies. But the hazards and strains are immeasurably greater
when examined in the light of population age group pyramids.[6]
(fig. 7·3). The population pyramids show a heavy proportion of
young age groups in the developing regions. This presages a continuing high population growth rate because these age groups have
yet to come to the reproductive phase. Once the first five years of life
are passed, the probability of reaching reproductive ages are high.
Children moreover represent a high consumer group in terms of
family support, clothing, food, education, medical care, welfare, etc.

In the developing nations the under fives represent a sixth of the
population, and the under 15 year age group 40–50 per cent of the
total population. They are a non-productive group which need a
heavy investment in medical care if the infant and child wastage
rate is to be prevented. These rates presently vary from 100 to 200
deaths per 1,000 births for infants. One third to one half of children
born die before the age of five! (see statistics at the end of the chapter).
In the U.S.A. children under five represent 11 per cent of the population
and account for 6 per cent of total deaths. By contrast it is to be seen
that children under five while forming 16–17 per cent of the population

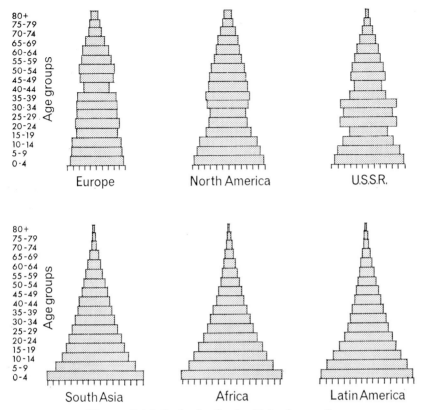

Fig. 7.3. Population by Age Groups, Major Areas, 1960.

(Percentage distribution of each area's total population by five-year age groups. Distribution by sex not shown. Each segment in the horizontal scale equals 1 per cent.)

In the developing countries, traditional fertility combined with declining mortality results in populations with a high proportion of children in the non-productive ages. This in turn creates great social and economic problems.

Source: Population Bulletin, Vol. XXI, No. 4, October 1965, p. 82 and 83.

in the underdeveloped territories account for 35–50 per cent of the total deaths recorded.

In Latin America deaths under five years account for 44 per cent of all deaths recorded with a range of 13–58 per cent for the individual countries. One third to one half of these deaths occur between the first and the fifth birthdays. This is a vulnerable age, with children under five responsible for deaths out of all proportion to their numbers. It would be better had these births been prevented rather than wasted. If *infant* mortality rates are higher than in the industrialised countries, *pre-school* mortality rates are immeasurably greater.

It is this age group that throughout the world offers the greatest potential for improved health services. It is this very group that tends to be relatively neglected. Maternal and child care services have been more oriented toward mother and infant care, school health services to the school age child. The pre-school child needs special care with emphasis on the continuity of the care throughout the whole pre-school era.

Medical care facilities in general do not reflect this predominance of the child and his needs.

Housing, Water Supplies and Sewage Systems

Population growth and urbanisation create an ever increasing need for housing, community water supplies, and sewage systems. A recent estimate places the need for the underdeveloped areas at 400 million dwelling units. In Latin America with its increasing flow to the towns, over half of the needs will be in the towns. In Africa and Asia, three quarters of the need lies in the rural areas, where the problem though less visible is equally urgent.

Only a quarter of this need is to overcome existing shortages, another one quarter to one third is to replace obsolecent and sub-standard housing. From one third to one half is required to provide for the increasing population.

The provision of water supplies to rural and urban areas creates entirely different stresses upon manpower and technology. The needs of the rural areas, where the bulk of the population lives, are for water supplies to homesteads and villages. Such projects rarely present engineering problems, but of costs, logistics and quantity. For example, in Thailand there are 45,000 villages comprising some 28 million persons of which less than 3,000 have protected water supplies. Rural installations can rarely be made self-costing: and rarely financed below $2–$5 a head of population. Protected and accessible water supplies are still, in many parts of the world, not regarded as a necessity, particularly in those areas where the woman is still the traditional labourer.

Yet, at Zaina, in Kenya where a rural community of 6,000 persons scattered over 588 farms and four villages was given improved housing, sanitation, and water supplies, the evidence from two surveys (1961 and 1965) indicated greater health gains in the control areas than in the neighboring non-improved areas. Such gains were measured in terms of point prevalence of illness, duration of illness and helminthic infestation. Despite such evidence, progress in providing protected water supplies and safe sewage systems to rural areas remains pitifully slow. In Guatamala in the rural areas which contain 85 per cent of the population, only 7·2 per cent have protected water supplies and 3·7 per cent serviced with sewage disposal. By contrast, in Guatemala *City* 42 per cent of persons are serviced with water and sewage disposal systems. The provision of water supplies and sewage disposal systems in rural areas of developing countries is difficult to assess, but the author's impressions are that such services rarely exceed 10 per cent of the population.

In urban areas the situation is easier to assess. In Asia it is estimated that over 60 per cent of town dwellers are *not* serviced, in Africa about one third and in Latin America about a quarter remain unserviced to water. The world urban population is expected to increase seven-fold by the end of the century. The need, therefore, is likely to become worse, not better. Such supply systems involve complicated engineering projects that make heavy demands on skilled manpower and money. The cost for Asia, Latin America and Africa are estimated at $6 billion, representing per capita expenditures respectively of $14, $23 and $24.[7]

Economic Aspects

An increasing population requires a corresponding increase in consumer commodities such as food and clothing. At the same time, a proportion of expenditure must be deviated to capital equipment for industry, power, communications, schools, hospitals, houses, etc. The world minimal economic growth rate requirement in gross national productivity is 5·5 per cent per annum, but the present figure is 4·5 per cent.[8]

In general, poverty appears to be associated with higher rates of population increase; and there appears to be an inverse relationship between population growth and composition, and economic development. Population growth appears to operate against the achievement of higher standards of living.

It is stated that some three to four times the rate of population growth rate is required for capital investment to promote adequate development. Thus, if the population growth rate is 3 per cent, capital investment should be between 9 and 12 per cent. Yet, it is those very disadvantaged countries with their high population growth rates that can ill afford to divert income to capital investment.

Coale has shown that if the birth rate is reduced by a half in 30 years, with investment continuing as before, there would be a gain in per capita income of 40 per cent.[9]

Enke states that economic resources used to reduce births can be a hundred times more effective in raising per capita incomes in underdeveloped territories than if the same amount of resources were invested in traditional development projects to increase output.[10]

Any rapid major advance in living standards, therefore, is dependent upon the adoption of wise population growth objectives as well as

P

economic investment. Unfortunately, the gap between the industrial-ised and underdeveloped countries seems not to be lessening, but becoming greater. In 1965 the gap between the less-developed and developed areas, by per capita income, was twelve times ($135: $1,675) whereas in the year 2,000 it is projected at 18 times ($325: $5,775).[11]

Birth rates in the developing areas have remained high whilst mortality rates have fallen, and are still falling rapidly. This creates a transition period until the birth/mortality ratio is restabilised at a lower and more equable level.

Organised health services have undoubtedly made major contribu-tions to this decline in mortality, as have other factors of improved living conditions, welfare, law and order, famine relief, improved agriculture, etc.

It is essential that health planning be undertaken with a sense of balanced realism and that health programs become involved in family planning. High death rates are but one of many factors; for example, traditional customs, religion, political – which tend to prevent the introduction of effective large scale family planning. The results of such programs are slow to perceive. As one African Health Worker in Africa stated to the author "parents must be convinced that spares (children) are no longer necessary." Family planning is an integral part of preventive and promotive family health programs.

Malnutrition

Chronic undernutrition of both calories and protein food affecting the young child exist in every economically underdeveloped area of the world. The classical syndrome of protein-calorie deficiency is generally known as kwashiorkor. It results in underweight, oedema, dermatitis, hair changes, apathy, misery, and in severe cases irre-versible pathological damage and ultimately to death. To actual food deficiencies are the added causative factors of prolonged wean-ing, maternal deprivation, diarrhea and infections.

In addition to chronic undernutrition there are the recurrent periodic famines brought on by droughts, floods and locusts. Other nutritional deficiencies of xerophthalmia, beri-beri, pellagra, rickets and nutritional anemias are still far too prevalent. Dental caries is also a growing problem: to an extent in some countries such as Polynesia and Guatemala where even the primary dentition is eroded, thus compounding nutritional aspects. The relationship between malnu-trition and infection is now universally recognised: the one precipi-tating and aggravating the other.

Such malnutrition in the underdeveloped world may be con-trasted with that in the developed world, where overeating leads to obesity, dental caries, and is associated with metabolic and cardio-vascular disorders.

In one Food and Agriculture Organisation World Survey 1963, it was estimated that by 1975 world food supplies would need to be in-creased by 35 per cent to maintain the present unsatisfactory level; and by 50 per cent to achieve adequate nutrition. By the year 2,000 supplies would need to be augmented threefold.

The Joint F.A.O./W.H.O. Expert Committee on Nutrition, which met in Rome in December 1966, noted that "in the less-developed areas food supplies would need to be quadrupled and supplies of animal protein should be nine times the present volume." It noted that since the Third World Food Survey "increase in food production had failed to keep pace with population increase – indeed the per caput world food production had decreased since 1962/63. Dif-ferences in regional trends exist but show an even greater decrease for developing regions, especially Latin America and Africa.[12]

Though 1967 showed commendable increased food supplies, largely overcoming the poor results of 1966 and 1965, the F.A.O. Director-General commented, "that continued uncontrolled population expan-sion could, however, still cause these hopes to be dashed." Total agricultural productivity in 1967 for the underdeveloped areas in-creased by 6 per cent, mainly in cereals. The minimal required in-crease in food productivity is 4 per cent per annum; yet, the average over the years has only been 2·7 per cent per annum.

The weaning of the peasant farmer from his traditional agricultural practices to adopting the newer high yielding strains of cereals (wheat and rice) – which under optimal conditions will double output with their increased number of crops per year – increased use of artificial fertilizer, and cooperative farming practices have contributed to the present success. The application of this scientific breakthrough has been most rewarding in those areas where it is most needed, for example Asia. High yielding strains of maize, sorghum and potatoes give promise of further increased agricultural productivity which will have particular applicability to Latin America and Africa.

Parallel increases in protein productivity have yet to be realised. There are indications that by selective breeding, it will be possible to increase the protein yield of cereals from the present 7 to 13 per cent to nearly double that proportion. Since cereals, not withstanding their low protein content, represent half of the world's total protein intake of 80 million tons, such an advance will materially relieve protein shortage in the underdeveloped areas of the world.

The intake of protein of animal origins represents a third of the world intake (approximately 25 million tons per year). Improving productivity along present lines because of its high cost and the slowness of the technological breakthrough in protein food processing, does not give rise to high hopes for immediate effective increase in supplies.

It is probable that a more effective rise in animal protein could be achieved by abandoning present domestic animal grazing practices and adopting balanced ecological grazing, such as occurs in nature. Wild game control and game-cropping is an avenue of supply not as yet exploited. Animal protein from the seas has been used for both direct and indirect (animal fodder) improvement of protein intake. Traditional feeding practices, technological processing and cost are again militating factors. Non-conventional methods of increasing protein such as algae, leaf protein and by growing yeast in petroleum are still in the early experimental stages.

The promise of all these advances for increased food productivity may ease present increasing food requirements over the next decade or two, but beyond that stabilisation of population growth rates is an invitable must if substantial and permanent gains in nutrition and health are to be sought, rather than a mere keeping pace with present inadequate levels of intake.

Social and Cultural Aspects

Many of the underprivileged countries are hampered in their attempts to achieve progress because they are not yet comprised of a homogeneous society, but rather a heterogeneous collection of disparate groups. Such groups derive from differing ethnic, religious and cultural origins. With the majority still wedded to the land it is also apparent that they are still wedded to their traditional beliefs and customs. Illiteracy, poor communication, feudalism and ruralisation aggravate and perpetuate the inate conservatism. The melting pot of urbanisation has yet to become effective in these countries.

Such urbanisation as is occurring is already at a rate that exceeds the ability of the towns to cope with the resulting economic, social and welfare aspects. The inevitable result is the "shanty town" and "septic fringe." The astonishing fact is not that delinquency, prostitution, crime, mental and physical disease occur, but that much more does not. Sex and age ratios are upset by the young, particularly males, migrating to the urban areas and by migrant labour retaining their families in the rural land holdings. Assimilation into the towns tends to be into the worst aspects of urban life, not the best; and new migrants tend to cluster in ethnic tribal groups. Tribal behavioral patterns thereby tend to persist.

In the rural areas illiteracy remains much higher than in the towns and ignorance persists. Definitions of literacy do not usually extend beyond technical accomplishments of limited reading and writing, to include an understanding and comprehension of what is read. Statistics do not reveal the breakdown between rural and urban areas, nor between the various social classes and groups. For example, in Guatemala where the literacy rate is assessed at 28 per cent overall, amongst the Indians who comprise 60 per cent of the population and are predominantly rural, the literacy rate is only 10 per cent. The extent of conservatism can be judged effectively by the persistence of beliefs in witchcraft, black magic, witch doctors and mysticism – which in themselves produce mental stress in the process of urbanisation.

Jamaica has adopted Christianity without abandoning its traditional African religious rituals. Pokomania is still widespread. Traditional African medicine men known as "Obeahs" still practice their art through herbalism, witchcraft and voodoo. In Guatemala adherence by the Indians to age old custom persists, because of historical factors of animosity to their Spanish conquerors. Dietary custom and food taboos prevent the use of animal protein, particularly for children, to full effect. Milk has become debased as a result of its potential as a carrier of disease and is classified as a "bad food." Milk is used for feeding pigs and for strengthening "whitewash." In some of the countries of Latin America, where the indigenous population is predominant, customs, traditions, and social structure date back to pre-Columbian times.

In Africa, animism is still rife and witch doctors, for good and evil, still abound. The Marabout of Senegal is both the religious leader and the medicine man: and will extract teeth and incise abcesses. The Mchawi and Mganga of Kenya represent the evil spell binder and the medicine man with his herbs and bones. Speaking in general terms, the uneducated African accepts Western medicine for its immediate relief of visible symptoms and signs of disease – but still resorts to the witch doctor for the eradication of the cause. He has yet to accept western beliefs in the aetiology and epidemiology of disease.

In Thailand, a country of a supposedly high literacy rate, "traditional practitioners" abound, numbering some 34,000 with an additional 13,500 traditional herbalists. This in a country of 4,500 modern physicians indicates the extent of tenaciously held beliefs. In India "ayerverdic" medicine still flourishes.

PATTERNS OF DISEASE

There is a common pattern in the underprivileged areas of the nature and extent of disease. It is not one of tropical diseases, except in small part, but one of diseases resulting from ignorance, poverty, fecundity and prejudice. They are the diseases from which people of the Western world suffered in past centuries; for example, plague and malaria were once rife in England. The broad picture is one of communicable and vector-borne diseases abetted by undernutrition affecting predominantly the younger age groups giving rise to morbidity and mortality trends two to three times greater than their proportions within the population. This contrasts with that pattern of disease in the industrialised countries, where it is one of overnutrition and the diseases of stress and degeneration. Trauma, alcoholism and drug addiction are common to the world!

Within this context there are two predominant variables: that relating to time and that relating to geography. In the time relationship there is observable a continuous and gradual change in the epidemiological picture from an endemic infectious disease situation with a high prevalence of parasitosis, gastro-enteritis, respiratory disease, undernutrition and malnutrition, and the vector-borne diseases; through a state where epidemics of measles, whooping cough, poliomyelitis and other bacterial and virus diseases dominate the picture due to rising standards of living; to a final state where the degenerative diseases of a cerebro-sclerotic nature, hypertension, heart failure, diabetes, psychosomatic diseases and cancer comprise the major portion of ill health. Undernutrition gives way to overnutrition and the severity of the disease pattern shifts from the child to the aged.

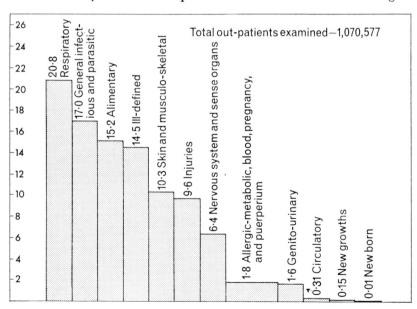

Fig. 7.4. Kenya. A histogram showing by disease groups the principal causes of morbidity among out-patients at Government hospitals. (Kenya: Ministry of Health Annual Report 1960).

A typical pattern of disease of an underdeveloped country can perhaps best be represented by that of Kenya,[13] which for its varieties of altitude and climate present a broad spectrum of disease and regional distributions. (figures 7.4, 7.5 and 7.6).

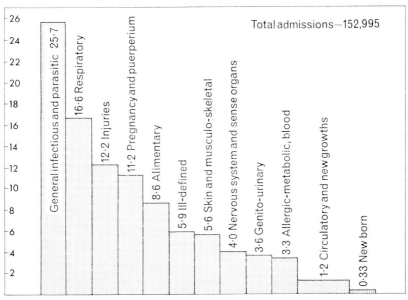

Fig. 7.5. Kenya. A histogram showing by disease groups the principal causes of morbidity among in-patients at Government hospitals. (Kenya: Ministry of Health Annual Report 1960)

Hospital mortality shows over a quarter of deaths due to general infectious and parasitic diseases, followed by respiratory diseases, alimentary diseases, the allergic and metabolic group (mostly kwashiorkor and anaemias) and trauma. The specific ranking causes of death of inpatients are pneumonia, gastro-enteritis (particularly under 2 years of age), respiratory tuberculosis, trauma, kwashiorkor, tetanus, malaria, pertussis and anaemia. The morbidity pattern reveals the predominance of infectious and parasitic diseases: tapeworm, hookworm and roundworm form the largest group, followed by malaria, pertussis, measles, chicken pox, mumps, venereal disease, tuberculosis, trachoma, otitis media, leprosy, dysentery, both bacillary and amoebic. Skin disease are common. Of the vector-borne diseases, apart from malaria, trypanosomiasis, kala-azar, filariasis and onchocerciasis (now eradicated) occur on a regional basis. Bilharzia is widespread, affecting probably 15 per cent of the population – again on a regional distribution governed by altitude. Lepers number some 35,000 mostly in the Nyanza-Lake Victoria area, but also on the coast. Tuberculosis is present at 10 to 11 cases per 1,000 of population – some 3 per

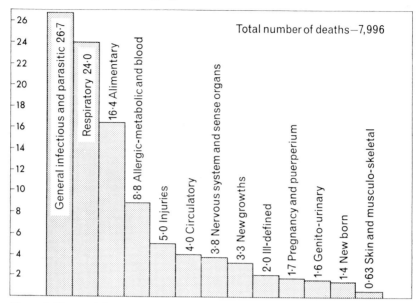

Fig. 7.6. Kenya. A histogram showing by disease groups the principal causes of mortality among in-patients at Government hospitals. (Kenya: Ministry of Health Annual Report 1960).

cent of children under five are infected. Poliomyelitis is changing from endemic to epidemic with an interval of three years, and an almost total incidence among the under three year age group. The zoonoses are prominent, including brucellosis and anthrax. Blindness is due to trachoma, infections and senile cataract. Some 80 per cent of blindness is considered preventable. Diseases of the ear are common, causing deafness to about 3 persons per 1,000 population. Dental fluorosis rather than dental decay is common. Of the quarantinable diseases, cholera had not been seen since the turn of the century until 1971, plague is regressing to well-known rural foci, relapsing fever and typhus are also disappearing, and yellow fever is an academic curiosity. Smallpox, however, is still endemic at an incidence of 1 per 100,000 population annually.

Morbidity of new growths is low, despite Burkitt's lymphoma of children. Chronic sub-nutrition is perennial, kwashiorkor prevalent and famine periodically devastates the country. Thyroid deficiency and Vitamin A deficiency occur. Lastly, mental ill health exists, consequent upon a breakdown of traditional tribal life with its communal living pattern, to one of individual responsibility. It has been estimated that 1 per cent of the population is in need of psychiatric attention.

The change of morbidity and mortality patterns in developing areas over a period of time are more difficult to chronicle since the classifica-

tion of causes of death has changed. There has been an improvement
in the extent and quality of registration of medical certifications.
It is seen for example in Hong Kong that respiratory diseases, infections and intestinal diseases have decreased and that neoplastic,
circulatory and nervous system diseases have increased (Figure 7.7).

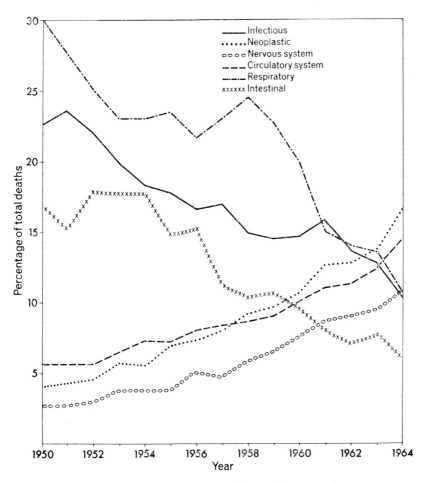

Fig. 7.7. Hong Kong. Major trends in mortality 1950–1964.
(Source: Official—Ministry of Health, Hong Kong).

In Jamaica the relative importance of kidney disease (probably
associated with malaria), pulmonary tuberculosis, syphilis, enteric
diseases and malaria have decreased. Pneumonia and bronchitis tend
to hold their place; whilst gastro-enteritis has increased its importance. Diabetes mellitus, nutritional deficiencies, hypertension, intra-
cranial vascular lesions, cancer and trauma all become relatively more

important. Heart disease retains a prominent place though probably the aetiology has changed (Figure 7.8).

JAMAICA 1945–61

Change in Relative Importance of 15 Diseases by
Medically Certified Causes of Death

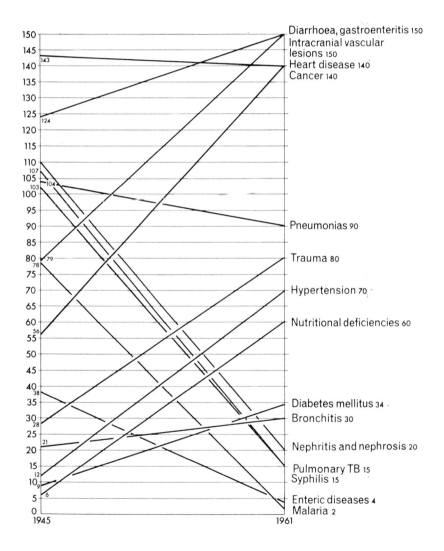

Fig. 7.8. Relative importance expressed as proportionate incidence in 1,000 deaths due to these causes in 1945 and 1961 respectively.

Geographic Epidemiology

In the context of the underdeveloped territories, as a whole malaria, cholera and tuberculosis rank as major causes of sickness and death, with yellow fever and smallpox still being scourges. Yellow fever is still endemic in areas of Africa and Latin America, cholera in Asia and has reappeared in Africa, smallpox and malaria in Latin America, Africa and Asia.

Smallpox has been virtually eradicated from the Americas, except for Brazil and Colombia. In Asia, from whence three fourths of the worlds cases are reported, almost all the cases emanate from Pakistan, India and Indonesia. In Africa few countries can claim complete eradication, though the prevalence is decreasing. In the world as a whole, smallpox has declined dramatically in the past several years but it has to be remembered that smallpox has a 5 to 7 year cycle.

In one survey of leading causes of death in selected countries of Africa, Asia and Latin America, the five major causes constituting 31 per cent were still gastro-enteritis, influenza and pneumonia, heart-disease, malignancies and accidents. Although tuberculosis did not rank amongst the five leading groups, in the 15–44 year age group it came second only to accidents.[14]

In Africa malaria, tuberculosis, leprosy, helminthic diseases, diarrhoea and dysenteries, onchocerciasis, trypanosomiasis, bilharzia, smallpox, venereal disease, and protein-calorie deficiency are commonly regarded as the diseases of major importance together with trachoma and otitis media.

In Asia the diarrhoeal diseases and dysentries, tuberculosis, malaria, leprosy, filariasis, smallpox, cholera, trachoma and malnutrition are considered the most important disease hazards.

In Latin America the disease profile is malnutrition taking precedence over the communicable diseases, then the diarrheoal diseases, schistosomiasis, Chaga's disease, venereal infections, and malaria. In certain countries of this region chronic degenerative diseases, mental disorders and alcoholism are regarded as major problems.[15]

It is a harsh commentary that many of the diseases which occur in these regions are not due to lack of knowledge regarding prevention, but to the lack of application of such knowledge. Many diseases are still extent that could be eliminated by intensive immunisation campaigns, yet others could be greatly reduced by the mass exhibition of prophylactic drug regimes. Finally, other conditions would succumb to simple but extensive improvement in environmental sanitation and water supplies.

In Latin America a minimum of one million children under five die annually, of which three quarters are alleged to be from preventable diseases. One third of the deaths occur in the one to four age group of which 90 per cent are classified as preventable diseases. Diarrhoea, measles and whooping cough are estimated to be responsible for approximately one quarter of the deaths: and another one quarter to the remaining infectious diseases, influenza and pneumonia. Nutritional deficiencies are an *important* contributory cause to these deaths.

Smallpox, despite the discovery of the prevention by vaccination in 1798 by Edward Jenner, claimed 122,098 victims in 1967. Of these cases 15,263 occurred in Africa, 4,376 in Latin America and 102,454 in Asia – the latter mostly in the sub-continent of India and Indonesia.

There are still some 11 million lepers throughout the world – a disease for which there is a cure by simple oral administration of a cheap and effective drug – di-amino di-phenyl sulphone. These lepers are distributed mostly in the underdeveloped world – 6.5 million in Asia, 3.9 million in Africa, and 0.4 million elsewhere. Of these cases only 2 million are under treatment. With this therapy, and the low communicability of leprosy, a whole new "open door" policy is feasible; medically, economically and socially. Leprasaria are institutions of a past era, yet there is failure in application.

Bilharzia affects some 150 million persons throughout the world mostly in the tropics. Yet this is a disease eminently responsive to improved environmental facilities. The provision of safe water supplies, combined with educational programs would produce an immediate effect in the reduction of the disease that predominantly attacks children between 5 and 15 years of age.

MEDICAL CARE AND FACILITIES

Shortages of personnel and maldistribution have already been isolated as one of the factors inhibiting the total outreach of medical care to rural areas. Although *services* are generally designed to attempt an overall coverage of the population, there is a heavy concentration of material resources and trained human resources, in and around the capital city of developing countries; and to a lesser extent secondary urban centers.

The table (7.5) on hospital and bed distribution shows the situation in five developing territories. Thus to an overall shortage of hospital beds as compared to the industrialised nations is an added factor of maldistribution. If these city facilities and resources were used for the whole country there could be no argument but, in fact, both the facilities and personnel are being used for the population in and around the immediate vicinity of the capital city. These hospitals should have a dual function: they should serve as general service beds for the local area and referral or consultative beds for the whole country. The extent, however, to which the beds are used in the latter capacity varies between 5 and 15 per cent. This figure includes both direct admissions and referred patients. Statistics on this are difficult to obtain.

In Senegal it was shown by records that of children hospitalised in three main hospitals of Dakar, some 85 per cent derived from the town itself. In Siraraj Hospital, Bangkok, it was estimated that 80 per cent of admissions were of city origin. Similar informed estimates were given in respect of the Kingston Public Hospital, Jamaica, and the Kenyatta National Hospital, Nairobi.

The outreach of these centralised *national* institutes is not in fact great, and from a consumer-usage viewpoint they do not justify being so represented.

In Jamaica over half the hospital beds are in the Kingston area which has about one third the population. In Guatemala, one half of the hospital beds are in the capital city which contains 15 per cent of the population. In Senegal a similar picture exists as indeed in other countries. In Kenya 20 per cent of the hospital beds are in the capital city which had 4 per cent of the total population and not more than 20 per cent of the patients derived from outside of Nairobi City and its environs.

The maldistribution of facilities of personnel is reflected in the differential between urban and rural vital statistics. In Ghana[16] for example the infant mortality rate in the two largest towns Accra and Kumasi is quoted as 37·6 per 1,000 live births. In other urban areas 123 and in the rural areas 167 per 1,000 live births. Maternal mortality rates reflect the same differences. Accra and Kumasi have rates of 4·5, other urban areas 22·3 and rural areas 35·6.

In Kenya the differences between Nairobi, the capital city, and the rest of the country are equally revealing.[17] The infant mortality rate for Nairobi Africans is 104 per 1,000 live births whilst for the country as a whole it is estimated at 170–200 per 1,000 live births.

In Jamaica in one rural parish 1,418 births were delivered through an official public service out of an estimated total births of 2,880; that is, just under 50 per cent. In the corporate area of Kingston, the capital city, 16,359 births were attended out of 22,344 births registered: that is nearly 75 per cent without taking into account the private practitioners of the urban areas.

Not only quantitatively is there a bias in favor of the urban dweller, but qualitatively as well there is a gross differential. The standard of service and facilities is much higher in the towns than in the rural areas. This applies to the ratio of staff/hospital bed, equip-

TABLE 7.5

Hospital and Bed Distribution

C 1965

Country	National			Capital City			Rest of Country		
	Total Hospitals	Total Beds	Ratio per 1,000	Hospitals	Beds	Ratio per 1,000	Hospitals	Beds	Ratio per 1,000
Jamaica	33	7,401[1]	4·1	12	2,065	5·4	21	2,409	1·7
Guatemala	44	10,250	2·5	18	5,018	8·0	26	5,232	1·3
Senegal	42	4,492	1·4	7	1,565	3·8	74	2,927	1·08
Thailand	95*	21,962	0·7	16**	6,294	2·7	79	15,668	0·5
Kenya	164	11,521	1·3	23	2,988	9·7	141	8,533	1·0

Jamaica: The total includes nearly 3,000 mental beds in Kingston. Thus the ratio of general beds is 2·3 per 1,000 persons.
Senegal: Additional 39 maternity units.
Kenya: Government 7,000; Mission 2,904; other 1,617.
*Plus 51 private and 25 municipal.
**Plus 24 private hospitals and 48 maternity units.

ment and facilities, such as laboratory facilities, x-ray apparatus, pharmacy and pharmaceuticals, and costs. Perhaps the most convincing illustration of what is in fact well-known can be conveyed by an example of costs.

In Guatemala where the hospital beds are divided in equal numbers between capital city and the rest of the country, whose population proportions are respectively 15 per cent and 85 per cent, expenditure proportions were 73 per cent for the city hospitals and 27 per cent for the remaining hospitals. In Kenya it has been estimated that approximately one third of personnel and money are utilized in the Nairobi area insofar as public services are concerned. In Senegal 40 per cent of the health budget goes to the support of the main teaching hospital at Dakar.

The facilities for medical care being provided in the rural areas outside of the hospital represent hardly more than a bare attempt to provide a building with a limited range of drugs. These facilities vary from health centers, health sub-centers, midwifery units, bedded dispensaries, to one room dispensaries and "lock up" units used periodically. The structure may vary from a well-built modern stone building with running water and electricity, as in Jamaica, to a mud and wattle building. But all of them have a paucity of diagnostic aids being mostly devoid of radiological equipment and laboratory facilities. There is generally a limited range and restricted quantity of drugs. These are not the facilities with which a professionally trained physician, trained in scientific medicine, trained to use advanced diagnostic tools, can be expected to be content. Given these conditions the physician resolutely refuses to work in the rural areas; and medical care under such conditions is inevitably the responsibility of the non-physician. Inside the hospital the physician is given time and some of the facilities; in the outpatients of a hospital he is given some of the facilities but no time. Outside of the hospital, excluding private practice, he is given neither the time nor the facilities.

So long as these prospects exist, so long will rural populations be deprived of a physician's attention. Either one must provide facilities and the tools to the degree of training or train to the facilities and tools which can be provided. It may be shown that despite the increased efforts made to expand and improve hospitals, the minimal facility that seems acceptable to the physician in less-privileged areas of the world in the public services, the rate of expansion and rate of improvement, is not adequate. It is not adequate either to attract the physician in sufficient numbers to rural areas nor adequate to stem the demands of the people – hence the resort to auxiliary personnel. Neither the professional environment nor the social environment, remuneration and housing, are in sufficient supply to attract the physician. One is attempting to place an elegantly trained person in an inelegant situation.

In Guatemala, despite the development programs in hospital construction over the past few years, the ratio of beds has actually decreased in relation to each thousand of population: from 2·9 to 2·5 per 1,000. In Thailand, the public service rural hospital facilities expanded from 2,512 beds in 1953 for 21 million people to 3,552 hospital beds for 26 million in 1964. The declared objective of reaching 5 beds per 1,000 population is totally unrealistic in the face of an expanding population and the resulting escalation of costs that this would involve. The total beds required in the 25 year period would be approximately 300,000. The budget for hospital services was appproximately $22 million, so that the expenditure envisaged for 1990 would be at least 20 times that of 1965 (i.e., to expand the ratio from .5 beds per 1,000 to 5 beds per 1,000 for twice the population), or $440 million per annum. But this rate of increase would be greatly in excess of the rate of increase of the gross domestic product. At the most a tripling of the ratio from 0·5 to 1·5 beds per 1,000 of population overall; (or from 0·3 to 0·9 in the rural areas) which would mean a sixfold increase in total number of beds over the period and an actual increase of 3,000 beds annually; could be expected to be achieved.

The same astronomical proportionate increases can be calculated for other countries. For example, Kenya would need to increase its beds from 10,000 to 40,000 over a period of 25 years, within which period the population would double if the ratio of beds to population were to increase from 1·25 to 2·5 beds per 1,000 of population. It is unlikely that during a doubling of the population facilities will be able to do more than double their ratio which means in effect quadrupling the facilities. It is inevitable then that medical care services will have to be discharged through other forms of facilities besides hospitals. To quote the figures for one continent, (namely, Latin America) of the three continental developing regions, hospital beds have increased from 685,000 in 1960 to 776,000 in 1966. The ratio of beds to population has remained constant at 3·2 beds per 1,000 of population. To keep pace with the growth rate an additional 154,000 beds will be required in 1971. To procure a slight improvement to say 4.5 beds per 1,000 of population will require 534,000 additional beds.[18]

In general, underdeveloped countries provide beds in a ratio from 0·5 to 6·5 beds per 1,000 of population. The urban/rural maldistribution is related to the population distribution. Those countries with a higher proportion of rural population having the greater disparity also in hospital bed distribution.

It was to correct this imbalance that the concept of the small bedded rural health center was introduced into many countries. For example, in Kenya there are some 150 such rural health centers each with 4 to 10 beds for emergency care, short stay patients, maternity and referral purposes.

As a generalisation, it may be said that medical care in the larger urban areas throughout the world, especially the capital cities, does not differ materially. There is a relative plentitude of trained personnel both at generalist level (with ratios of physicians in the region of 1:1,000 to 1:2,000) and specialist cadres. There is relatively good provision of hospital and medical care facilities, with hospital beds averaging 5 to 10 per 1,000 persons. Such hospitals are well-equipped with facilities to conduct advanced diagnoses and treatment. There is also an adequate supply of medical personnel and facilities in the private sector.

In the rural areas on the contrary, both personnel and facilities are in poor supply. Specialist services are not available. At the best, a generalist physician may be found supported by one or more paramedical personnel and trained or untrained auxiliaries. Such a physician may serve anywhere from 5,000 persons upwards. In most countries 25,000 persons or upwards is a better approximation. Hospital beds rarely exceed 2 per 1,000 and are poorly equipped for diagnostic and operative techniques: often inadequately supplied with therapeutic drugs. Communications are poor, and the cost of transport to a medical center may exceed the value of the service rendered. For example, in Western Nigeria the expenditure on drugs and dressings per head of population in the public sector (which is the principal source of medical care) is a little over 6 pence (U.S. $0·15). In England the expenditure is in the neighborhood of 50 shillings (U.S. $6·50 or 100 times as much.

THE CHURCH AND MEDICAL CARE

The church has had a respected and valued role to play in introducing modern medicine to the less-developed areas of the world. It has perhaps made its major contribution in taking medical services to the *rural* areas rather than the urban. It has attempted to fill the gaps of inadequate public services. It has frequently been the first in the field.

Its activities in medicine have been limited almost entirely to medical care programs through hospitals and dispensaries. Special efforts have been made in selected fields such as maternity and leprosy. In Malawi the church provides 2,027 hospital beds out of a total

Q

of 5,074 existing in the country; in Kenya, 2,207 out of a total of 10,368 and in Ghana 1,622 out of 7,037.

In association with these medical care programs, and from necessity, the church has entered the realms of medical training, mostly auxiliaries in nursing, midwifery and medical assistants. It has not so far been active in the training of physicians with one or two notable exceptions. Its professional and supervisory personnel are still largely expatriates.

The contribution that the church can make in developing medical and health services should not be underestimated in planning for the future. It does require, however, that the churches themselves should coordinate their efforts and not plan from a sectarian viewpoint. Coordination with government can then be achieved on a planned basis through a formal committee procedure rather than on a haphazard and piecemeal basis. The areas within which the church can most advantageously operate likewise need to be defined. Personal health services offer one such field but would necessitate church personnel conforming to government policies and being responsible to the District Medical Officer of Health. The majority of mission medical personnel are motivated by the desire to render services to the individual, and are not trained in public health activities. There is a pressing need for health and welfare activities to deprived and handicapped children, infirm and handicapped adults, the aged and the long-term care patient.

These are activities which the official public services find it difficult to encompass and for which voluntary and church organisations are particularly suitable. Activities in these fields have been initiated already in some countries; for example, the deaf child and the blind child. They could well be expanded!

MEDICAL CARE WORKLOAD AND NATURE OF SICKNESS

In determining the requirements for health in the underprivileged territories a distinction must be drawn between needs as seen by the health authorities and the wants as expressed by the people. The former is control of communicable diseases, the improvement in protein-calorie nutrition, and a more stabilised and equable fertility pattern. The latter are for care when sick, particularly the child, relief when hurt, and reassurance and help during maternity. Failure to supply to the "wants" is inevitably to ensure failure of attempts to improve the "needs." The faith of the people is in the magic of curative medicine and the whole superstructure of preventive and promotive medicine is based on this faith.

In an unsophisticated society the community can hardly be said to be aware of health, much less positive health. There is, however, a demand for the absence of disease. Though medical care is an expensive item, the cost of such programs should be judged in terms of the consequences of foregoing them. That prevention is better than cure is undoubtedly true; but to attempt to attend to the needs without catering to the wants is unrealistic. Priority for preventive medicine is generally advocated by those who are themselves assured of effective curative services.

Medical care in the United States averages 5·1 physician/patient visits per year for urban populations; 3·6 visits for persons living on farms in rural areas, and 4·5 for rural non-farm residents. The average number of physician/patient visits for the United States as a whole was five per year.[19] In another study the authors conclude "data for medical care studies in the United States and Great Britain suggest that in a population of 1,000 adults (sixteen years and over), in an average month 750 will experience an episode of illness, 250 of these will consult a physician, 9 will be hospitalised, 5 will be referred to another physician, and 1 will be referred to a university medical centre."[20]

In an illiterate and ill-informed community, where there is much more ill health, it is patently obvious that there will be a much greater demand for care and attention at a much more simple level than in a sophisticated society. In the latter, much illness is self-diagnosed and self-treated via the druggist and pharmacy – a facility that is lacking in the rural areas of many of the under-privileged peoples.

THE TIME ELEMENT

In an article advocating an initial approach through a program to achieve *minimal* medical care, before *adequate* medical care is accepted as the goal Cordero stated "that Puerto Rico requires one physician per 3,000 of population. The time required per patient was calculated as approximately 15 minutes."[21] Minimal care is defined as "providing the patients with care that would be at least barely or minimally adequate *for their more manifest conditions,* that is for conditions that could be picked up by a physician without a *complete* clinical evaluation." Auxiliaries are advocated to diagnose and treat uncomplicated illness, whilst physicians are used for consultation and referred cases.

Taking a standard less than this minimal care provision advocated, one can postulate that one physician could handle a population of 5,000 persons at 2·5 visits per patient per year. This would entail the physician working exclusively on clinical aspects on a 5 day week of 48 hours. Allowing 10 minutes per patient he would average

50 patients per day. Manpower requirements at 1 : 5,000 would involve considerable stresses, financial and educational, to achieve this *sub-minimal* standard.

In East Africa to achieve this figure of 1 physician per 5,000 persons would require 600 physicians per year output from the three medical schools. An input to achieve this would absorb a very high proportion of the high school graduates: a situation that would obviously lead to an unbalanced ecological development program.

Services and physicians themselves generate an increasing demand through their integral educational factor. Nowhere in the world has supply, either of service or health personnel, caught up with demand. The medical auxiliary in such circumstances can be the first "agent provacateur" to supply to an immediate quantitative need and generate a "qualitative" demand : and thus accelerate health progress.

THE DISTANCE FACTOR

Communications in the underprivileged countries are notoriously inadequate and the isolation of rural areas needs to be measured, for sickness purposes, in terms of time comfort and cost, as much as in distance. Studies in Kenya[22] showed that three quarters of admissions to hospital and 95 per cent of outpatients derive from within a 25 mile radius. Half the inpatients and 90 per cent of the outpatients came from within the small township itself. The area and distance serviced varies directly with the size of the medical unit.

THE COST FACTOR

Hospitals

The cost of hospitalisation is high throughout the world so that the selection of patients for hospital care should be limited to those for whom alternative methods of care will not suffice.

Figures have been quoted earlier of the disparity between per capita incomes, gross national products, expenditures spent on health services, and rates of economic development between the developed and underdeveloped world. It would be unrealistic to suppose that the developing countries will be able to increase both their proportionate and absolute expenditures on health services dramatically. It has taken Kenya some 15 years to increase its proportionate expenditure from 1.1 per cent to 2.1 per cent of the G.N.P. and from 3 shillings per head to 13 shillings per head. In some countries the proportionate expenditure has actually decreased; in others, for example Guatemala, it has remained constant.

The cost of treating patients in hospitals is high everywhere, the less-developed areas will not be able to afford a major expansion of these facilities – either quantitatively or qualitatively. It will certainly be many decades before the ratio of hospital beds to population can achieve the accepted norms of industrialised countries. In effect, such hospitals must be so situated and managed that they are located at the center of communications and serve the whole area, not merely populations in their immediate vicinity. Such hospitals need to be "protected" by peripheral medical units of lesser excellence and lesser cost where the less seriously ill can be filtered off and treated.

Health Centers

It is clear that hospitals in themselves do not provide the solution to medical care requirements in underprivileged society. Nor indeed, from the ambulant nature of much of the sickness, is it necessary to blanket the country with such institutes.

If sub-minimal standards of care with total outreach are accepted as a primary step towards achieving minimal medical care, then one can postulate that a medical care unit, staffed with two medical care auxiliaries, allowing $7\frac{1}{2}$ minutes per patient, can serve a population of 20,000 at 2·5 visits per person per annum. Each medical auxiliary would see 100 patients, both primary and reattendances, daily (250 working days per year).

Such case loads for the physician and auxiliary are common in many medical institutes, e.g., a polyclinic in Dar-es-Salaam, a district hospital in Kenya, a health center in Jamaica, an outpatient department in Khartoum, and an outpatient center in Guatemala. Such is the common pattern rather than the uncommon. From personal observation the properly trained medical care auxiliary can cope under such conditions, almost as well as the registered physician, at a fraction of the cost.

In Kenya costs per illness varied from U.S. 24 cents at a dispensary and U.S. 64 cents at a rural health centre to $53 at the National hospital, Nairobi.[23]

Such costs can, of course, be only very approximate. For example, in the Thailand health centre if other personal health services are included, such as deliveries, child health visits, home visits and school children examinations, the cost per personal service rendered falls to U.S. $0·75. If in addition the number of immunisations is included the cost per service decreases still further to U.S. $0·06.

SPECIAL DISEASE PROGRAMS

Special disease programs have been an integral part of health progress since the discovery of specific "tools." First came the vaccines, then specific prophylactic drugs, and within the last quarter of a century the residual insecticides. These tools have contributed much to the reduction of disease and thus are part of medical care systems. Such programs are complementary to the development of general health services. Whereas the latter are a long-term process requiring extensive investment in human resources and facilities, the former offers quick results. However, the consolidation of gains from such special disease programs requires a minimal basic health service. There is an interplay of benefits whereby in some countries, notably Latin America, the early campaigns against yellow fever, hookworm and leprosy, have led to the development of local health services. In others, notably East Africa, the development of rural health units has permitted the introduction of several disease programs on a concurrent and regional basis.

The Vaccines

Many of the diseases susceptible to immunisation procedures still rank as major causes of child mortality and morbidity. A concerted and continuous effort in applying vaccines would undoubtedly give a good return for a modest expenditure. The quarantinable diseases of smallpox, cholera and yellow fever still exist. Tetanus, tuberculosis, typhoid, pertussis, measles and poliomyelitis are major scourges. The prophylactic use of such vaccines, for example, BCG without prior tuberculin testing have to be weighed against the consequences of non-usage. Even with the development of ambulant anti-TB drug regimens at a tithe of former hospitalisation costs they are still considerably more than B.C.G. programs.[23] Such techniques have to be considered in that the greater outreach permitted in terms of economic and human resources, achieves in the long run a greater reduction in the total reservoir of disease extant.

In many developing countries poliomyelitis is changing from endemic to epidemic status, and is truly an "infantile paralysis" affliction. The use of live oral vaccines in mass campaigns as a preventive epidemic measure can be justified not only in terms of cost-effectiveness, but also as avoiding the life long tragedy of incapacitation in the physical labour environment of a peasant society.

During 1960 an epidemic of considerable proportions occurred in Kenya. Oral poliomyelitis vaccine was administered to 1·7 million persons, including 661,000 children out of the 1·4 million in this age group. The campaign was organised and executed *through the pre-existing health services and personnel*. The attack rate of the vaccinated children was less than half that of the non-vaccinated. In the following year the attack rate was five times greater in the non-protected.[24]

236

The Prophylactic Drugs

Drugs are the next most economical tools in these specific disease campaigns, and have been used on mass scales ever since the days of bismuth for yaws. Other examples are penicillin in venereal diseases, the sulphones in leprosy, tetracycline for trachoma and isoniazid and thiocetazone for tuberculosis. The advent of oral drugs has materially lessened the costs and organisational aspects. In such campaigns it is necessary to weigh what is the optimal treatment for least cost against the council of perfection in relation to the total reservoir of disease present.

Tuberculosis

Fox writing on tuberculosis states that the developing countries have derived very little benefit from advances in the treatment of pulmonary tuberculosis.[26] He gives two reasons: firstly, the gross shortage of medical resources and secondly, that "relatively little attempt has yet been made to adapt current knowledge to their special problems." He refers to the misapplication of knowledge without relevance to local factors: the attempt to apply the latest discoveries without relevance to costs. He concludes that expenditure on tuberculosis must be related to overall health priorities and that developing countries should concentrate on ambulatory chemotherapy.

Experience from Madras showed that standard chemotherapy given over a one-year period to patients in very poor environments at home was nearly as good as that of those patients in sanitoriums. In East Africa, after considerable studies and trials, a cheap and effective dual drug regime (consisting of isoniazid and thiacetazone) was determined suitable for domiciliary treatment. Recently a suggestion has appeared that by adding streptomycin to treatment during the first two months, the treatment success rate will be improved from its present 80 per cent level to 90 per cent. To achieve this improvement, treatment costs would double. To this cost still must be added the costs of hospitalisation for the two months of daily injections.

With 60,000 new cases of tuberculosis a year occurring in East Africa, one third being diagnosed, and only one sixth being treated, and with total health and medical care expenditures currently at ten shillings per head of population, can a doubling and more of costs be accepted for a 10 per cent increase in success? Since tuberculosis is highly communicable, it is important to achieve total outreach if the reservoir of infection is to be materially reduced: and this has to be accomplished within existing resources of money and trained manpower. So, doubling the outreach will achieve a greater total success and make greater inroads on the reserves of disease than will doubling the cost of treatment. That is, society and future generations will benefit while some individual patients (10 per cent) will suffer.

Yaws

In Thailand, population 30 million, the prevalence of yaws in 1950 was cited at 350,000 cases annually or about 18 per 1,000. An anti-yaws campaign was mounted in that year which by the year 1962 had reduced the figure to 2,000 cases annually, or 0.07 per 1,000. The total cost amounted to $4.5 million. The cost per case treated fell from $8 in 1950 to a low point of 50 cents per case in 1957; and then began to rise again with the effort to achieve complete eradication to $40 per case treated in 1962.

Meanwhile, in Kenya, population 10 million, which also was heavily afflicted with yaws the following occurred. Yaws was hyper-endemic to the extent that amongst the Kikuyu in 1920 mission physicians estimated that 90 per cent of the population had at one time or another been affected by yaws. In the early 1920s treatment campaigns commenced with Novarsenobillon. By 1923, with the introduction of bismuth and lowered costs, the campaign was intensified and between 30,000 and 70,000 cases a year were treated. Following this, the incidence dropped to between 10,000 and 12,000 cases a year and remained at that level until around 1950 (in which year 11,163 cases occurred). From that year forward, without any specific anti-yaws campaigns and despite increasing epidemiological returns from a growing rural health service, the number of cases reported annually began to decrease. In 1962 the case load had decreased to 1,050 – a reduction of from 2 per 1,000 to 0·125 per 1,000.

The known factors were the development of the rural health center programs, which grew from 0 to 150 centers in the 12 years, and the introduction and distribution of penicillin throughout the service.

It is reasonable to suggest that part of the reduced incidence in both countries was due to factors such as expanding health services, general availability of modern therapeutic drugs, improved living standards, clothing and personal hygiene. Further, there appears to be a "break-point" at which the law of diminishing returns begins to operate, without the need to continue specific efforts at mounting costs. At this point as the Ministry of Health, Thailand, noted in its 1961–62 Annual Report "It is evident that yaws control is more justifiably to be integrated into the rural health services."

The Residual Insecticides

Though these are more recent in the discovery of their application to disease control, they have been quickly appreciated and extensively applied. Anti-malaria campaigns are too well-known to warrant more than but passing mention in their contribution to medical care.

Malaria

Malaria, which was a scourge in Thailand reputedly causing 20 per cent of deaths has been under attack since 1949. The campaign started as a focal project near Chiengmai and expanded to a national one with some 24 million persons protected by 1964. The death rate has been reduced from 210 per 100,000 persons in 1949 to 23 per 100,000 in 1963. Despite this, malaria was still rife in 1963, some 120,000 cases being reported; and 350,000 cases of "fever" being recorded. The costs of the campaigns from 1949–64 were $18·6 million. The anticipated additional expenditure up to 1972 was put at $43 million.

In a report of an assessment of the National Malaria Eradication Project, Howard and McDowell state[27] "Eradication is the most exacting and difficult public health project that the nations of the world have ever attempted. It demands perfection. It requires the finding and spraying of every house and the search for all fever suspects. It requires a large organisation with the discipline of an army. It is more expensive than control because of its larger personnel force, but it is limited in time and therefore it is less expensive to the government over a long period of time."

The expenditure for anti-malaria in 1965 was estimated at just over $6 million or 20 cents per head of population. As against this the per capita expenditure on general medicine and health services was 65 cents. And in the rural areas it was estimated that only 25 cents per caput was being spent,[28] on curative and preventive needs.

It is still an open question as to whether such "perfection" can be achieved or whether drug administration could have been equally effective in suppressing malaria. Trends in Ceylon indicate a breakdown in the eradication program in that country. In East Africa malaria eradication on a regional basis was suggested in the early 1960's, but was rejected because it was considered that technical and scientific knowledge of the vector's habits was inadequate, the logistics of a campaign were too severe for strained medical and health services, and the costs too high in relation to the per capita expenditure on total health services. The estimate at that time was $1 per head per annum for 5 years as against a then expenditure of $1.40 per head for *all* medical and health services. Such a campaign would have meant either a 60 per cent increase in annual expenditure or a comparable recession of other health services. The failure of the Pare-Taveta anti-malaria experiment has since proven the rightness of the decision. An editorial in the East African Medical Journal[29] in commenting upon this and upholding past decisions against embarking upon a malaria eradication program writes "those who by the very nature of their long experience must spend much of their time dealing with the multitudinous health problems that face us cannot afford to be allowed to indulge in the luxury of restricting their activities to a single disease."

A recent report[30] on a malaria eradication project in Peruvian Amazonia cites some of the operational difficulties hindering the program. These are: lack of communication facilities, tribal languages, aboriginal tribes, isolation, migration, floating houses, houses without walls, destruction of housing and mosquito nets after spraying with DDT, difficulties in surveillance and case detection, limited personnel resources. These factors added to inadequate entomological data have led to failure to achieve eradication. On the merit side it is averred that valuable experience has been gained for the establishment of more comprehensive health services in the future.

A much less known but completely successful story was the eradication of onchocercosis from the Kenya Lake Victoria Basin by eliminating the vector S. neavei from rivers by the use of DDT. This has saved countless children from blindness, but was based upon thorough and painstaking research to elicit the complete epidemiology of the disease before embarking on the project.

ENVIRONMENTAL FACTORS IN SPECIFIC DISEASE PROGRAMS

Tickborne Relapsing Fever

Walton[31] in his review of "Ornithodoros moubata" in relation to the epidemiology of human relapsing fever reveals a dramatic picture of the influence of home living conditions on the incidence of disease. The number of cases in Kenya decreased from 1200 in 1945 to only sporadic cases by 1960.

He points out that the incidence of relapsing fever is highest amongst the Bantu-speaking tribes in Kenya. The Bantu in recent times live under static conditions on a mainly vegetarian diet, and the women as the "hewers of wood and drawers of water" have little time for the more domestic duties of normal housewives. Such conditions encouraged tick infestation. Pastoral tribes, on the other hand, restricted their womenfolk to home activities, and by constant repair to their houses keep the huts free of vermin.

Walton stated "generally the use of BHC (benzene hexachloride) convinces the African that the European means what he says. The

African also knows that supplies of BHC could not be relied upon in rural areas and is interested in any simple and effective remedy. In all areas the simplest remedy is good housekeeping; in other words the adoption of the methods used by the pastoralist tribes, but in improved dwellings. Frequent repair to plastered walls and floors, the use of bedsteads, the elimination of domestic animals and fowls from the house, introduction of windows and, above all else, improved design of houses. In Kenya the process of improvement has been going on imperceptibly for a number of years."

Improvement in housing, sanitation and water supplies is at least as important as special or specific anti-disease measures. The contribution of these environmental factors to health are incalculable. In the deployment of slender resources the balance between expenditure on environmental improvements and on attacks on specific diseases must be carefully weighed.

Conclusions

Many other situations and diseases could have been mentioned to illustrate facets of planning for medical care. Some examples are the changing epidemiology of poliomyelitis from endemic to epidemic, the advent of oral vaccines, the emergence of kala-azar from low endemicity to high epidemicity in Kenya, and the need for epidemiological research, the approach to hookworm, tapeworm, and beef cysticercosis, the common infectious diseases, nutrition – poverty in the midst of plenty – the general disease distribution of leprosy and campaigns for prevention, trachoma and the pastoral areas, the superimposition of "Rhodesian" type of sleeping sickness on the existing "Gambian" form and planning for eradication and settlement rather than control of sleeping sickness.

But sufficient information has been presented to delineate the stresses of planning for a limitless array of demands with strictly limited manpower and finances and to underline the advantages of an approach based on the development of a health center, the fundamental unit in the structure of a health service.

Smallpox may be used to measure the adequacy and sufficiency of health services to contain disease. In Kenya over the years 1911–62 it is observable that whenever an extra strain was imposed on the health services smallpox broke through from endemic to epidemic state. These periods occurred during World War I, the recession in the mid-nineteen thirties, World War II, and the mid 1950's when civil strife was paramount. During these times there were financial economies, reduction in manpower, and additional workloads imposed. This picture reveals the very thin margin between adequacy and inadequacy that prevails, in the health services of most developing countries. It emphasises the care that must be exercised in planning for the deployment of the limited trained manpower, and financial resources available.

In arriving at a decision as to whether a specific disease campaign is justified in terms of cost-benefit, as opposed to deployment of the monies in general medical care and health services, the following indicators are useful guidelines:

1. Prevalence, age incidence, and whether the disease is a killing, crippling or social disease.
2. Mortality and morbidity trends of the disease.
3. The social pathology.
4. The tools available and their effectiveness.
5. The state of current knowledge of the disease.
6. Manpower and training considerations.
7. The administrative and organisational aspects.
8. The cost, and alternative deployment of such monies.
9. The effect of the campaign on the general medical and health services.
10. The feasibility of consolidating gains once achieved.
11. The end result.
12. The advantages and disadvantages of control versus eradication of the disease.
13. The consequences inaction.

It is perhaps pertinent to reflect upon comparative costs of what might be described as the means of delivering the quantitative and qualitative needs of medical care through the health centre and the hospital. The latter is for care of those in more urgent need, and the former for those less seriously ill. The health centre also acts as a screening device to ensure that where resources are slender, each patient is treated at a level of care that is adequate but not excessive. It also provides the means through which special disease programs may be mounted.

In terms of capital costs, one health centre equates with some 5–10 hospital beds or less. On recurrent costs very roughly equivalent money would support either one health centre or 8 – 15 rural hospital beds. If one accepts the premise that only 2 per cent of total outpatient attendances need referral to a hospital, then a community of 100,000 persons (at 2.5 medical visits per person) would need five health centres (each with 5–10 beds): and a 100 hospital beds; that is, 1 bed per 1,000 of population – allowing an average inpatient stay of 7 to 8 days.

The more seriously ill patients not suited for the rural district hospital would be referred to a regional hospital serving say a population of 2·5 million. The regional hospital would be of 500 beds, a ratio of 0·2 beds per 1,000 of population.

At the national centre one could provide a complex of hospitals for specialised services. Such a complex would need to encompass 1,000 to 2,000 beds, i.e., 0·1 to 0·2 beds per 1,000 of population. Thus, for 10 million persons there would be 500 health centres (with 2,500–5,000 beds), 100 district hospitals with 10,000 beds, 4 regional hospitals with 2,000 beds (or 8 of 250 beds each) and 1 central hospital complex with 2,000 beds.

Such a system would admittedly provide sub-minimal care as a first goal. The second objective would be to double this service so that there was one health centre per 10,000 persons (0·5 to 1 H.C. bed per 1,000 population) and 2·8 hospital beds per 1,000 population. Such a system, if strategically planned, having regard to population scatter and density, adequately supported by mobility, especially at the health centre level, and staffed with a mixture of auxiliary, para-medical and professional personnel would at least provide a balanced medical care service: it would permit of logical development plans being formulated.

Given this pattern, not only can ambulant care and hospital care be provided, but special disease and prevention programs can be mounted. Fendall and Southgate[32] illustrated how such a service can operate in relation to a sleeping sickness program. Any specific disease eradication or control program can be partly executed and supplemented through a well-planned public health and medical care organisation. Through such an organisation it is possible to provide vigilance, service, treatment, prophylaxis, and follow-up activities, whilst at the same time reinforcing general environmental activities and promoting medical care services. Such integrated programs are mutually supportive and beneficial.

In the planning of medical and health services there are four cardinal steps.[33] These steps are the collection and analysis of data through an epidemiological research and evaluation component: a policy and planning unit; a training organisation for all levels of health manpower; and a service organisation with total outreach. To be effective a health plan must be integrated, if not fully compre-hensive, embracing curative medicine, preventive medicine and pro-motive medicine. Perhaps of these the greatest need is for fundamental education in better living practices.

In planning for health one must take cognizance of the five common factors; an excessive and wasteful population growth rate, limited economic resources and growth, a paucity of educational resources and trained manpower, the pattern of disease and malnutri-tion, and the cultural pattern of traditional societies.

243

Lack of long-term planning, and resort to short-term idealistic demonstration projects, not capable of nationwide replication leads only to frustration and lack of real progress in the delivery of medical care programs. The qualitative and quantitative aspects must progress in harmony. Curative medicine provides the foundation of faith, and the spearhead of the attacks on ill health.

Some Additional Comparative Statistics

DEATHS UNDER 5 YEARS BY AGE AND PROPORTIONS OF ALL DEATHS IN THREE DEVELOPING COUNTRIES

Age in years		Jamaica 1958 Numbers	% of all deaths	Guatemala 1961 Numbers	% of all deaths	Thailand 1962 Numbers	% of all deaths
Under 1	....	3,945	26·6	17,485	28·7	43,489	19·7
1 –	....	1,237	8·3	7,971	12·7	12,187	5·5
2 –	....	254	1·7	4,656	7·7	8,583	3·9
3 –	....	108	0·7	3,032	4·8	6,752	3·0
4 –	....	92	0·6	1,880	3·1	4,831	2·2
0 – 5	....	5,636	37·9	35,024	56·8	75,842	34·3
All deaths	....	14,813	100·0	62,287	100·0	221,157	100·0

Source: From official government documents.

MEDICAL CARE FIGURES FOR SEVEN DEVELOPING COUNTRIES (1962)

Country	Population millions	Inpatient	Admissions per Thousand Population	Outpatient Attendances Hospital Health Centers & Dispensaries	Average visits per Person per Year
Jamaica	1·8	68,828	38	1·08M	0·6
Guatemala	3·8	136,154	36	0·85M	0·2
Senegal	3·1	65,673	21	7·80M	2·5
Thailand	28	541,000	19	17·5M	0·6
Kenya	9·3	146,740	16	5·2M*	0·5
Tanganyika	10	231,598	23	25·97M	2·6
Uganda	7·2	172,279	24	9·63M	1·4

NOTE: These figures ignore the private sector of physician visits – which are considerable, but are related to urban areas and the paying patient.

*Estimate – probably underestimated.

PATTERNS OF DISEASE

A typical picture presented by the analysis of patients attending a
health sub-center in Thailand (1964–65)*

Diarrhea	....	21	Adenoma	....	1
Influenza	....	21	Simple Goiter	....	3
Traumatic Contusion	....	1	Menopause	....	3
Cut Wound	....	2	Climacteric (M)	....	1
Traumatic Wound	....	7	Endometritis	....	1
Common Cold	....	9	Newborn Baby	....	1
Otitis Media	....	7	Malnutrition	....	1
Otitis Externa	....	2	Debility	....	1
Acute Tonsillitis	....	6	Conjunctivitis	....	1
Acute Pharyngitis	....	17	Appendix Abscess	....	2
Acute Pharyngitis and			Abdominal Pain	....	1
Tonsillitis	....	3	Ulcer Vulva	....	1
Upper Respiratory Infection	....	6	Enteric Fever	....	5 (group)
Fever of Unknown Origin	....	2	Vertigo	....	1
Cellulitis	....	1	Eczema	....	2
Flatulence	....	7	Contact Dermatitis	....	2
Myalgia	....	3	Palpebral Space Inf	....	1
Pregnancy	....	21	Morning Sickness	....	1
Tinea Corporis	....	1	Colic	....	1
Leprosy	....	1	Convulsion	....	1
Pyoderma	....	1	Placenta Previa	....	1
Miliary Tuberculosis	....	1	Rhinitis	....	1
Premature Baby	....	1	Senile Arthritis	....	1
Well Baby	....	41	Beriberi	....	4
Neurosis	....	3	Arthralgia	....	1
Neurogenic palpitations	....	1	Joint Pain	....	1
Neuralgia	....	1	Anorexia	....	1
Burns	....	1	Epistaxis	....	1
Hypertension	....	1	Snake Bite	....	1
Hyperventilation	....	1	Hematoma	....	1
Dyspepsia	....	3	Dressing	....	3
Stomatitis	....	1	Caries	....	1
Hepatitis	....	1	Herpes Zoster	....	1
Gastritis	....	1	Bronchial Pneumonia		1
			Total	....	233

* 12% sample – 233 cases out of 1,922

References

1. Moser, C. A. "The Measurement of Levels of Living," Colonial Research Studies, No. 24, 1957. H.M.S.O.
2. *World Health Chronicle,* Vol. 22, No. 3, March 1968, pp. 105–106.
3. "Population and Economic Growth," A Chart Guide from the Conference Board, National Industrial Conference Board, Inc., New York 1966.
4. "World Population Projections 1965–2000," *Population Bulletin,* Vol. XXI, No. 4, October 1965.
5. Hance, W. A., "The Race Between Population and Pressure," *Africa Report,* January 1968.
6. *Population Bulletin,* Vol. XXI, No. 4, October 1965, p. 82–83.
7. "Population and Economic Growth," p. 22 (ref. 3).
8. Science, Vol. 156, No. 3782, June 1967.
9. Coale, A. J. and Greep, R. O., "Human Fertility and Population Problems," Cambridge, U.S.A., 1963, Schenkman.
10. Enke, S., "Economic Aspects of Slowing Population Growth," Cosmo Club, Economic Journal, 1966, 76, 44–56.
11. Harbison and Meyers, "A Look Into the Future".
12. Joint F.A.O./W.H.O. Expert Committee on Nutrition. 7th Report, Rome, 1966, W.H.O. Trs. No. 377, 1967.
13. Fendall, N. R. E. and Grounds, J. G. "The Incidence and Epidemiology of Disease in Kenya," *Journal of Trop. Med. and Hyg.* Vol. 68, pp. 77–84, 113–120, 134–141, April–June 1965.
14. *World Health Chronicle,* Vol. 18, No. 11, 1964.
15. Third Report of the World Health Situation, *World Health Organisation,* Geneva, 1967.
16. Sai, Fred, "Health and Nutritional Status of the Ghanian People," Mimeographed Document, 1965.
17. Fendall, N. R. E., "Public Health and Urbanisation in Africa," *Public Health Reports,* 78, 7, pp. 569–584, 1963.
18. "Facts on Health Progress," P.A.H.O./W.H.O., Washington, D.C., 1968.
19. "Health Statistics: Physician Visits in the United States 1957," U.S. Department of Health, Education and Welfare, Washington, D.C.
20. White, K. L., "The ecology of Medical Care," *New England Journal of Medicine,* 265, 885–892, 1961.
21. Cordero, Ana Livia, "The Determination of Medical Care Needs in Relation to a Concept of Minimal Adequate Care," *Medical Care,* Vol. II, No. 2, 95–103, April–June 1964.
22. Fendall, N. R. E., "Planning Health Services in Developing Countries," *Public Health Reports,* Vol. 78, No. 11, pp. 977–987, 1963.
23. ibid.
24. Fendall, N. R. E., "Poliomyelitis in Kenya", *Journal of Tropical Medicine and Hygiene,* Vol. 65, 245–255, 1962.
25. Egsmose, T., "Epidemiological studies of some Tuberculosis Control Measures in a developing Country," Dept. of Epidemiology, University Institute of Hygiene, Copenhagen, Denmark, 1969 (Doctoral thesis).
26. Fox, Wallace, "Realistic Chemotherapeutic Policies for Tuberculosis in the Developing Countries," *British Medical Journal,* Vol. I, pp. 135–142, 1964.
27. Howard, L. M., McDowell, J. W., et al., U.S.O.M./Thailand, A.I.D., 1963.
28. Kahn, Lt.-Col. Rafique, "Pakistan Army Medical Corps S.E.A.T.O., Report on Health Conditions in North Eastern Thailand With Particular Reference to the Problems of Ubol," 1963 (Mimeographed Document.)

R

29. *East African Medical Journal*, Editorial, Vol. 42, 719–720, 1965.
30. "Malaria Eradication in Peruvian Amazonia," *World Health Organisation Chronicle*, Vol. 22, No. 12, pp. 530–533, 1968.
31. Walton, G. A., "The Ornithodoros moubata Superspecies Problem in Relation to Human Relapsing Fever Epidemiology," *Symposium Zool.* Society London, No. 6, pp. 83–156, May 1962.
32. Fendall, N. R. E., and Southgate, B. A., and Berrie, J. R. H., "Trypanoso-miasis Control in Relation to Other Public Health Services," *World Health Organisation Bulletin*, 28, 787–795, 1963.
33. Fendall, N. R. E., and Southgate, B.A., "Principles, Priorities and Public Participation in Planning a Program for Health," U.N. Conf. on the Application of Science and Technology for the Benefit of the Less Developed Areas, World Health Organisation Geneva, 1962. Mimeographed Document.

Chapter 8

Medical Care in Australia

H. N. Robson, f.r.c.p.e.
Vice-Chancellor, University of Sheffield, England
Formerly Professor of Medicine, Adelaide, Australia

THE COUNTRY AND ITS PEOPLE

Geography

Continental Australia has an area of some 2,967,909 square miles – as large as Europe and only slightly smaller than the United States. Lying between longitude 113°E to 153°E and between the latitudes of 10°S and 44°S, climatic conditions range from tropical in the north to temperate in the south. The outstanding topographical feature is the large central arid desert area which occupies about one third of the continent. About a further third has such low rainfall that human settlement is very sparse. Extensive urban settlement is to be found only in southern and eastern coastal areas and close to the large river systems of the Darling and the Murray which drain south westwards from the spinal mountain range which lies near the eastern coast of the continent.

History

The first European settlements in Australia occurred late in the eighteenth century with the establishment of British penal colonies in New South Wales and Tasmania. Other settlements were established later and separately at Melbourne, Perth, Adelaide and Brisbane and from these centres the States of Victoria, Western Australia, South Australia and Queensland were developed. In 1901 these six sovereign states agreed to federate to form the Commonwealth of Australia under a federal constitution somewhat similar to that of the United States. Until recently the Australian economy was primarily based on agriculture with large exports of wool, wheat and meat. Since the Second World War, however, considerable industrialisation has occurred, very extensive mineral deposits have been found and are being exploited, and discoveries of oil and natural gas in various parts of the country have further encouraged technological development.

Constitutional Structure

Under the original federal constitution, the central or Commonwealth Government, based in Canberra, is responsible mainly for defence, external affairs, customs and quarantine, and the central collection of taxes. The latter are then distributed as allocations which form by far the main revenue of the six State Governments. The latter exercise full authority over all matters not specifically consigned to the federal government. Thus each State is autonomous in areas such as education, housing and development, public order and many others, including hospital services and public health.

Without formal constitutional amendment but by agreement with the State Governments, the Federal Government has progressively assumed responsibilities in the fields of education especially technical and tertiary aspects and of health and social security. In these latter areas old age, disability and unemployment benefits are federal matters as are certain specific national health problems such as tuberculosis and poliomyelitis and the whole of the national health insurance scheme as described later.

Economic Structure

The increasingly mixed economy has been buoyant in recent years. Since World War II there has been a sustained policy of national development and rapid industrialisation. A controlled immigration system together with national population increase has produced a growing home market.

At the last census (1966) 27 per cent of a labour force of about 5 million were employed in manufacturing industries, 16 per cent in commerce, 9 per cent in primary production, 11 per cent in community and business services, 9 per cent in building and construction, 8 per cent in transport and communications, 6 per cent in catering and hotels and the remaining 14 per cent in other industries and in public authority.

Australia supplies nearly one third of the world's wool and also exports large amounts of wheat, meat, sugar, dairy produce and fruit. The continent is rich in minerals. Iron and coal have formed the basis of a steel industry which ranks thirteenth in size in the world and the motor vehicle production is the ninth largest in the world. Copper, bauxite, nickel, lead, zinc, uranium, rutile, oil and natural gas are the basis of other growing industries.

Australia is one of the few countries in the world where most wages are fixed by law and a Commonwealth Commission determines Minimum Total Wages for most industries. The average standard of living is high. The statistically "average" home in Australia has more than five rooms, with less than one person per room. More than 70 per cent of homes are occupier-owned. Eighty per cent of homes have television and 99 per cent have electricity or gas or both. The number of motor vehicles averages about one to every 2·7 persons, and there is about one telephone for every four people in the population.

Social Security System

The major social services in Australia are financed from a National Welfare Fund appropriated annually from federal revenue by the Commonwealth Government. In addition to the health insurance arrangements which are detailed later, there are comprehensive provisions for retirement and old age pensions, family allowances and child endowment, unemployment and sickness benefits, and widows' and invalid pensions. There are individual State governmental provisions for Workers' Compensation in case of injury or death. Ex-Servicemen and their dependants are entitled to comprehensive health and social security benefits under federal provisions.

Population

The population of Australia is now approaching 12·5 million. The average population density throughout the country is about four people to the square mile. The annual increase is about 2 per cent, half of this being due to net migration. The last major census results (1966) showed that 58·14 per cent of the population lived in metropolitan areas: 25·08 per cent in other urban areas and 16·61 per cent in rural areas. At the census there were 5,816,359 males and 5,734,103 females. The age distribution was as follows:

| % | Years of age | | |
	Under 15	15 – 64	65 and over
Males	29·88	63·03	7·09
Females	28·86	61·3	10·1
All persons	29·37	62·09	8·54

Vital and Health Statistics

Life expectancy at birth in Australia is between 67 and 68 years for men and about 74 years for women. Recent figures showed the birth rate at 19·3 and the infant mortality was 17·7 per 1,000 births. The general death rate was 9·1 per 1,000 of mean population. The major causes of death were arteriosclerotic and degenerative heart diseases, neoplasms and vascular lesions of the central nervous system.

There are some 14,000 medical practitioners in the country of whom about 60 per cent are self-employed in private medical practice.

HEALTH SERVICES

Principles and Philosophies Underlying Medical Care

The Australian health insurance system was established in the early 1950's with the object of enabling the public to obtain protecttion against the cost of medical treatment, of hospitalisation and the services of medical practitioners. The National Health Acts (1953–1968) registered non-profit making societies with whom individuals could insure on a voluntary basis. Those who so insured became eligible for Commonwealth Government hospital and medical benefits which supplemented the amounts obtainable from the insurance schemes. To these provisions were added, by the Commonwealth Government, arrangements to provide for medical services to pensioners and a pharmaceutical benefits scheme whereby all necessary drugs were provided free or at nominal cost on a doctor's prescription.

In 1968 the Commonwealth Government set up a committee to review this insurance system. This committee, which came to be known by the name of its chairman, Mr. Justice J. A. Nimmo, reported at length, and its recommendations formed the basis of new legislation (National Health Act, 1970) which extended considerably the national health service provisions.

It may be noted that the reasons which prompted the federal government to mount this enquiry and subsequently to extend quite considerably the national arrangements were as follows:

   (i) The operation of the insurance based schemes had become unnecessarily complex.
   (ii) The benefits received by contributors were frequently much less than the cost of hospital and medical treatment.
   (iii) The contributions had increased to an unreasonable extent.
   (iv) Operating expenses of the various organisations were unduly high.
   (v) A considerable range of services such as home nursing, physiotherapy, optometry, dentistry and others had not been covered by the insurance system.

The legislation of 1970 while providing for a considerable extension of the national health service, still retained the basic principle of voluntary insurance which then automatically attracted the governmental additions. Commonwealth Government expenditure in 1969–70 on National Health Benefits totalled $A324·7 million.

Under the present arrangements, annual premium payment of about $A35 (£15 sterling) will cover a whole family against the greater part of all medical, hospital and ancillary costs. The scheme is nation-wide and covers the whole population. Additional provisions (see later) are made for the elderly, the incapacitated, and for those suffering from certain diseases.

The entire scheme is financed on the basis of voluntary insurance supplemented by large central (federal) government funds. The individual is entirely free to choose whether to insure, with which fund to insure, and when insured there is freedom of choice of medical practitioner.

Structure and Administration of Health Services

Although the Australian community is predominantly urbanised and although substantial numbers of the population are relatively recent immigrants, the pioneering history and traditions of the country are still very influential. Thus there is emphasis on personal responsibility in health matters. As described, the national health service provisions are based on a system of voluntary insurance. Something of the same principle may be discerned in the relations in the health field between the Commonwealth (federal) Government and the various State Governments. The latter are predominantly responsible for the provision of hospital services, community services and general public health measures. Federal financial assistance is from time to time offered or may be attracted on a matching basis. Thus if a State Government is prepared to find money for a particular project, the Commonwealth Government will provide a similar amount. Examples where this system has operated recently include the development of mental health institutions (a state responsibility), the provision of public nursing homes, the provision of paramedical services, such as physiotherapy, occupational therapy, speech therapy, chiropody and similar services. Other areas which though primarily state responsibilities have received federal governmental support are home nursing schemes, blood transfusion services, child health centres and the provision of free milk for school children.

The Commonwealth Government is responsible for all external relations in the field of health e.g. with international bodies such as WHO. Quarantine is a federal responsibility. The central government maintains a number of laboratories for standards purposes and for the production of vaccines. There is a National Health and Medical Research Council. Tuberculosis and leprosy are the subject of special federal provisions. Otherwise each State is responsible for all health provisions under its own legislation.

State governments are therefore usually the licensing authorities for personnel – medical, nursing and paramedical – and for institutions, including hospitals and nursing homes.

Health Resources

Australia has highly developed and sophisticated services both for personal and for environmental health. Some illustrative statistics would include the following.

Beds in public hospitals totalled 63,500 (in 1969) to which should be added 12,600 in private hospitals. In addition there are large numbers of nursing homes both public and private, licensed under the various state authorities and subsidised in varying degrees.

Medical practitioners total some 14,000 and the medical schools in the country now produce nearly 1,000 graduates annually. The nursing profession includes some 80,000 members and about 5,000 new nurses are registered each year.

The medical centres, in addition to medical and nursing schools nearly all have dental schools and in most centres there are physiotherapy, orthoptic and other ancillary training facilitites.

Medical Care (Personal Health Services)

(a) *Informal health services system*

Since the greater part of the Australian population is urbanised the patterns of self care and of family medicine are very similar to those of Western Europe or North America. Well-stocked pharmacies provide a wide range of proprietary preparations for self-medication. There are no recognised services at a level other than that of medically-qualified personnel, except for the specialised nursing services in midwifery, home visiting and in psychiatry.

(b) *First contact services*

General practitioner or family physician services are a well-developed and prominent part of the Australian medical scene. With an overall doctor/population ratio of better than one in a thousand, access to these first contact services is readily obtained. (There are exceptions to this in some of the sparsely populated country areas). The majority of city practitioners belong to group practices, many of which are conducted from specially-designed clinics or surgeries. The provisions of the 1970 National Health Act should ensure that there is no serious financial barrier to access by all to these services of first contact.

(c) *Specialist services*

Again, in the urban areas, specialist services of a generally high standard of competence are readily available. Specialist training and recognition are largely controlled by professional colleges and associations along the lines of the British pattern. In the capital cities the large public hospitals are teaching institutions and are staffed by very high calibre personnel whose services are available both on an in-patient and an out-patient basis. The National Health Service provides for the refund of the greater part of specialist fees where the patient has been referred by a family doctor. A register of specialists has now been established in each State.

(d) *Hospitals*

The Australian hospital service is well-developed and indeed some of their recently constructed facilities match the most advanced anywhere in the world. The public hospital system is the responsibility of the various State governments and such hospitals range from the large teaching complexes in the capital cities to the small community-type arrangements in the country towns. The public system also includes modern well-equipped specialist hospitals, particularly for maternity and for children's diseases. As mentioned earlier, the Commonwealth Government assumes special responsibility for tuberculosis and special hospital facilities are provided in each State. Also, the Commonwealth Government through the Repatriation Department provides both general and special hospitals for ex-servicemen and their dependents. The system is similar to the Veterans Administration arrangements in the United States.

In addition to these state systems there is a large system of private hospitals. These vary from large city institutions, some of which are included in the teaching complexes of the medical schools, to small nursing-home type institutions. Many of the private hospitals are associated with religious or philanthropic foundations and many specialise in the care of geriatric or long-stay problems.

(e) *Community Home Care*

Until recently, home care services lagged somewhat in development relative to the generally advanced level of other provisions. This was no doubt in part due to the fact that, before 1970, such services were not directly included in the national health service coverage.

255

As part of its direct community health responsibility each State government provides home nursing and health visiting services but these have tended to be somewhat over-worked and under-staffed. Since 1969, however, Commonwealth financial assistance has been available on a matching basis, broadly related to population, for the provision of paramedical services in the home, especially for the aged.

A considerable amount of home care is provided by voluntary organisations of various types, some specialising in home nursing, others in areas such as food provision, e.g. the Meals on Wheels Scheme. Many such organisations receive subsidies from their local State governments and in recent years the Commonwealth Government has increasingly offered financial assistance.

As a result, home care services have expanded and improved considerably in recent years.

Provision of Drugs, Appliances etc.

An early part of the development of the Australian national health service was a pharmaceutical benefits system founded by the Commonwealth government. An approved list of pharmaceutical preparations was set up. This list is regularly reviewed by a non-governmental advisory committee. The list, which is extensive, basic-ally consists of all drugs which can be regarded as essential in defined medical conditions. Any drug on this list can be obtained at a nominal charge of 50c on a medical prescription. In 1969–70 some 60 million prescriptions were filled and the cost of this Pharmaceutical Benefits Scheme was $A136·7 million.

There is no general system for the provision of appliances but special categories such as pensioners (hearing aids), widows, incapacit-ated persons, unemployed, ex-servicemen and their dependents can be provided for usually under Commonwealth arrangements. State governments through their public hospital systems provide appliances. If necessary a number of charitable organisations can be approached for assistance.

Public (Environmental) Health

Provisions for the safeguarding of public health are organised similarly to those in the United States or in Western European countries. The Commonwealth government provides a number of central laboratory services, operates the general quarantine arrangements and maintains records and statistical services.

Each State government is responsible for its own legislative and administrative arrangements. These include all the usual vaccination and inoculation services for the control of infectious diseases:

the inspection and control of water and sewage: of food production, processing and handling: and the multifarious activitites necessary to protect a modern community.

The standards of community health are high and compare with most advanced societies. Poliomyelitis has been virtually eradicated and the tuberculosis rate is one of the lowest in the world.

Community and Regional Planning

Planning problems in Australia tend to be relatively uncomplicated. The division of a very large area into six states divides a comparatively small population into manageable groups. The further concentration of the population into large city areas in and around the capitals of each state makes for very close relations between the state authority and the urban authorities responsible for the more detailed arrangements. The very large area of some of the cities has created some difficulties in the provision of hospital services at the periphery and conversely some of the older established hospitals in the centre of citites have become separated from the main residential areas. These problems, however, have been relatively small compared with those facing some of the older cities of Europe, Britain and America.

Rural Health Services

The rural communities of Australia face problems of very great distances. In the less remote areas medical services are provided by general practioners who face hours of travelling to reach their patients and who have to be prepared to undertake when necessary a wide range of emergency procedures. Air transport is increasingly available and used to transport complicated or difficult cases to the metropolitan centres.

In the most remote areas, radio and air transport have been utilised to produce the well-known Flying Doctor Service. Started by voluntary effort, this remarkable organisation now receives both state and federal support. Operating from bases around the great empty heart and north of Australia regular radio contact is maintained with even the most remote settlement. Medical advice is available at any time and medical and nursing personnel are transported in aircraft belonging to the Service to deal with emergencies. Hospitals are maintained at the main Flying Doctor Service bases.

Categorical Health Services

(a) As mentioned earlier, the Commonwealth government undertakes special responsibilities for the treatment of tuberculosis and leprosy. These responsibilities go beyond the provision of hospital facilities and include diagnostic services, out-patient clinics and the granting of living and family allowances. Mental health services are provided by the State authorities, though Commonwealth subsidies are now offered for some purposes on a matching basis. Hospital, out-patient and home care provisions are made by the various State governments.

There are no national dental health services in Australia and special provisions for cancer sufferers are not yet regarded as state responsibilities.

(b) There is a well-developed Pensioner Medical Service, funded by federal finance under which all pensioners are entitled to free medical, pharmaceutical and hospital services. In addition there are federal subsidies for nursing homes, both public and private, which undertake the care of the elderly. At June 1970 – 9·5 per cent of the population was covered by this Service. School health services are provided by State authorities throughout the state educational system. The federally supported free milk service has been mentioned already.

In 1970 the Commonwealth government made provision for financial assistance to families on low incomes (up to $A45 per week): to unemployed persons: to migrants during the first two months in the country such that these groups became entitled to free hospital and medical insurance. Mention has already been made of the arrangements whereby the Repatriation Department (federally financed) provides a wide range of medical and social security benefits to ex-servicemen and their families.

(c) Rehabilitation services are provided by both federal and state authorities and are generally of a high order of efficiency and comprehensiveness. Such services usually extend from the fitting of appliances and prostheses through to re-training for employment. A number of voluntary organisations are also active in this field.

(d) In the area of preventive medicine again both the federal and state governments are active. The Commonwealth government maintains a central service for the production of vaccines and immune globulins, including poliomyelitis, tuberculosis, cholera and the usual infectious diseases. The State governments are generally responsible for the immunisation programmes in schools and in the community at large. The State health departments also conduct community educational exercises in a variety of preventive health fields.

Voluntary Organisations

Voluntary effort is still more prominent in the Australian scene than is the case in the United Kingdom. In a wide range of health and educational activities voluntary or community organisations are to be found. In very many instances state and federal responsibilities have been met by financial subsidy of the previously existing voluntary organisation. Notable examples of this are to be found in the areas of maternity and child welfare, handicapped children, the adult incapacitated, the elderly, cancer sufferers, special diseases such as asthma, haemophilia, tuberculosis, diabetes and others and the somewhat unique Flying Doctor Service for people living in the outback.

Relation to other Community Services

The health services are generally well integrated with other community services. The State governments, which have the primary responsibility for the provision of health facilities are also responsible for education services and for a wide range of welfare provisions, though in the latter areas the Commonwealth government plays a large part, as it does in the financing of personal health services.

Financing

(a) As outlined earlier the basis of the Australian national health scheme is a system of voluntary self-insurance which, if effected, attracts substantial supplementary subsidy from federal sources. These provisions now apply to medical, hospital and paramedical costs. The individual pays the insurance premia and is then automatically covered. At present an annual payment of about $A35 will cover a family. (these payments are tax deductible). Under present arrangements the maximum further payment which may have to be made for any medical or hospital service should not exceed $A5. Similarly the maximum further amount to be paid for a visit to a doctor's surgery is 80 cents and for a home visit not more than $A1·20. Under the Pharmaceutical Benefits Scheme there is at present a nominal charge of 50 cents per prescription.

(b) Those supplying the services whether they be family doctor, specialist, paramedical or hospital authority, render an account directly to the patient. The latter takes or sends this account to the Fund with which he or she is insured and receives, in one payment, the insurance entitlement together with the Commonwealth contribution. Payment is then made by the patient to the provider of the service. In the case of pharmacists, they receive payment directly from the Commonwealth, to cover the full costs of substances prescribed together with prescribing costs.

(c) Income guarantee insurance schemes are available commercially and are used by professional groups. Generally, illness and disability periods would be covered by the unemployment and sickness benefits to which all employed persons are entitled under the Social Services Act. There are also provisions under Worker's Compensation Acts in case of industrial accident or injury. As described earlier, there is a Commonwealth government scheme whereby those on low income, for whatever reason, can receive assistance with health insurance payments.

(d) Commonwealth Government sources indicate that in the financial year 1966–67 the recurrent health expenditure in Australia was $A538·8 million from private sources and $A579 million from public sources – totalling $A1118·6 million. This represents a figure of about $A95 per head of population. The G.N.P. for the corresponding period was $A21,612 million.

Medical Personnel

Medical

There are 9 medical schools associated with the universities in the capital cities of Australia. Admission to medical school is selective and competitive. Performance in school leaving and in matriculation examinations is the main factor determining selection. The medical curriculum extends over six years as a rule and most states require a year's hospital training in addition before full registration. Clinical training is carried out mainly in the large state hospitals which are associated with the medical schools. The system is similar to that found in Britain.

Specialist training programmes are generally prescribed by the professional colleges and specialist associations.

Nursing

Most of the large hospitals, both public and private, run nurse training schools. Training courses are usually 3 or 4 years in duration. Examinations and certification are the responsibility of individual State governments. Registration in one State is reciprocally recognised by the others.

Other Paramedical

In the large medical centres there are usually training centres for other paramedical personnel such as physiotherapists, social and psychiatric social workers, dietitians, occupational therapists, optometrists etc. Arrangements for education and training vary in different centres. In some the training is part University; in others it is entirely hospital-based. Again, registration is a matter for State authorities.

Research

Medical research is actively pursued in all the university and large hospital centres throughout the country. There are a number of specialised research institutes of which the Walter and Eliza Hall

Institute in Melbourne is a notable example. A prominent feature of the medical research effort is the John Curtin Medical School of the Australian National University in Canberra. This is an entirely post-graduate institution which has an international reputation in a number of fields.

The Commonwealth government, which finances the National University also provides considerable sums for medical research throughout the country. This is distributed mainly through the National Health and Medical Research Council. This Council, in addition to supporting medical research, is a forum for the discussion of national health problems and also is concerned with the recording of medical statistics.

The Commonwealth Bureau of Census and Statistics in Canberra is the national centre for records, statistics and information. Each State also maintains record and statistical offices. The Commonwealth Department of Health also provides a focal information point about health statistics and health services organisation in Australia.

Planning, Evaluation, Quality Control

Various national organisations, including those mentioned above, both governmental and non-governmental are interested in and engaged in the study of health services in Australia. Such activity has undoubtedly contributed to the present situation whereby the quality of health service provision in Australia ranks among the best in the world.

Section Three:

The Administrative Problems of Medical Care

Chapter 9

The Status of Medical Care in America

Wilbur J. Cohen
*Presently Dean, School of Education, University of Michigan,
and formerly Secretary of the Department of Health, Education and
Welfare in the Johnson Administration, and Architect of Medicare*

American health care is a dynamic pluralistic mosaic of programmes which offer both many advantages for experimental development, and serious problems in the delivery of care. Some of these problems such as shortages of personnel are not easily corrected but deficiencies in organisation and financing can be effectively improved and in particular health insurance both public and private could be expanded to provide comprehensive protection for all. Health insurance might cover ambulatory as well as hospital services, hospital costs might be better contained and with the removal of impediment to group practice and an expansion of the numbers engaged in health care some of the current problems in U.S. health care might be overcome.

The Pattern of Development

Interest in health insurance began to develop in the United States about the time the National Health Insurance Act in Great Britain was implemented (1910–12). Although the German Health Insurance programme was well known to the few American social insurance experts then, it was the adoption of the British legislation which gave special impetus to the first American movement for health insurance.

The period 1910–43 was marked by the pressure for health insurance on a State-by-State basis. When it became clear that a national social insurance programme was constitutional (1937), interest began to develop in a national health insurance plan. The appearance of the Beveridge Report in England reinforced this interest and in 1943 the Wagner-Murray-Dingell bill was introduced in Congress which proposed a comprehensive national social insurance system, a key part of which was a national health insurance programme.

President Truman endorsed this type of national health insurance in 1945. A vigorous ideological and propaganda battle ensued which resulted in the plan failing to get off the ground (1950). As a result, a shift occurred and the immediate legislative proposal in this area became national health insurance for the aged (1952–60).

Presidents Kennedy and Johnson endorsed this proposal which was enacted finally in 1965 as Medicare. At the same time another programme called Medicaid was enacted which provided Federal subsidies to the States for helping to finance medical costs of indigent persons.

After 55 years of debate, and controversy, a national health insurance plan for 10 per cent of the population became a reality. The fight had been acrimonious, bitter, and heated.

The Rubicon had been crossed. Within a year or two (1967–70) the political and psychological dam broke, holding back the waters of national health insurance, and individuals and groups which had been opposed to national health insurance began to develop their own version of national health insurance.

The Recent Changes

We have made thus considerable headway in recent years in the conquest of this frontier. The executive branch of the federal government, the Congress, the States and the public have acted to attack some of the ancient enemies of mankind – hunger, disease and human blight. As I look back over the past decade I see some noteworthy milestones of progress. In 1960 there were 40 million persons in poverty; today, there are 15 million less than in 1960. Whereas there was then no co-ordinated attack on poverty, today, the poor have a better chance to find decent jobs, homes, health care and education for their children. Ten years ago, millions of Americans over the age of 65 were without adequate health care because they could not afford it. Today, 20 million older Americans are protected by Medicare. In the past decade Congress has enacted over 50 new health laws designed to help assure the right of every American to high-quality health care. In the last 19 years – the life of a teenager – we increased the proportion of our gross national product spent on health, education, welfare and social security – private and public – from just over 13 per cent to almost 22 per cent. In 1970 we invested over 67 billion dollars on all health services, research and construction – 7 per cent of the gross national product.

In human terms, these new laws, programmes and increased expenditures have helped to bring about major improvements in the health of the American people. Infant mortality is now at the lowest rate in United States history, and the lives of thousands of children

266

have been saved that would have been lost to diseases in early infancy and childhood. The death rate from heart disease has been reduced 20 per cent in the past four years. New developments in computer technology make possible mass health screening, medical diagnosis, monitoring of patients, improved laboratory procedures and other improvements in the actual delivery of health services. Dramatic declines have been recorded in the number of resident mental-hospital patients.

These improvements are a result of the increased investment that the American people are making in one of their most important resources: good health. "The first wealth," Emerson once said, "is health." However, the most affluent Nation on earth still cannot claim to be the healthiest one. For there are still too many obstacles, some of long standing and some recent, that bar many citizen from recciving even barely adequate health care.

Americans are fully aware of the rapid advances in medical care and fully expect to benefit from them. When they find their access blocked, the entire health care system comes under attack, and that is precisely what is happening today. The public is dissatisfied with the gap between what it knows is possible and the reality of what is available. Inaccessibility, fragmentation and the high cost of health services, combined with a lack of concern for the total well-being of the individual, are legitimate grievances of too many Americans. And society is beginning to demand that these grievances be redressed. The challenge is clear: steps must be taken to make the health care system more responsive to the needs of all Americans rather than only the privileged few.

American health care is not really a "system" but is essentially a mosaic of public and private health programmes – one that has grown piecemeal to meet needs as they arose. A multitude of people, institutions and arrangements is involved. There are a total of over 3 million health workers, including 300,000 physicians in a variety of practices and 700,000 nurses. There are 7,000 hospitals varying greatly in size and in operation, and some 20,000 long-term care facilities; there are local and national voluntary health agencies, and professional groups, medical schools, hundreds of insurance companies, local, state and federal agencies, consumer groups and a variety of payment mechanisms, including fee for service, repayment and charity, which further complicate the system.

This dynamic, pluralistic arrangement has definite advantages. It provides opportunities for innnovation and competition for quality development, and incentives for organisational and quality improvements. And it has produced amazing medical miracles.

The Serious Problems

But out of it has evolved a number of serious problems that are likely to continue to face us in the decade ahead. Among the most serious, I would include the fact that the supply of certain services, such as those of physicians, dentists and nurses, is inadequate. There is often an excess in supply – duplication – of some services and facilities for high-income individuals including some very expensive hospital services, and health facility planning is not now performed adequately. Also, children, the poor, the disadvantaged, the blacks, and other minority groups, often have inadequate access to medical care. There are often shortages in less costly alternatives to hospital care such as out-patient care, home health services, extended-care facilities and nursing homes. Some costly services, especially hospital services, are sometimes utilized unnecessarily. Many private health insurance plans produce undesirable incentives to use the most expensive methods of care; there are substantial gaps in the coverage of health insurance. The cost of many drugs is too high. Many possible hospital management improvements have not been adopted. The growth of group practice has been retarded by legal bars and restrictive attitudes. Productivity in the provision of medical care has not been defined and measured. Insufficient attention is given to preventive care and health education. There are insufficient financial incentives to restrain mounting hospital costs while maintaining high-quality medical care. Ignorance of quality comparisons or the failure to undertake them have resulted in the purchase of high-priced drugs or unnecessary services. There has been unsatisfactory organisation of activities at all levels – public and private – in the health field, and there are serious deficiencies in the organisation, financing and delivery of health care in the United States.

The point is driven home in vivid contrasts – in the terrible wastage one sees within cities that can boast, for their most favoured residents, of very low rates by any standard. In New York City, for example – where the overall infant mortality compares with the national average of about 24 per 1000 – there are neighbourhoods where the rate is as high as 47 and others where it approaches 12. The difference of 35 annual deaths per 1000 infants under one year of age must be considered excessive. It is a rather difficult thing in the United States to realize that we are only 14 or 15 in the world in our rate of infant mortality; that is, there are 14 or 15 other countries which have a lower infant mortality rate than we have.

We also happen to know that out of the $3\frac{1}{2}$ million women who deliver a child each year, there are somewhere in the neighbourhood of seven hundred thousand by sample studies that do not have comprehensive prenatal care at the present time. Most of these are women in the low-income groups, among the black members of our society, among the Appalachians, among those with low educational attainment, with little health education, but the fact is they still produce 700,000 children a year, and without comprehensive prenatal, and possibly even postnatal care. Nevertheless during the past two decades the extension of private health insurance protection to the working population and their families has been impressive. At the end of last year between 75 and 85 per cent of the population under 65 years of age had some coverage of hospital and surgical expense. But despite this impressive coverage, health insurance benefits in 1967 met only about 33 per cent of all consumer expenditures for health services.

Advances in the medical sciences have tremendously increased the ability of modern medicine to cure or relieve disease. But the costs of care have multiplied, and can be prohibitive for everyone. People with low incomes need the protection of health insurance more than those with high incomes. Yet the extent of health insurance coverage varies in reverse degree. In 1967 only 35 per cent of persons under the age of 65 with family incomes under 3,000 dollars had some hospital insurance, and 57 per cent of those with incomes between 3,000 dollars and 5,000 dollars as compared with 90 per cent among those with incomes of 10,000 dollars or more.

The expansion of health insurance to its present dimensions testifies to the need for and the popularity of insurance protection against health care costs. Nevertheless, private insurance still falls seriously short of the mark. Some 15 to 25 per cent of the population under the age of 65 have no health insurance protection. Among these are millions of otherwise self-supporting people who must rely upon public or private help when serious illness strikes, or go without care.

Moreover, health insurance emphasizes reimbursement for care and medical services in the hospital. In fact, in the great majority of cases, when there is any protection against out-of-hospital health care expenses, it is so seriously limited that only a small part of the expenses is reimbursed. By encouraging hospitalisation rather than appropriate alternative types of care, private health insurance has a major effect on health costs. Private insurers must find ways of increasing the proportion of health and medical expenditures that is met through voluntary insurance. The need and the opportunities are present. Improvements in private health insurance protection would limit the need for expanding Medicaid. Higher levels of employment and income should provide more opportunities for people to take advantage of voluntary health insurance.

We need more doctors, nurses, technicians and other health workers. Other countries are producing more than the United States. Russia, for example, with a population of 235 million graduated 35,000 doctors last year, whereas we, with a population of 200 million, graduated only 8,000. I say we can do better. I believe that every boy or girl who qualifies for medical school should have the opportunity to enter medical school. This would involve a doubling of the entrants into medical schools. The American Medical Association and the American Association of Medical Schools has endorsed this proposal. I believe we should make this our objective during the next decade.

A New Ideology

The passage of Medicare brought to an end one of the most bitterly fought ideological battles in the political history of this country. Today the emotional content is no longer present and the major issue is how to deliver access to health services for everyone. Even the American Medical Association, the most active adversary of publicly sponsored national health insurance legislation, has presented a legislative proposal which is designed to broaden and improve health insurance coverage.

Keys to Health Insurance

National health insurance involves several key principles of significance:

1. Eligibility to services as a matter of legal right supported by statutory enforcement of such rights by administrative and legal procedures;

2. Financing the programme in such a manner as to distribute the costs in a more equitable manner than voluntary insurance;

3. The assumption of major responsibility by the Federal rather than the State or local government;

4. The development of incentives for economical and efficient delivery of service.

Effective implementation of a national health insurance programme requires increasing medical manpower and supporting staff, training of many additional individuals from black and other minority groups, expansion of services, hundreds of additional neighbourhood health centres, universally accessible family planning units, and an effective health education programme.

In addition to the implementation of the right to health services, the seventies undoubtedly will see the adoption of the universal right to a minimum income. This development will be accompanied by a vigorous and comprehensive programme to reduce and abolish the root causes of poverty, to eliminate hunger and malnutrition, and to eliminate racial and all forms of discrimination.

A national income supplement plan became financially and politically feasible during the decade of the nineteen-sixties when the number of individuals with incomes below the poverty line began to fall below 20 per cent of the total population.

The poverty level in 1969 according to the Bureau of the Census ranged from 1,749 dollars for one person age 65 and over to 6,034 dollars for seven or more persons. The amount for four persons was 3,721 dollars. As shown in Table 9.1, the proportion of the population below the poverty line dropped between 1959 and 1969 from 22 per cent to 12 per cent and from 39 million to 24 million persons.

TABLE 9.1

PERSONS BELOW THE POVERTY LEVEL, BY RACE
1959–70

| Year | *Number below poverty level (in millions)* | | | *Percent below poverty level* | | |
	Total	White	Other	Total	White	Other
1959	39·5	28·5	11·0	22·4	18·1	56·2
1965	33·2	22·5	10·7	17·3	13·3	47·1
1969	24·3	16·7	7·6	12·2	9·5	31·1
1970	25·5	17·5	8·0	12·6	9·6	32·1

Source: U.S. Department of Commerce, Bureau of the Census, Current Population Reports, Consumer Income, Series P. 60, No. 77, May 7, 1971.

The basic concept of a national guaranteed income is really not new. The payments to veterans and Social Security and Railroad Retirement beneficiaries embody the same principle as a national income guarantee. The payments under State welfare programmes have been based on the principle of the residual responsibility of the public to provide income to individuals below a given level of income.

The new feature of more recent proposals has been to make payments universal to all individuals with incomes below a given level rather than limit such payments to certain categorical groups such as the aged, blind, disabled, or to children only in families where one parent is dead, disabled, unemployed or absent from the home.

The basic features of a new national income supplement are: (1) complete financing by the Federal government, (2) administration by a Federal agency, (3) eligibility determined by Federal law and administrative procedures with appeal to the Federal courts, (4) financial incentives for individuals who work, and (5) incentives to break the cycle of poverty such as training, employment, and appropriate child care services.

Social Security Increase

A national income supplement programme cannot do the whole job of meeting income deficiency by itself. Social Security benefits must be increased and benefits under private retirement and welfare plans must also be adjusted to meet current needs and rising expectations.

In addition, we must find the means of reducing and removing the great inequalities which exist between income levels in America. There are millions of people whose earnings fall in the lower middle-income brackets. Their wages are too high for them to receive assistance from government, but too low to fully partake in the full benefits and opportunities offered by the American economy.

As part of the solution to this problem, there must be a significant attempt made to remove the wide disparities which exist among states. Table 9.2 shows the range in income and services which exists between different parts of the country.

TABLE 9.2

INEQUALITIES AMONG STATES IN INCOME, HEALTH, EDUCATION, AND WELFARE

State	Per capita income 1968	Physicians per 100,000 population 1967	Infant deaths per 1,000 live births 1969	Per capita State and local expenditures for all education 1967–68	Welfare aid per child, April, 1970
Highest	.... $4,256	222	30·6	$348	$67
Average	.... $3,421	158	20·7	$206	$46
Lowest	.... $2,081	74	13·2	$141	$12

Source: Ranking of the States, 1971. National Education Association, Washington, D.C., 1971.

Finally, the elimination of racial and sex discrimination would increase incomes by some $30 billion a year and would aid in the reduction of poverty, the increase in productivity, and the enhancement of individual dignity, and self-reliance.

The decade of the seventies is destined to be that period in this century when many long-emerging trends come to a convergence in institutional changes. Health services, education and income to all become a right, not a privilege; a right grounded in human and community responsibility and not a handout or gratuity – or part of a policy of "noblesse oblige".

The security of these rights will not be an easy or an inexpensive task. During the last two decades the proportion of the gross national product devoted to health, education, and welfare has risen from 13·5 per cent to 21·6 per cent (See Table 9.3). We may reasonably expect that before this decade closes approximately one-quarter of each year's gross national product will be devoted through public and private sources to health, education, and welfare as compared to 20 per cent at the present time.

TABLE 9.3

PUBLIC AND PRIVATE EXPENDITURES FOR HEALTH, EDUCATION AND WELFARE, PERCENT OF GROSS NATIONAL PRODUCT, 1950–70

Fiscal year			Total	Health	Education	Welfare
1950	....	....	13·5	4·6	4·1	4·9
1955	....	....	13·3	4·7	3·7	5·1
1960	....	....	16·0	5·3	4·4	6·5
1965	....	....	18·0	5·9	5·2	7·1
1967	....	....	19·0	6·2	5·7	7·4
1968	....	....	19·6	6·5	5·8	7·6
1969	....	....	20·3	6·7	5·9	7·9
1970	....	....	21·6	7·0	6·3	8·5

Source: Social Security Bulletin, December 1970, p. 17. Totals adjusted to eliminate duplication resulting from use of cash payments received to purchase medical care and educational services.

An American National Health Program

The adoption of a universal national health insurance plan is a necessary and inevitable development in the United States for the decade of the seventies. Such a plan would cover a major portion of medical costs for everyone in the nation from birth to death – the rich and the poor; the employed and the unemployed; those in middle-incomes and those in middle-age; those who live in urban areas and those who live in rural areas; those working for large corporations or small businesses or who are self-employed.

The following are essential elements of a feasible national health insurance plan at this time covering a wide range of medical services:

1. *Breaking the barrier between the paying for health care and eligibility for service.* We must create a system where the individual is

not forced to meet the total cost of health care at one particular time. The use of an insurance system allows the individual to contribute for medical services while working so that financial considerations are not a major problem during illness.

2. *Requiring the government to contribute part of the cost.* This would enable individuals without incomes or with low incomes to receive equal access to health services on the same basis as those with more adequate incomes. Thus, the stigma of poverty and welfare would be removed from the medical care system.

3. *Requiring the employer to pay part of the cost of health care so the immediate financial burden is not so great on the individual.* Good health is a valuable asset for the employer as well as the employee. This fact has been recognized by many employers who today are contributing to the private health insurance protection of their employees and their families. It is something which should be extended to the general working population.

4. *Assuring that eligibility for service would be determined by Federal rules.* The operation of a medical insurance programme by the Federal government would insure that all persons would receive the same benefits, be eligible under the same standards, and be required to contribute on the same basis no matter where they live in the United States. A Federally administered programme would also assure an individual of a fair hearing on matters in dispute before a Federal agency and an appeal for judicial review by Federal courts. Thus, due process and equal treatment would be assured every individual irrespective of his colour, age, sex, education or background.

5. *Providing for new, innovative, economical and efficient methods of organising and delivering medical care.* Financial incentives should be provided for expanding ambulatory and out-patient care, improving emergency services and group practice plans and salary and capitation plans. Funds should also be provided to allow for experimentation with different models of medical care so that new procedures for allocating scarce medical resources may be discovered. Medical care organisation changes with the times. We must be willing to adapt to new needs, new inspirations, new life-styles.

6. *Providing for expansion of preventive medical techniques.* The scope of coverage of medical services must be broad. At the same time it must be recognised that not every element of medical service can be provided in unlimited quantity. Multi-phasic screening, periodic examinations, and community sponsored co-ordinated plans for health, education, family planning, nutrition and environmental concerns should be supported and encouraged. The most economical and humane method of dealing with illness is to prevent its occur-

rence. Medical research must continue to be encouraged and supported, and undoubtedly will have a tremendous impact on changes in services, costs, and arrangements.

7. *Encouraging and accelerating plans for increasing health personnel.* Financial incentives should be provided for expanding the training of more physicians, nurses, dentists and other health personnel including physicians' assistants, aides, technicians and allied health personnel. Methods must be developed which will provide for the most effective use of para-medical personnel so that doctors, dentists and nurses can devote their full attention to their respective professional tasks. Particular attention should be paid to encouraging more black persons and individuals from other minority groups to be trained, and for more women to have opportunities to participate in the delivery of services.

8. *Providing opportunities for the various groups in society to play a significant role in policy formulation and administration of the health system.* Health care is too important to be the sole province of any one professional group no matter how well trained or well intentioned. Therefore, mechanisms must be developed where concerned parties-employers, labour unions, and the consumer himself can make a contribution in determining the amount of money to be spent, the efficiency of care, the priorities to be met first, and a host of administrative, psychological and procedural factors essential to good health. This involvement must be present at all levels of the health care system – at the local, regional and national levels.

9. *Assuring health personnel reasonable compensation, opportunity for professional practice, advancement, and the exercise of humanitarian and social responsibility.* The various components in a national health insurance programme should be designed so as to foster the highest quality of medical care with individual and group responsibility for initiative, advancement, and a sense of creative and social responsibility.

10. *Encouraging effective professional participation in the formulation of guidelines, standards, rules, regulations, forms, procedures and organisation.* There should be widespread participation by all health personnel in the formulation of policy at every level of administration. A co-operative sense of participation should be fostered which would overcome hierarcial considerations and individual distinctions based on income, education and prestige. The importance of professional and administrative competence must be fostered and encouraged.

11. *Fostering a pluralistic system of administration.* There are widely different ideas in the different parts of the United States and among different groups as to how medical care should be administered. As science and technology continue to develop new methods

of diagnosis and treatment, as new drugs are developed, and as new systems of delivery of care are established, we should be willing to adapt our arrangements to new needs and new opportunities. We must be open to the development of different methods of treatment and new forms of medical care organisation. It is essential that various procedures be tried so that we can evaluate which methods prove to be the most effective for different types of situations and changing conditions. There must be opportunities for institutional self-renewal.

12. *Recognising administrative reality and administrative competence.* National health insurance is not a panacea for all the problems of medical care. The continued increase in demand for medical services while the increase in supply remains inelastic will certainly create increasing price and cost pressures for the foreseeable future. Changes in organisation, delivery, and access to services will not occur overnight. Changes in medical school curricula, admissions, and orientation will take time. The administrative implementation of all these components will be difficult and errors of judgment will occur inevit‧ably.

Meanwhile, we must make a more effective effort to distribute medical services in a more rational socially conscious manner than at present. National health insurance is a mechanism to focus our planning and our priorities for a more intelligent distribution of the miracles of medical science to the millions of our people. Medical needs are almost infinitely expansible. Medical services are a scarce resource. The allocation of scarce resources to priority needs involves planning, judgment, administrative capacity, and above all self-restraints.

This all involves a considerable investment in time, money, effort and manpower yet one that we must and can make if we are to assure that the basic components of human dignity and well-being are to be provided to all citizens of our country.

Bibliography

New Eng. Journ. Med., (1969), 281, 193.
Journ. Ind. State Med. Assn., 1310, November (1969).
Patient Care, 92, March (1970).
Congressional Record, 117, 19, Feb. 19 (1971).

Chapter 10

Government and Medical Care

RT. HON. KENNETH ROBINSON
Former Minister of Health, London, England

No country in the world possesses what it would regard as adequate resources to meet the demand for medical care. The relation of resources to demand, or to potential demand, varies from country to country between extraordinarily wide limits. Taking the crude ratio of doctors to total population, the United Kingdom has 1:870, the United States 1:660 and the U.S.S.R. 1:460. In each of these countries strenuous efforts are being made to increase the ratio by training more doctors or by encouraging the immigration of doctors from elsewhere. Even the U.S.S.R., with nearly twice as many doctors relative to population as the U.K., was aiming a year or two ago to double its medical school intake. At the other end of the scale, in Indonesia and Nigeria for example with one doctor per 30,000 population, the shortage is manifest and unarguable.

There is no indication that the need for more medical care resources will be satisfied anywhere as far ahead as one can see. As standards of living rise, so inexorably does the demand for medical care. As everyone who has had responsibility for administering health services must know, improvement in the level and quality of services itself generates increased demand. We have therefore a seller's market for medical care virtually everywhere in the world. At the same time it is a service which of necessity is costly. The acquisition of medical skills is a lengthy and expensive business, medical equipment tends to become more sophisticated and costly as science and technology forge ahead, and medical establishments are bound to be expensive in terms of manpower and on other counts as well.

These inescapable facts lead to the inevitable conclusion that the economic cost of medical care, at least in cases of serious illness or accident or of chronic disorder, is likely to be beyond the capacity of most people to pay. Moreover it tends to rise at a faster rate than that of commodities in general and faster than the standard of living. To

277

leave access to medical care to be determined by a free market could only mean that the majority would be denied the services they need. It is self-evident that the element of consumer choice enters the picture hardly at all. No one chooses to be ill or to suffer injury, but once serious illness or accident has overtaken them the need for treatment becomes imperative.

No civilised nation would today tolerate a situation whereby its people died simply because they could not afford medical treatment and it is for this reason above all that conscious effort has to be made to organise the distribution of medical care so that it can, to some extent at least, meet need. In this way there is inevitable distortion of the market economy in medical care, and of the distribution patterns that would result if the consumer were required to pay the economic price. To organise distribution to meet need requires intervention by authority and in practice the authority can only be governmental or para-governmental. The accompanying costs are of such an order and the social consequences of maldistribution so potentially serious that government can hardly help becoming involved. The extent of involvement will vary with the social philosophy of the particular country and to some degree with the extent of the nation's resources.

Some element of subsidy will certainly be involved which can only be met by taxation. It may extend only to the old or the very poor, or it may cover the entire population as in the British National Health Service or the services of communist countries. Even where the problem is tackled principally through insurance, government cannot opt out. Along with subsidies derived from taxation goes the need for accountability, and this in turn predicates further involvement by government. Thus a relationship develops between government on the one hand and the medical and ancillary professions on the other. By its very nature it can never be a particularly easy relationship.

In Britain since the advent of the National Health Service relations between government and medical profession have been stormy and bitter at times, quiescent and moderately co-operative at others. Doctors seem rather more suspicious than most groups of the motives and intentions of government, but in view of the nature of their calling, the individualism which their whole training tends to stimulate, this need occasion no surprise.

To overcome these suspicions should be the primary objective of government in this situation, and perhaps the best way of doing so is by making absolutely clear that there will be no government interference with clinical freedom. This freedom has in fact been preserved under the National Health Service to a quite remarkable extent. When one reflects that, broadly speaking, the doctor prescribes and the State pays the bill whether for hospital treatment, for medicines or for long-term care, there is surprisingly little inhibition of his right to determine what is best for his patient, regardless of cost. Some controls there must be on costs met almost entirely by the state but they are applied with a broad brush, and to a far greater extent upon institutions than upon doctors as such. Adherence to these principles ought to lead to a steady growth of mutual confidence between profession and government, which is essential for the healthy development of a vast human enterprise in which neither party can do without the other.

The most important task of government in the organising of medical care is to determine the total amount of resources which can be made available to this end in a given period of time. Quite the most difficult task is to select priorities within the total allocation available, which will always be less than is required to meet all the desirable objectives put forward.

Ultimately decisions on priorities have to be made by one person, the Minister in charge of the Service, though he can and does call upon a wealth of advice both administrative and medical. It should be remembered that by far the greater part of a year's estimated expenditure, at least 95 per cent, is automatically committed in advance. This represents the remuneration of all who work in the service at the current negotiated rates of pay, the maintenance and replacement of buildings and equipment, the drug bill and the like. Unless one is prepared to curtail or eliminate some part of the existing service, the existing service has to continue and be paid for at the going rate. The real problem for the Minister is to decide what additional services or developments can be provided and to choose between the various options.

These options can take a variety of forms. A new, and probably somewhat expensive, form of treatment has been developed, or perhaps a new vaccine or immunisation. There may be a crying need to improve the standard of hospitals for the mentally subnormal. A widespread campaign may have been launched to provide more accommodation for the chronic sick, or to expand local authority services for discharged psychiatric patients. It may be desirable to step up the hospital building programme. More financial help may be urgently needed for modernising general practice. All these things, all costing additional money, may well be desirable, even urgent. Their cost will certainly add up to far more than the Minister has available for new developments. So he has to choose and, as will have been seen already, to choose between disparate alternatives.

On what basis does he assess the priorities? How does he make a choice? What factual information and advice can he call upon to assist the process of decision making? It is difficult to generalise since

T

no two Health Ministers approach this dilemma of priorities in the same way, and however much each tries to make a wholly objective assessment it is likely that some element of subjectiveness, or possibly instinct, will creep into decision-making.

Even with all the factual information and advice that a Minister can call upon, needs in the health field are notoriously hard to evaluate. Perhaps the most agonising problems are those which quite literally involve life and death. A new treatment is discovered for a condition which carries a high mortality rate. Claims are made for the efficacy of the treatment and are likely to be widely publicised. Whether such claims are substantiated or exaggerated, or even in some instances unfounded, there is bound to be public pressure for the treatment, which may well be expensive and make a substantial demand on resources, to be made available under the health service. In a democracy and in a service where there is specific public accountability, it is not wrong that pressure of public opinion should be a factor taken into account in determining priorities. But it should not be the only or even the decisive factor. There are other searching questions which the Minister must ask himself and his advisers.

In this competition for a share of limited resources, it is not enough for example to know that the new treatment could save lives which would otherwise be lost. A minority of heart transplant patients have survived for at least a matter of months, but one must ask oneself whether they are living in the full sense of the word or merely ekeing out a bare existence. Can such an outcome justify the very heavy expenditure of skills and money that every heart transplant operation involves? Thus one takes into account the quality of life that a new treatment can offer. The reverse side of this coin appeared when there was public and parliamentary pressure in Britain for the provision of facilities for intermittent dialysis. Here it was demonstrable that sufferers from kidney disease which would otherwise be fatal (kidney transplants were still relatively untried) could through dialysis be enabled to live almost completely normal and full lives. Though the cost per patient of providing facilities was extremely high, it would hardly have been possible in these circumstances to resist the pressure for doing so. In retrospect the decision to go ahead was undoubtedly right.

Even in the less dramatic area of preventive medicine, it is necessary to take a long, cool look at a proposition before committing resources. Skilled medical manpower is one of the scarcest resources in the health service and proposals for multiple screening for example can make extravagant demands on medical manpower. Here one must ask whether the results likely to be achieved will justify the diversion of these resources from some other valuable channel of patient care. Is a particular morbid condition susceptible to early diagnosis and to effective treatment? Are treatment facilities available in sufficient quantity to meet increased demand? Is the condition potentially serious or disabling? These are a few questions to which affirmative replies need to be given before scarce resources are committed. They could be so given in the case of screening for cervical cancer, at the time when a decision had to be made whether or not such a service should be provided. As a result the service was established. Demands for other forms of screening were rejected because they failed on one or more of the criteria mentioned above, and in these cases public pressure had to be resisted.

These few illustrations may give some indication of the way in which decisions as to priorities are reached. In the more general aspects of health service developments there will be a desire not to see some elements of the service falling seriously behind the standards of the whole. At one moment the Minister may consider that developments in the care of the mentally subnormal have been somewhat neglected perhaps because so much of the additional resources available have been channelled into providing new district general hospitals. He may therefore slow down the hospital expansion rate in order to divert money into improving the quality of care of the mentally handicapped. Or the time may have come, as indeed it did around 1965, to try to rescue general practice from a steady decline in status and morale. Broad decisions such as these cannot be based on precise quantifications of need. They are taken on the judgment of the Minister and his senior advisers both lay and medical.

The Minister will have many roles to play, not all of them easily reconcilable with each other. He has of course ultimate responsibility for his Department and for the health service itself. He is accountable in Parliament and through Parliament to the public at large, for the total administration of the health service. He cannot of course be held responsible for the clinical decisions and actions of the service's doctors but he may be called upon to institute enquiry into complaints made about a doctor's actions or omissions. Established procedures at different levels have been developed for this purpose.

The Minister is also a member of the Government and perhaps of the Cabinet. In this context he shares responsibility for all decisions of Government whether they affect his Department or not. He remains a Member of Parliament with responsibilities to his constituents and is expected, despite his Ministerial burdens, to make himself available to advise them and deal with their problems.

As head of his Department he is theoretically responsible for every action of his staff from the Permanent Secretary down, and in practice responsible for all major decisions of policy and for many of the more important executive decisions as well. The day to day administration of the Health Service is in the hands of bodies who are agents of the Minister, responsible to and to a large extent appointed by him. It is most desirable that a Minister should, despite all the duties which tend to keep him at his desk and in Westminster, travel around the country from time to time in order to meet those who administer the service as his agents and to see their problems at first hand. This contact with the services's grass roots is essential if a Minister is to have full understanding of the service for which he is responsible and to see it in a perspective which his office in the Ministry can never provide.

The ideal administrative structure for the health service simply does not exist, though there is a constant search for improvement. Too many irreconcilable factors have to be accommodated. Reasonable devolution of power has to be equated with the central provision of broad financial resources and with centralised policy-making. Consumer representation and a democratic element have to co-exist with the pressing need for managerial efficiency in a service which is at once a human organism and a large-scale business enterprise. The medical and para-medical elements must have their say in administering the service but any syndicalist tendencies have to be suppressed. Voluntary representation on health service bodies should ideally reflect the make-up of the population at large but in practice is largely limited to the minority who have the necessary time to spare for what is a fairly demanding kind of public service. The structure must at the same time encourage the closest co-operation and recognise the disparate parts of the service and the special requirements of each. Finally, change must be generally acceptable, or at least not inimical, to the principal elements of the service. Small wonder that a new structure has been at the time of writing some four years in gestation with no certainty yet of parturition.

In a complex organisation such as a national health service, catering for people at their most vulnerable moments, there will always be problems for the Minister, problems of a clinical nature, problems of resources, problems for the administration, problems for those who give voluntary service and for many others. The service will be criticised for its shortcomings, government will be blamed. All this is inevitable and on the whole healthy, for it would be a sad day when this great social service was simply taken for granted. The essential point is that today almost no one questions the fundamental principles on which the service is based. They are quite simply that in a civilised democracy medical care must be organised and distributed equitably among those who need it, as far as possible in accordance with their need; and that access to a high standard of medical treatment and care no longer depends upon the patients' ability to meet the economic cost. These concepts have become embedded in our social thinking and few would challenge them today.

Chapter 11

Health Planning—A View from the Top with Specific Reference to the U.S.A.

PHILIP R. LEE, M.D.
Professor of Social Medicine, School of Medicine,
University of California at San Francisco, and
Chancellor, University of California at San Francisco,
San Francisco, California, U.S.A.

and

GEORGE A. SILVER, M.D.
Professor of International Health,
School of Medicine,
Yale University,
New Haven, Connecticut, U.S.A.

Introduction

The health of the people of the United States has long been the concern of the federal government and has been expressed in a variety of ways: federal medical care programs for selected beneficiaries (e.g., armed forces and veterans), federal financial support for public health and medical care programs, legislative authorisation and appropriation of funds for a growing range of health and health related activities, Presidential messages and a host of other ways. Although of continuing concern, health care and the right of all citizens to health services has only recently emerged as a major national issue in the United States. In enacting the Comprehensive Health Planning and Public Health Service Amendments of 1966 (Public Law 89–749) Congress declared:

Fulfillment of our national purpose depends on promoting and assuring the highest level of health attainable for every person, in an environment which contributes positively to healthful individual and family living; that attainment of this goal depends on an effective partnership, involving close intergovernmental collaboration, official and voluntary efforts, and participation of individuals and organisations; and the Federal financial assistance must be directed to support the marshaling of all health resources – National, State and local – to assure comprehensive health services of high quality for every person.[1]

The purpose of this chapter is to discuss the formidable obstacles in the way of translating these goals into reality. We will review some of the major issues of public policy; examine the roles of the Congress and the executive branch; particularly the Department of Health, Education and Welfare (DHEW) in health policy; comment on the various forces that influence policy development and the allocation of resources; speculate on the likely paths for policy direction in the 1970's; and finally, propose changes in the organisation of the federal government to improve health policy making.

In examining health care in this country we find a number of problems. First, there are serious defects in the organisation of health services. Second, there is both a shortage and a maldistribution of health manpower. Third, significant financial barriers to adequate health care exist for many millions of Americans. Fourth, medical care costs are rising rapidly due to price inflation, particularly for inpatient hospital care and physicians services. Fifth, many of our existing institutions are old, poorly designed and often ill equipped to provide modern medical care. Sixth, planning and program developments have been too often in discrete categories, with the result an increasing fragmentation of services.

These obstacles are a reflection of the problems in health care and the dissatisfaction which is expressed in a growing number of professional and lay publications, as well as in increased public pressure for more federal intervention to combat the problems.[2, 3, 4, 5, 6, 7]

The federal relationship to and within the health care system is vital to the success of the entire venture. The federal role within the health field has changed significantly in recent years and is exercised in three primary areas:

1. The developement of health resources (e.g., new knowledge, education, facilities construction and organisation);
2. The provision of hospital and medical services; and
3. The prevention and control of disease.

A number of strategies within these areas of federal responsibility have been proposed to overcome the major obstacles to improving health care. There are significant differences in the approaches taken or proposed during the Kennedy and Johnson Administrations to those advocated under President Nixon.

The long range plans and strategy proposed by DHEW in 1968 reflected a two-fold strategy:

1. To maintain and promote a strong base for improving the general health; and

2. To strive for a level of health protection and services comparable to the general population for those who are inadequately served by the existing health system.

The goals stated by the Nixon Administration in their first five year plan for health were similar.[8] The strategy for achieving the goals, however, revealed the Nixon Administration's preference for action by the private sector rather than government. The strategy statement of the Nixon Administration, "Towards a Comprehensive Health Policy for the 1970's," illustrated both the complexity of the policy making process and the inadequacy of efforts to date. On the fundamental issue of public versus private effort the Nixon Administration made its position clear:

> Preference for action in the private sector is based on the fundamentals of our political economy – capitalistic, pluralistic, and competitive – as well as upon the desire to strengthen the capability of our private institutions in their effort to provide health services, to finance such services, and to produce the resources that will be needed in the years ahead.[9]

The role of the private sector, the balance between public and private effort, and the scope and nature of the federal government's role all remain vital questions in relation to the achievement of health goals. There are those who would like to see an expansion of the federal government's role, particularly in the financing of health services, while others favor maintaining the present limited range of responsibility and authority. One significant difference between the major political parties is the degree to which they would stress a broader role for the federal government in dealing with our health care crisis.

The Congress, rather than the President or one of the executive departments, ultimately determines federal health policy through legislation authorising programs and legislation appropriating funds to carry out programs. These are two separate processes, although a continuing effort is made to relate the two through the budget. The role of Congress and the importance of the federal budget in health policy were recently reemphasised by the Senate Appropriations Committee in its report on the fiscal year 1972 appropriation for DHEW. The Committee, and later the Senate, added more than $700 million to the amount requested by the Administration. The Committee commented critically on the budget submittal in support of the Administration's "health strategy". They stated:

The Committee recognised that increased funding alone is not the sole answer to providing an adequate level of health for all of our people. But the Committee is equally persuaded that this budget which, with few exceptions, shows a year to year decline in real dollars and level of effort, fails to deal effectively with the magnitude of the problem. Consequently, for the third successive year, the Committee must express grave concern about the apparent downgrading of health as reflected by the budget request.

The Committee concluded its introductory comments on the budget with these words:

Reduction in health services, health research and training funding to control inflation is tantamount to balancing the Federal budget by the sacrifice of human lives.[10]

These critical and emotional comments reflect the great differences of view between the Congress, with its control in the hands of the Democratic Party, and the Republican led executive branch on critical questions of national health policy and program priorities.

The differences of view between the Congress and the President also illustrate the vital role played by the federal budget in formulating and implementing health policy. The process of budget development has been described by an experienced public servant as "the handmaiden of the political process of deciding who gets what, when and how."[11] The budget remains the best means available to the federal government for reaching a workable consensus among groups holding divergent views.[12, 13]

The federal budget includes items referred to as "controllable" and "uncontrollable". The uncontrollable items require an appropriation of general funds to meet an entitlement provided by law, such as federal formula grants to states for public assistance and Medicaid. The appropriations for the National Institutes of Health, the Food and Drug Administration and other programs within the Public Health Service are in the controllable category and are responsive to the budgetary and political processes. Even these items pose problems for those responsbile for the total federal budget. Writing of his experience as former Director of the Bureau of the Budget, Charles Schultze noted some of the difficulties:

Planning a coherent strategy for even the "controllable programs" became extremely difficult. By the close of the 1960's HEW was administering dozens of specific categorical programs, each of which has developed a supporting clientele in Capitol Hill and in the field. Vocational educators lobbied hard for vocational education. Librarians organised to increase aid to libraries, manufacturers of instructional equipment extolled the benefits of equipment programs. Hospital associations fought for hospital construction money and so forth.[14]

We will have more to say about these vested interests, the lobbies, the professional associations, industry and consumer groups later in this chapter. Their influence is felt on the budget, in the development of new programs and in the carrying out of programs after enactment and appropriation of funds.

Policy is also proposed, debated and defined in legislation which either extends existing programs, modifies these programs or defines new areas of federal responsibility. Some legislation, such as that authorising the research programs administered by the National Institutes of Health, does not require periodic legislative review and renewal by Congress, but only an annual appropriation.

Health policies are then defined through the appropriations process. Most of the other grant-in-aid programs, such as those for health professions education, regional medical programs, comprehensive health planning, hospital construction and migrant health, require new authorisations every few years. In the review and renewal process the programs are evaluated in relation to the achievement of goals and objectives and in relation to new needs and costs. The process is an imperfect one.

Many Congressional committees are involved, in both the Senate and the House of Representatives, because the jurisdiction of the committees varies and health related legislation involves a number of different agencies and a variety of authorities. For example, Medicare was considered by the House Committee on Ways and Means because new Social Security taxes were required to finance it. For the same reason, it was considered by the Senate Finance Committee. Medicaid was also considered by these committees because it was presented as an amendment to the original Social Security Act. Most of the legislation authorising programs administered by the Public Health Service is considered by health subcommittees in the Senate and House of Representatives. In the Senate the parent committee deals with Labor and Public Welfare, while in the House of Representatives it is the Interstate and Foreign Commerce Committee.

The development of legislative proposals, including the review by the President's staff, both Special Assistants and the Office of Management and Budget and the presentation to Congress, is a task of the Secretary of Health, Education and Welfare. Legislation dealing with health policies and programs is handled jointly by the Assistant Secretary for Health and Scientific Affairs and the Assistant Secretary for Legislation. Agency heads and staff are also involved in the development of proposals and in the close working relations with

Congressional committees and their staffs in assuring consideration, and hopefully, enactment of the proposals.

The long list of proposals translated into laws and new programs during the 1960's illustrates the magnitude, scope and complexity of this task during a period of major change in the role of the federal government in health and medical care (Appendix one). The legislation enacted in a single year often exceeded the output of two or three Congresses in the preceding two decades. Not only was there a great deal of legislation presented, discussed and enacted, but major new policy directions emerged in mental health, medical and health professions education, the organisation of health care, the financing of health care, consumer protection and environmental health.

The policies as determined by Congress are executed through many federal agencies. The DHEW is the principal federal department involved. Major health and health care programs are carried out or financed directly or indirectly through the Public Health Service, including the Food and Drug Administration and the National Institutes of Health; the Social and Rehabilitation Service; and the Social Security Administration. Major medical care programs are carried out by the Department of Defense and the Veterans Administration, while the Office of Economic Opportunity supports health care programs for the poor. Research is supported from a variety of sources outside DHEW, including the Agency for International Development, the National Science Foundation, the Atomic

TABLE 11.1*

FEDERAL EXPENDITURES FOR MEDICAL AND HEALTH-
RELATED PROGRAMS BY AGENCY
(in millions of dollars)

Agency	1966 actual	1967 estimate	1968 estimate
ADMINISTRATIVE BUDGET			
Department of Health, Education, and Welfare:			
Public Health Service:			
National Institutes of Health	738·8	929·9	989·2
National Institute of Mental Health	164·3	194·9	217·6
Other	633·5	866·2	1,095·2
Welfare Administration	863·8	1,196·7	1,407·9
Social Security Administration	—	971·8	917·6
Other	141·1	198·6	238·6
Proposed legislation (net)	—	—	42·0
Total, Department of Health, Education, and Welfare	2,541·5	4,358·1	4,908·1

Table 11.1*—contd.

FEDERAL EXPENDITURES FOR MEDICAL AND HEALTH-
RELATED PROGRAMS BY AGENCY (in millions of dollars)

Agency	1966 actual	1967 estimate	1968 estimate
Department of Defense			
Army	436·8	666·2	716·5
Navy	367·9	428·1	461·3
Air Force	398·7	440·7	445·7
Other	9·0	7·8	7·3
Total, Department of Defense	1,212·4	1,542·8	1,630·8
Veterans Administration	1,306·7	1,381·7	1,471·5
Agency for International Development	120·0	198·7	223·9
Atomic Energy Commission	93·9	98·6	102·8
Department of Agriculture	126·7	141·1	154·0
National Aeronautics and Space Administration	73·0	81·8	85·7
Department of Housing and Urban Development	27·5	28·6	103·0
National Science Foundation	24·2	25·0	25·0
Civil Service Commission	29·2	36·6	40·7
Office of Economic Opportunity	48·2	120·2	140·5
Department of Commerce	·5	3·8	25·2
Department of State	21·0	25·3	26·7
Department of Labor	30·4	48·9	71·4
Other Agencies	60·4	74·9	66·3
Contributions by Federal agencies to Federal employees' health benefits funds not included above	139·8	185·1	189·1
Interfund transactions	....	−1,021·8	−991·6
Total net budget expenditures for health	5,864·3	7,329·4	8,237·1
TRUST FUNDS			
Department of Health, Education, and Welfare:			
Social Security Administration	64·5	3,525·8	3,971·6
Proposed legislation	—	—	200·0
Civil Service Commission, net	1·5	−3·0	−14·3
United States Soldiers' Home	7·2	8·4	10·1
Total trust fund expenditures for health	73·2	3,531·2	4,167·4
Total budget and trust fund expenditures for health	5,927·5	10,860·6	12,440·5

*Special Analyses H, Federal Health Programs. From the U.S. Budget for Fiscal Year 1968.

Energy Commission, the National Aeronautics and Space Administration and the Department of Defense. Environmental health programs were recently shifted from DHEW to a newly created Environmental Protection Agency, while health manpower programs are supported in DHEW as well as in the Departments of Defense and Labor and the Office of Economic Opportunity. The bulk of federal health expenditures are within DHEW and the relative importance of the Department in relation to other departments and agencies has increased in recent years (Table 11.1).

The Evolution of the Federal Role in Health Policy and Health Care

The slow emergence of federal policies and programs related to health and health care in the United States has generally followed the pattern of other industrialised countries, particularly those in Western Europe. At least three stages in the process have been identified:

1. The phase of private charity, individual contract between user and provider, and public apathy or indifference;

2. The public provision of such necessary health services as are clearly not being provided by voluntary effort and private contract; and

3. The substitution of public provision of services or the financing of services for private, voluntary and charitable effort.[15]

The federal government has been a provider of medical and hospital services to a limited number of beneficiaries, such as merchant seamen and members of the armed forces, since the founding of the republic.

The public provision of necessary health services began to develop after the Civil War. Not only were state and local health departments established to provide such traditional public health services as sanitation, communicable disease control and the collection of vital statistics, but systems of public medical care developed at the local, state and federal levels. Medical care for the poor became a responsibility of local government rather than charity. The same was true for patients with tuberculosis and some other communicable diseases. The confinement of the mentally ill gradually became the responsibility of state government and large numbers of state mental hospitals were established. The federal government continued its commitment to members of the armed forces and merchant seamen and accepted the responsibility of war veterans with service-connected disabilities. Later the care of veterans with nonservice-connected disabilities were added. These systems of medical, hospital and custodial care were not only separate from each other, they were largely separate from the provision of private medical and hospital care for the bulk of the population.

The role of the federal government in public health, but not in medical care, expanded significantly in the early decades of the twentieth century. The U.S. Public Health Service emerged with a broader role from its limited beginnings as the Marine Hospital Service. This period has been described as the "nationalisation of public health" in the United States.[16]

The contemporary role of the federal government in health care had its origin in the Social Security Act of 1935. This legislation established a national program of compulsory old age, survivors, and disability insurance, and it provided federal grants to states for public health, maternal and child health and crippled children's services. It also created our present day system of welfare, or public assistance, by providing federal grants to the states for payments to the poor who were aged or blind and to families with dependent children. The Social Security Act represented a major change in public policy in this country and it initiated a pattern in federal/state relations and in program development that was to be followed for more than thirty years. Medicare, perhaps the most important federal health care legislation in the 1960's, was an amendment to the Social Security Act providing protection against the rising costs of medical and hospital care for the aged.

Another significant step in the involvement of the federal government in medical care was the Hospital Survey and Construction Act of 1946. Through this program a unique public-private partnership was established between federal, state and local government and non-profit community hospitals. The legislation provided federal financial support to states for the construction of needed hospitals and other health care facilities. Since the inception of the program federal funds have aided more than 3,000 communities for the construction of hospitals, nursing homes, public health clinics and rehabilitation centers. The partnership concept has been carried over into many other health programs. The policy of supporting the development of necessary resources for health care, whether it be new knowledge, manpower or facilities, is a major element in present day federal health policy.

One of the keystones of federal health policy has been the support of biomedical research. This policy was first clearly established by Congress in 1937 with the passage of the National Cancer Act. This legislation created a national institute focused on cancer. The institute was authorised to conduct research in its own facilities, to provide grants for nonfederal research projects, and to award fellowships for advanced study and training, all under the guidance of a National Advisory Cancer Council comprised of nonfederal leaders in science and public affairs. This authority was expanded broadly by Congress in 1944, providing authority for the Public Health Service to foster, conduct, support and cooperate in research relating to health and disease. Authority to award funds for nonfederal research and research training, hitherto limited to cancer research, was extended to health problems generally.

The basic rationale for the support of biomedical research has not always been the conquest of specific diseases. Although the policy has been given repeated emphasis in Congress it has not always been clearly understood or fully supported by the scientific community.

The key role of Congress in promoting the growth of federal support for biomedical research and the vital role played by Mrs. Mary Lasker and her "health lobby" have been well summarised by Strickland. He observed:

> In large measure then, medical research became an important national effort in the post war years because scientific talent, political interest, popular concern about health, and potential federal dollars for health had virtually no place else to go. The National Institutes of Health became the most important vehicle for federal support. In fact, NIH was shortly to become the center of a new research empire. In the seven years between the war's end and Dwight D. Eisenhower's inauguration as President, the NIH budget climbed from $7-plus million to $70 million. That was a growth pattern that was to continue for almost two decades.[17]

In the two decades that followed, national expenditures for biomedical research grew from $87 million to over $2 billion annually. The federal share grew from approximately 30 per cent to over 70 per cent, while that of the National Institutes of Health grew from approximately 10 per cent to 40 per cent. Gradually a national health policy had evolved that was to have a major impact on health care and health professions education.

Evidence of the changes produced by this growth rate are clear. We see it in the expansion of research manpower and facilities; in the size of graduate academic enrollments in the basic biomedical sciences; in the extent and diversity of publications and conferences; in the growth of medical specialities; in the changing patterns of undergraduate and graduate medical education; in the improvements and increasing complexity of medical care, particularly hospital based services; and in the growing complexity of administrative mechanisms to assure public accountability for these large expenditures. During this period of phenomenal growth the relationships of investigators and institutions to the political process has profoundly altered.

As the federal role in health policies and programs began to take shape more clearly, four broad areas of federal support and activity emerged. The first was continued and balanced support of the development of health resources, including manpower, facilities and biomedical knowledge, with national priorities determined in relation to the changing health needs of the people. The second was systematic encouragement to support regional, state and local initiatives – public and private – in comprehensive health planning, assignment of priorities and the design and execution of programs for meeting local health needs. The third was expansion of the national program of research and development designed to improve the organisation, delivery and financing of health care. The fourth was further reduction of the barriers to equal access to health care, whether they be financial, geographic, social or cultural.

These broad areas of federal support were reflected in a long list of laws enacted relating to health and health care in the 1960's (which is listed in detail at the end of this chapter). The changes were also reflected in a rapid increase in federal expenditures for health and medical care. Not only did the expenditures increase, but they represented a growing percentage of national expenditures for health and medical care. Federal outlays for health and medical care programs increased from $3·5 billion in fiscal year 1960 to an estimated $22·2 billion for fiscal year 1972 (Table 11.2). As a percentage of the

TABLE 11. 2*

Federal outlays for health and medical care compared to total national
expenditures for health and medical care
(*billions of dollars*)

Fiscal Year	1960	1962	1967	1968	1970	1971	1972
Federal outlays for health	3·5	3·7	10·8	14·1	18·1	20·7	22·2
Total Federal budget	92·2	106·8	158·3	178·9	196·6	212·8	229·2
Total national health expenditures	26·4	30·2	47·9	53·6	67·2	—	—
Federal health outlays as percent of—							
Total Federal budget outlays	3·8	3·5	6·8	7·9	9·2	9·7	9·7
Total national health expenditures	13	12	23	26	27	—	—

*Special Analyses K, Federal Health Programs. From the U.S. Budget for Fiscal Year 1972.

federal budget, health expenditures rose from 3·8 to 9·7 per cent, indicating a shift in resource allocation priority within the federal government. As a percentage of national health expenditures, the federal share rose from 13 to 27 per cent between 1960 and 1970. As the federal share increased those of state and local governments were maintained, while private expenditures, as a percentage of the total, declined. Actual dollar expenditures increased significantly from both public and private sectors.

The distribution of the federal expenditures for health and medical care also illustrate the shifts in policy, with major increases for the provision of hospital and medical services and increases for support of training, research and programs of disease prevention and control (Table 11.3).

TABLE 11. 3*
FEDERAL OUTLAYS FOR MEDICAL AND HEALTH-RELATED ACTIVITIES BY CATEGORY
(*in millions of dollars*)

	1968 actual	1969 estimate	1970 estimate
Development of health resources, total	2,803	3,057	3,496
Health research	1,547	1,476	1,639
Training and education	687	841	932
Construction of hospitals and health facilities	470	595	728
Improving the organization and delivery of health services	100	145	197
Provision of hospital and medical service, total	10,764	12,518	13,977
Direct Federal hospital and medical services	2,738	2,896	2,996
Hospital and medical services, indirect	8,025	9,622	10,981
Prevention and control of health problems, total	565	741	804
Disease prevention and control	386	506	522
Environmental control	54	83	102
Consumer protection	125	151	180
Total outlays from Federal and trust funds	14,132	16,316	18,277

*Special Analyses L, Federal Health Programs. From the U.S. Budget for Fiscal Year 1970.

In spite of the significant policy and program developments in the 1960's, the United States has yet to reach the third stage of public policy evolution which has been developed in a number of European countries. There are some who believe, however, that the enactment of the Medicare amendments to the Social Security Act in 1965 represented the first major step in substituting public financing of health care services for private, voluntary and charitable efforts. The

U

rapid growth in public expenditures for health and medical care followed the enactment of Medicare and gives some substance to this impression (Tables 11.2 and 11.3). Only time will tell if the assumption is correct.

The Role of the Department of Health, Education and Welfare in Health Policies and Programs

The Department of Health, Education and Welfare was established in 1954 in order to bring together a variety of health and health related programs with those of social security, welfare, vocational rehabilitation and education. At the time the Department was organised the Office of the Secretary had only a small staff to provide the leadership and to achieve the coordination of program efforts. The Secretary was dealing with agencies like the Public Health Service and the Food and Drug Administration, with long histories and strong, independent constituencies.

The DHEW has grown progressively in size, complexity and scope since its establishment. Its growth since 1961 has been particularly impressive and has been accompanied by a series of agency and departmental reorganisations to accommodate the new responsibilities. The number of programs administered has risen from approximately 100 to over 250 in the last decade. Total expenditures from general fund appropriations and trust funds grew from $20·3 billion to $53 billion in fiscal year 1969. Health expenditures grew even more rapidly in this period from $1·6 billion to over $19 billion from general appropriations and trust funds. While health programs have grown in DHEW, they have also emerged in a number of other agencies such as the Office of Economic Opportunity, the Veterans Administration and the Department of Labor.

Within the Department, health and health service programs are the responsibility of the Public Health Service, including the National Institutes of Health; the Social and Rehabilitation Service; and the Social Security Administration. The Public Health Service has as its basic mission the maintenance and protection of the health of the American people and the development of the resources necessary to advance the nation's health to higher levels. This mission is carried out through more than 100 grant-in-aid programs which range from grants for the development of state and local Comprehensive Health Planning agencies to the support of individual investigators conducting basic research. The Public Health Service also operates a series of hospitals and clinics to provide care for Native Americans (Indians, Aleuts) and merchant seamen. Its staff of more than 40,000 is located throughout the United States in federal institutions as well as assigned to state and local health departments. Personnel are also working in a variety of international health programs.[18]

The Medicaid program provides federal matching grants to the states to pay for hospital, medical, dental, pharmacy and other health services for the poor who receive public assistance payments. It is administered by the Social and Rehabilitation Service, which also administers public assistance and vocational rehabilitation programs. The Medicare program, which finances about 35–40 per cent of the costs of medical care for those aged 65 and over, is administered by the Social Security Administration because it is financed primarily through Social Security payments from employers and employees rather than through general tax revenues and it is limited primarily to Social Security beneficiaries.

Consumer protection activities within DHEW are primarily the responsibility of the Food and Drug Administration which is an agency within the Public Health Service.

The role of DHEW goes far beyond the administration of specific programs. In describing the role of a Departmental Secretary, Wilbur J. Cohen commented:

This Department handles the major portion of federal grants-in-aid funds for social programs. He administers the largest insurance program in the world. So the shape, direction and style of Departmental programs in many ways sets the course for state, local and nongovernmental agencies.

He went on to note:

...the Secretary of Health, Education and Welfare must review and approve budgets, allocations, priorities. He must approve and issue innumerable reports and recommendations on topics ranging from prescription drugs, to smoking, to desegregation of schools, to payments made to people in need.[19]

To assist the Secretary in dealing with the wide range of health problems and health policy issues, a Special Assistant for Health and Medical Affairs served in the Office of the Secretary from the time the Department was established in 1954 until major organisational changes were made in 1965. This was a staff position and the duties did not impinge on the responsibilities of the Surgeon General of the Public Health Service or the other agency heads such as the Commissioner of Food and Drugs or the Commissioner of Social Security. These line agency heads reported directly to the Secretary and were responsible for the administration of large, complex agencies.

In 1965 the position of Special Assistant was elevated to Assistant Secretary for Health and Scientific Affairs. Two major reorganizations of health agencies followed in 1966 and 1968, giving the Assistant Secretary line authority over the Public Health Service, which was broadened to include the Food and Drug Administration. The Surgeon General, the principal career official in the Public Health Service, became the Assistant Secretary's deputy. Although a professional, the Assistant Secretary was a political appointee and served at the pleasure of the President. The Surgeon General was appointed for a four year term in a career service.

Additional changes made in the organisation of the Secretary's office in 1965 provided the Secretary with a better means to influence legislation, program planning and implementation and the budget. An Office of Planning and Evaluation, under the direction of an Assistant Secretary was established to introduce the planning, programming and budgeting systems into the Department. The point was made by William Gorham, the first Assistant Secretary for Planning and Evaluation, that if this process succeeds "it will be perceptible only over the long haul." He also observed:

> In theory, a shift in program priorities could be translated into a drastic alteration in the budget and if necessary in the laws of the land. In fact, the laws of the land normally change slowly and each year's budget looks a great deal like last year's ... except a little larger.[20]

The growth of programs, the rapid increase in federal expenditures in health and medical care and the new emphasis placed on problems such as narcotics addiction and drug abuse led to growing concern about the capacity of the federal government to provide the necessary leadership in the field of health. Indeed, there has been increasing concern about the failure of DHEW to get its own house in order.

The Nixon Administration removed environmental health programs (e.g., air pollution control) from the Department and merged them with other programs to create a new environmental protection agency. It also supported legislation removing the Cancer Institute from the policy and program direction of DHEW. This legislation was to create a new Conquest of Cancer Agency with the director reporting to the President. Drug abuse has also emerged as a major national issue and the Administration has proposed a new agency in the White House to direct and coordinate federal efforts. At the same time, the Administration has proposed that DHEW be reorgansied as the Department of Human Resources. One of the major agencies would be in health but it would be without authority in relation to Medicare and Medicaid.

The Senate Appropriations Committee, in its report on DHEW's budget for fiscal year 1972 had a number of critical comments about Departmental organisation and management which are shared by many.[21] Their concerns are in part due to the number and variety of health programs enacted by Congress in the past decade.

Program Implementation and Coordination—Relationships Among Government Agencies and the Private Sector

The establishment of goals, the setting of priorities, the development of a legislative program and allocation of resources through the budget process are only part of a process of achieving program objectives and national health goals. The ultimate test is what the plans, the funds and the efforts accomplish. Programs must be carried out.

The field of health care illustrates very well the complex set of relationships between the public and private sectors and the various levels of government necessary for the achievement of program goals and objectives. As the role of the federal government in health care began to expand, the varying elements of the internal relationships between agencies and departments within the federal government became more evident and the relationships with the forces outside the federal government – professions, hospitals, insurance companies, state agencies, planning bodies, consumers, university medical centers, voluntary agencies and industry – took on increasing significance. As new programs emerged, new relationships had to be established. None were more complicated than those required for the success of Medicare. Hundreds, indeed thousands of people, were involved in the year of planning and the development of regulations, relationships and mechanisms that were to pay the Medicare beneficiaries' hospital and medical bills on time. The preparations required were more complex and extensive than those for the invasion of Normandy in World War II.

Medicare was not an isolated example. Much of the legislation affecting the health field enacted in the 1960's required cooperative action by many agencies. The establishment of interagency cooperation required unusual tact as well as technical and administrative skill. The cooperative efforts between the Public Health Service and the Social Security Administration to apply the Civil Rights Act of 1964 to the Medicare Program is an example of what was required. Several thousand hospitals in the United States had to eliminate racial discrimination in hospital admissions, bed assignments, staffing and professional privileges if they were to participate in the Medicare Program. The Social Security Administration did not have the expertise or the relationships with public health agencies and hospitals necessary to effect the changes in hospital policies and practices. The Public Health Service had the professional manpower and a long history of cooperative relationships as a result of the Hill-Burton hospital construction program. The job of desegregating hospitals practicing racial discrimination is not yet complete but through a wide-ranging effort, which ultimately required the full support of the President, the process was begun and sufficient progress made to permit most of these hospitals to participate in the program and provide services for Medicare beneficiaries. The ability of the Social Security Administration to withhold payments for services proved to be a powerful incentive for desegregation.

In DHEW it became evident that policy development and program direction had to be more closely coordinated. If the Assistant Secretary for Health and Scientific Affairs was to develop policy and see that it was carried out, it was necessary to join the leadership and managerial roles. To achieve this kind of direction and coordination, the major organisational changes took place in DHEW in 1965, 1966 and 1968. The Public Health Service was placed under the direction of the Assistant Secretary for Health and Scientific Affairs, with the Surgeon General as his principal deputy. It was evident even before this move that a more encompassing structure was needed. Some changes have been proposed by the Nixon Administration in its reorganisation plan to create a Department of Human Resources. A major agency within this department would be a health agency with a broad range of responsibilities.

Next it became clear that in addition to relationships that had to be rationalised within the federal establishment, particularly within DHEW itself, there had to be a rationalisation of the relationships among the Department and the various groups in and out of government who were involved in health services, research or training. This meant state and local governments with whom health services had to be rationalised because a good deal of the health services activities in state and local areas were determined by federal acts. Even though only a portion of the funds available for state and local services came from the federal government, that portion made the federal role tremendously important because of legal demands that required state and local governments to provide matching funds and established regulations and changes in law to conform to federal policy. The Medicaid program, with its multibillion dollar expenditures from federal, state and local revunes has had a major impact in other policy areas because it has preempted funds that might otherwise have been used for a variety of other purposes.

In addition state health agencies and officials had relationships to local government similar to those that the federal agencies and officials had to the states. The problems of fragmentation were magnified at every level. The competency or incompetency of state and local executive agencies often made a crucial difference in the way in which federal laws were carried out and whether or not goals were achieved.

There are also the professional agencies with which it is necessary to maintain contacts. These range from the professional associations such as the American Medical Association (AMA), American Nurses Association, American Pharmaceutical Association and American Dental Association; though those agencies that represent hospitals such as the American Hospital Association; the professional schools, such as the Association of American Medical Colleges, the National Association of State Universities and Land Grant Colleges, the American Council on Education; professional organisations that represent minority groups such as the National Medical Association and the National Dental Association; student groups such as the Student American Medical Association or Student Health Organisation, the Student Nurses Association; a host of professional groups representing medical or other specialists, such as the American College of Physicians, the Academy of Pediatrics, the American College of Surgeons, the College of Obstetrics and Gynecology; and those representing many professional groups, such as the American Public Health Association.

While the growth of federal programs multiplied the difficulties because it created innumerably greater occasions for contacts with these professional groups and, therefore, took up a great deal more time of the Assistant Secretary's Office, the Surgeon General and the operating agencies, it also had some beneficial aspects. In the first place, when the American Medical Association found itself first among equals, rather than the only voice for medicine, it became much less aggressive in its dealings with DHEW, although it continued to maintain an independent position and strongly advocate its views to the public, Congress, the Department and the President. The debate on Medicare was a long and bitter one, but once those amendments were passed, the AMA worked vigorously and cooperatively to assure that the program was appropriately administered, with due consideration to the role and responsibilities of the physician. The AMA was also sincerely cooperative and helpful in the development of health manpower proposals, once it got beyond the point of insisting that there was no manpower shortage.

With most of the specialised professional groups, relationships were warm and cordial. It may well be that the less financial stake there is in the relationship and the less regulating power of government, the easier it is for the relationship to prosper. The relationship with the drug industry, for example, was constantly stormy. Drugs currently represent well over $8 billion of national expenditures in the health field, and, as a consequence, anything that approaches the possibility of change in the profit relationship touches an open nerve. The Pharmaceutical Manufacturers Association was constantly at odds over the operation of the Food and Drug Administration and the policies of the Secretary's Office with regard to supervision and control of advertising, of drug efficacy and safety, drug testing and related matters. Clearly, policy elements that have important consequences on total earnings and total profits will often create agonising confrontations.

The voluntary health agencies often played a complementary role to government. They often advocated greater federal activity in their particular areas of interest, such as cancer or heart disease, but they seldom had a major impact on federal policy. Perhaps the principal exceptions were the groups interested in mental illness and retardation. Here both the professional groups and the voluntary agencies worked with their primary constituent agency, the National Institute of Mental Health, to expand its legislative authority and programs. It included within its scope the full range of program responsibility for research and professional education to community service.

There is another area of lobbying or public advocacy which is difficult to describe clearly and specifically. In this area advice can be given and action stimulated by those who never make an appearance in the mainstream of public or lobbying activity. They include Presidential advisory commissions, various task forces and advisory committees set up by the President; his special assistants, cabinet officers and agency heads. In recent years there have been five Presidential commissions: heart disease, cancer and stroke, mental retardation, health manpower, health facilities and mental health of children, examining all or parts of the health care system.

The Secretary of Health, Education and Welfare has had special advisory committees on hospital effectiveness, environmental health and related problems, alcoholism, health protection and disease prevention, as well as on Medicare and Medicaid. Task forces have been used to examine a host of problems, including those related to prescription drugs. Program analyses have emerged as another important tool for the study of health needs and program alternatives. This approach has been used both by the Assistant Secretary for Planning and Evaluation in DHEW and the operating agencies.

A White House Conference on Health was held in 1965, and similar national and regional conferences sponsored by the federal government in recent years have examined medical care costs, private health insurance, medical group practice and family planning. A number of less public task forces, advisory committees and individual consultants have also helped to shape federal policies and programs.

There have been major studies on social issues relating to health, health professions education, and health care by the independent National Commission on Community Health Services, the Carnegie Commission on Higher Education, the AMA, the Academy of General Practice, the Board on Medicine/National Academy of Sciences, the National Commission for the Study of Nursing and Nursing Education, the Commission on the Survey of Dentistry in the United States and a number of small groups supported by private foundations.

The health field, particularly biomedical research, has been the beneficiary of a unique citizen lobby led by Mrs. Mary Lasker. For more than 30 years she has worked tirelessly and effectively to increase the federal role in support of biomedical research, particularly related to disease categories such as heart disease and cancer. Gradually the group's interest broadened to include federal aid for medical education and programs to speed the application of research advances. Congressmen, Presidents, cabinet officers and agency officials felt the effective pressure from this group. Members of the group were frequent witnesses before Congressional committees, they served as members of advisory councils to the various institutes within the National Institutes of Health, they served on Presidential commissions and Departmental committees. Their role in the development of the National Institutes of Health has been particularly important and impressive.[22]

Each of these approaches has some usefulness. It often appears that when a President or cabinet officer samples the views of experts, generalists or interested citizens, it is primarily to blunt a particular public demand. In such instances the activity of a committee, Presidential commission or task force over a period of a year or two allows the heat and rancor, which resulted in the formation of the task force, to be dissipated and by the time a report is made it can be carefully put on the shelf and forgotten. In other instances, the nature of a report and the nature of the group that has prepared it are of such dignity and stature that the deliberations and recommendations come out with great force and actually produce administrative or legislative action. In any case, the reports of these commissions often contain valuable information which eventually, if not immediately, results in action. The President's National Advisory Committee on Health Manpower, for example, produced a landmark report and a substantial number of the recommendations have borne fruit since the 1967 report of the Commission.[23]

One group only now beginning to grow in importance is the consumer group itself. Its impact on policy development has been recognised very slowly and it is possible that its impact is related to the increasing concern in the United States for adding wide-scale participation by consumers to the traditional form of representative government. This may be attributed in part to the civil rights movement which has swelled in force since the 1950's. In any case, consumers have demanded more and more to be heard in addition to professionals and vested interests; to have the consumer's point of view an established part of the decision-making process; and, in many instances, to be certain that consumers are represented on the boards and commissions that make policy and program decisions. While professionals have been loathe to permit this kind of consumer participation, the Congress has been much more sympathetic. As a consequence, much of the new legislation provides specifically for consumer representation.

A Health Policy for the 1970's?

A. A Social Report

In looking at the future and attempting to sort out a national health policy and its implementation, it is well to remember one major difficulty is still the lack of adequate indicies that would signal success or failure. Too frequently we have merely described program inputs in terms of dollars, people or facilities. Services have also been enumerated as if they represented an achievement in and of themselves.

In some other areas policies can be evaluated. One can recognise the state of the economy. Indices, standards and criteria have been developed and an annual economic report is submitted to the President on the basis of which a policy direction is taken. The wage-price freeze policy of the Nixon administration was a dramatic example. The social philosophy and style of a particular administration will certainly color the goals, direction and policies that it adopts in response to the economic conditions of the country, but at least the meaning of the events is perfectly clear. Inflation does occur, is noted, and can be measured. Employment is noted and can be measured. Actions can be taken in response.

The problem is that an equivalent "social" report is not available. Efforts in this direction were undertaken by DHEW as early as 1967, and in January, 1969 the Secretary published "Toward a Social Report" which attempted to undertake the establishment of such criteria in a number of areas, including health. This report was not altogether successful inasmuch as the Secretary himself admitted, in the introduction for example, "There is no government procedure for periodic stock-taking of the social health of the nation. The government makes no social report." He goes on to say, however, "These are not easy questions, since all major social problems are influenced by many things beside governmental action, and it is hard to disentangle the different causal factors."

In the chapter "Health and Illness" it is noted that "In the absence of extraordinary scientific breakthroughs in the treatment of degenerative diseases, the gains and expectations of life will not begin to match those achieved during the first half of this century." The report goes on to note that we cannot blame our health status on lack of total expenditures for medical care, health manpower or biomedical research. It places blame on environmental factors, the American style of life, socioeconomic deprivation and the distribution of medical care as major causative elements. And it ends with a policy challenge: "There can be little doubt that appropriate public policy decisions can help to alleviate some of the factors adversely affecting the health status of our population. Public policy can aim to redress the imbalance in health resources, prevent and control harmful environmental factors, and even influence our thinking about those personal habits and forms of behavior which may prove detrimental to our health."[24]

These critical questions must be examined in the formulation of health policy. What should the goals be? How can priorities be properly established? How should resources be allocated?

A national health policy cannot be developed or evaluated without the essential basic data. The National Center for Health Statistics has proven an invaluable resource of health statistics and better economic data are becoming available gradually through the Social Security Administration, the National Center for Health Services Research and Development and the private sector. These social indicators are of increasing importance in program evaluation and in assessment of priorities. Unfortunately, they are not yet adequate to meet the needs.

B. Defining Health, Health Services and Health Maintenance

Agreement on terms or definitions is also important. In recent years we have seen a shift from the use of the term medical care to the term health care. We must first ask what is health and what is health care?

Defining health has never been easy. In recent years two concepts of health have emerged – one relates health to man's adaptation and balance with his environment and the other in the definition adopted by the World Health Organisation which includes not only the absence of disease, but social well being. Historically, the medical profession has been preoccupied by disease. Even the preventive efforts have focused more on specific diseases than on the promotion or maintenance of health.

Health Planning

The President's Commission on Health Facilities provided an excellent definition of comprehensive health care and it also set forth certain principles that should be applied in developing such services. Comprehensive health care was defined as "a system of services for individuals and families, including four essential components: health education, personal preventive services, diagnostic and therapeutic services, and rehabilitative and restorative services."[25]

The Nixon Administration, in developing its health strategy, placed strong emphasis on health education and prevention, even using a new term, "health maintenance organisation," to describe it. The Nixon Administration also focused its efforts on improving the delivery of health care. In the analysis of need two major problems emerged: (1) inequality in health status, health care, and access to financing and (2) the pervasive problem of rising medical care costs.

These major issues relate to the goals of better health and access to high quality health services at an acceptable cost. To achieve these goals requires that both the capacity of the health care system be improved and that adequate access be provided for every citizen.

If an emphasis on preventive medicine and health maintenance is to develop it need not displace the traditional focus of medicine on disease, but it must deal with both the patient's and the physician's tendency to emphasise treatment. In this setting, one must ask if our existing institutional forms and arrangements – indeed the delivery system – will be able to accommodate this shift of focus. Even if we accept that the present system is adequate to deal with the diagnosis and treatment of patients' diseases on an episodic basis, we must examine carefully alternatives that exist or can be developed to shift to a "health maintenance" strategy.

When we examine the social and environmental factors in health and disease, we recognise how ineffectively the present system applies existing knowledge. There are, of course, other avenues to reach the public on such matters as smoking, nutrition, accident prevention, air pollution and overcrowding. Often effective action depends not on the physician but on decisions and measures that are more social than medical, directed not so much at the care of patients as the treatment of society. In recent years major steps have been taken by the federal government to deal with some of these health related problems. Efforts include food stamps, new urban renewal policies (called model cities), welfare reform, auto and traffic safety and air pollution control.

C. The Health Care System – Access, Distribution of Services, Costs

The health care system is both part of the problem and part of the solution. Improvements in the capacity of the system can be

306

achieved in part through the production of more manpower, the expansion of existing health care facilities or the creation of new ones, advances in our knowledge of health and disease through research, and finally, through improved organisation of services. Except for better organisation, which should improve productivity, all other approaches to expanding the capacity of the system are likely to increase the costs of health care. Some research advances, such as poliomyelitis vaccine, have a striking impact in reducing costs. Others, such as renal dialysis and kidney transplantation, increase costs because they provide a new range of services.

The magnitude of medical care costs and their growing importance is evident both in an examination of the course of events in the past decade (Figures 11.1, 11.2 and 11.3) and in future projection of cost

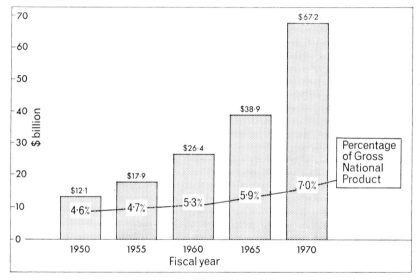

Fig. 11.1

increases. Health and medical care expenditures rose from $26·4 billion in 1960 to $67·2 billion in 1970. As a percentage of the Gross National Product these expenditures rose from 5·3 per cent to 7·0 per cent. Per capita expenditures have risen from a little more than $140 per year to $324 per year. Without inflation the per capita costs in 1970 would have been $216 per year in 1960 dollars.

A recent study in the Department of Health, Education and Welfare has estimated that total health and medical care expenditures will rise to $105 billion by 1974. They will comprise an increasing percentage of the Gross National Product and price inflation will contribute a significant share of these increases.[26]

To provide adequate access to the system, greater attention must be paid to those whose needs are greatest and who have the most difficulty utilising the services. In spite of the progress of the past decade through a variety of organised efforts, including community mental health centers, neighborhood health centers and other efforts

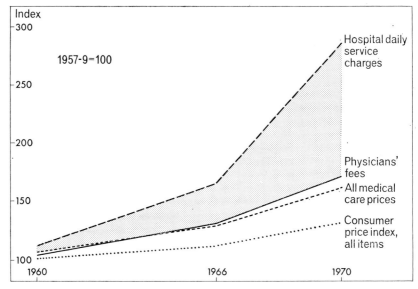

Fig. 11.2

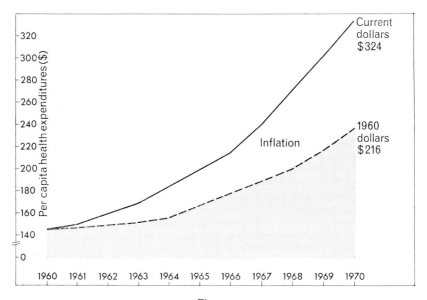

Fig. 11.3

to better organize and provide community health services, major gaps remain. Removal of major financial barriers, through private health insurance, Medicare and Medicaid has helped but it has also made it clear that financing alone is not enough.

Maldistribution of physicians and other health workers remains a major unresolved problem. Not only are there too few primary physicians, but there are too many specialists in a number of communities, while others are short of both. To correct problems of maldistribution, changes were needed in both the educational institutions and programs as well as in the financing and organisation of health services.

D. Health Care Policy Alternatives

The policy alternatives available to the Nixon Administration in health care, after a period of rapid expansion of the federal role, included:

1. Continuation of existing programs, organisation, budget and legislation without substantial change;

2. Setting as a major objective the improvement in and expansion of the capacity of the health care delivery system; and

3. Setting as an objective the removal of the financial barriers to access through universal coverage of the population with health insurance.

Although the federal government has developed two major programs for financing health care services to target groups, Medicare for the aged and Medicaid for the poor, substantial needs continue for low income, medically needy groups, for those with high cost catastrophic illness and for growing numbers of middle income families who are gradually being priced out of the market by inflation. At the same time that these needs become more evident, rising federal and state expenditures, particularly in the Medicaid and public assistance programs, have created a crisis in the ability of federal and state governments to continue to finance an uncontrolled Medicaid program and to simultaneously finance other programs to improve the capacity of the health care system.

The crisis in financing has resulted in a reduction in services. There have emerged a variety of approaches to cost control through administrative action to reduce physician services and hospitalisation in the Medicaid programs of many states, while stimulating the introduction in Congress of a host of proposals for national health insurance. Some of the proposals would merely expand private health insurance with governmental subsidy for the poor. Others would finance the bulk of hospital and medical services through a federal program designed to make major modifications in the delivery of health services. Some of the proposals, including those proposed by the Nixon Administration

and Senator Edward Kennedy, appear to have given insufficient attention to the problems of administering the programs. All the proposals
would increase the costs to the federal government; all would increase
demand and inflationary pressures.

Most of the legislative proposals for national health insurance or
universal coverage would exert only an indirect effect on the delivery
of health services. The cost of the various proposals, although not easy
to estimate with accuracy, is far easier to define than the possible
benefits. Increased budgetary expenditures, increased utilisation of
services, price inflation and administrative costs can be measured.
Benefits, whether expressed in morbidity or mortality, days of disability
or in terms of greater access to service for the target population, are
more difficult to measure in relation to the financing system.

The Nixon Administration developed what it has called the
"health maintenance strategy" to attempt to deal with both the
organisational problems and the rapidly rising costs. In addition to the
emphasis on prevention the Health Maintenance Organisation
provides for prepaid medical care on a capitation basis. The concept
has been widely tested in such organisations as Kaiser-Permanente,
Health Insurance Plan of Greater New York, Group Health of Puget
Sound and in other pioneering group practice prepayment programs.

The concept goes well beyond the arrangement for care and financing. It is based on the assumptions that the federal government should
assert its leadership to initiate change in the organisation and delivery
of health services; that the health care crisis can only be resolved by
structural and organisational changes and that the health industry
should be self regulating in terms of cost and quality control. The
hope is that through organised groups of providers, services will be
provided on a capitation basis and greater emphasis will be placed on
preventive services and the health of the individual, rather than an
episodic care at the time of illness. It is also hoped that more effective
cost control will be achieved because of a decreased need for in-
patient hospital care.

The Nixon Administration in its proposals on financing has emphas-
ised those in financial need. It has not proposed a federally financed
program of universal coverage. The policy problems related to the
financing of health care were clearly described in the summary report
of the Sun Valley Forum. The report notes:

Participants in the symposium disagreed as to two major aspects
of the financing problem, specifically with respect to: (a) The extent
of the needed changes in the financing system: and (b) The extent
to which changes in the delivery system should be tied to basic

changes in the financing system. Essentially three positions emerged:

(i) Some participants believe that a universal publicly supported system of paying for health care should be adopted and specifically designed to bring about major changes in the health delivery system.

(ii) Other participants agreed that a universal publicly supported system should be adopted to assure equal access to care for all, but believe that this financing system should be designed separately from needed changes in the delivery structure and that such changes should be accomplished independently.

(iii) A third group of participants believe that a universal publicly supported financing system is neither needed nor desirable, but that substantial improvements should be made in publicly supported provisions of health care services for the poor and near poor, leaving the financing of health care services for others primarily in the private sector. This group also believes that restructuring the delivery system should receive high priority.[27]

This latter course was adopted by the Nixon Administration. The policy debate continued because Congress had made no major decision on the Nixon Administration's proposals or on other proposed financing alternatives. These alternatives will be debated and discussed in the early 1970's. It is likely that the policies on financing for the next decade will emerge by 1973 or 1974. Our history as well as the diverse forces at work suggest that the changes that evolve will build on existing financing systems and will represent a host of compromises.

E. *Proposals for Changing the Structure and the Process*

Health policy in the United States continues to develop in a haphazard way that reflects the diverse forces and processes at work within our federal system. It assigns certain powers to the federal government and others are reserved for the states. Gradually some of these authorities and responsibilities have become blurred. It is still true that a variety of professional, bureaucratic and other vested interests and concerns are more influential in the creation of policy than rational planning or what some might view as the broad public interest. As more attention has been paid to health policy development, program planning and budgeting by a variety of disciplines and the public at large, the issues involved have become clearer and alternative routes to the solutions are being explored more fully.

A major obstacle is the lack of a clear focus for federal health policy development and program execution. To overcome this problem we propose three steps.

x

Health Planning

Our first suggestion is the establishment of a Department of Health, either as a separate department or within DHEW. We do not believe the proposals by the Nixon Administration to establish a health administration within a Department of Human Resources would meet this need.[28] A reorganised Department of Health, Education and Welfare with an Undersecretary of Health responsible for health policies and programs might be an appropriate transition from the present organisation to departmental status.

The Department of Health should have responsibility for federal health policy development and coordination; for major programs related to health resources development (e.g., research, education and facilities construction); environmental health and pollution control; preventive medicine; health education and occupational health and safety; comprehensive health planning; the organisation and delivery of health services; nutrition and food stamp programs; food, drug, cosmetic and product safety; and financing of medical, hospital and other health care services. Health programs which are now scattered in a number of departments and agencies, except for the Veterans Administration and the Department of Defense, should also be transferred to this new department.

Second, we suggest the establishment of a policy coordinating committee chaired by the Secretary of Health. In 1968 an attempt was made to establish a Federal Interagency Health Policy Council to fascilitate improved policy decision and program coordination. The Federal Executive Order drafted at that time was never carried out because of the vigorous political objection of veterans' organisations who feared that the Secretary of Health, Education and Welfare was attempting to take over veterans' medical care programs. The need is evident and such a council should be established, even without the other changes we propose.

Third, a high level council of health policy advisors should be established, as recommended by the Committee on Government Operations of the United States Senate and the National Advisory Commission on Health Manpower.[29, 30] The Council should be composed of non-government experts who could serve on a full-time basis for terms of three to five years. The Council would be responsible for formulating a national health policy and evaluating the performance of federal departments and agencies in achieving policy objectives. The council would also recommend to the President actions to carry out the policies.

Summary

The present system for national health policy formulation and implementation in the United States has been reviewed and found seriously deficient. Formidable obstacles stand in the way of translating into reality broad national goals, such as the right of access to health care for all. One obstacle is the lack of a clear focus for federal policy development and program execution.

To correct the present deficiencies we have proposed the establishment of a federal Department of Health, a health policy coordinating committee and a council of health policy advisors.

References

1. Comprehensive Health Planning and Public Health Service Amendments: Hearing before the Committee on Interstate and Foreign Commerce, House of Representatives, 89th Congress, 2nd Session on HR 13197, HR 18232, S 3008, October 11, 1966. Serial No. 89–52. Washington, D.C.: U.S. Government Printing Office.
2. Greenberg, S. *The Troubled Calling*. New York: The MacMillan Company, 1965, p. 398.
3. Rutstein, D. *The Coming Revolution in Medicine*. Cambridge, Mass.: The MIT Press, 1967, p. 180.
4. Cohen, W. J. Statement before the Subcommittee on Executive Reorganization of the Committee on Government Operations, U.S. Senate, April 26, 1968.
5. Richmond, J. B. *Currents in American Medicine, a Developmental View of Medical Care and Education*. Cambridge, Mass.: Harvard University Press, 1969, p. 136.
6. Lee, P. R. Social Demands Upon Health Care Delivery. *Jour. Med. Educ.* **45**: 61–68, November, 1970, Part 2.
7. Anonymous, It's Time to Operate. *Fortune*, **81**: 79, January, 1970.
8. Finch-Endorsed "Five Year Plan" is Key Health Document to Emerge So Far From Nixon Administration; No New Departures Indicated. The Blue Sheet. Washington, D.C.: Drug Research Reports, March 4, 1970, pp. S-2 to S-12.
9. Richardson, E. L. Towards a Comprehensive Health Policy in the 1970's. Washington, D.C.: Department of Health, Education, and Welfare, May, 1971, p. 52.
10. U.S. Senate, Committee on Appropriations, Department of Labor, and Health, Education, and Welfare, and Related Agencies Appropriation Bill, Report to Accompany HR 10061. Report No. 92–316, 92nd Congress, 1st Session, July 29, 1971.
11. Lewis, I. J. Science and Health Care—The Political Problem. *New England Jour, Med.* **281**: 888–896, October 18, 1969.
12. Schultze, C. *The Politics and Economics of Public Spending*. Washington, D.C.: The Brookings Institution, 1968.
13. Schultze, C. *Setting National Priorities, The 1971 Budget*. Washington, D.C.: The Brookings Institution, 1970.
14. *Ibid.*, p. 60.
15. World Health Organization (Regional Office for Europe). Health Services in Europe. Copenhagen: World Health Organization, 1965, p. 325.
16. Smillie, W. G. *Preventative Medicine and Public Health*: 3rd Edition by (the author and) Edwin D. Kilbourne. New York: MacMillan, 1963, p. 11.

17. Strickland, S. P. *The Integration of Medical Research and Health Policies.* Paper presented to the 137th Annual Meeting, American Association for the Advancement of Science, December 28, 1970.

18. Annual Report of the Department of Health, Education and Welfare, Fiscal Year 1968. Washington, D.C.: U.S. Department of Health, Education, and Welfare, 1969.

19. Cohen, W. J. Secretary's Introduction, Annual Report of the Department of Health, Education, and Welfare, Fiscal Year 1968. Washington, D.C.: Department of Health, Education, and Welfare, 1969, pp. 1–3.

20. Gorham, W. *Sharpening the Knife that Cuts the Public Pie.* Lecture 2, H.E.W. Forum, December 20, 1967.

21. Senate Report No. 92–316, *Op. Cit,* pp. 5–7.

22. Strickland, *Op. cit.*

23. Report of the National Advisory Commission on Health Manpower. Washington, D.C.: U.S. Government Printing Office, 1967, p. 93.

24. Cohen, W. J. *Toward a Social Report.* Washington, D.C.: U.S. Department of Health, Education, and Welfare, 1969, pp. 22–46.

25. National Advisory Commission of Health Facilities: A Report to the President. Washington, D.C.: U.S. Government Printing Office, 1968, p. 85.

26. *Dire Forecast on Health Cost,* San Francisco Chronicle, Friday, August 6, 1971, p, 5.

27. Nimetz, M. Sun Valley Forum on National Health: Report of Symposium on Personal Health Care and Financing, July 21, 1971.

28. Papers Relating to the President's Departmental Reorganization Program. Washington, D.C.: U.S. Government Printing Office, April, 1971, pp. 116–118.

29. *Federal Role in Health:* Report of the Committee on Government Operations, U.S. Senate, 91st Congress, Senate Resolution 320, April 30, 1970. Washington, D.C.: U.S. Government Printing Office, p. 32.

30. Report of the National Advisory Commission on Health Manpower, *op. cit.*

General References

1. Lee, P. R. Role of the Federal Government in Health and Medical Affairs. *New England Jour. Med.* **279**: 1139–1147, November 21, 1968.

2. Shannon, J. Federal Role in Health: Report of the Committee on Government Operations, U.S. Senate, 91st Congress, Senate Resolution 320, April 30, 1970. Washington, D.C.: U.S. Government Printing Office, pp. 507–533.

3. Lewis, I. J. Government Investment in Health Care. *Scientific American* **224**: 17–25, April, 1971.

4. Kissick, W. L. Health Policy Directions for the 1970's. *New England Jour. of Med.* **282**: 1343–1354, June 11, 1970.

5. Gardner, J. W. HEW Progress Report: A Report from the Secretary to the Department's Employees. Washington, D.C.: Department of Health, Education, and Welfare, 1969, p. 51.

SIGNIFICANT HEALTH LEGISLATION IN USA

1935–1960	*Public Law*	*Title*
1935	74–271	Social Security Act
1937	75–244	National Cancer Act
1938		Food, Drug and Cosmetic Act
1946	79–487	National Mental Health Act
1956	84–835	Health Research Facilities Act
1956	84–911	Health Amendments of 1956
1961–1962		
	87–692	Migratory Labor Act
		Kefauver-Harris Drug Amendments of 1962
1963–1964		
	88–129	Health Professions Education Assistance Act
	88–104	Mental Retardation Facilities and Community Mental Health Centers Act
1965–1966		
	89–74	Drug Abuse Control Amendments
	89–92	Federal Cigarette Labeling and Advertizing Act
	89–97	Social Security Amendments of 1965
1965–1966		
	89–105	Community Mental Health Centers Amendments
	89–115	Health Research Facilities Amendments
	89–181	Gorgas Memorial Laboratory
	89–234	Water Quality Control Act
	89–239	Heart Disease, Cancer and Stroke Amendments
	89–272	Clean Air and Solid Waste Disposal Act
1965–1966		
	89–290	Health Professions Educational Assistance Amendments of 1965
	89–291	Medical Library Assistance Act
	89–384	Medicare Extension (1966)
	89–554	Transportation, Sale and Handling of Dogs and Cats for Research
	89–563	Traffic Safety Act of 1966
	89–675	Clean Air Act Amendments of 1966
	89–709	Veterinary Medical Education Act of 1966
	89–749	Comprehensive Health Planning and Public Health Services Amendments of 1966
	89–751	Allied Health Professions Personnel Training Act of 1966
	89–793	Narcotic Addict Rehabilitation Act of 1966)
1967–1968		
	90–31	Mental Health Amendments of 1967
	90–148	Air Quality Act of 1967
	90–170	Mental Retardation Amendments of 1967
	90–174	Partnership for Health Amendments of 1967
	90–489	National Eye Institute
	90–490	Health Manpower Act
	90–574	Health Services Act
	90–602	Radiation Control for Health & Safety

Chapter 12

The World Medical Association and Medical Care

S. S. B. Gilder, t.d., b.sc., m.b., b.s.
Secretary of World Medical Association

A number of factors have combined to increase the demand for medical care in recent years so rapidly as to overwhelm the traditional providers of care almost everywhere in the world. Problems have arisen to which no entirely satisfactory solution has been found, although enthusiasts for various systems would have us believe that they have the correct answers to everything.

In efforts to solve these problems it has been necessary to involve the medical profession individually and collectively, and The World Medical Association as the only international body representing the whole profession has therefore been concerned with these problems from its foundation in 1947.

The factors which have produced a crisis in the provision of medical care in many geographical areas, ranging from the poorest of the developing countries to the richest, the United States of America, were identified at the First Socio-Economic Conference of the World Medical Association in Paris in June 1969, notably by Professor Péquignot (see *World Medical Journal,* 1969, *16,* 112). He classified them under four headings:

1. Demographic factors, including population growth and changes in age structure, with increase in children and the elderly, both of which groups need more than average medical care;
2. Technical progress, in general and in medicine;
3. Cultural factors, including improved health education and easier general access to good quality medical care;
4. The intrusion of medicine into new areas, such as the management of social maladaptation and the control of reproduction.

The changing climate

He might have added that there has been a gradual but definite change in the public attitude towards medicine which has increased demands on doctors. This change, for example, has been marked in

316

Japan, where the practice of medicine has rapidly changed from the exercise of a benevolent art by charitably minded persons to the satisfaction of a basic human right to medical care, if not to health. When the public decide that access to medical care is a right, they demand this right through their elected representatives, and in consequence medicine enters the political arena. As Garfield (*New Engl. J. Med.* 1970, *283*, 1087) put it recently: ".... times have changed. Now there is a new game – and its name is 'medical care as a right'." The concern of organised medicine should be to achieve a reasonably smooth transition from the old to the new without sacrificing the quality of medical care, either from the humane or the scientific point of view.

In outlining the role of the World Medical Association in this field, the writer is not forgetful of the part played by specialist international organisations, such as the International College of Surgeons or the World Psychiatric Association, whose influence however has been more limited and mainly exercised through efforts to raise standards of education and care in their own speciality.

Doctors on the whole are conservative rather than radical by nature, and this has been repeatedly reflected in the debates of the professional organisations, either at national or international level. Moreover, it is only in recent years that in some areas younger doctors have begun to play an active part in the national association and thus to some extent to leaven the conservatism of their elders. This trend is being slowly reflected in the age of delegates to the W.M.A. Assembly, which at first tended to consist of rather senior statesmen. The W.M.A. in its formative years laboured under the handicap common to all international bodies, namely the greatly different political and professional systems prevailing in the countries of its member associations. In addition, efforts to frame meaningful statements about the provision of medical care involved the need to compromise between the North American philosophy of medical care, in which such terms as "social security" were suspect, and the European philosophy with its acceptance, although sometimes a grudging one, of social security arrangements and either direct or indirect government intervention in the practice of medicine. Thus the earlier pronouncements about provision of medical care tended to be vague and confined to generalisations of a harmless nature. The climate of opinion in North America is now changing; Canada has already taken steps towards national health insurance, and the subject is under debate in the United States. It is therefore now possible to stage more effective debates on medical care, as the conferences on the economics of medical care at the Paris Assembly in 1969 and on general practice at the Oslo Assembly of 1970 showed.

The structure of W.M.A.

For those unfamiliar with the World Medical Association, it should be said that this organization with its headquarters in New York and five regional secretariats, serviced on a voluntary basis by national medical associations, has a structure common to many international bodies. Its court of final appeal in policy matters is the Assembly which meets once a year in a city chosen after consideration of invitations from host member associations. To this Assembly come delegates from the national medical associations which are members; the membership includes most countries outside Eastern Europe, where the absence of national medical associations has limited participation to the sending of observers. The executive body of the W.M.A. is its Council of less than twenty persons who meet each spring for a week, and also directly before and after an Assembly. Council in turn operates in part through smaller committees, of which the most intimately concerned with medical care systems has been the rather quaintly named Socio-Medical Affairs Committee, whose able secretary, Dr. Schloegell of West Germany, has over the years provided a focal point for its work and also contributed useful working papers based on his own experience as secretary of the German association of insurance doctors.

Medical Education

But this is not the only committee to study medical care. The W.M.A. has involved itself in the field through its medical education activities, whose chief achievement has been the preparation of four World Conferences of Medical Education. The first of these in London in 1953 discussed undergraduate education, while the second in Chicago in 1959 dealt with continuing education of the doctor, coining the phrase – "Medicine – a lifelong study". The third conference held in New Delhi in 1966 was more loosely structured and was concerned with the integration of medical education into the social and economic framework of a country. The fourth, to be held in Copenhagen in 1972, has as its theme: "Educating tomorrow's doctors", and will therefore try to look forward into the medical education of the future. Obviously, these conferences, which have made an impact particularly on countries in which the education of doctors is still a rather new activity, have also affected thinking on the provision of medical care.

Medical Ethics

The excursions of the W.M.A. into the area of medical ethics, an increasingly important activity, are also not without significance for medical care systems. This work began with the framing in the fifties' of the Declaration of Geneva, an updated version of the Hippocratic oath, some of whose clauses limit or restrict the doctor in carrying out some of the tasks recently imposed on him by progressive societies, notably in the field of the control of reproduction. The later Declaration of Helsinki, concerned with a code of ethics for human experimentation is perhaps not so pertinent, but the later declarations made in Sydney in 1968 on the definition of death, and in Oslo in 1970 on therapeutic abortion certainly affect the ordinary practice of medicine. The W.M.A. Committee on Ethics is currently studying a subject of significance to the data-bank society, namely the preservation of traditional medical confidentiality in the face of growing application of computerisation to medical records. It will also study human sterilisation and artificial insemination, both medical activities likely to add to the workload of the medical profession.

Malpractice

A worrying phenomenon in a number of countries is the rising tide of litigation against doctors for alleged medical malpractice or negligence. While it is admitted that doctors should bear a responsibility for their actions, a way must be found to ensure that frivolous or vindictive litigation, such as is commonplace in the United States, does not hamper the proper practice of medicine by creating an atmosphere of fear in which self-preservation rather than the patient's interests is paramount. This subject has been debated twice at Assemblies, and is currently under study by an international committee including American, British and French experts.

Influence on medical care patterns is also exercised through the official liaison maintained between W.M.A. and such bodies as the World Health Organisation, International Labour Office, International Social Security Association, International Red Cross and the International Law Association. Effective cooperation with these bodies has been gravely impaired in the past through lack of funds, for the budget of the W.M.A. is small and much of the liaison work done on an ad hoc basis by volunteers. Probably the closest cooperation has been with W.H.O., whose help with the conferences on medical education has been gratefully received.

Social Security

The most direct impact of the World Medical Association on the provision of medical care has of course been in the field of social security and medical economics, mainly through the Socio-Medical Affairs Committee.

The first document to emerge on social security, the *Twelve Prin-*

ciples of Social Security and Medical Care, was revised and adopted by the Assembly in 1963. Its preamble states that the ideal is provision of the most up to date medical care while entirely respecting the freedom of both doctor and patient. It also states that it is not the duty of the W.M.A. to pronounce judgment on the various social security systems in existence but to determine with the greatest possible precision on what terms the medical profession can collaborate with government health services. The Twelve Principles are as follows:

i. The conditions of medical practice in any social security scheme shall be determined in consultation with the representatives of the professional organisations.

ii. Any social security scheme should allow the patient to consult the doctor of his choice, and the doctor to treat only patients of his choice, without the rights of either being affected in any way. The principle of free choice should be applied also in cases where medical treatment or a part of it is provided in treatment centres.

iii. Any system of social security should be open to all licensed doctors; neither the medical profession nor the individual doctor should be forced to take part if they do not so wish.

iv. The doctor should be free to practise his profession where he wishes and also to limit his practice to a given speciality in which he is qualified. The medical needs of the country concerned should be satisfied and the profession, wherever possible, should seek to orient young doctors towards the areas where they are most needed. In cases where these areas are less favourable than others, doctors who go there should be aided so that their equipment is satisfactory and their standard of living is in accordance with their professional responsibilities.

v. The profession should be adequately represented on all official bodies dealing with problems concerning health or disease.

vi. Professional secrecy must be observed by all those who collaborate at any stage of the patient's treatment or in the control thereof. This should be duly respected by authority.

vii. The moral, economic and professional independence of the doctor should be guaranteed.

viii. When the remuneration of medical services is not fixed by direct agreement between doctor and patient proper consideration should be taken of the great responsibility involved in the practice of medicine.

ix. The remuneration of medical services should take into consideration the services rendered and should not entirely be fixed according to the financial status of the paying authority or as a result of unilateral government decisions and should be acceptable to the agency which represents the medical profession.

x. Control in medical matters should be carried out by doctors only.

xi. In the higher interest of the patient there should be no restriction of the doctor's right to prescribe drugs or any other treatment deemed necessary.

xii. The doctor should have the opportunity of participating in any activity directed toward improving his knowledge and status in his professional life.

There is a world-wide trend for doctors to congregate in urban areas where the amenities of life are easily obtainable and to leave rural areas without adequate medical care. An excellent example of this is the situation in Uruguay, the Latin American country where social security arrangements have for a long time been in advance of the rest of the reigion, and which possesses the demographic structure of a well developed society coupled unfortunately with the economy of an underdeveloped country. The capital city contains about 45 per cent of the total population of about two and a half million; it also contains almost all the country's specialists and 77 per cent of its doctors. Because this phenomenon is even more marked in developing countries, in some of which it is difficult to find a doctor outside the cities (this is for instance one of India's big medical problems), the W.M.A. studied the problem and eventually produced *Recommendations concerning medical care in rural areas* in 1964. This document may be summarised as follows:

The W.M.A. states that rural populations are entitled to the same medical care as people living in urban areas; it urges that efforts be made to raise the quality of rural medical care to the highest level in the nation. It considers that voluntary self-help and cooperative effort will solve most of the health problems of any community, and that in rural areas health goes hand in hand with education and economic and social levels. It believes that the duty of the State is to ensure that health workers in rural areas are offered sufficiently attractive terms and that the health programme should incorporate preventive and curative medicine, environmental sanitation and health education. It insists on maintenance of the doctor-patient relationship in rural areas and wishes to see responsibility in the hands of qualified medical practitioners, with medical auxiliaries used only temporarily to provide medical care (It is likely that this clause may need revision in the light of changing conditions in many areas). It calls upon the medical profession to give leadership in health education and to cooperate with other professionals in related fields. It enjoins national medical associations to take steps to ensure that rural doctors are not working at a disadvantage, and to play an active part in developing plans for improving rural health conditions.

An example of the way in which these principles have been implemented is furnished by the Philippines, where the national medical association for some years has taken a lead in what are known as MARIA projects. In these the national association has taken steps to establish doctors in outlying areas, not only to give medical care but also to give the often backward population a lead in education and community projects to raise cultural and economic levels. The W.M.A. has even started a similar pilot project in Indonesia, with the cooperation of the rather impoverished Indonesian Medical Association, providing a medical officer to an area totally bereft of medical care. This MARINDA project has proved somewhat difficult to maintain because of the inaccessibility of the site and the difficulty of supervising a project from a distance. It has however an emotional appeal to those who would like to see international medicine actually doing something for people rather than making academic pronouncements about medical care.

General practice

In recent years the W.M.A. has taken an increasing intereste in general practice, culminating in the two-day conference at the Oslo Assembly in 1970.

The Socio-Medical Affairs Committee looked into problems of general practice in 1968 and 1969, aided by two working papers by its secretary, Dr. Schloegell, among other documents. In the first of these (The general practitioner and his problems, *World med. J.* 1969, *16*, 26) the author points out that prophecies of the demise of the general practitioner have been proved false, that in various countries attempts are being made to modify his training in accordance with his new role, and that group practice is being encouraged. His problems include his increased workload, most of which he handles alone, less than 5 per cent of his patients being referred to specialists, and the fact that in some countries he is economically discriminated against by social security bodies.

In a second paper (*ibid.* 1969, *16*, 29) the author examines the status of the G.P. in relation to the social security system, analysing the factors which affect his standing. These include the legal structure of the system, the way benefits are obtained, the extent to which the population is covered by the system, the extent of benefits, and the general status of doctors within the system in terms of their right to practise within it, their level of payment, their freedom of prescribing, their supervision, and the activities of hospital outpatient departments in competition with the G.P.

The subject of group practice is discussed in *World Medical Journal* for March–April 1968, and that of the medical profession's attitude to unacceptable social legislation in the January–February 1968 issue, in which Dr. Schloegell reports on results of a questionnaire from W.M.A. to its members, in which they were asked how they had reacted or would react to governmental legislation affecting the practice of medicine and which they found unacceptable or undesirable. All respondents agreed that in no circumstances could doctors completely refuse medical care (the strike weapon) but a number thought that doctors might refuse to give services under the unacceptable conditions and treat patients outside this framework. Others felt that refusal to issue certificates or to cooperate in organisational measures was sufficient. From the variety of responses it became clear that W.M.A. could make no general recommendation to its members in this matter. It did however suggest that the profession should make closer contact with various social and political groups and with legislators or parliamentarians interested in questions of health policy, that it should keep the public informed of its thinking, and that it should ensure that individual doctors were well informed on medicopolitical issues.

From time to time, other aspects of medical care have come before the Council and the Assembly, as individual member associations have introduced resolutions asking for W.M.A. study of a topic. Subjects have included occupational medical services, the use and abuse of drugs (this was the subject of a two-day discussion at the Ottawa Assembly in September 1971), hours of work of hospital physicians, family planning (W.M.A. has pronounced in favour of this but added that the decision to plan a family should belong to the couple involved and not the State), total health planning (the Manila Assembly of 1966 was concerned with this), minimal standards for salaried practitioners, and the arrangement of emergency services.

Medicine and money

It must be clear to everyone that there is no limit to the amount of money that can be used for health services, and that costs of medical care are doomed to increase regularly. The final session of the Socio-Economic Conference at the 1969 Paris Assembly was devoted to the theme of the rising cost of medical care and designed to provoke discussion by national medical associations among themselves and with their governments and social security organisations. The session revealed that the rise in cost seems to be independent of the social security system prevailing and of the economic state of the country. Yet medical care does not cost as much as some luxuries considered almost indispensable to modern man, and a civilized country ought to be prepared to spend at least as much on health as on education and more than on defence.

Previous sessions had dealt with the increased demand for medical care, described by Dr. Gibson (U.K.) as "an awesome picture of grave problems facing the medical profession both the short and the long term"; requirements for medical manpower; the role of institutions in medical care; and the form and financing of medical care. Details of these sessions will be found in *World Medical Journal* for September-October and November-December 1969.

General practice

The conference on "Has the general practitioner a future?" in Oslo in 1970 concluded on an optimistic note. Only a minority of delegates thought that the general practitioner was doomed to extinction; the majority took the view that the modern family doctor forms a focal point in a world of bewildered patients blinded by science and seeking for a word of comfort. It is however necessary to revise drastically both the educational curriculum for general practice and the way in which it is organised. The debates included discussion of the scope of general practice, a highly controversial subject; the organisation of primary health services; education and motivation for general practice (the two go hand in hand); and research in general practice.

Conclusion

In a world which is becoming steadily more uniform, medical care is likely to cease to show the extreme variations it still displays, as those responsible for its provision and their advisers inside and outside medicine find it possible to define more exactly the requirements of an ideal system. It therefore seems likely that the role of an international organisation such as the World Medical Association in making proposals about such matters as the most economical medical care system, the one most acceptable to both patient and doctor, the relation of primary medical care to hospital and specialist care, the optimum utilisation of auxiliaries, the relation of health to welfare, and the best type of education for the job will become more important.

But this presupposes a growing internationalisation of outlook among doctors in place of the parochial view of life so many still adopt, and their interest in and support of supranational bodies whose significance and effectiveness depend more on the enthusiasm of their supporters than on the quality of their secretariat or the organisation of their meetings. The advance of scientific medicine is steady and sure. What is equally necessary is the will and ability to bring the benefits of these advances to the general public. The public is aware of this point and often in critical mood. To counter this criticism, organised medicine at the national and international levels has a star part to play.

Chapter 13

Comparisons, Implications and Applications

JOHN FRY, M.D., F.R.C.S., F.R.C.G.P.

*Consultant, World Health Organisation, and
Family Physician, London, England*

What Lessons?

A number of systems of medical care have been described. None is perfect. Everywhere there are problems in endeavouring to make the best use of available resources, yet nowhere is there evidence that this has been achieved successfully.

Nowhere is there evidence of any system of qualitative or even quantitative mensuration by which proper utilisation of resources can be assessed. There is a desperate need for the development of techniques by which quality and quantity of medical care resources can be measured in such ways that international comparisons can be made readily. At present we have to rely on crude data, ill defined and roughly interpreted.

In the utilisation of resources, these will always continue to be less than completely adequate to meet insatiable wants and total needs. Decisions on priorities have to be taken at all levels. From the medical workers in continuing contact with the public who have to decide how best to spend their available hours to the top ministerial administrators and politicians who have to decide between building new hospitals, new houses, new schools or buying more planes, guns or industrial machinery, or improving public health sanitary measures, or investing in ways of improving natural resources. Faced with much human suffering and human misery how can such priority decisions be taken without the human feelings of politicians and administrators being aroused.

No system of medical care can be transported wholesale across national borders. Each nation has to evolve its own, with due regard to local and national characteristics.

Evolution is very much better than revolution in matters of medical care. New systems and techniques and methods that have evolved gradually and logically from the old have tended to be much more sound and stable than those introduced by sudden and drastic revolutions.

The British National Health Service of 1948 was a more universal evolution and flowed from the immediately preceding National Health

Insurance Scheme that had existed from 1911. Although there was much that was new in the Soviet system of medical care introduced in the 1920's, it continued to use feldshers who had proved their value over more than two centuries. The Indian and Chinese systems have taken care to evolve using both traditional and indigenous forms of care as well as the newer and more scientifically based methods. The future system of medical care in the U.S.A. almost certainly will evolve from its present and past patterns, namely, an extension of a pre-paid national health insurance scheme to cover almost the whole population, but retaining considerable freedom of choice and action by the public, physicians and hospital and other facilities, and with the physicians choosing the ways in which they are to be paid agreed fees or salaries.

Evolution of medical care systems must recognise national historical, cultural, philosophical and political features.

Available resources of money, manpower and facilities and their growth potentials are important influencing factors as are the resrouces of education and training and the numbers of individuals whom it is possible to train.

Ideally growth of resources should keep ahead of population growth and some form of population control seems essential in any successful system of care.

Common Basic Components in Medical Care

Running through all the different systems of medical care there is a certain common basic structure that is necessary for a sound system to function.

These common basic components can be defined most readily as levels of care and levels of administration.

The flow of medical care and the various levels of care are related closely to population size and geography, to the nature and complexity of the morbidity and to the administrative structure.

In all systems there are clearly recognizable *levels of care* but much less distinct and recognizable *levels of administration*. This lack of compliance creates problems.

Levels of Care

1. *Self Care in a Family Unit* (1–10 persons)

The first level of care is self care. It is a most important level of care and one that has been neglected and left to develop without support and encouragement in most systems. Less than one symptom in every four is taken to a physician or other professional adviser in developed nations such as U.K., and U.S.A. The proportions are very much less in other nations with less adequate and available

327

resources. For self-care to be effective it requires to be encouraged as a national policy, as is being done in U.S.S.R., through a very extensive system of health education and health maintenance. The family should know what can and should be treated by themselves and which symptoms must be taken to skilled and trained practitioners. There must be facilities and medicines available for self care. There must be accessible pharmacies or their equivalents where home remedies can be obtained. It would be a great step forward if in Africa with its great shortage of medical manpower simple drugs were made available for people to treat themselves for malaria and other well-known local diseases, and if simple analgesics and similar symptomatics were available. Such actions might be cheaper and more effective at the present time as crash measures whilst doctors and nurses are being trained and hospitals and medical centres built. Village "health shops" might be considered.

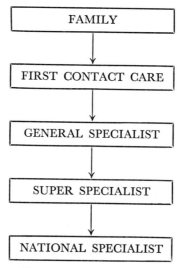

Fig. 13.1 Flow of Medical Care

2. *First Contact Care* (for 500–50,000 persons)

Once the individual or family decide that medical attention or advice is required some trained person has to act as the "doctor (or nurse) -of-first-contact" or the "primary physician".

The features of this level of care are – direct access of physician to patient.

   – first contact care and the assessment and care that this involves.

   – small and relatively static community with the physician and patient coming to know each other.

– longterm and continuing care, not only of the patient but the whole family and local community.

– the disease spectrum, the morbidity, is that which will occur in the small population cared for, common diseases will commonly occur and rare diseases rarely happen.

Who should be the worker of first contact?

It may well be a physician but it also may be a medical assistant or nurse or fledsher or indigenous doctor.

In developed nations it is usually a physician who acts as the doctor-of-first-contact, but in Africa the medical assistant carries out similar roles in a satisfactory manner as do the feldshers in U.S.S.R. and nurses in outlying regions of Sweden and Canada.

What Sort of Physician?

Should he be a *"generalist"* as in U.K., Scandinavia and Western Europe, or a *"specialoid"* as in U.S.A. and U.S.S.R., or a recognised *"specialist"* to whom the patient has direct access?

Providing that the special features of work in this field are recognised, namely, small population at risk and limited range of morbidity experience then each nation should work out its own views. Whatever those views are attention must be paid to define clearly what the roles of these workers are to be and what tools they require to carry them out satisfactorily. Such tools must include attention to education and training and access to hospital facilities.

Recent Trends

Recent trends in this field include this continuing debate over what type of physician is best deployed at this level – *generalist or specialoid?*

Everywhere there are moves away from solo practice to working in *groups of physicians.*

More than group practice the establishment of *health teams* of physicians, nurses, social workers and secretariat is being successfully accomplished in U.K., U.S.A., and U.S.S.R.

Purpose built premises, such as polyclinics (U.S.S.R.), health centres (U.K.), and groups (U.S.A.), are now considered essential for good practice. Their form and structure have not reached any uniform pattern yet.

The *relations with hospitals* are varied. In U.S.A. and other places such as outlying areas of Africa, Australia and Canada, primary physicians also work in their local hospitals. This is not so in most urban societies in U.K., Western Europe and U.S.S.R. Here this is a problem that has to be re-examined and corrected.

3. *General Specialist* (50,000 to 500,000 persons)

Specialisation is one of the features of modern medicine, but in relation to the provision of medical care it is important to relate specialisation to the availability of enough clinical material on which to practice. Some specialities can serve populations of 50,000 and others require populations of millions. These can be referred to as general specialities and super-specialities.

The general specialists are general physicians (internists), general surgeons, obstetrician-gynaecologists, psychiatrists and paediatricians. In the British National Health Service there are approximately one of such general specialists to 50,000 to 200,000 of the population. Not only is it in the clinical field that general specialists occur but also in public health, nursing and social services. Once more the key to such groupings are the populations cared for.

Current problems in this level of general specialist care are relations and communications with the first-contact and super-specialist levels of care. On the siting of units should general specialist work entirely from hospitals as in U.K., or should they move out into the community as in U.S.S.R., U.S.A., and developing nations? Should the public have direct access to specialists or should access be only be referral from other physicians?

How are specialists to be recognised and registered? What should be the place, if any, of private practice? It exists in all countries, even in U.S.S.R. These are questions and problems for future deliberation.

4. *Super-Specialist* (500,000 – 5 million persons)

There are some specialities that require large populations to make them worthwhile. For example, the clinical material for a neurology – neurosurgery, plastic surgery and thoracic surgery units is around 2 million, that for open heart surgery is more around 3–4 million and that for a spinal injuries unit at some 5 million. The problems with such units is their relative isolation from the community and other levels of care. For best use of resources there should not be any duplication or competition between such units as exists in some large cities in U.S.A., where such super-specialist units have become almost status symbols for some hospitals and may have insufficient clinical material to remain viable.

There will be in all nations some units and some individual physicians of such excellence as to become national centres for care, research and development.

5. *National Level*

There will be in all nations some units and some individual physicians of such excellence as to become national centres for care, research and development.

Levels of Administration

Side by side with levels of care there emerge levels of administration.

1. *The Family Unit* (1–10 persons)

The family is accepted everywhere as the basic social unit. This is accepted administratively through family welfare schemes, family housing plans and family physicians.

2. *The Locality of Neighbourhood* (500–50,000 persons)

In rural areas this is the administrative levelof the village or small town but in urban areas any distinctions become less clear. In U.S.S.R. there is a definite delineation of uchastoks (or neighbourhoods) on which primary or first-contact care is based.

The neighbourhood level is the level of first-contact medical care, but it is also the level of primary education, welfare and communal self-help, or preventive and public health, of housing schemes and roadwork and of social and other activities. It is a level that is considered too small to be recognised statutorily but important to recognise functionally and worthy of some administrative autonomy in planning and direction.

3. *The District* (50,000–500,000 persons)

This is a readily recognisable administrative unit of local government. It is large enough for elected councils and other bodies. It is large enough for hospitals and public health and sanitation centres. Medically there are problems of administration, control and planning. In U.S.S.R., with its planned society there is a Chief Physician of the Rayon (District) who is responsible for the integration and working of all the medical and public health services in his district.

4. *The Region* (500,000 to 5 million persons)

The regions are large administrative units, often immediately below the national government level.

The medical care regions offer considerable opportunities for major planning as in the Regional Hospital Boards in U.K., and the Oblast Health Committees in U.S.S.R.

In very large nations such as U.S.S.R., and U.S.A., there is further administrative level, the State (U.S.A.) or the Republic (U.S.S.R.) which may have as many as 50 million or more persons.

5. *The National Level*

This is the level of the National Ministry (or Department) of Health responsible for the whole policy of medical and health services in the country.

The Twin Peaks of Medical Care

One factor to success in the organisation of a medcial care system is the integration of levels of care and administration (Figure 13.2). Such an integration should be aimed at but cannot take place separately from the general national administrative structure.

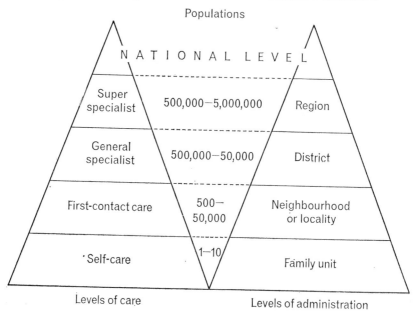

Fig. 13.2 The Twin Peaks of Medical Care

Questions to be Tackled

What Sort of System?

There are spectra in the types of systems of medical care that have to be matched to national characters. From a nationalised system as in U.S.S.R. and Eastern Europe and U.K., we pass through partly nationalised systems as in Western Europe, Australasia and Canada, with combinations of State and private insurance, to a free-enterprise system where the individual is responsible for arranging and paying for his medical care – this would seem to be quite impossible for the ordinary man today; the costs are much too high.

How is the profession to be paid? Here again there is a range from full salaries, through capitation fees, agreed fees on an item of service basis to a full free-enterprise basis.

How is the system to be financed?

There are many possible ways of raising money to pay for medical care. Do they really matter? In developed nations between 5 and 10 per cent of G.N.P. is devoted to medical care. Does it matter whether it is raised at source, by direct or indirect taxation, by insurance or by fees? The totals are similar. What should matter is that no individual or family who are sick should have in addition a massive financial load and anxiety to bear in meeting medical costs. Some form of taxation, insurance and subsidies are inevitable. The exact forms are best left to each country to work out.

How to achieve maximal utilisation?

This must be our goal. Success requires continuing and available data for implementation of changes. Such changes, however, have to take note of and allow for professional freedom so that physicians can be able to practice their clinical and scientific skills according to international professional edicts and concepts. However, it is quite unrealistic to expect this "freedom" to be so total as to lead to a completely disorganised and independent system where every physician is on his own. Within any sound system of care there have to be controls and directives to ensure best deployment of resources and these include the distribution and supervision of medical manpower. The medical and paramedical professions have to accept some controls and arrive at some compromise with governments.

In all systems and places there are problems of maldistribution. Some areas are less attractive than others. No one has solved the problem of attracting or directing medical workers to such places and the problems persist.

Appendix

Death and Disease in a British General Practice community

Moving away from the astronomical numbers of world deaths and disease, it is salutary and illuminating to turn to the experiences over one year in a typical British general practice providing care for some 2,500 persons. The reasons for choosing British general practice are that under the National Health Service there are no financial or other major barriers to available and accessible medical care and because there is considerable data available on the prevalence of disease in this field.

Use of Services

In such a practice of 2,500 we know that in any year approximately 70–75 per cent of the population will consult their general practitioner once or more, that 15–20 per cent will receive hospital treatment and one per cent will die.

Deaths

There will be approximately 25 deaths in the practice population in a year and of these:

9 will be from cardiac and circulatory diseases
5 „ „ cancer of all forms
4 „ „ strokes
4 „ „ pulmonary disease
1 „ „ some accident or violence
2 „ „ other causes.

Morbidity

The patterns of disease that an average and representative general practitioner will see in a year are as shown in Tables 1–5.

ANNUAL MORBIDITY EXPERIENCE IN AN AVERAGE AND
REPRESENTATIVE BRITISH GENERAL PRACTICE OF
2,500 PERSONS

TABLE 1

Minor Illnesses (of short duration and minimal disability)

	Persons Consulting Per year
Upper Respiratory Infections	500
Common Gastro-intestinal 'infections' and 'Dyspepsias'	300
Skin Disorders	300
Emotional Disorders	250
Acute Otitis Media	50
'Acute Back'	50
Acute Urinary Infections	50
Migraine	30
Hay Fever	25

TABLE 2
Acute Major Illnesses (life threatening)

	Persons consulting Per year
Pneumonia and Acute Bronchitis	50
Acute Myocardial Infarction	7
Acute Appendicitis	5
All NEW Cancers	6
Severe Depression	12
(Suicide 1 every 4 years)	
(Suicidal, attempts 2 every year)	
Acute Strokes	5

TABLE 3
Chronic Illnesses

	Persons Consulting Per year
Chronic Arthritis and Rheumatism	100
Chronic Mental Illness	55
Chronic Bronchitis	50
Anaemia	40
High Blood Pressure	25
Asthma	25
Peptic Ulcer	25
Chronic Stroke (after effects)	15
Epilepsy	10
Diabetes	10
Parkinsonism	3
Multiple Sclerosis	2
Pulmonary Tuberculosis	2

The "*social pathology*" of this community is computed in the following Table.

TABLE 4
Social Pathology in Community of 2,500 Persons

	Persons
Poverty (persons receiving supplementary benefits)	100
Aged over 75	100
Lonely old persons (over 75) living alone	50
Broken Homes (children under 15 living with only one parent)	60
Illegitimate Births	4
Problem Families	5–10
Divorce	1–2
Adult committed to Prison	1
Juvenile Delinquents	5
Chronic Alcoholics (known)	5
Chronic Alcoholics (probable)	25
Male Homosexuals (probable)	50
Registered Blind	5
Registered as Physically Disabled	5

Appendix

The numbers of persons with *undiagnosed diseases* as determined by mass-screening studies are approximately as in Table 5. The significance of these is uncertain because it is not yet known whether early treatment will affect the final outcome.

TABLE 5

Undiagnosed Diseases in Community of 2,500

	Persons
High Blood Pressure	250
(Of these 15 will have evidence of some complications.)	
Anaemia	200
Chronic Bronchitis	150
Bacteriuria	100
Obesity	60
Diabetes	10
Cancer of Cervix in-situ	3
Pulmonary Tuberculosis	1
Glaucoma	1

These numbers represent the expectation of annual morbidity facing an average British general practitioner. He will meet and manage all the morbidity that is presented to him by the patients who consult him but he will deal with only a small proportion of the social pathology that exists in his practice community and unless he undertakes extensive pre-symptomatic screening exercises he will not begin to detect and manage the many with diseases at early stages.

Some of the questions that face physicians of the future are whether and to what extent they should become involved in early detection and management of every physical, mental and social disorders in their own communities.

Index

References to countries indicate information on general aspects of medical care. See subject entries for specific topics. Main entries in italics.